IN THE SHADOW OF LIBERTY

IN THE SHADOW OF LIBERTY

The Invisible History of Immigrant Detention in the United States

ANA RAQUEL MINIAN

VIKING

VIKING
An imprint of Penguin Random House LLC
penguinrandomhouse.com

LIBRARY OF CONGRESS CATALOGING-IN-PUBLICATION DATA
Names: Minian, Ana Raquel, 1983– author.
Title: In the shadow of liberty : the invisible history of immigrant detention in the United States / Ana Raquel Minian.
Description: [New York] : Viking, [2024] | Includes bibliographical references.
Identifiers: LCCN 2023033975 (print) | LCCN 2023033976 (ebook) |
ISBN 9780593654255 (hardcover) | ISBN 9780593654262 (ebook)
Subjects: LCSH: United States—Emigration and immigration—Government policy. |
Noncitizen detention centers—United States—History. |
Immigrants—United States—History. | Immigrants—United States—Social conditions.
Classification: LCC JV6483 .M57 2024 (print) | LCC JV6483 (ebook) |
DDC 365/.470973—dc23/eng/20240131
LC record available at https://lccn.loc.gov/2023033975
LC ebook record available at https://lccn.loc.gov/2023033976

Printed in the United States of America
2nd Printing

Book design by Daniel Lagin

To my parents for their love and support.

And to Chi Hao, Ellen, Gerardo, Fernando,
and all the other migrants who shared
their stories in the hope that others don't have
to endure the horrors of detention.

CONTENTS

Part III
DETERRENCE

Part IV
WHERE WE ARE, WHERE WE'RE GOING

PREFACE

The cement floor was cold, and loud sobs echoed throughout the room, but that night Fernando Arredondo was too tired and shell-shocked to let much bother him. Ignoring his surroundings, he wrapped his gray sweatshirt tightly around his chest as if he were an infant draped in a warm blanket, pulled the hoodie over his head, and fell asleep on the floor.

He had not gotten much sleep the night before. Or during the past year, for that matter. It was back then, in the spring of 2017, that his troubles had begun. That was when he and his family—or at least those who had survived—had fled their home near Guatemala City after being targeted by gang members.

But now, Fernando thought, he and his twelve-year-old daughter, Andrea, were at last safe. Earlier that day, the two of them had finally crossed the US-Mexico border and pleaded asylum at the Laredo Processing Center on the bank of the Rio Grande in south Texas. The paperwork had been endless and the officials derisive. They had forced Fernando to strip down to his underwear and then searched him. They had demanded that he dispose of his shoelaces. And, worst of all, they had taken Andrea to sleep in the "children's section" of the immigration station, despite her pleadings and fear. Fernando had complained but had been powerless to stop it. All he could do was wait to be reunited with her the following day. And so it was that Fernando found himself uneasily asleep in a locked room alongside more than a dozen other adult refugees.

Rest was not in the cards, however. At around 4:00 a.m., earsplitting screams stirred him from his slumber.

"They are taking the kids! They are taking the kids!" a woman was yelling.

Fernando jumped up from the floor and rushed to the door, which had a little window that looked out onto the station's quarters. Cramming himself against the other refugees, he could glimpse children being lined up and herded toward the building's exit. Andrea was in that line. So was a toddler who could barely stand by herself.

The shrieks inside the locked room became louder. Parents banged on the door, on the walls, demanding to be with their children: "What's happening?" "Where are you taking our kids?" More banging. More screaming.

No response. No one came to provide an explanation. And they couldn't escape, no matter how hard they pounded on the door. Trapped in that room, the parents saw their children leave the building one by one.

A woman sobbed desperately. "My baby! My baby!" she yelled. "Where did you take her? Brutes!" Her sequestered daughter, who had made the long journey with her from Honduras, was not even two years old. Still, no one came.

IN THE LAST DAYS OF JUNE 2018, IN WHAT WAS TURNING OUT TO BE AN UNusually hot summer, thousands of Americans stepped outside to attend one of the more than seven hundred demonstrations that erupted throughout the country to protest the Trump administration's zero-tolerance policy that was separating children from their parents while in detention. The marches took place in both liberal cities like Los Angeles and New York and conservative strongholds like Appalachia and Wyoming. Zero tolerance was one of Trump's most unpopular policies; only one-quarter of Americans supported it. Even a politically divided country, it seemed, could agree that Trump's family separation policy had gone too far.

But though hundreds of reporters descended outside the gates of the nation's detention centers, their cameras failed to capture what lay just beyond their frame. They didn't reveal that family separation constituted only one aspect of a much broader and more insidious issue, one that has been an affront to America's most fundamental democratic principles for more than a century.

Individuals detained without trial. Caged without explanation and without having been accused of committing any crimes. Denied basic constitutional rights. Unaware of when they will be released or if they will be released at all. Subjected to beatings and other torture. Americans have long pinned these abuses to far-off regimes and distant times: Nazi Germany, Pinochet's Chile, the Soviet Union. They do not happen here. If our leadership perpetrates these acts, we have believed, it does so for profoundly specific reasons and in marginal spaces outside the country: in legal black sites like Guantánamo Bay—a so-called island outside the law where terrorist suspects have been detained with limited access to rights.

In reality, however, Guantánamo-like facilities have arisen in towns and cities across America since the nineteenth century. Every day in the heart of the self-described "greatest democracy on earth," people are incarcerated without charges for indefinite periods of time, under horrific conditions and without basic constitutional protections. This is the hidden world of immigrant detention centers.

To understand how America came to be crisscrossed by a vast network of facilities where people are detained without basic rights, we have to look back almost 150 years to when Congress passed legislation that spawned what is now known as the "entry fiction." According to this doctrine, migrants stopped at the border are legally considered to be outside the country. When these "entrants" are detained in the United States while the government decides their fate, they are treated as if they are not here. This is the case whether the detention centers are near the border or deep within the country. The detention centers exist on the US map, but the "entrants" within them are presumed to be held outside the nation. Since they are "not here," detainees are not guaranteed basic constitutional protections—even when subjected to the laws and forces of the state. This fiction continues to dictate conditions for asylum seekers and migrants stopped at the border to this day.

Not all migrants caged in detention centers have been classified as "entrants" lacking rights. Unauthorized migrants who evade apprehension at the border and are only later detained—for example, those caught living without papers in Los Angeles—hold a different legal status. They are considered to have entered the nation and as such are accorded constitutional rights. Even these migrants, however, are caged in spaces originally conceived as sites where rights can be flouted.

Abuse is built deep into the bedrock of detention centers. Nowadays, federal statutes and regulations are supposed to guarantee at least baseline protections against inhumane conditions in immigrant detention facilities. Nonetheless, detained migrants have regularly been subjected to sexual and physical abuse from guards, forced to sleep outside in the snow or without airflow in sweltering heat, denied medical attention, and, as we know, torn from their children, who are caged elsewhere.

Much of this torture is by design. Since the 1980s, the US government has used the threat of detention to deter potential migrants from attempting to come into the country. Detention centers are purposely made to be horrid under the fallacious logic that the ghastlier such sites, the more successful they will be in dissuading foreign nationals from setting out for the United States.

Like the nation's prisons, immigrant detention centers tend to be located far from urban hubs, beyond the easy reach of most reporters, visitors, and lawyers. Given the shrouded nature of these sites, the vast majority of Americans are unaware of the horrors that happen inside these facilities or the astounding number of people caged there. In 2012, the Obama administration confined 477,523 migrants, and by 2019, the Trump administration held almost 511,000. Because of the pandemic, the number of detained migrants fell during the first year of the Biden administration to about 190,000, but by 2022, it had risen to approximately 307,000.

Indeed, since 1891, when the government first introduced federal immigration detention, millions of foreign nationals have been locked up. Computing the exact number of detentions over the years is impossible, because immigration officials employed arbitrary and changing counting methods over time and, even worse, failed to report detention figures for multiple years. Still, existing statistics show that between 1941 and 2022, there were at least fourteen million foreign nationals held behind bars. This means that more migrants have been detained over time than the current population of the entire state of Pennsylvania. It is no surprise, then, that the United States has created the largest immigrant detention system in the world.

Ignoring the existence of sites where people can be imprisoned and deprived of basic rights puts the rights of all people in America—including citizens—at risk, just as ignoring the presence of a cancer in a particular part of the body allows for metastatic growth and fatal spread elsewhere. In fact, immigrant detention has already helped shape other sites where basic rights are not guaranteed, regardless of citizenship. One of them is the prison system. For instance, the first private prison in the United States was originally a detention center. Since then, for-profit prison companies have lobbied to increase the incarceration of both American citizens and migrants in order to boost bottom lines.

The interconnectedness of prisons and immigrant detention centers is particularly notable because, in theory, the purpose of these two institutions is distinct. Unlike those held by the criminal justice system, detained migrants are not being penalized for breaking the law; they are being held until they can be deported or released. Nonetheless, the nation's detention and prison systems have grown side by side, buttressed by the same logic and arguments, to the point that they are now virtually indistinguishable.

The ability to deny rights to detained "entrants" upon arrival even paved the way for the development of Guantánamo Bay as a quintessential site of rightlessness. In 1991, President George H. W. Bush used the naval base in Guantánamo Bay, Cuba, to detain Haitian refugees. Both because Haitians were understood to be entrants and because Guantánamo was outside the United States, the government held that it did not have to provide detainees with full constitutional rights. When the war on terror broke out, George W. Bush merely continued the practice of interning and torturing individuals at Guantánamo.

From immigration to mass incarceration, from counterterrorism to constitutional law, the history of immigrant detention is ultimately America's history writ large. Even though most Americans have been oblivious to migrant incarceration, the effects of this system have been so far-reaching that they have come to endanger all our rights.

But it doesn't have to be this way. As this book will show, the history of immigrant detention also contains moments in which our leaders recognized the system as antithetical to the notion of justice and attempted to move away from it. During the period between the mid-1950s and early 1980s, US leaders spoke forcefully against immigrant incarceration and sought to curtail the practice. In 1958, the Supreme Court, in *Leng May Ma v. Barber*, even held that "physical detention of aliens is now the exception, not the rule," and pointed out that "certainly this policy reflects the humane qualities of an enlightened civilization." It is once again time to shine a light on our shared humanity and reject detention. There are, as we will see, more effective and just alternatives.

In the Shadow of Liberty unpacks the long, complex evolution of the federal detention of "entrants" by following Fernando's journey, as well as the stories of Fu Chi Hao, Ellen Knauff, and Gerardo Mansur—all migrants who were stopped at the border and thus stripped of basic rights. These four individuals were part of the most important transformations in the history of immigrant detention in America. Chi Hao migrated during the era of Chinese exclusion, when inland detention and the "entry fiction" originated. Ellen was a Jewish war bride who migrated from Germany to the United States after escaping the Holocaust, only to be detained on Ellis Island—the iconic site of hope and opportunity inviting the world's "poor, huddled masses." But Ellen's story also brought a reckoning: the national embarrassment of her very public case spurred a waning of the immigrant detention system that lasted for decades. The push to incarcerate migrants only returned in full force following the Mariel boatlift of 1980, which brought Gerardo to America. At this point, the system changed its logic. Previously, immigrants had been detained while the government decided whether they could stay or not; after 1980, the explicit goal of detention became to dissuade future migrants from embarking for the United States in the first place. Harm became detention's ready weapon. It was this deliberately pitiless system that Fernando and his daughter experienced when they sought asylum in 2018.

Given how invisible detention centers are deliberately made to be, it is not surprising that there is a dearth of available information on the experiences of migrants who have been held behind bars. To write this book, I conducted weeks-long oral history interviews with Gerardo and Fernando, as well as with their family members. I also consulted Chi Hao's and Ellen's meticulous memoirs, which detail not only their detentions but also their lives in their home countries, their migrations, and their arrivals in America.

Chi Hao, Ellen, Fernando, and Gerardo are people whom most Americans will find sympathetic. But likeability, or lack thereof, should not be a factor when it comes to detention. With this in mind, I also conducted over a hundred oral history interviews with Cubans and Central Americans who were detained from the 1980s to the present; analyzed thousands of letters that imprisoned migrants wrote to their lawyers as well as court decisions and legislative debates; and examined newspaper articles, government archives, personal collections, and unpublished ephemera. Together, these sources allowed me to document the experiences of not just the four individuals this book follows but of all their fellow sufferers fighting for their lives, determined to change their destinies. Their stories inform every page.

Ultimately, this book shows that if the United States is a nation of immigrants, then it is also a nation of prisoners. Coursing through the body of the country is a hidden history unlike the one most of us have been shown. From the late nineteenth century to the present, America has incarcerated migrants from all corners of the world, whether they be south-of-the-border asylum seekers or European migrants. They have been imprisoned under the most inhumane of conditions, without trials and often without even knowing why they are being held. America's history is not complete without their stories.

Part I

A DREAM DETAINED

1

CHRISTIAN LAND

Fu Chi Hao

SUMMER 1900

A horde of shirtless boys fell to the ground with a thud. Then, responding to a signal that only they could hear, they scrambled back to their feet. Next, the frenzy: a surging mass of boys, wild, hungry, and ready, pumping their fists into the air, flinging long, arcing kicks at no one but the gods to whom they were offering their urgent bodies. Their spasms were a ritual calling for the gods to possess them and infuse them with the necessary strength and invulnerability to fulfill their campaign.

By then, Fu Chi Hao had heard much about these infamous martial artists, known as Boxers, who were killing Christians throughout northern China, looting homes, and burning churches. But this was the first time that the lanky young Chinese teacher was seeing them in person. As if in a trance himself, Chi Hao pushed through the crowd, trying to see past the flock of onlookers like his life depended on it.

To be fair, it kind of did.

Chi Hao was not just any man among the hundreds of spectators watching the Boxer ritual. No, he was the target of these very practices. He was a stranger among strangers: a Christian in a country where many detested Christians and a Chinese native who lived and worked with foreign missionaries.

IT BEGAN WITH AN ILLNESS, A PIERCING PANG DEEP INSIDE MR. FU'S CHEST. Back then, Chi Hao, Mr. Fu's youngest son, was only a baby, and all Mr. Fu wanted was to admire his youngest child. Instead, he spent his days stooped and in agony, visiting physician after physician, searching for relief and finding none. He knew the pain would soon kill him.

Desperate, Mrs. Fu burned incense in the temples, begging the gods to cure him. She vowed to eat only the blandest of food until he recovered. When that didn't work, she bid the implacable gods to take twenty years of her life and give them instead to her beloved husband. She even followed the orders of the town's shaman, performing a complex ritual in the serpent-infested yard of a derelict temple, but her husband still did not recover.

After two years of this misery, a neighbor returned from a trip with information: he had heard that English doctors in the port city of Tianjin could remedy any illness. The family did not have much money, so Mrs. Fu sold some valuables for her husband's travel. There, at last, the miracle for which they'd searched: the doctors performed a painful but successful surgery. Mr. Fu was finally cured.

Now, for the doctors, this was not just a surgery. It was an opportunity to convert a "heathen." That was why they were in China in the first place.

"Your recovery is due not alone to the skill of doctors, but also to the grace of the true God," they told Mr. Fu. And, little by little, Mr. Fu became convinced that the evangelists were right.

Mrs. Fu? Not so much. At first, she wanted nothing to do with Christianity, fearing that her friends and neighbors would judge her harshly if she converted. Mr. Fu solved this issue by hiring a cart and relocating the family to a mission in Tongzhou, near Beijing, where they would not only be accepted but would also be able to reap the advantages that the missionaries provided. Living there, Mrs. Fu, too, became a disciple of Christ.

Growing up, Chi Hao knew no other life. His parents sent him to mission schools and then to the North China College, an academy that trained Chinese students to become Christian teachers. When he graduated, Chi Hao headed to Shanxi Province in northern China to teach in a Congregationalist mission run by a tight-knit group of missionaries from Oberlin College in Ohio.

One April day during his first year in Shanxi, Chi Hao woke up with a terrible headache. By the next morning he could barely stand up: a brutal bout of typhus fever was ravaging his body. The disease was known for its ruthlessness, and people were rightly scared of contagion. But one of the Oberlin missionaries, Dwight Howard Clapp, stayed by his side and nursed him back to health while other missionaries cooked for him and sent him gifts. Such kindness, he later wrote, "I can never repay, I can never forget."

Just like his father had experienced, the benevolence that the missionaries exhibited in the face of illness transformed Chi Hao. Perhaps this was why he was now willing to stand by the missionaries' side in their time of need.

AFTER SEEING THE YOUNG BOYS PERFORM THEIR POSSESSION RITUALS, CHI Hao tried to calm himself. His fear was not so much for himself as for his parents, who still lived near Beijing. A few weeks earlier, he had received a letter from them, telling him that the Boxers were gaining power in that region and had already disturbed their church. Since then, he had received no new messages.

Breathing in, Chi Hao reminded himself that the uncharacteristic silence did not necessarily mean something had happened to his family. Since the end of May 1900, roving bands of Boxers had severed communication between foreigners in different parts of China by tearing up rail lines, pulling down telegraph poles, and beating or killing anyone they caught carrying letters or dispatches written in a foreign language.

But Chi Hao did have reason to worry. After weeks of waiting, he finally received news, and it was worse than what he had feared. The Boxers had destroyed the North China College in Tongzhou, where he had studied and where his parents lived. He was immediately overcome by worry: Was his father alive? What about his mother? And his beloved teachers and friends from the college?

He needed answers. He needed to rush back home. Before he did so, however, one of the missionaries warned him about the dangers of making the trip and the likelihood that he would be stopped along the way. Chi Hao knew the missionary was right. And so, against his will, he stayed in Shanxi. Nothing was more excruciating than not knowing. He was filled with an impenetrable sense of hope and terror and loss.

"FU QING MIE YANG." (SUPPORT THE QING, DESTROY THE FOREIGN.) THIS WAS the slogan under which the Boxers first rose to prominence in 1899. It was an unequivocal cry against imperialism. And for most Chinese people, Christianity was the face of the foreign, the face of imperialism.

Missionaries were, in fact, imperialist actors. Their very efforts to convert Chinese to Christianity were efforts to impose Western values and culture upon them. Missionaries were also vital to imperialist projects, regularly working, for instance, as translators in treaty negotiations with Western powers. Under the "unequal treaties," China was forced to concede many of its territorial and sovereign rights to various powers, including Britain, France, and the United States. It had to cede Hong Kong to Britain, open its ports for foreign trade, and legalize the importation of opium. It also had to give foreign nationals in China extraterritorial rights, which allowed them to have their own legal, judicial, and police systems. It was these very treaties that gave Christian missionaries the right to propagate their faith in China without having to abide by Chinese laws.

As Chinese villagers' frustration toward imperialism grew, so did their resentment toward the foreign Christians living among them and trying to convert them. This anger enabled the Boxers to convince local villagers that the foreigners were responsible for any ills that might befall them—including the catastrophic drought that was destroying their livelihood.

Unsurprisingly, the rise of the Boxers caused much consternation in Europe and the United States. In mid-April 1900, warships from several European countries began arriving in China to protect their envoys. Two months later, an army composed of American, British, German, Russian, French, Japanese, Italian, and Austrian forces set out to capture Beijing. Although they failed to do so, they did manage to occupy the Dagu Forts, a key strategic site for their military efforts.

In retaliation for this occupation, on June 21, Empress Dowager Cixi named the Boxers yimin, "righteous people," and issued an official declaration of war against all foreign powers in China.

A wild wind was rolling through the country, and Chi Hao was caught up in its storm.

THE SCHOOL YEAR HAD NOT YET FINISHED, BUT CHI HAO AND HIS COLleagues understood what was happening that day in Shanxi when fathers showed up to take their sons home. The declaration of war had dramatically expanded the Boxers' reach, and violence had spread throughout the region. Before the end of June, the mission school closed its doors to protect the Chinese teachers and missionaries who remained inside. Every day, a mob gathered along the perimeter, yelling: "Kill the foreigners, loot the houses!"

From the mission, Chi Hao could see the anger in the streets. It was terrifying. The Boxers had already stormed other Christian compounds and brutally murdered everyone within them. They had tortured their victims; they had beheaded adults and children alike; they had burned down the missions with people inside.

The Boxers were not alone in perpetuating violence. In early July, Shanxi's governor issued a proclamation calling on Chinese Christians to end their association with foreigners, leave the missions, and recant their religion. Those who did so received state-issued certificates proving that they had renounced Christianity, which they pinned on their jackets. Those who did not knew that their decision might cost them their lives.

That very month, Chi Hao and his colleagues learned that the governor was heading toward their mission with three hundred soldiers and two hundred Boxers, intending to kill everyone who remained at the compound. Upon hearing this, most of the Chinese converts who were still there bolted, but Chi Hao could not force himself to do the same. As he silently paced back and forth across the schoolyard, trying to decide what to do, Charles Price, the mission's reverend, approached him with instructions to flee at once: "We foreigners would be recognized wherever we might go, so it is useless for us to flee. If there were hope, we would run too. There is hope that you might escape, and you cannot save us by remaining here."

Chi Hao had to agree. He walked out of the mission's gate just as rain began to fall. But he did not go far. A few hours later, he was back. He was not going to abandon his friends. If necessary, he would die with them.

BACK INSIDE THE COMPOUND, CHI HAO WAITED ALONGSIDE THE MISSIONARies for the siege. But as the nights passed, all they heard was the howling of invisible wolves deep in the nearby mountains. Chi Hao let himself wonder if the "news" they had received had been false. Perhaps they would be safe.

Then came the official order: a band of soldiers was to escort Chi Hao and the missionaries from the station in Shanxi to the port of Tianjin, where they would be expelled from the country. Once again, the missionaries instructed Chi Hao to flee, reasoning that, unlike them, he might have a chance of escaping to safety. But all Chi Hao could think was: "If I do not go with them, I am afraid their difficulties on the journey will be still greater. Perhaps I can help them a little."

On the day that the missionaries were to be exiled, Reverend Price reluctantly agreed to let Chi Hao join them, but not before making him promise that "When danger comes, if there is a chance for you to escape, you will make every effort to save your life so that, afterward, you can tell our story to others." Charles then gave Chi Hao several ounces of silver, as well as a small piece of blue cloth on which he had written: "This is a trustworthy man; he will tell you of our fate. C. W. Price." He told Chi Hao, "Hide this on your person, and if you get through to Tientsin [Tianjin], give it to any foreigner whom you may find. . . . They will take you to an American official."

His words, his signature, a little money. Charles was handing over to his friend not an entire life but what would remain if that life were snuffed out.

At nine that morning, four carts arrived at the compound's front gate to take the missionaries away. Thousands of villagers had also come to observe the exodus. Chi Hao and his friends mounted the carts, knowing how vulnerable they were. As they charged away, a gentle breeze caressed Chi Hao's face, reminding him that they had finally escaped their confinement. It was the first time that most of them had left the damp mission in weeks or even months. "It was all so beautiful and peaceful and strength-giving. So as soon as we were out in the country air, our spirits rose and fresh life and joy came to us," Chi Hao remembered years later.

The soldiers broke the peace. "Lend me your boots to wear," one ordered Chi Hao.

"Don't demand them of him; won't they be ours in a little while?" another soldier asked, laughing.

None of the English-speaking missionaries seemed aware of this conversation, but after the soldiers made a few more ominous comments, Chi Hao knew he and his friends were in danger. "If anything is going to happen, please tell me," he begged the soldiers.

There was a lengthy pause. The carts rolled forward; the only sound was the wheels whining on their axles. Finally, one of the soldiers spoke to his fellow countryman. "You ought to escape at once, for only a short distance ahead we are to kill the foreigners."

Chi Hao knew that this time there would be no reprieve. Almost instinctively, he jumped from the cart and began running. As he fled, he heard a rifle blast, but he kept going, trying not to think about his friends. He ran for miles and miles, even as his feet ached and his mouth cried for water.

When his energy was finally depleted, Chi Hao stopped at an inn. He was ravenous, and the place was lively, which allowed him to sit unnoticed in the press of bodies and listen to the chatter happening around him. The inn's guests were laughing at the massacre of foreigners that had just occurred a few villages away. At the killing of his friends. Chi Hao kept his face and body immobile as the details accumulated: The missionaries had been shot and slashed with swords. The soldiers had even murdered their children.

Just then, the waiter arrived with Chi Hao's food. But, as he later described, "had the emperor sent me the choicest viands from his table, I could not have swallowed a morsel."

HIS BODY WAS EMACIATED, HIS FACE SUNBURNED, HIS CLOTHES RAGGED, AND his feet bubbled with painful blisters, but after traveling more than three hundred miles, Chi Hao finally made it to Tianjin. From what he could see, the great city was ruined and deserted. Not a house remained standing on either side of the street. But here the foreign armies were still in control, and he was safe.

Chi Hao approached a group of American soldiers and produced the blue cloth that Charles had given him. For the next few days, the US Army fed him, and officials from the provisional government, composed of the eight foreign nations invading China, interviewed him. Chi Hao told his anguished story, time and time again, hoping that these officials would send help to any foreigners still in Shanxi.

Even so, he knew not to expect much. Soon after arriving in Tianjin, he learned that some of his family members had encouraged his parents to commit suicide so that they would avoid a worse fate. Before his mother died, Chi Hao was told, she had said: "My heart is very anxious for my youngest son . . . for I know not whether he is living or dead. If he ever returns to our village, will you for the sake of his old parents care for him and help him?"

Everyone Chi Hao loved was gone. Everyone who had loved him—gone.

Under the fog of a deep depression, he found little joy or meaning in life. Weeks turned into months. Then, on one dismal day, he received a letter from his old schoolteacher Luella Miner. She had written to inform him that she was taking K'ung Hsiang Hsi, whom Chi Hao had known since childhood, to America in a few weeks.

A direct descendant of Confucius, Hsiang Hsi was a handsome young man who would years later become a major figure in the Chinese Nationalist government, even serving as China's premier for a short stint. But at the time, no one could foresee that. Hsiang Hsi had recently worked in a Shanxi mission close to the one where Chi Hao had taught. Like Chi Hao, he had stayed with the missionaries for as long as he could, building barricades around the compound and running errands on the outside when necessary. The missionaries had given him letters they had written to their families to deliver in the future if he survived them.

In the end, leaving the mission was not Hsiang Hsi's choice. Two weeks before the Boxers massacred everyone at that station, his relatives kidnapped him and imprisoned him in their home. It was through the latticed window in the room where he was confined that Hsiang Hsi heard the howling crowd outside the mission and the rifle reports. Trapped, he listened to the murder of his friends.

Like Chi Hao, Hsiang Hsi was overcome by sorrow and trauma, but one thought kept him going: he must get to America and deliver to the families of the martyred missionaries the letters entrusted to him. After that, he thought, he should go study at Oberlin College, the very site where his beloved missionaries had come from.

As soon as he read Luella's letter, Chi Hao's sense of purpose returned: he had to join Luella and Hsiang Hsi. Chi Hao had studied English for ten years now, hoping to one day attend an American college. Now, his father and mother were gone, and he had no more ties to his homeland. Chi Hao reached out to Luella, and she agreed to take him to the United States as well.

CHINESE MIGRANTS BEGAN TRAVELING TO THE UNITED STATES IN SIGNIFICANT numbers following the discovery of gold in California in 1848. They came primarily from the Pearl River Delta region in Guangdong, which saw approximately one-quarter of its population head overseas in the nineteenth century. Turmoil pushed many to migrate. During the 1850s, the Red Turban Rebellion swept through Guangdong, and then the even more devastating Taiping Rebellion killed more than twenty-five million in southern China between 1850 and 1864. Other migrants boarded vessels headed to America with the dream of becoming rich after hearing popular stories about California's Gold Mountain, where solid gold nuggets supposedly covered the land.

The American steamship companies that transported Chinese migrants across the Pacific did actually secure mounds of gold and avidly fomented this migration. In 1867, the Pacific Mail Steamship Company began to offer regular service between Asia and San Francisco. It promoted these trips in a newspaper it published, describing the glorious opportunities that awaited Chinese émigrés in the United States.

But even as Western steamship companies profited from Chinese migration, many Americans, and especially those in California, detested the new arrivals. Reports written by American diplomats, traders, and missionaries in China influenced many Americans to view Chinese people as heathens who had inferior bodies, facial features, customs, foods, and morals—and who should not be welcomed in the United States.

Anti-Chinese sentiments amplified in the 1870s as a result of rising unemployment in California. White workers accused Chinese migrants of stealing jobs, lowering wages, reducing living standards, and bringing women from China for prostitution, thus slashing the nation's moral fabric. In 1877, a group of white workers formed the Workingmen's Party of California. Its rallying cry? "The Chinese Must Go!" Others adhered to similar calls. San Francisco lawyer H. N. Clement stood before a California State Senate committee and said: "We have a great right to say to the half-civilized subject from Asia, 'You shall not come at all.'"

These calls altered the course of US immigration. Up to that point, the federal government had not passed and enforced policies to regulate immigration at the national level. In 1852, the Supreme Court had even held: "This country is open to all men who wish to come to it. No question, or demand of a passport, meets them at the border. He who flees from crimes committed in other countries, like all others, is admitted; nor can the common thief be reclaimed by any foreign power. To this effect we have no treaty." Anti-Chinese demands changed that. In 1875, Congress passed the Page Act, prohibiting the entrance of convicted criminals, Asian laborers brought involuntarily, and women imported for prostitution. This last provision primarily targeted Chinese women, whom officials believed were trafficked to the United States for sex work.

Seven years later, in 1882, the government shut the nation's door still further through the passage of the Chinese Exclusion Act. This law barred Chinese laborers from entering the country and expressly allowed only a few "exempt" classes of Chinese people to continue to migrate: merchants, teachers, students, diplomats, and travelers.

But why should Chi Hao and Hsiang Hsi worry about this? The two men had already proven their worth and loyalty to America and its citizens through valiant action. They also had personal invitations from US missionaries and Oberlin College. And if that was not enough, they were coming as students, one of the exempt categories under which Chinese migrants could enter the United States.

CHI HAO FELT TERRIBLY NAUSEOUS AS HE AND HSIANG HSI MADE THEIR WAY to America aboard the *Doric*. Crammed with cargo and throngs of other passengers, the overcrowded steerage quarters lacked privacy and proper ventilation, which fomented the spread of disease. Most of the voyagers around Chi Hao were Chinese. On these trips across the Pacific, white people were discouraged—and sometimes even prevented—from traveling in the lower decks of the vessels.

On Thursday, September 12, 1901, the ship finally reached the welcoming lips of the Golden Gate—that long-awaited strait that connects the Pacific Ocean to the San Francisco Bay. Burnt-red and green cliffs, steeper than any wave through which the boat had sailed, put an end to the vast ocean. "The peril of the water, the seasickness on the boat, were both ended," Chi Hao recalled of his relief. He had arrived in Christian America—a country whose citizens would accept him because of, not despite, his beliefs.

A smaller boat appeared in the distance and glided toward the *Doric*, disturbing the serenity of the moment. From it emerged an inspector who boarded the much larger steamer. If this man concluded that even one person aboard carried a transmissible disease, the *Doric* would have to raise a yellow flag and head to quarantine at Angel Island, just as it had five months earlier over a case of smallpox.

The quarantine officer examined the passengers. After spending more than three weeks in the foul steerage quarters, Hsiang Hsi had fallen terribly ill. But the officer did not stop the boat because of it. Even if Hsiang Hsi was sick, he was presumed not to be contagious—and that was all this "doctor" cared about. Before long, the officer announced that the *Doric* was clear to proceed to the wharf.

Chi Hao's body tensed once more with anticipation, even though he knew he had to be patient. Luella had warned him and Hsiang Hsi that they were unlikely to disembark as soon as the vessel arrived, as white people were always first to leave. And so it happened: the two friends watched Luella and the other passengers from the first and second classes descend happily onto America's shores while those in the third class were kept inside. Hours passed. Everyone else had disembarked, but those in steerage still had not received any instructions. Chi Hao and Hsiang Hsi fell asleep that night aboard the still-rocking ship, left to imagine their new lives in America.

When they awoke the next morning, the steerage passengers were finally summoned to the deck. Inspectors from the Chinese Bureau had boarded the vessel to interrogate the migrants and determine whether they had the right to enter the country. Chi Hao and his friend headed up the stairs, carrying with them paperwork confirming that they were coming to the United States as students and were thus exempt from Chinese exclusion. When their turn came, the men handed their papers to the inspectors, ready to be waved into Christian land.

The inspectors examined the documents. Then they gruffly told the two men that they could not exit the boat.

Chi Hao and Hsiang Hsi could barely believe what they were hearing. Many of the other passengers around them had been allowed to disembark. Why hadn't they? The inspectors provided them no explanation.

It was not until later that afternoon that the two friends learned what was wrong. To enter the United States as a member of an exempt category, a Chinese migrant had to hold a certificate issued by the Chinese government and endorsed by the American consul. The immigration inspectors in San Francisco were claiming that the wrong Chinese official had issued the paperwork and that the American consul had made some errors when endorsing the permits.

Because of these purported mistakes, the two students were to be deported on the *Doric*, which was heading back to China the following week. In the meantime, they were to be detained aboard the steamer.

Their valiant sacrifices to save the lives of American citizens during the Boxer Uprising. Their legal right to enter the country. Their verifiable status as students. None of it mattered: they would still be detained; they would still be deported.

2

LADY LIBERTY GREETS EUROPEAN IMMIGRANTS

Ellen Knauff

AUGUST 14, 1948

Ellen gazed at the dazzling fantasy that emerged before her, breaking the evenness of the horizon. It looked almost as if a massive spider were extending its leg out of the thick ocean brume, but Ellen was too much of a realist to believe that. For the last ten days, she had been aboard the ironically named USAT *Comfort*. All she had felt was nausea, and all she had seen in the distance was water and fog. As the ship sailed on, she finally recognized the image before her: it was not a spider's leg but the Parachute Jump at Coney Island.

Like thousands of immigrants before her, Ellen had dreamed that the Statue of Liberty would be her first glimpse of the United States, even though her husband, Kurt, had warned her that it would not be. How she wished he were with her now, introducing her to his country, welcoming her home. After all, he was the reason she was coming to America.

Just then, a band began to play. The *Comfort* had arrived. All around her, the other war brides aboard the ship started cheering. They had come from across Europe, but they were now arriving in their new homeland. Among them was Rosi Dyer, a short twenty-six-year-old Romanian woman with brown hair and green eyes who had recently married a GI from small-town Texas. There was also Jadwiga Osowicz, who was traveling with her two teenage daughters. And then there were war brides like Katherine Martinoff, who was lucky enough to be traveling with her GI husband by her side.

The loudspeaker boomed throughout the ship, briefly distracting Ellen from thoughts about Kurt. All war brides were to go to the main cabin, a voice instructed. Feeling seasick and tired, Ellen walked there slowly and joined a long line of women who were waiting for officials to inspect their passports.

As she waited, Ellen barely noticed the officer entering the cabin, until he began to yell. "I want her," the man hollered, pointing his finger at a name on the list. He then turned around and looked at the women. "You! You sit over here!" he said, gesturing wildly. None of the war brides felt called upon. "Get a move on! What are you waiting for?" he bellowed again, now pointing directly at Ellen.

Ellen did as he ordered, but the hollering did not stop. "Where are your documents? I want them," the inspector yelled. Then, after reviewing them, he asked loudly: "How many husbands have you got?" And, without allowing her time to answer, he shouted: "Two! Two husbands!"

If this were true, it would have been a huge problem, given that Ellen was trying to enter the United States as the wife of an American GI. But it wasn't true.

"May I show you my divorce papers?" Ellen asked politely, realizing the potential source of the confusion.

"I am not interested. You know what's wrong with you," the man roared before adding, "I am sending you to a place where they will look after you."

I am sending you to a place where they will look after you. That is what the Nazis had told Jews as they herded them into freight cars—the exact scenario that Ellen, a Jewish Holocaust survivor from Germany, was trying to leave in her past. Those very words were probably what the Nazis had told her parents, she thought. Against her will, Ellen broke down.

THE FIRST TIME ELLEN FLED—IN A MOVE THAT LIKELY SAVED HER LIFE—she did so for a man, Edgar Boxhorn. But that, of course, was not the whole story.

The year was 1934, and nineteen-year-old Ellen was in love. Her parents, however, felt differently. Her father was a prosperous clothing manufacturer; Edgar was an insolvent traveling salesman. Both her father and her mother were German; Edgar was Czech. Both her parents were Jewish; Edgar was only part Jewish. Edgar could not be trusted, Ellen's parents insisted as they tried to prevent her from seeing her handsome suitor.

Life outside Ellen's home was even harder. Hitler had only risen to power a year earlier, but for German Jews, everyday life had already changed dramatically. The Nazis had banned Jews from taking jobs as civil servants, lawyers, farmers, or editors, and from studying medicine, dentistry, or pharmacy. They had organized boycotts against Jewish shops and businesses and ordered public burnings of Jewish books. In the industrialized city of Dortmund, where Ellen and her family lived, Nazis had placed billboards on Jewish houses, stores, and synagogues denouncing Jews as vermin.

And so Ellen made a decision. Without her parents' blessing, she nonetheless married Edgar and relocated with him to Prague.

Unfortunately, she soon realized that her parents had been right about her new husband. Edgar preferred spending time in nightclubs to being at home. He had girlfriends in every town to which his business took him. And he had numerous debts. Ellen put up with his behavior until one day, during a fight, he threatened to call Germany's secret state police, the Gestapo, on her father.

That was it. At a time when almost no one divorced in Czechoslovakia, Ellen decided that she would. She fled her home with Edgar as if it were ablaze. She had no job, no place to live, and no family in Prague, yet she knew that she could not return to Dortmund. Since her departure, the situation for Jews in Germany had only become direr, in part because the Nuremberg Laws had stripped them of citizenship, designating them instead as "subjects" of the state. And so Ellen remained in Prague and took a job handling English correspondence for a leather business. She found a place to live and friends to call family.

Back home, the situation continued to deteriorate. On November 9 and 10, 1938, in an episode known euphemistically as Kristallnacht, civilians and Nazi paramilitary storm troopers attacked Jewish people throughout Germany and destroyed their synagogues, businesses, homes, hospitals, cemeteries, and schools. Amid the chaos, the Nazis arrested thirty thousand Jewish men aged sixteen to sixty and sent them to concentration camps. Peter Hans, Ellen's only sibling, was too young to be taken, but her father, Gustav, was not.

"Arbeit Macht Frei" (Work Makes You Free) read the sign on the front gate of the Sachsenhausen concentration camp, where the storm troopers took Gustav and six thousand other Jews following Kristallnacht. Escaping was almost impossible. A three-meter-high wall and an electric fence surrounded the camp's perimeter. Outside that wall, Ellen's family worried about Gustav, knowing almost nothing about his state; inside it, Gustav and the other imprisoned men were forced to sleep in overcrowded barracks and to toil in SS workshops. They were provided little food and had to wear old, ragged uniforms unsuitable for the bitter cold of that particularly frigid November.

After several weeks of this torture, the Nazis gave the men's families a way out: they could pay an exorbitant extortion fee for the release of their loved ones. Gustav and most of the other men were released, but by then the guards at Sachsenhausen had killed 450 prisoners, including 17 from Dortmund.

The terror soon reached Prague, where Ellen still resided. In March 1939, only four months after Kristallnacht, Germany occupied Czechoslovakia. Ellen did not think twice: it was time to flee again. She got her hands on a visa to enter England and headed there as soon as possible. Within a few weeks of her arrival, she managed to get hired as a cook and housekeeper and began helping the Women's Voluntary Services. She would remain in England for the rest of the war.

It was not until May 1946 that Ellen relocated again. This time, she was not fleeing Nazism. By then, Hitler's Wehrmacht had been defeated. The United States, Britain, France, and the Soviet Union had carved Germany into four zones, each to be administered by a victorious power. To govern its zone, the US Army of Occupation in Germany needed workers, and Ellen decided to apply for one of its jobs. She passed the US Army's security clearance and was hired to work in its Civil Censorship Division. She was moving back to Germany with one goal: to unearth the truth about what had happened to her family.

The country to which she returned was nothing like the one she had left. Between one-quarter and one-half of all the houses had been destroyed. Millions of homeless German refugees roamed the streets. Factories were closed. Inflation was rampant and food scarce.

Ellen could not focus on the misery she saw; she had a mission. During the workday, she performed her job, listening to German telephone calls and reporting any infringement of the military government's rules and regulations. In her spare time, she searched for her family. It did not take her long to find out what had happened to her loved ones. The Red Cross listed the news, and the Jewish community in Dortmund confirmed it: her parents and her brother had been murdered in an extermination camp near Riga.

LIKE MOST GERMAN JEWS, ELLEN'S PARENTS HAD TRIED TO ESCAPE AFTER Kristallnacht, but Nazi bureaucratic roadblocks obstructed the ways out of Germany, and other countries' immigration restrictions made it difficult to enter them.

In the United States, President Franklin D. Roosevelt had already recognized the plight of German Jews and called for an international conference to discuss how to aid those seeking to flee Germany. In July 1938, delegates from thirty-two nations met in Évian-les-Bains, France, to discuss the issue. In the end, however, most countries—including the United States—refused to admit German refugees, even Jewish ones.

At the time, the United States did not distinguish between immigrants and refugees, and it severely limited immigration. The Immigration Act of 1924 capped the number of annual immigrants from each country based on the number of foreign-born persons from that country who had resided in the United States in 1890. The quota for those trying to flee Nazi Germany was abysmally low given the need. After March 1938, when Germany annexed Austria, America's immigration quota for people born in those two countries was 27,370 per year. Yet between 1939 and 1941, more than 300,000 Germans—most of whom were Jewish—asked for immigration visas to enter the United States. The wait time for these refugees was years long—time they didn't have.

Attempts to allow more German Jews to immigrate to America beyond the quota system failed in great part because of existing antisemitism. In February 1939, New York Democratic senator Robert Wagner and Massachusetts Republican congresswoman Edith Nourse Rogers introduced legislation to admit, outside the quota system, twenty thousand German refugee children who were under the age of fourteen. But polls quickly revealed that most Americans opposed the proposal, and Congress never voted on the bill.

That May, the transatlantic liner *St. Louis* sailed from Hamburg, Germany, to Havana, Cuba, with more than nine hundred Jewish passengers. The travelers planned to stay in Havana until their turn came up on the long wait list for US visas. But when the liner arrived in Havana, Cuban officials refused to allow the refugees onto the island. The

St. Louis then headed to Florida, with those aboard hoping the United States would take them. But soon after it anchored in Miami, US officials forced it to turn back to Europe with its passengers. An estimated 254 of those people were later murdered in the Holocaust.

Ellen's parents, Gustav and Elisabeth, and her nineteen-year-old brother, Peter Hans, were among those who would never find a way out of Germany. They stayed in Dortmund until 1942, when they received the dreaded notice to report to a collection camp. From there, they would be deported by train to a ghetto in Riga, Latvia.

We are sending you to a place where they will look after you.

The ghetto had been created in the summer of 1941, when the Nazis had forced Riga's thirty-three thousand Jews to relocate to a rundown suburb that was big enough for only a third of them. The Jewish population did its best to survive, assembling a small hospital, forming its own police force, and creating a committee to assign jobs. But order was short-lived. On the evening of November 29, SS paramilitaries stormed into the ghetto. They threw children from windows, pushed women down the stairs, and fired indiscriminate shots into crowds. They then marched more than fifteen thousand of the ghetto's residents toward the Rumbula Forest, where graves had already been dug.

It took days to kill them all. Under close watch, the victims waited for their turn in the forest's biting cold as their fellow Jews were massacred. One managed to scrawl a little note: "Don't forget us—take revenge."

Almost a week later, the Nazis returned to repeat their carnage. In total, they murdered between twenty-four and twenty-nine thousand Jews on these two occasions. By December 9, only five thousand people remained in the ghetto, most of them men who held jobs vital to the war effort.

The inhumanity of this bloodbath did not faze the Nazis, but the resultant scarcity of laborers in the region did. Not long after the massacre, they decided to repopulate the ghetto by bringing in Jews from Germany, Austria, and Czechoslovakia.

The first Jews from Western Europe to arrive in Riga were appalled by what they saw. The houses that they were to now inhabit still held the remnants of those who had just been killed. Gertrude Schneider, who was deported from Austria to the Riga ghetto, described finding "food, frozen solid, still on plates, dentures frozen in glasses of water." It took months to scrub off the many bloodstains that marked the walls, floors, and steps of their new homes.

The ghetto was still reeling on February 1, 1942, when the last train bringing Jews from Western Europe lurched into the station. It was the one from Dortmund, carrying Gustav, Elisabeth, and Peter Hans.

Twenty thousand people, all besieged with hunger, diarrhea, frostbite, and swollen feet, now teemed the ghetto. They were only allowed to leave to perform arduous work in the city and its surroundings, such as shoveling snow or unloading goods in the harbor.

Murder was a regular affair. In the spring of 1942, the Nazis informed a group of detained Jews—primarily comprising those who were elderly, sick, or had young children—that they would be sent to labor in another city's fish canneries. Many welcomed this news, believing that the canneries might provide access to food and a reprieve from the cold.

As the Jews boarded the trucks that were supposed to take them to the canneries, an SS soldier asked a boy for his name and age. "Rudy Nadel, drei Jahre, ledig, und gesund!" (Rudy Nadel, three years old, single, and healthy!) responded the kid gleefully. The SS soldier could not help but laugh and gave the boy a piece of candy. He then urged him and his father to get back in line so that they would not miss their truck.

When the trucks returned to the ghetto a few days later, the Nazis ordered a group of Jewish women to unload their contents. The trucks contained clothes, baby bottles, toys, photographs, and eyeglasses. The women immediately recognized what they were unpacking: the belongings of their family members and friends who had surely been murdered. The stories they had heard about the Latvian Jews were now happening to them.

There are no records of how Gustav died, but as the Red Cross had informed Ellen, he was killed in Riga. Contrary to what the Red Cross had reported, however, her mother and younger brother were murdered in another camp.

On July 23, 1944, the Soviet Army pushed past German forces and entered Lublin, Poland. There, they came upon the Majdanek extermination camp. The camp's staff had fled Majdanek in haste, without taking time to dismantle incriminating evidence. Virtually all of its horrors remained intact: gas chambers, a warehouse packed with shoes, ovens with half-cremated bodies. War correspondents swiftly descended on the camp to document and publicize German atrocities through interviews with some of the five thousand individuals the Nazis had incarcerated but left behind.

After that, SS commander Heinrich Himmler resolved to prevent the Nazis from being exposed again. He ordered the evacuation of all concentration camps and subcamps within the Soviet Army's reach. Those in captivity were to be moved to camps within the interior of the Reich. On August 9, 1944, the Nazis transferred Elisabeth to the Stutthof concentration and extermination camp near Danzig and on October 1 sent Peter Hans there as well. Twelve days later, the Soviet Army liberated Riga.

A rotten smell greeted Peter Hans when he arrived at Stutthof. It wafted from the gas chamber and crematorium used to massacre those who were too sick or weak to work. Nazi soldiers regularly told their victims that the gas chambers were showers and ordered them to disrobe before entering. Once the prisoners were inside, the soldiers locked the doors and released the lethal gas.

It is likely that this is how Peter Hans was killed. As with Gustav, no records remain that disclose how he or Elisabeth died. But we know that Peter Hans did not make it past his second week in Stutthof.

As for Elisabeth, her records indicate that she perished in the camp on December 30, 1944, probably having succumbed to the typhoid epidemic rampant in the camp that winter. A Stutthof survivor recalled:

"The girls fell ill and lay in their filth, no longer able to get up. We relieved ourselves in the bowls from which we ate, and we threw the excrement out of the window. When a hand trembled and the girl did not have the strength to turn the bowl outside, the excrement spilled onto the heads of others."

Ellen might not have known the details of her family members' deaths, but what she knew was more than enough. Germany, a country she would forever associate with the horrors of the Holocaust, was not a place where she could settle permanently.

ELLEN MET KURT KNAUFF AT A PARTY SHORTLY AFTER RETURNING TO GERmany. He, like Ellen, worked for the US Army of Occupation in Germany. And, like Ellen, he was a native German who had opposed the Nazis. Kurt had migrated to the United States in 1929. After the war broke out, he naturalized as a US citizen, enlisted in the US Army, and fought against his country of birth. He had been awarded all sorts of ribbons and medals for his service, but he never placed them on his uniform, which he still wore regularly. In truth, he did not need to sport his honors: the small scar on his chin already conjured images of courageous heroism.

Ellen was not the only woman who found Kurt mesmerizing. Admirers competed for his favor and clung to his every word. When Ellen first met him, he was going on regular dates with a woman named Eve and, on occasion, with other women as well. No one faulted him for it, as the onus of sexual respectability fell on women. Indeed, the US Army and the domestic press regularly accused fräulein (single German women) of being promiscuous in the hopes of seducing American GIs who might take them to the United States.

Knowing about Kurt's entanglements, Ellen did not expect much when she first started dating this particularly handsome GI. But they had a special connection. They loved the same music, and both were interested in photography. The two enjoyed hunting and fishing: Kurt had taught Ellen how to cast, and she had reeled in an eight-pound pike on her very first throw. Noting that she was a natural, Kurt gifted her a large tackle box, identical to his. Ellen distinguished the two boxes by marking them as HIS and HERS with nail polish.

To the ire of other women, it was clear that they belonged together.

The war had taught the lovers not to waste time, but they could not marry in haste: the Army of Occupation, for which they both worked, required them to get security clearance before they could marry. It was a long process, but each complication only made them more resolved to tie the knot. On February 28, 1948, they finally did.

Even though the newlyweds lived in Germany, Kurt wanted to eventually return to the United States. If Ellen wished to follow—and she did—it was best that she head to America immediately. In 1945, Congress had passed the War Brides Act, which allowed foreign spouses of GIs who had fought in the Second World War to be admitted to the United States without needing to go through the onerous visa process. But the act was set to expire imminently, in December 1948. Before it did, the couple decided Ellen would go to the United States, become a US citizen, and then return to Germany to be with Kurt until they could permanently relocate to America.

And so it was that Ellen opted to migrate once again for a man. The last time she had done so, she had lost her parents and Peter Hans forever. This time, it would be different. This time, she was moving away from the country that had killed her family and going to the country that had come to represent democracy. And she was doing so for the only person alive whom she could now call family.

It was with these thoughts in mind that Ellen embarked aboard the USAT *Comfort*.

3

CUBANS ARE WELCOME

Gerardo Mansur

SPRING 1979

Gerardo Mansur observed Rafael carefully. Once a gangly boy who would lose every time he played marbles, the man who now stood before him flashed swanky clothes and talked with confidence. And although Gerardo had trouble focusing on his old friend's monologue, it was easy to catch the gist of what he was saying. "In America, there is freedom. . . . No one is watching you, and you can say and do whatever you want without risking prison for it."

Gerardo, who had never left his home country, knew Cuba's prisons firsthand. While completing his military service, he'd refused a sergeant's order, and the officer had retaliated by canceling his leave, which had led Gerardo to protest by setting a mattress on fire. Nine years had passed since then, but Gerardo still blamed Fidel Castro's regime, rather than his act of vandalism, for his imprisonment.

It wasn't just prison. Castro's government expected everyone to join the Committees for the Defense of the Revolution (CDRs), which consisted of state-affiliated associations that existed on each block in Cuba and acted as the "eyes and ears of the Revolution." Members of the CDRs were always on the lookout, ready to report "suspicious" or "criminal" behavior, like having unknown visitors, buying red meat, or dressing unconventionally.

To Castro, such surveillance seemed indispensable: it was the middle of the Cold War, the US surely had spies secreted all over the island, and Cuban citizens needed to remain loyal to the spirit of the Revolution. But like many in Cuba, Gerardo begrudged neighbors watching his every move. As he recalled years later, "They kept an eye on you. It was constant. They checked what you carried in and out, at what time you were coming back, at what time you were leaving, what you were doing." The CDRs made him feel as if he lived in a panopticon, where people's behavior was shaped by the knowledge that they were regularly monitored. Like Gerardo, all those who did not fully support the Revolution and its ideals lived in fear that they would be accused by the CDRs and arrested.

His friend carried on: "In America, if you work, you become rich. . . . I own two cars and a big house with all the comforts . . . a washing machine."

Rafael was one of the hundred thousand Cuban exiles who descended on the island in 1979 to visit friends and family after the Cuban government suddenly began allowing émigrés who had fled the country to return. The visitors wore fashionable clothes and carried suitcases bulging with books, records, televisions, and stereos to gift to their relatives. They stayed in posh hotels and drank alcohol at fancy bars, such as El Floridita, where Ernest Hemingway had once sipped frozen daiquiris. These were luxuries few islanders could enjoy.

Gerardo had heard about the wonders of America since he was a child. In 1960, Castro's government passed an urban reform law to address Cuba's housing inequalities that stripped landlords of their rental properties. Cubans were only permitted to retain possession of their places of residence. Before that law came into being, Gerardo's grandparents and primary caretakers had been well-to-do real estate investors who took great pride in their elegant portfolios. Afterward, they whispered to Gerardo of a magical place where the limitless horizon glistened with skyscrapers. If Gerardo ever had a chance, they told him, he must flee across the Florida Straits. He must go to America.

Gerardo had yearned to migrate since those early days, and his desire to do so had only increased over the years. By then, his father and grandparents had already died, and he had divorced. Only his children would miss him if he left—Gerardo knew that his ex-wife would never allow their kids to migrate with him. But imagine if he could provide them with all the worldly goods America had to offer. He envisioned himself in Rafael's position, his arms heavy with presents, his pockets brimming with dollars.

In his longing to live the American dream, Gerardo resembled thousands of others throughout Latin America and the Caribbean who desperately wanted to migrate. There was an important difference, however. Mexicans, Dominicans, Central Americans, and others had difficulty migrating because the US government would not allow them entry. But the United States welcomed Cubans, holding them up as symbols of the failures of Castro's regime. The Cuban government, however, did not allow its citizens to leave the island. Though most Cubans supported the Revolution and had no desire to flee, thousands of others would have jumped at the opportunity—so much so that Castro feared mass emigration would drain the nation's labor force and give rise to movements that aimed to topple his government from abroad, as had happened in April 1961 with the Bay of Pigs invasion.

Gerardo turned his attention to the harbor, looking past the gray seawall toward the horizon. About one hundred miles away lay America, the country everyone talked about as the land of freedom. A place where riches abounded; where the CDRs did not hang over citizens like low, ominous clouds; where no one had to live in fear of being imprisoned for no good reason. It was almost at Cuba's doorstep yet felt impossibly distant.

IT WAS THE SPRING OF 1980, AND RADAMÉS GÓMEZ WAS HURRYING TO VISIT his friend and neighbor Héctor Sanyustiz. The opportunity they had been waiting for had finally arrived: their chance to leave Cuba and the regime they abhorred.

Rumors had spread through the capital faster than the Havana sky changed colors at dusk. Two days earlier, a driver had crashed his bus through the gates of the Peruvian embassy after hearing that the Andean country would grant asylum to anyone deemed deserving. Now, Cubans were whispering that all those aboard the bus would soon be on their way to Lima—and Radamés had concocted a scheme to join them.

The plan was simple: Héctor had been a bus driver in Havana for many years. If he could convince one of his former coworkers to provide him with a bus sturdy enough to break through the embassy's fence, he and Radamés could present themselves to the Peruvians and plead for asylum. All they had to do was pray that the bus would withstand the gunfire that would surely be unleashed on them by the Cuban guards who surrounded the compound.

Less than a week later, on April 1, the two friends tried their luck. Together with three companions and the driver whose bus they used, they pointed the vehicle toward the Peruvian embassy and hit the gas. Immediately, a barrage of bullets pummeled its metal exterior. Héctor continued to accelerate until the bus came to a halt. Almost as if in slow motion, the shooting also stopped. Héctor looked around. Radamés was slouched behind him, bleeding from his head and back. Héctor's own leg was injured from the crash. Outside the compound lay Pedro Ortiz Cabrera, a Cuban guard who had been killed in the crossfire. But the bus had made it across the fence line and into the embassy. They might be safe.

The Peruvian ambassador had already received orders to support Cuban asylum seekers. At once, he sent the injured bus passengers to a military hospital under the care of the Peruvian government. When the head of Cuban state security arrived at the embassy to apprehend Héctor and his conspirators, the Peruvians refused to hand them over.

Behind closed doors, Castro plotted out a plan of his own. When he heard of the guard's death, according to one of his aides, "his face turned deep red" with anger. On April 4, Castro ordered the police to tear down the barriers protecting the embassy. After pulling out all guards, he announced in *Granma,* the official state newspaper, that his government would no longer risk the lives of its soldiers to defend the embassy from the "common criminals, lumpen, and antisocial elements" who sought to leave Cuba. If all went according to plan, Castro thought, hundreds of Cubans would head to the compound seeking asylum. The logistical nightmare would force Peruvian officials to change course.

But it did not go according to plan.

As if under a spell, cooks dropped their spatulas, factory workers shut off their machines, office employees laid down their pens, and one bus driver even stopped his daily route and instructed the passengers to wait for the next bus. They flocked to the embassy by the thousands. Within two days of Castro's announcement, approximately 10,800 people had taken refuge in the Peruvian embassy.

Gerardo prowled around the perimeter of the compound, wondering whether he should go in. What would happen to those inside? Would the government allow them to leave the country, or would the police arrest them all? Would the military shoot them? Gerardo scanned the embassy one more time and then skulked away, scared that one of his neighbors would see him there. Perhaps he would return the following day.

BY APRIL 6, IT WAS TOO LATE FOR GERARDO. THAT MORNING, THE CUBAN police erected barricades around the embassy and prohibited anyone else from entering. Those inside continued to await word about their fate. Students, babies, housewives, construction workers, farmers, and office employees were pressed up against each other in tight quarters, without shelter from the tropical sun. Some climbed on the roof to get some space, dark shadows against an unfeeling sky. "There were too many people, ten thousand or around ten thousand five hundred in a small square, and we were all there piled up one on top of the other, without showering, without eating, without being able to wash ourselves or anything," recalled Carlos Pardon, who had taken refuge inside. "It was depressing."

Lacking supplies, the crowd was soon beset by hunger. The refugees devoured the embassy's plants and roasted anything they could catch—from cats to the ambassador's pet parrot. Eventually, Cuban officials sent cartons of food, but the quantities were always insufficient. "Only the children could eat, because there was simply not enough," Pardon explained.

Outside the embassy, CDRs and other state organizations coordinated protests to vilify the refugees. "Let the lumpen go!" they yelled. "Cuba for the workers!" Not a day went by without masses taking to the streets to demonstrate against the "parasites," "scum," and "delinquents." On April 19, the government celebrated the nineteenth anniversary of the Bay of Pigs invasion with a national rally against the refugees. Che Guevara's father was one of the million attendees. A similarly thunderous rally on May 1, International Workers' Day, brought together figures such as Nicaraguan leader Daniel Ortega and Nobel Prize–winning author Gabriel García Márquez. The crowds enveloped the plaza with pro-Fidel chants, colorful banners, and placards.

Buoyed by this wave of support, Castro decided to rid the island of those who fell into the category of his despised "scum": queer people, sex workers, counterrevolutionaries. On April 21, he announced in *Granma* that he would allow Cuban Americans and Cuban émigrés living in the United States to sail into the port of Mariel to collect their relatives and friends. He urged all Cubans who wished to leave to apply for exit permits from newly opened government offices and to call their relatives in the United States to come pick them up.

Thus began a historic rush: from Florida, émigrés dashed to the nearest port, found boats, and sped to Cuba, where thousands swarmed government buildings for permission to leave the island.

Gerardo's opportunity had arrived. Now he could leave Cuba legally, and there was no question that he would be welcomed in the United States. Americans had long celebrated Cuban exiles as defectors from a Communist regime, and on May 3, more than two weeks before Gerardo departed, President Jimmy Carter delivered a speech promising that the United States would embrace the people fleeing Cuba with "an open heart and open arms."

It looked to Gerardo like the beginning of a glorious new day.

GERARDO SLOWLY STROLLED ALONG THE CRACKED SIDEWALK, HOPING NOT to look suspicious. People's homes were festooned with signs that read "Scum! Let Them Go!" From a block away, he spotted his friend Paulito waiting for him in his best attire, twitching with nervousness. Gerardo grinned. He could not blame his high-strung friend for such lack of guile. "Let's do this," Gerardo muttered. The two men took deep breaths, clasped hands, and marched into the station.

Inside, a pungent stench of sweat assaulted their nostrils. People packed the building—all desperate to leave Cuba. Gerardo and Paulito took their place in line, which crawled along at a snail's pace. One man wore a dress; others held letters from their CDRs certifying that they were dissidents or "antisocial." Like Gerardo and Paulito, they had no family members in the United States who could sail to Cuba to claim them, but if the government found them to be sufficiently undesirable, it still might allow them to flee. A man at the front of the line pranced flamboyantly in front of the officers, who snickered with disgust. Gerardo's mind returned to the same question: If he could not convince the officers to give him an exit permit on the basis that he was an undesirable, what would happen to him?

Gerardo and Paulito approached the head of the line. "Step forward," the officer commanded. It was now or never.

"We are seeking to leave Cuba because we are homosexuals," Gerardo lied. "He is my boyfriend."

The officer looked skeptically at Gerardo and then at Paulito. "Is he? Then kiss him."

Without thinking twice, Gerardo grabbed his friend and passionately met his lips. The officer smirked. He stamped both men's identification booklets with an *R*, a letter that would open the gates of Cuba for them. It signaled that they had begun the process of leaving the country. However, it was also a scarlet letter: if they failed to depart, the government would make their lives miserable. The officer instructed the men to go home and await further instructions. Above all, he said, they should stay indoors. Right-thinking citizens were already retaliating against the "scum."

The following morning, Gerardo awoke to shouting. Pulling back a corner of his threadbare yellow curtain, he saw a scrum of twenty to thirty people, many of them neighbors with whom he had played as a young boy. They cursed him and lobbed eggs at his house, the yolks splashing against the walls.

Thousands of other houses in Cuba were similarly befouled. Nara Roza, who lived on the highest floor of her apartment building on the other side of Havana, recalled the protests as a daily occurrence. One day, Nara watched, stupefied, as a mob chased a family friend down the street, pelting her with stones as she ran.

GERARDO HID IN HIS HOUSE FOR THREE DAYS BEFORE HE HEARD A KNOCK ON the door. A police officer stood outside—his time had come. "Let's go," the officer said when Gerardo opened the door. "You are getting out of here." There was no time to say goodbye to his family or friends. Gerardo climbed into the patrol car, which took him to a bus depot. The officer instructed him to board one of the idling coaches.

As the bus inched through the impressive Miramar neighborhood, Gerardo saw sidewalks teeming with children wearing neckerchiefs symbolizing their membership in the pioneros, the mandatory state-led youth organization. Its aim was purportedly to aid in the children's "spiritual and moral development," but at that moment, the children were chucking eggs and tomatoes at the buses. Gerardo wondered how they could justify wasting so much food during a time of such economic hardship.

Despite the best efforts of the mobs and pioneros to intimidate the defectors, the bus arrived at "El Mosquito" after a seemingly interminable ride. This tent camp by the port of Mariel would be the exiles' final way station. Dazed, Gerardo drifted through the crowd. All he wanted was a place to sit, but this sea of people felt as vast as the ocean that was to take him away. Tarps covered large parts of the camp—some even had bunk beds nestled inside—but there was no space to be found anywhere he looked. Eventually he perched himself on some rocks and futilely tried to remain calm.

The sun beat down as Gerardo's thoughts circled around the same fears: "Oh my God, I said I was a homosexual. If I don't leave now, I'll be considered a homosexual . . . and also a counterrevolutionary. I'll be in so much trouble." Being at El Mosquito, he knew, was no guarantee that he would be allowed to leave.

The sense of dread was universal throughout the camp. Nara remembered seeing guards with dogs approach a family of five. "You can all go, but the woman has to stay," the guards said. It could happen to anyone. The refugees' dreams of the future, the sadness of leaving loved ones behind, the melancholy of departing from their homeland—all receded before the dreaded prospect of having to stay in Cuba with the scarlet *R* on their identification cards.

Their distress increased as conditions worsened. Every day, state officials would distribute boxes of food and water, but they were always "a pittance," recalled Gerardo. One day, he watched a small but boisterous rabble beseech the officers for more food. The guards let loose their dogs. One snarling animal ripped the thigh muscle off a young man as if his flesh had been silk. Horrified, Gerardo fled to his refuge on the rocks.

Days passed, stifled by heat, hunger, thirst, and fear. He later remembered, "It was like being Robinson Crusoe," subsisting without enough food or water, exposed to the elements, "but with thousands of people around." Then, three days after he arrived at El Mosquito, a voice on the megaphone boomed, "Gerardo Mansur!" It was his time to leave.

BY THE LOOKS OF THE MOTORBOAT, GERARDO GUESSED IT COULD SAFELY fit nine passengers. As he hopped aboard, he counted almost twice that number already huddled on the deck. The boat's owner was an émigré who had come for his relatives and had not expected to be transporting strangers. "These people are not my family," he kept complaining, "and there's too many of them." His boat might sink under the weight. "You have to take them if you want to leave this place," insisted the lieutenant. The boat's owner had no choice but to agree.

Similar scenarios transpired throughout the port of Mariel. As émigrés sailed in to collect their relatives, Cuban officials informed them that they would not be allowed to depart unless they also transported others. In some cases, the Cuban government forced émigrés to return to Florida with a boatload of strangers and no relatives at all.

As Gerardo's boat set sail, no one spoke. Looking over his fellow passengers, Gerardo noticed two who appeared like they had just been released from prison, based on their harsh expressions and ill-fitting clothes. Whatever their situation, they sat crammed alongside the others, everyone holding their breath as they bobbled their way toward the open ocean.

And then they reached international waters. "Down with Fidel!" they bellowed. "Long live America!" Castro could no longer reel them back. They laughed, they celebrated, they hollered. They no longer needed to censor their disdain for the regime. They were, they believed, free.

As the hours ticked by, the speedboat quieted. The only thing the passengers could hear was the drone of the vessel cutting through the waves. Other boats skimmed into and out of sight, charting similar voyages from the port of Mariel to Key West. All told, 21,611 Cubans made this same journey the week Gerardo did. The shouting resumed whenever they saw these other Cubans—they, too, were traveling toward freedom.

Their howls, however, soon switched from ecstasy to terror. The motorboat could not withstand so much weight. Water poured over the gunnels. They were sinking. Acting quickly, the skipper radioed for help, and the US Coast Guard arrived before anyone drowned. A massive aircraft carrier rescued Gerardo and all the other passengers from the small, foundering watercraft.

They were lucky that the Coast Guard was near and the waters were calm. The following day, on May 17, 1980, ten people drowned when an overloaded thirty-five-foot pleasure boat capsized and sank in the choppy seas approximately twenty-eight miles north of Havana. By early June, the Coast Guard had conducted 989 search-and-rescue operations of Mariel Cubans; at least twenty-five people had died on the journey.

UNBEKNOWNST TO GERARDO AND THE OTHER CUBAN EXILES, ANOTHER DANger lurked onshore. As Cuban émigrés sailed off to the port of Mariel on yachts, tugboats, and shrimpers, only to return to Key West jammed with the hungry, the hunted, and the ill, US immigration officials began to worry. They could not know exactly who these new arrivals were. Not only that, but as the days passed, the men entering the country seemed "rougher in appearance" than earlier exiles. On May 14, President Carter officially accused the Cuban government of "taking hardened criminals out of prison and mental patients out of hospitals" and forcing "boat owners to take them to the US." While he had previously asserted that America would receive Mariel Cubans with "an open heart and open arms," he now vowed: "We will not permit our country to be used as a dumping ground for criminals who represent a danger to our society, and we will begin exclusion proceedings against these people at once."

Newspapers published story after story about Castro shipping hardcore felons to America. "Convicts among the Refugees" read one headline from *The Boston Globe*. It went on to explain, "Dade County Sheriff Bobby Jones said yesterday that more than half the 200 'high risk' refugees interviewed by his department—single men under 40 without relatives in this country—had acknowledged criminal records," which ranged from "petty theft to murder."

These stories ignored the fact that most arrivals had no criminal records and that many who did had served time for crimes not recognized in the United States. Between April, when ships began sailing from Cuba to Key West, and September, when the Cuban government closed the port of Mariel to potential emigrants, more than 124,000 Cubans landed in the United States. Although 26,000 of those who arrived were recorded as having criminal records in Cuba, only 2,000 had committed serious felonies. Many of the others had been imprisoned for such offenses as homosexuality, gambling, "extravagant behavior," and participating in the black market. Nevertheless, *The New York Times* captured the feeling of most Americans that Castro had duped their leaders and "pulled a fast one by dumping many criminals and perverts on American shores."

Public opinion turned abruptly against the arriving Cubans. No longer seen as courageous refugees fleeing Communism, they were now characterized as "maniacs" and brigands. A poll conducted by the *Miami Herald* showed that in Dade County, 68 percent of all non-Hispanic white residents and 57 percent of Black residents considered the Mariel boatlift detrimental to their community and the country.

With so many refugees disembarking in Key West daily and fears about who they were on the upswing, the Carter administration declared a state of emergency and opened military bases to question, register, and house the refugees until they found sponsors to care for them. The government used Krome, a former missile base in Florida, as well as the Fort Chaffee base in Arkansas, Fort Indiantown Gap in Pennsylvania, and Fort McCoy in Wisconsin.

Gerardo was sent to Fort Chaffee. Despite his confinement, he still believed that he had arrived in the land of freedom. Many refugees had similar feelings, rejoicing that they had survived the journey and believing that their stay on the bases would be short. By then, they had heard that Castro had sent criminals along with them, and they understood why the government was submitting them to a rigorous interview process.

American generosity seemed endless. The US military provided them with more food than they had been able to acquire in Cuba. They could finally eat meat. Churches donated clothes. Gerardo picked a blue Fruit of the Loom T-shirt from a pile of clothes—blue was his favorite color. The United States could do no wrong in his eyes.

Gerardo waited in the camp alongside thousands of others like him, hoping that someone would soon sponsor him. He had reasons to be upbeat. His family in the United States would probably support him, and for most refugees, the process passed relatively quickly. By the month of May 1980, 86,000 Cubans had arrived, and 42,000 had been resettled. By June, there were 21,000 arrivals and 33,000 resettlements, while in July, 2,600 refugees arrived and nearly 21,000 were released from the camps.

Still, the excitement that Gerardo felt at starting a new life was tempered by an overwhelming sense of boredom. The monotony of camp life demoralized even the most optimistic Cubans. The refugees would gather to eat, chat, or play dominoes or baseball to pass the time, but the emptiness of their days ground down their spirits. Camp administrators tried to entertain them by teaching them English and organizing sporting events. The administrators also installed TVs, but as one refugee recalled, given their limited English, they only watched baseball games. The base published Spanish-language newspapers to teach the refugees about American life or, at least, about the idealized life that the administrators imagined. One article in *La Libertad*, the newsletter published at Fort Indiantown Gap, offered women the following advice: "Today I am going to give you some tips on women's clothes; or, what the well-dressed average American girl wears. I realize that there are a lot of ways to dress here, and many people go to extremes in their apparel, but I'm sure we wouldn't want to look like them. We want to look nice and acquire that clean, freshly scrubbed look most American girls have."

For Gerardo, it was not these activities but a chance meeting that shattered the tedium. One day, as he was socializing outside his barrack, he saw two men carrying a beautiful lady on a stretcher. "It was Julia," he recalled years later. "She was young, a stunning mixed-race woman." He immediately approached her.

"Hey there, what's going on?" he asked.

"My heart hurts," responded Julia, putting her hand on the right side of her chest.

Gerardo grinned. "You must be special, having your heart on the right side," he said as they bore her away. He had to see her again. He asked around until he found out where her barrack was and awaited her return, intending to win that seemingly misplaced heart.

Within a week, Gerardo and Julia were officially dating, and he had moved into her barrack. At night, they would lie together and tell each other about their previous lives. Like Gerardo, Julia had been married and divorced in Cuba. She had two children whom she had tried to bring with her to the United States, but her ex-husband had prevented her from doing so. Devastated, Julia had debated what to do but ultimately decided to leave. Life in Cuba was hard. There was no political freedom, and more urgently, she regularly went hungry. Some nights, she had to drink sugary water just to fill up her stomach enough to sleep. She did not want that for her children: she would go to the United States and return with presents and money. Julia had told Cuban officials she was a sex worker so that they would let her leave. Shortly thereafter, she found herself in a motorboat heading for Florida and then at Fort Chaffee, next to Gerardo.

FAR AWAY FROM THE FORT CHAFFEE CAMP, TWENTY-THREE-YEAR-OLD GELET Chevalier waited in Krome South, another processing center in Florida. Like Gerardo, Gelet passed the hours any way he could, joking with other refugees, playing dominoes. Whenever a beautiful woman walked through the camp, he took note.

Gelet was a Haitian exile. A *Chicago Tribune* article from October 6, 1980, compared Gelet's experience with that of a Mariel refugee: "Caribbean cousins, they were two people on their way to somewhere else when fate stepped in and swept them along on a tide of history. One is mulatto; the other black. Different in language, dress, and manner, they now live a half-mile apart in federal refugee camps in the Florida Everglades."

Haitian refugees had embarked on their own, flimsier boats, heading toward Florida in order to escape their country's despotic government, poor living conditions, and high rates of unemployment. But if Mariel Cubans had blazed to the forefront of the nation's attention, Haitians were almost an afterthought: between April and October 1980, more than 124,000 Cubans arrived from the port of Mariel, while only 10,000 Haitians landed in Florida. As such, immigration officials simply subsumed Haitian migration into that of Cubans. In July 1980, the White House ordered the creation of the Cuban-Haitian Task Force to deal with these groups simultaneously.

This did not mean, however, that the two groups received the same treatment. Cuban exiles had advantages that Haitians lacked when they arrived in the United States. A vibrant Cuban community with plenty of political capital already resided in the United States. Haitians had no such equivalent. Moreover, US citizens had long viewed the arrival of Cuban exiles favorably. Fear of Mariel Cubans was an aberration. In contrast, Americans had long opposed the migration of Haitians. Not only were they considered "blacker" than their Cuban counterparts, as the *Chicago Tribune* noted, but Americans were also discomfited by the implications of their flight. Haitians had begun arriving in 1972, asking for asylum from the repressive regime of Jean-Claude Duvalier. This had dismayed US officials, who viewed Duvalier as an ally against Communism in the Caribbean. If the migration of Cubans had seemed righteous, that of Haitians seemed problematic and inconvenient.

The differing resources and perceptions of the two groups manifested in drastically divergent processing conditions. The centers where Cubans were held were in a much better state than Krome, where most Haitians were housed. Some Mariel Cubans were also interned at Krome, but they were held in Krome North, while Haitians were confined to the deteriorated southern part, almost half a mile away and separated by a wild stretch of Everglades.

"The conditions here are very bad," said Joseph Innocent, a young Haitian man who had ended up at Krome South alongside Gelet. "We live like animals. The food is bad. At night there is no light, and we fight the snakes. There are no telephones. We have no way to let our families know that we made it here alive." He was not exaggerating. Over a thousand Haitians occupied Krome South, a facility built for only 150. In June 1980, a State Department spokesman who visited Gelet and Joseph's "residence" maintained: "I saw women sleeping under blankets so soiled and threadbare I mistook them for the contents of vacuum cleaner bags; guards so indifferent to suffering that they snickered at the helpless; sanitary facilities so squalid that they turned your stomach."

Despite these conditions, most of the Haitians detained at Krome were determined to make their way in America. Like the Cubans, they, too, had good reason to hope. By November 28, 1980, 92 percent of all Haitians had left Krome and been resettled, an almost identical percentage of the Cubans sponsored at that point.

ON MAY 24, 1980, THE SUN'S RAYS GLISTENED BRIGHTER THAN USUAL ON FORT Chaffee, a welcome sight for the Cuban exiles accustomed to their island's tropical weather. Laughing and chattering, they left their barracks and went outside to relax in the heat. At first, only a few heard the discordant chants that pierced the day's harmony, but soon enough, hundreds of heads turned to see what was happening.

There they were: the white-hooded, white-robed men about whom the Cuban government had spoken relentlessly. The face of US racism and violence. The essence of what Castro had said was wrong with the United States. A group of Klansmen had gathered outside the camp, spouting hate, seeking, perhaps, to beat them up or even lynch them.

Terrified, Julia fled to her barrack, where she peeked through her small window at the disturbance. As she recalled years later: "Imagine my fear. . . . I knew they were racists. That they killed. And I said to myself, 'Oh my! Now I am in the hands of the Ku Klux Klan.'" She refused to leave the barrack for the rest of the day.

Gerardo was not scared. If anything, the group of a dozen or so individuals, which included a fourteen-year-old boy, seemed ridiculous, clad as they were in their ghostlike robes while trying to antagonize thousands of Cubans. It was apparent to many of the refugees that the Klansmen would not stand a chance in a fair fight. The exiles might not have been able to read the Klansmen's English-language signs, emblazoned with racist slogans like "White Power" and "Racial Purity Is America's Security," or comprehend the shouts that the Cubans should be returned to their country. But they knew that the Klan was protesting against them, and they were not going to simply stand by and watch.

A pack of refugees headed toward the Klansmen, yelling insults in Spanish. Some drew their fingers across their throats while shouting that they would "kill them [the Klansmen] and take their cigarettes." Gerardo stood some fifteen meters apart from the crowd. He did not want to be involved in any violence, but he wanted to see what would happen.

Over the camp's loudspeakers, guards barked commands: "Keep to yourselves; leave them alone." If anything, such orders enraged the Cubans. A group of about two hundred dashed to their barracks, emerging with strips of metal ripped from their bunk beds, and charged the Klan.

When the Klansmen saw the mass of Cubans advancing, they dropped their placards and fled. The exiles were elated by their victory. According to Gerardo, they even took trophies: the morning after the incident, Cubans were selling hoods the Klan had left behind along the camp's main boulevard.

Years later, Gerardo reflected that those detained at Fort Chaffee had never heard of the First Amendment or America's guarantee of freedom of speech when they threatened the Klan members. As he said, "What did Cubans know about constitutional rights or anything else?" Soon enough, however, he and thousands of other Mariel Cubans would come to learn the costs of not being protected by the Constitution.

THE KLAN'S VISIT PUT A DENT IN THE MONOTONY OF CAMP LIFE, BUT IMPATIENCE soon returned. In Cuba, few had dared to protest against the government, but after two months of seeing the sun rise and set over Fort Chaffee, the refugees voiced their discontent. It began as an experiment. A few exiles talked back to the guards. When nothing happened, more challenged their captors. Others strayed into the camp's forbidden areas. Then, on the first night of June, a large group of refugees decided to escape. Gerardo was not among them; he was frightened of anything that might endanger his ability to stay in the United States. But between two hundred and a thousand of the eighteen thousand refugees put their fears aside and set out toward freedom.

The escapees marched down the grass-lined main street of the base, yelling, "Freedom!" Once they reached the edge of the camp, they jumped a five-foot-high chain-link gate and continued down Route 22 toward the small nearby city of Barling, Arkansas.

When the residents of Barling heard that the escaped Cubans were heading toward them, five hundred civilians armed themselves with shotguns, pistols, and clubs, then headed out. They were not going to let these "criminals" take over their state.

State troopers amassed on the highway, ready to restrain the Cuban escapees on one side and stop the armed Barling men on the other. They fired at the Cubans, forcing them to rush back toward the base. Inside, the refugees set both mess halls and some of the barracks ablaze, illuminating the camp in a destructive splendor. The incident only ended when federal police and military personnel rained tear gas on the compound and a fire truck quenched the flames.

The anger Arkansans felt toward the refugees was not so quickly extinguished. To the surprise and fury of the residents of Barling, two months after the incident, President Carter announced that his administration would "begin consolidating the Cuban population" that still resided at the multiple military bases in Fort Chaffee. By then, most Cubans had been sponsored and left the camps, but those who had no family or acquaintances in the United States found that few people were willing to trust them enough for sponsorship. Now, as Arkansans saw with dismay, this population would be relocated to their state.

"It is no longer reasonable or economically feasible to keep the remaining individuals in four separate camps, each of which cost nearly $5 million a month to operate," the Carter administration stated. The government had chosen Fort Chaffee only "after carefully reviewing the situation and assessing the existing facilities, as well as numerous others."

The Eglin Air Force Base facility, which was comprised of tents, was dangerously vulnerable to hurricanes. Other bases were not adequately winterized. Carter insisted that consolidating the remaining Cubans at Fort Chaffee would have "a favorable economic impact on the Ft. Smith area" and was expected to "bring an additional $50 million to the area."

Such promises did little to appease the local population. A Barling weapons store started selling not only rifles, pistols, and machine guns but also T-shirts that depicted a group of Cubans at Fort Chaffee, seen through a gunsight. "My wife thinks they're a bunch of thieves," said Bill Crawford, a gun owner, as he fiddled with a rifle at the store. "They'll never make good citizens." Bill Clinton, who was the governor of Arkansas at the time, wrote in his memoir that to say the locals were scared "is an understatement."

Arkansans never forgave the government for consolidating the exiles in their state. A month later, Clinton lost the gubernatorial election to Frank White, in large part because Arkansans believed that Clinton had done too little to stop the move of Cubans to Fort Chaffee. A few months after the election, White House staff released a memorandum that put it bluntly: "The use of Ft. Chaffee as a refugee center became highly controversial in Arkansas. It is the opinion of the Governor, his political advisors, and those of us who have analyzed the 1980 election that Governor White was elected solely on the basis of this issue."

If news of the consolidation disturbed the residents of Barling, it tormented the Cuban refugees set to be transferred. Julio Unfonio Vades Viera was one of those exiles. An unaccompanied man with no relatives in the United States, Julio had not found a sponsor and so remained at Fort Indiantown Gap. He lived in a two-story wooden barrack with broken windows. Thirty other men shared his floor. To create some privacy, he hung three orange sheets around his bed. Despite the terrible living conditions at the camp, he feared Fort Chaffee would be worse. He had heard about the disturbances there and believed that he would be relocated to a more dangerous space, where he would be treated like a prisoner. A disaster specialist at Fort McCoy noted that this sentiment was widespread: "In general, I feel the logic of consolidation is understood among the refugees," but "Chaffee has had 'bad' press. There is the feeling that the refugees will be going to a more 'penal' environment and that there is the possibility that it might be a 'permanent' camp." Lying on his bed in his dimly lit barrack, Julio tried, between cigarette puffs, to communicate his anguish to a reporter. "They will have to drag me there," he warned.

Julio and the other refugees had good reason to be afraid. Government officials did, indeed, intend to turn Fort Chaffee into a more punitive space to guarantee that the refugees could not riot or resort to violence again. They had crafted a multiagency plan that involved the Federal Protective Service, the Immigration and Naturalization Service, the US Marshals Service, the US Park Police, and the Bureau of Prisons. The Department of Defense would handle the "security of the enclave" and would erect a fence around the camp. Before the refugees were transferred to Fort Chaffee, they would be "physically searched" to ensure that they did not smuggle in weapons or contraband. Once within Fort Chaffee, those refugees who did "not conform to the established rules" would face "confinement in administrative detention, a stockade or a federal correctional institution."

Fort Chaffee had gone from being a resettlement camp—intended as an interim location for refugees awaiting sponsorship—to a punitive detention center for those who had not been sponsored. The refugees who were moved to Fort Chaffee starting in October 1980 were treated as criminals who needed to be imprisoned.

4

A SAFE HAVEN

Fernando Arredondo

NOVEMBER 2016

The moon reflected white against the ashen houses of Peronia, a colonia, or suburb, of Guatemala City. Every evening at eight, a group of twelve to fifteen men and women dragged a heavy, unwieldy tree branch across the only road that permitted access to the colonia. Then, in the deepening darkness, the group split up—five of them remained to pull back the branch when cars they recognized drove up, and the remainder headed out to patrol the suburb's streets.

Fernando, a charismatic forty-one-year-old with shining black hair and an inviting smile, had helped organize the neighborhood watch a few months earlier. Having grown up in the area, Fernando felt more devoted to this place than most of his neighbors. His parents had been among the first people to move to Peronia, which at the time was only a small, ambitious settlement clinging to the outskirts of the sprawling city of nearly three million residents. Fernando had watched Peronia grow from dirt piles and empty lots into a bustling town. He had attended school there; his closest friends all lived in the neighborhood. It was a poor community where parents could not afford to buy toys or bicycles for their children, but Fernando and his friends found joy in building rickety wooden carts and racing them down the new streets.

It was also in Peronia where Fernando had encountered Cleivi. She was a child when they first met, the sister of the boys Fernando ran with, invisible to him until one day she was not. Those same brothers would become an impediment for Fernando: when he tried to kiss the girl he loved, there they'd be, spying and teasing and trying to ruin everything with good-natured bullying.

By the time Fernando and Cleivi married, the town had become too expensive for them, but they wanted to remain nearby. So they bought land in an undeveloped area above the hills called Colonia El Mirador de San Cristóbal. Fernando and Cleivi built a home and had four children there. And, just like their parents, the couple saw El Mirador grow from seventy houses to almost a thousand. Though it was still a humble residence, it felt like theirs.

Gangs were changing that. While vigilantes had existed since Fernando was a teenager, before the mid-2000s, they did not extort businesses, much less kill people. In the ensuing years, though, organized gangs became so violent that everyone in the greater Guatemala City region lived in fear.

Years later, Fernando still recoiled at the memory of the first time gangs targeted him. He was a taxi driver and liked to start work at 4:00 a.m., which allowed him to earn the money he needed and still spend evenings with his family. But one morning in 2015, he drove to the Peronia taxi stand where he usually collected his first passengers and saw the drivers in a frenzy. Two mareros, as the gang members were called, had come by and given one of the drivers a small flip phone. This, everyone knew, could only mean one thing: the drivers were about to be extorted.

A few hours later, the call came: each of the twenty men who worked at that taxi stand was ordered to pay one hundred quetzales daily. The drivers discussed what to do. "We should pay!" one cried. "I simply can't afford it," another objected. The ransom was a lot of money for men who made around four hundred quetzales per day working from dawn to dark. In the end, most drivers refused to pay.

Nearly two months later, two armed men on a motorcycle rushed toward the stand and fired on everyone they saw. The cabdrivers ran for cover, but one of them was struck in the chest. The mareros jumped off their bike to rip a gold chain from the wounded man's neck before zooming away.

The drivers dispersed for a month, but they were finally forced back by necessity—the taxi stand in Peronia remained the best spot to pick up clients. From then on, though, they all always paid up.

Not long after the shooting, Fernando and Cleivi's oldest child, Marco, approached his mother to show her his phone. Marco had been receiving Facebook messages pressuring him to join the Caballos, a local gang with connections to M-18, also known as Barrio 18, one of Guatemala's most vicious gangs. Cleivi looked at her son. He was so young, only seventeen—but that was precisely what put him in harm's way: mareros recruited youths. Marco had big dreams, a stable family, and no intention of joining up. Cleivi knew this, but she and Fernando still worried. What happens when a child says no to a gang?

It got worse. Even though Marco stayed away from the mareros, they did not always stay away from him. One day, the normally jovial teenager returned home looking miserable. Two gang members had walked up to him and threatened to kill him if he didn't hand over his cell phone. Marco had done as he was told and was not harmed, but the encounter shook him.

Over the next couple of months, gang members robbed Marco three more times. On one occasion, they punched him, leaving him with a bruised eye.

Marco, who wanted to be a mechanic, worked the night shift at a McDonald's in Peronia. His parents tried to protect him as best they could, picking him up in the taxi after work so that he did not have to walk alone in the dark or ride the local minibus, which was a prime target for the mareros.

Then came the final straw. Mareros started extorting businesses in El Mirador. Until that point, the gang had restricted its activities to the town of Peronia and had largely ignored the residences in the hills. If mareros operated in El Mirador, Fernando worried, all his children would be at risk—not just Marco, who spent the most time in Peronia.

The residents of El Mirador could not count on the police to help them, because law enforcement and gangs were closely intertwined. A local cop even used his house as a drug den. As the then mayor of greater Peronia described: "The Guatemalan national police," known as the PNC, "is saturated with corrupt personnel, and also suffers from insufficient resources and poor training. The PNC is distrusted by the civilian population of Guatemala, and for good reason. PNC officers are often complicit in gang- and drug-related crimes, including murder and extortion."

If they wanted to keep the mareros out, the residents of El Mirador had to take matters into their own hands. Someone suggested creating a neighborhood watch program. Fernando and Cleivi immediately agreed to join, as did all their neighbors. Fernando felt he owed it to his community, to the place that had seen him and his wife become adults. But most of all, he wanted his four children to grow up in peace. The issue mattered so much to him that he became vice president of the program.

Fernando felt a sense of pride in what he and Cleivi had built and desperately wanted to protect it. He had earned enough to buy a house for his family, with a proper stove and a TV, a far cry from his childhood shack, with its dirt floors and cardboard insulation. And their four children brought them such joy—along with Marco, they fawned over their three daughters: Keyli, a fashionable sixteen-year-old; Andrea, a reserved and studious eleven-year-old; and the family's baby, six-year-old Alison.

That night, as he always did, Fernando carried a baseball bat with him; a woman who lived a few doors down from him brought a machete.

Others held metal rods. Nothing as deadly as the arsenals the gangs had amassed. But they didn't need guns, they believed. Their presence alone would surely be enough to keep the gangs out, to show the mareros that this was their colonia and they were ready to protect it.

Marco was also there. Just like his father, he wanted to protect his loved ones and his home.

MOST GUATEMALANS VIEWED THOSE WHO BELONGED TO M-18 AS VIOLENT sadists and lived in terror of gang members like Miguel Martínez.

Miguel was a product of the carnage of history—a history directly shaped by US intervention in Guatemala. In 1951, Jacobo Árbenz became the president of Guatemala and almost immediately implemented policies that threatened the interests of the United Fruit Company, an American corporation that owned land in the small Central American country. To protect its interests abroad, the US government engineered a coup, which successfully ousted Árbenz in 1954. The new military-led government revoked the policies implemented by the previous president and cracked down on his supporters.

A brutal civil war that killed as many as two hundred thousand citizens ensued. During the early 1980s, the Guatemalan government—with the continued support of the United States—accused entire villages, and particularly Mayan ones, of aiding rebel forces. The government dispatched elite units with orders to torture and kill. Soldiers entered towns and decapitated children with dull machetes in front of their parents, raped women and children, ripped pregnant women's stomachs open, burned towns down to their foundations, and slaughtered entire villages.

Miguel's parents were indigenous Mayans who lived in the Alta Verapaz department of Guatemala, an area that saw much of this brutality. In 1982, the military set up an outpost in Sepur Zarco, a Mayan village in the region. The army descended upon the village, killed all its men, and forced its women into sexual slavery. Maria Ba Caal, one of those women, recalled: "When my husband and my fifteen-year-old son were taken away, they were working men. The army came in the afternoon and took them away. . . . That was the last time I saw my husband and son." The army ordered the women to cook and wash uniforms while continuously raping them and forcing them to take medicines and injections to prevent pregnancy. "We were forced to take turns. . . . If we didn't do what they told us to, they said they would kill us," Maria recounted.

The conflict forced thousands of Guatemalans, like other Central Americans whose countries were experiencing civil wars, to flee to the United States to escape the bloodshed and crumbling economy, which had cratered as a result of the violence in the region. By 1985, between three-quarters of a million to 1.3 million Central Americans lived in the United States; approximately one-fifth came from Guatemala.

Many refugees settled in poor neighborhoods in Los Angeles, where gang violence dominated. Gangs offered young refugees a way to gain respect, friendship, and, most important, protection. Although many gangs did not welcome them, one did: the Mexican American outfit known as 18th Street, which later came to be known as M-18 and Barrio-18.

But gang members did not always remain in Los Angeles. In 1996, the same year that the civil war ended in Guatemala, the US Congress passed the Illegal Immigration Reform and Immigrant Responsibility Act, which led to the deportation of thousands of gang members to their "home countries" in Central America.

Bearing the lasting scars of gang life, those who returned to Guatemala found a country primed for disruption. The civil war was the perfect incubator for violent gangs. Over 1.5 million people had been dislocated; the country's youth had been raised in chaos; orphaned children roamed the streets; and thousands of citizens had become inured to violence. M-18 soon became responsible for much of the carnage in Guatemala.

Miguel's parents, like other indigenous families in their area, raised their son against the backdrop of civil war. His childhood was additionally punctuated by his parents' instability. His mother struggled with terrible mental health issues. His father became an abusive alcoholic. Miguel left home when he was only eleven. By then, he recalled, "I already knew what it meant to be a gang member. If you went to the store, they wouldn't charge you. If you wanted something, you asked for it and they gave it to you . . . sardines, bean cans, cream, bread."

Boys like Miguel were ideal recruits. Just a few years earlier, children and teenagers had been considered fit to fight in the civil war. Now they were soldiers in a new kind of army, with M-18 stepping in to fill the void at home. As Miguel later said: "My family are the people who are with me during the day and the night." By "family," he meant gang members.

It was boys and teenagers like Miguel whom Fernando and his neighbors, armed with baseball bats and machetes, sought to keep away from El Mirador.

PERONIA'S TRAFFIC SEEMED WORSE THAN USUAL, BUT THERE WAS NO ESCAPE. The only road in and out of El Mirador led directly to the only road in and out of Peronia. Fernando was hoping to pick up passengers in downtown Guatemala City, so there was nothing for him to do but wait in the long line of cars, baking under the morning's blazing sun.

A bus was blocking both sides of the street to allow straggling passengers to board. Something suddenly caught Fernando's attention: two young men with shaved heads, tattoo sleeves, baggy blue pants, and shiny, oversize T-shirts were approaching the taxi. Mareros regularly prowled traffic-congested streets to demand money from trapped drivers, often targeting commercial vehicles like soda trucks and cabs.

Fernando watched through the window. He was ready to give them the money he had made that day, even if it meant working more hours. Better pay than be killed, he thought. One of the mareros bent down to talk to him through the window, but the other one interrupted. He had recognized Fernando from the neighborhood patrol.

"Aren't you from the group of those over there from above?" He meant from El Mirador, which lay just above Peronia. "Of those who are organizing themselves?" Without waiting for an answer, the marero continued. "Because you know what's going to happen to those there? We are going to go kick their ass."

Fernando tried to sound calm. "No, I only came to leave a passenger here. I am not from the area."

The men sized him up, deciding whether to believe him. The bus blocking the street finally lumbered off, and traffic started inching forward. The two gang members stepped aside, allowing Fernando to proceed. As he drove away, the men made a hand gesture to signal that they were keeping an eye on him.

He had always known that participating in the neighborhood patrol was dangerous. In addition to standing up to M-18, the residents of El Mirador were also making enemies in the municipal government and the police force by shining a light on both institutions' failure to protect the neighborhood. Fernando was terrified: Did the mareros know that he was the vice president of the neighborhood watch? Had they actually recognized him? Was he safe? And for how long? But he knew that he had to continue patrolling the streets, for his family and for his community.

The danger would only increase. In early 2017, a few months after his run-in with the mareros, municipal officials, members of the national police, and the local gang affiliated with M-18 established a formal partnership to gain full control of the area. The partnership took a strong interest in the neighborhood watch program.

On Friday, April 28, 2017, Fernando's life would change forever.

Around 4:00 p.m., he was dropping off a regular client about forty minutes from Peronia when his eldest daughter, Keyli, rang. School had ended early, and she was visiting her ailing maternal grandmother in Peronia; Cleivi, Marco, and Alison were already there.

Keyli was a responsible girl. After arriving, she greeted her family and then headed outside to sit with Marco on the curb, where she called her father to let him know that she had safely reached her grandmother's home.

"I arrived—" Keyli began but was suddenly cut off.

Pop. Pop. Pop.

To Fernando, the shots sounded like firecrackers. But then he heard Keyli scream Marco's name. Then, indistinguishable shrieks, followed by silence.

"Hello? Hello!" Fernando screamed through the phone. "What happened?" There was no answer.

Fernando hung up and dialed his wife. No answer. He called his sister-in-law. No answer.

Fernando sped back, his mind blank. By the time he made it to his mother-in-law's house, a crowd had assembled in the streets. He pushed his way through. Amid the commotion, he saw Cleivi kneeling in the middle of the street, holding Marco tightly. Alison and Keyli were hovering over a pool of blood, screaming but unharmed.

"What happened?" he implored again. But Cleivi did not stop wailing. She could not speak.

A neighbor told him that Keyli and Marco had been sitting on the stoop when two mareros drove by on a motorcycle. They pulled out guns and aimed at Marco. He tried to run away but only made it a few steps before the mareros shot him dozens of times and then took off. Keyli screamed, frozen in place, but the gang members did not attack her. Cleivi burst out of the house, saw her dying son lying limp on the street, and rushed toward him. Marco was still breathing. For a second, he opened his eyes, and she kissed him.

A moment later, he died in her arms.

NO ONE KNEW FOR SURE WHY THE MAREROS KILLED MARCO, BUT FERNANDO suspected that they did so to punish him for participating in the neighborhood watch. This type of violent retribution was commonplace, as the gangs effectively instilled fear by going after the families of their enemies. As one gang member in Guatemala explained to an ethnographer the same year Marco was murdered: "If someone betrays you, you must make them pay for it, and make sure that everyone knows that you will stop at nothing. . . . You go after their family, their brothers, their parents, their wife, their mistress, and their kids so they feel the pain, and so everyone knows that anyone who fucks with you will die crying."

The brazen nature of Marco's murder, which took place in public during broad daylight, sent a message to everyone in El Mirador. After the killing, the neighborhood watch dissipated. As one neighbor explained, "After they killed Marco, the community patrols and our confidence just fell apart. We could not risk our lives or the lives of our children. We had no support from anyone."

It was clear that the police had no intention of apprehending Marco's murderers. When officers arrived at the crime scene, they asked some basic questions, such as Marco's name and age, but then left without investigating further.

The morning after the killing, Cleivi stood outside her mother's house looking at the spot where her son had been shot. She could not shake the image of Marco lying on the ground and then dying in her arms. Keyli, Andrea, and Alison stood by her side as they waited for Fernando to finish making the arrangements to retrieve Marco's body. They, too, were in shock.

The flash of a camera brought them back to the present. Two men on the other side of the street were surreptitiously snapping pictures. Cleivi herded the girls inside. She felt detached from everything around her, even her own body.

That night, as neighbors and friends gathered to pay their respects, an unfamiliar gray car kept driving up and down the street, passing the house. Someone was watching them. For the rest of the night, Fernando couldn't focus on mourning his son. He was scared.

Then, the morning after Marco's funeral, Fernando was unloading the trunk of his taxi when two gang members drove up on a motorcycle. Fernando could not make out their faces through their darkly tinted helmets. What he could clearly see were the guns they held.

"Are you going out to work?" one of the mareros asked Fernando.

"No," he responded as politely as he could. "Not today."

"Okay. Well, we are going to tell you something: if we find out that you place a police report or that you place a complaint against anyone, we are going to come and we are going to snuff out the rest of your family."

"No, that will not happen," Fernando said, trying to reassure them.

One of the men pulled out photos of the family and identified Fernando's three daughters. Fernando stood there in silent terror after the two men sped off.

Back at home in his kitchen, Fernando resolved not to tell Cleivi what had just happened. She was already falling apart. How did the men know so much about his family? He would obviously not go to the police. But how, then, could he protect the people he loved?

Less than two hours later, two officials from Guatemala's public prosecutor's office showed up. The gang had clearly infiltrated the office, Fernando thought as he opened the door.

"We are here to ask your daughter Keyli a few questions about what happened," one of the men said.

Fernando had little patience. "Look, sir," he replied, "first of all, my daughter is a minor, so you need to ask my consent before talking to her. Second, she is not here."

After a few minutes of back-and-forth, Fernando said: "I will bring Keyli to the station when she is doing a little better." With that, the officials left.

Alone in his kitchen, Fernando understood what he had to do. The police and the gangs were colluding, and they were keeping a close watch on all of them. Keyli had seen the murder. Everyone knew that gangs always sought to eliminate all witnesses.

His family could no longer stay in El Mirador.

Fernando closed the door and told his daughters to pack clothes that would last several days. He then prepared a bag for himself and his wife and drove them all to downtown Guatemala, about an hour away from Peronia.

From then on, the traumatized family lived in hiding. They slept in one motel one week and in another the next. Every day, Fernando would depart the motel early in the morning to work, leaving Cleivi and their daughters behind. The girls had to stop attending school; it was too dangerous.

Cleivi's brother, who remained in communication with the family via cell phone, reported that gang members were driving motorcycles up and down the family's street, trying to find them. This continued for weeks after Marco's death.

Fernando took every precaution he could. He insisted that the family not hold the customary Mass for Marco nine days after his death. Instead of going to church, they prayed for their slain boy in a shabby motel room. Fernando also took care not to be recognized while he was outside. Every night, he would park his taxi far from where the family was staying, in case mareros identified it. Eventually, he realized that he had to sell it, since the risk was too high. With the proceeds, he rented a different taxi so he could continue working.

As the days elapsed, Fernando thought through his family's options. He reached out to a close family friend who let them stay in a house that his brother owned in another town, which saved them the motel costs and constant movement. Yet Cleivi and the girls still needed to stay inside all day, hiding. They could not live like this forever.

A friend of Cleivi's living in Washington, DC, first seeded the idea that the family should head to the United States. The friend had written Cleivi a Facebook message offering condolences. When Cleivi thanked her, the woman wrote back, describing her trajectory north. Her ex-husband had been physically abusive, so she had fled from Guatemala to the United States and asked for asylum. Cleivi and her family should do the same.

Fernando thought about it. Thousands of Guatemalans headed north every year to escape the violence and poverty they experienced in their own country. He knew plenty of them. But he also knew how hard it was for Central Americans to reach the United States. Many died on the way. How could he take his wife and three daughters on such a journey? Besides, could they really live so far from the place where their son was buried?

When Marco's gravestone was ready, Fernando decided that they should come out of hiding and say their goodbyes. They headed out early, hoping to avoid crowds. They brought flowers and sat around the stone, crying and telling stories of the boy they had loved.

When Fernando left to get them some food, Cleivi noticed a man standing a few graves away, staring at Keyli and talking on his cell phone. She was likely anxious over nothing, she told herself. But shortly after, a motorcycle rumbled into the cemetery and pulled up near them. The rider stayed on his bike, looking intently in their direction, his hand on top of the long, slim crossbody bag slung over his shoulder.

Cleivi grabbed her daughters' hands and ran toward the cemetery's entrance. Fernando was just returning with the food. When they saw him, they jumped in his car. "Take off! Take off!" they screamed.

The man on the motorcycle did not follow them.

After that, Fernando and Cleivi concluded that they would never be safe in Guatemala, no matter where they went. M-18 mareros were still after them, and the gang was everywhere in the country. They had to flee to America like Cleivi's friend had suggested.

The journey through Mexico to the United States was both dangerous and extremely expensive. The family needed money. A lot of money. And so Fernando started selling their belongings. Their most valuable possession was their house, which took several months to sell and went for much less than it was worth.

But now they could attempt the passage with some chance of success.

WHY WAS IT SO HARD AND EXPENSIVE FOR FERNANDO AND OTHER GUATEMAlans to cross through Mexico and reach the US-Mexico border?

It began with a Faustian bargain: in the early 1980s, US policymakers worried about the increasing number of Central Americans heading to the United States and came up with a plan to stop them—they would convert Mexico's territory into a buffer zone where Central Americans were interdicted before they even reached the US border. In 1984, US Secretary of State George Shultz warned Mexican officials that if Central Americans kept migrating north, the US government would further fortify the US-Mexico border, which would obviously also prevent Mexicans from entering the country illegally. This would severely depress Mexico's economy, which had come to depend on Mexican migration. Mexican officials succumbed to this pressure. Constricting Central Americans' journeys seemed a small price to pay to ensure that their citizens could keep entering the United States.

Since then, US officials have continued to cajole the Mexican government into stopping Central American migration. Indeed, since the 1980s, more Central Americans have been deported from Mexico than from the United States. The deportations of Central Americans from Mexico rose from 14,000 in 1988 to 133,000 in 1991. By contrast, in 1991, the United States removed 5,000 Central Americans. Similarly, from 2004 to 2018, Mexico deported 1.7 million Central Americans back to their home countries, while the US deported 1.1 million. In other words, for Central Americans, Mexico presents the greatest threat of deportation.

Increased immigration enforcement in Mexico has led Central Americans to hire expensive smugglers to help them evade apprehension by Mexican officials. But coyotes, as the smugglers are known, charge heavily for their services. When Fernando and Cleivi decided to head north with their daughters, coyotes were charging around $8,000 to take a person from Guatemala all the way to the United States. The problem was that after selling their house, they had only made $10,000, enough to cross one family member. There was no way they could hire professional smugglers.

Migrants who cannot afford coyotes often embark upon a dangerous ride atop freight trains, otherwise known as La Bestia (the Beast). María García, who boarded La Bestia in 1994, recalls that when the train passed through checkpoints in Mexico, migrants jumped off to evade officials and then ran to jump back on afterward. A ladder dangled from the rear of the cars, and migrants pulled themselves up. When María was trying to jump on the train, she slipped and "destroyed" her chest. Although she recovered from the accident, an uncounted number of migrants have lost their lives and limbs to La Bestia.

Fernando and Cleivi could not subject their three girls to La Bestia. They would have to cross Mexico by bus and use the money they had made from selling the house to bribe Mexican officials along the way.

At the end of February 2018, Fernando and his family set off, leaving everything behind. It was midday, and the sun shone brightly on the murky waters of the Suchiate River, which divides Mexico from Guatemala. They boarded a crude "raft," which consisted of a few wooden slats laid across floating car tires. Once it left the shore, those aboard swayed like a pendulum in a grandfather clock. There was nothing to hold on to, so Fernando told the girls to squat for stability. He and Cleivi held on to them as tightly as they could.

When they reached the shore, they pressed through a crowded market full of brightly colored vegetables and rich aromas before rushing into the first taxi they saw on the other side. They were headed to Tapachula, from where the buses going north departed. It was pitch-black by the time they boarded the bus, and they were terrified. This, they knew, was the most dangerous part of the route—full of immigration checkpoints.

But Fernando and Cleivi had a strategy. To keep the girls safe, Fernando would sit with Andrea, the middle child, at the front of the bus. Behind them would be Keyli, the oldest, and Alison, the youngest. Cleivi would sit right at the back, watching them all. The two parents had also made a pact: if any of their girls were apprehended, one of them would go with the child while the other would continue the journey with the other daughters.

The family sat in silence so as not to draw attention to their foreign accents. Fernando hoped that they could blend in with the night and the bus seats. That they would be invisible.

Mexican immigration authorities boarded the bus about six times between Chiapas, in southern Mexico, and Puebla, located in the central part of the country. On each occasion, the agents asked to see the papers of passengers whom they considered suspicious. Whenever agents asked to see one of the family members' visa or residence papers, Fernando called them over to where he was sitting. "She is my wife, and these are my daughters," he said, handing the agents their passports. Inside each, he had placed a fifty-dollar bill. The total amounted to $250, approximately half of what a full-time immigration agent made per month after taxes. Time and time again, the officers took the money, returned the passports, and moved on to question other passengers.

Then came the mobile immigration checkpoint at the entrance to Veracruz. The bus slowed to a stop once more, and two stout, balding agents came aboard. They looked over the passengers and asked Fernando to step off the bus for questioning. They did not notice the rest of the family—not even Andrea, who was sitting with him. Fernando descended slowly, making sure that the passports had bills inside to bribe the agents. To his surprise, as soon as he disembarked, the bus closed its doors and sped away.

"My dad, my dad!" yelled Alison.

Cleivi ran up to the driver and pleaded with him to wait. Surely this was all a mistake, and her husband would be allowed back on.

"Forget about it," the driver said. "He will soon be deported."

Then something remarkable happened: About half an hour after the bus had taken off without Fernando, a police van from Mexican immigration enforcement rushed past and pulled in front of the bus, forcing it to stop. The van's door opened, and Fernando emerged from the passenger seat. He had paid the officers enough money that they not only allowed him to continue the journey but also drove him back to the bus that was transporting his family.

Once in Puebla, the family felt much safer, since immigration checkpoints tended to be near the country's southern and northern borders. But by then they had paid so many bribes that they were short on cash. They decided to stay in the town to replenish their financial reserves before moving on. Fernando managed to get hired by a small tortilla factory, where he worked for three weeks. In the meantime, Cleivi and the girls stayed inside the motel room, dormant as its furnishings, hiding from anyone who might call immigration agents on them.

After they collected some money, they continued their trajectory north, stopping in the state of San Luis Potosí, where Fernando worked construction for a few weeks before they headed to the industrial city of Monterrey, in northern Mexico. After two months crisscrossing Mexico, they finally reached the last leg of their trajectory: a four-hour bus ride to the city of Nuevo Laredo, which lay on the banks of the Rio Grande.

THE BUS SHUDDERED TO A STOP. MEXICO'S CHECKPOINT 26 WAS SIXTEEN MILES away from the US-Mexico border. Through the windows, Cleivi and Fernando could see officials from Mexico's armed forces, the federal police, and immigration enforcement. Some held big dogs, probably to sniff out drugs. Two immigration agents boarded the bus. They walked past

Fernando and Andrea. They walked past Keyli and Alison. They walked past Cleivi to the back of the bus.

"Documents?" one of the agents asked Fernando on his way back to the front of the bus.

Unlike on past occasions, Fernando only gave the officer his own passport, with the fifty dollars tucked inside. Now that they were so close to the border, Cleivi and the girls could continue even if he were stopped.

The agent opened the passport and saw the money. Then he said, "I have to ask you a couple of questions. Can you get off the bus?"

"Yes, of course."

The agent then turned to Andrea, who was sitting next to Fernando. "Is she with you?"

"Yes, she is my daughter."

"She should get off too."

Cleivi and the two other girls stayed quiet, and the agents did not notice them.

Fernando and Andrea were escorted off the bus, which then departed with Cleivi, Alison, and Keyli still on it. Fernando pleaded with the officer to let him and Andrea continue the journey, but the agent simply replied: "Okay. We now have to wait for my superior to arrive and examine your case, but what will probably happen is that you and your daughter will be sent to a detention center in Mexico City and then, from there, be deported back to Guatemala."

After informing Fernando that his superior would arrive the following day, the official took him and Andrea to a small room with a long cement bench along the wall. He gave them two bottles of water and locked the door behind him.

For a few minutes, they sat in silence as Fernando worked through their options in his head. After a while, Andrea interrupted his thoughts. "What about Mom?" she asked.

Fernando held her. "Don't worry about it," he answered. "We will figure out a way to reunite with her soon." He tried to sound calmer than he felt.

At dinnertime, another agent brought them egg burritos and sodas but had no more information to give them. Fernando tried to cheer his daughter up as they ate. Once they finished, they lay down on the hard bench, without sheets or blankets, and tried to sleep.

"What about Mom?" Andrea asked again upon waking the following day. That was the only thing she had said since they had been taken off the bus.

Hours passed. Around 2:00 p.m., Fernando heard voices. He peeked through a small window in the door and saw a man who he thought must be the station's head immigration official.

"Can I talk to you?" Fernando called out, raising his voice so that the man could hear him through the door but also trying to sound as polite as possible.

"Who are you?" the official said.

"I am a man in need. I would really like to talk with you. I came basically running away from my country, and I am so close [to the United States]. I almost made it."

The official opened the door. "Well, it's just like when they catch you on the other side [of the border]. You are almost there. But if they catch you, they catch you."

Fernando tried again, but the officer interjected. "Is that your daughter?" he asked contemptuously. "Aren't you aware of how dangerous it is to cross her all the way from Central America to the United States without papers?"

"Sir," Fernando began graciously, "when the agents stopped us yesterday afternoon, my wife and two other daughters were also on the bus."

"And they didn't catch them?"

"No, they didn't. But we were all fleeing Guatemala because of what happened to us there." Fernando told the officer about Marco being murdered in front of his sister and how the mareros had stalked the family. He pulled out copies of the police records he had brought with him. They included photographs of Marco's body, lying on the street, shot. "I never thought about coming, much less with my wife and daughters. Of putting them at risk," Fernando said as the official looked over the documents. "But I had no other option."

"I am sorry, man," the official said after a pause. He turned to Andrea. "Is this true?"

"Yes," Andrea muttered quietly.

"What was your brother's name?" the officer asked while examining the documents.

"Marco."

"And where did you live?"

"In El Mirador de San Cristóbal, in a village in Guatemala."

"How old was your brother?"

"Seventeen."

The official looked at Fernando. "You know what? We are going to do something. Nothing has happened here. We have no record that you were ever here. Today, when the next bus comes by on its way to Nuevo Laredo, you will board it. From then on, it's up to your luck."

ON MAY 16, 2018, FERNANDO GAZED OUT AT THE INTERNATIONAL BRIDGE, steeling himself with the courage to cross it. He and Andrea had arrived in Nuevo Laredo the previous evening, but he had decided to pass the night in the northern city before heading over to the United States. This would give him a chance to see if Cleivi and his two other daughters were waiting for them in Nuevo Laredo. Fernando and Andrea spent all morning searching for them but found nothing. In the late afternoon, they gave up. The rest of his family had probably already crossed over, Fernando told himself, trying to put his worries aside. He had heard that members of the Zetas cartel were kidnapping Central Americans, but he knew he couldn't think about that. He had to focus on the task at hand. If Cleivi and the girls were already in the United States, he and Andrea had to head there now.

Clasping his child's hand, Fernando ambled to the bridge's pedestrian walkway, almost as if they were out on a promenade. Once above the Rio Grande, however, father and daughter sped up, fearful that the Mexican military or immigration officials would once again stop them. Andrea gripped Fernando's hand tighter. "Don't worry, daughter, I am here with you," he told her. She did not reply.

Fernando carried only Andrea's backpack. They had left everything behind except for the documentation they needed and a change of clothes for each of them. He was wearing a gray hoodie; she, a pink one. After all, like most Central Americans, Fernando knew that in the United States, asylum seekers were often kept in extremely cold rooms, which they called hieleras, meaning iceboxes, before being allowed in.

The minutes it took to cross the 1,050-foot-long bridge felt like an eternity. On the other side, a balding US official stood ready to welcome some and snub others. "Papers," the man uttered in Spanish. From his features, Fernando could tell that the man was Latino, even though he didn't speak Spanish well.

"We are here to beg for asylum," Fernando declared.

ALTHOUGH MANY AMERICANS VIEW ALL ARRIVING CENTRAL AMERICANS AS lawbreakers trying to bypass immigration rules, in reality, US laws confer the right to seek asylum. Asylum is a protection granted to foreigners who are already in the United States or who arrive at the border and meet the international legal definition of refugees. The 1951 UN Convention Relating to the Status of Refugees and its 1967 Protocol define a refugee as someone who cannot return to their country of origin owing to a "well-founded fear of being persecuted for reasons of race, religion, nationality, membership of a particular social group, or political opinion."

The core principle of the 1967 Protocol, which the United States ratified, is that of non-refoulement—or nonreturn—which establishes that refugees "should not be returned to a country where they face serious threats to their life or freedom." This standard is now deemed a rule of conventional international law. It is also national law. In 1980, the United States passed the Refugee Act, which instituted the United Nations' definition of a refugee and established that those seeking asylum would not be deported until their cases were judged on an individual basis.

Like other asylum seekers arriving at the border, Fernando and Andrea had the right to ask for asylum and the right to remain in the country while their case was examined.

FERNANDO AND ANDREA'S TURN FINALLY CAME, AND A SHORT FEMALE OFficer led them to a waiting area. And wait they did. Andrea remained silent while Fernando held her tight. As time ticked by, more asylum seekers arrived. They, too, sat silently, waiting, scared.

"Undress," a male officer ordered Fernando, who was allowed to keep only his underwear on as his body was searched. He burned with humiliation but did as he was told. With all the drugs coming in, Fernando thought, it made sense to search him. When finished, the officer allowed Fernando to put his clothes back on but took away the small backpack he had been carrying, his belt, and their shoelaces. Most important, the officer also took the little scrap of paper on which Fernando had scrawled the phone numbers and addresses of all the people he knew in the United States.

The official led him and Andrea inside a building where there were dozens of other asylum seekers and gave them paperwork to fill out. Hours passed. Another official called their names. To Fernando, it was clear that the man could not care less what happened to them. He interrogated Fernando and took their fingerprints. More hours passed without explanation. When Fernando asked for water for his thirsty daughter, the man told him there was none.

Perhaps the long wait was intended to wear them down.

Fernando and Andrea had crossed the bridge at three in the afternoon. At around ten that night, the officer returned, looking as bored as always. "Your daughter is coming with me," he said. "Follow me," he ordered Andrea.

Father and daughter would be detained—separately.

Part II

FROM EXCLUSION TO REPRIEVE

5

ENTRY FICTION

FU CHI HAO

SEPTEMBER 1901

If Chi Hao and Hsiang Hsi's weeks tossed around by rough sailing across the Pacific Ocean had been fraught, their confinement aboard the ship on which they had arrived was even more unbearable. The cots remained uncomfortable and the food unpalatable, but now they were not even moving toward their goal. To make matters worse, a thick layer of dust soon begrimed the vessel, as enormous piles of coal were shoveled from the dock to the ship.

As the two men waited to be deported, the injustice of their situation enraged Chi Hao. How could America not welcome them after they "had loyally stood by her citizens at the very gates of death"? How could they, out of all people, be "denied the privilege of landing on American shores"?

Back on land, Luella Miner, who had helped arrange for the two men's arrival, was now doing everything in her power to stop their deportation. With feverish energy, she reached out to the Chinese consul general in San Francisco, sent telegrams to the Chinese foreign minister in

Washington, met with the collector of the port in San Francisco, and appealed to the chief of the Chinese Bureau. Everywhere she turned, she encountered courteous and sympathetic officials, but none were able to help.

Bureaucracy trumped reason. While the purpose of the papers was to show that Chi Hao and Hsiang Hsi were coming to study, the officials refused to accept the word of the teachers from Oberlin College, where the men were enrolling as students. The absurdity of it all was not accidental: since 1897, the commissioner of immigration had set out to reduce Chinese migration by constricting merchant and student arrivals, even though, by law, both of these categories were exempt from Chinese exclusion and supposed to be allowed in the United States.

Luella had one last recourse: to appeal to the Treasury Department in Washington, which oversaw the office that dealt with immigration. The petition would halt her friends' imminent expulsion, as officials from the Chinese Bureau could not deport migrants while their cases were pending. But this option came at a high cost: while awaiting the decision from Washington, Chinese migrants who disembarked in the Bay Area were imprisoned in a wooden detention shed owned by the Pacific Mail Steamship Company.

Luella agonized about what to do. "If the appeal failed, they would still be deported," she recalled, "with the additional hardship of having endured at least three weeks of suffering in a hell" of detention. In the end, she decided to make the appeal. At least this way, Chi Hao and Hsiang Hsi stood a chance.

IMMIGRATION RESTRICTION DEMANDED IMMIGRATION DETENTION. OR SO legislators believed. When members of Congress leaned into anti-Chinese sentiment and passed the Page Act in 1875, they added a provision that prohibited an "alien to leave any such vessel arriving in the United States" until an inspector certified that the migrant could legally enter the country.

In other words, legislators implicitly mandated that detention take place on arriving ships.

Detaining migrants aboard the vessels on which they had sailed, however, created problems. Sometimes a ship stationed at the Port of San Francisco needed to depart for its next destination before a person's case was determined. This was a regular occurrence, as Chinese migrants who were denied entry upon arrival frequently filed habeas petitions, which were based on the provision that the government cannot hold people without informing them why it's doing so or giving them the right to challenge their detention in court. Chinese migrants asserted that they were citizens or belonged to an exempt class and were thus being unlawfully detained. Habeas corpus cases often took weeks or months to resolve, during which time the migrants were supposed to remain in detention, preventing the ships holding them from departing.

To solve this issue, steamship companies would shift the detained individuals from vessel to vessel. On occasions when there were no other vessels in port, however, even this arrangement did not work. In these cases, immigration inspectors would generally send women and children to a Christian mission and men to San Francisco's county jail, or simply release them on bond.

San Francisco's county jail was ghastly. It was built for 140 individuals but at times held up to 230. The dark, putrid cells lacked ventilation, and there was only one bathtub in the entire facility. Bronchitis and tuberculosis lingered from season to season, perpetually attacking new victims. Within the jail, Chinese men were assigned the grimmest quarters: the roofs of their cells hung so low that occupants could not even stand upright.

The jailing of these early Chinese migrants reveals how, from its inception, immigration detention was linked to the nation's criminal justice system. Migrants—many of whom had the right to enter the United States—were incarcerated not because they were accused of breaking the law but because they were waiting for a decision on whether they could enter the country or not. They were nonetheless treated as "criminals," showing that individuals' race, rather than their actions, determined what criminality meant.

During this same period, the system of convict leasing was running at full force in the US South, also demonstrating the connection between race and incarceration. Through this system, state governments arrested Black people and then leased them to local planters, railroad companies, or mining magnates, who used them as forced laborers. The scheme was so profitable that state governments increased the number of activities classified as felonies so that they could arrest more Black people and lease them out.

Legislators in California sought to put detained Chinese migrants to work in a similar manner. In 1892, they passed the Geary Act, a federal law that required all Chinese laborers living in the United States to apply for certificates of residence that demonstrated they were in the country legally. Thereafter, any Chinese person found without such a certificate would be "imprisoned at hard labor for a period of not exceeding one year and thereafter removed from the United States." This law operated until 1896, when the Supreme Court ruled in *Wong Wing v. United States* that it was unconstitutional to subject "aliens to infamous punishment at hard labor, or by confiscating their property" without first providing them with judicial trials to establish their guilt. While the Supreme Court ruled that migrants could not be subjected to hard labor without judicial trial, it affirmed that they could be detained without trial.

Not only was immigrant detention legal, but it no longer had to happen solely on ships. In 1891, Congress had passed an immigration act that explicitly authorized detention on land. This law stated that officers should inspect all arriving migrants but could "order a temporary removal of such aliens for examination at a designated time and place, and then and there detain them until a thorough inspection is made."

There was, however, an important twist to the 1891 act: even though migrants could be detained within the country's landmass, they were to be treated as if they were not there. As if they had never landed. As if they were not legally present in the nation. The law stated: "Such removal shall not be considered a landing during the pendency of such examination." According to this provision, which created what came to be known as the entry fiction, the detention site was simply an extension of the border, a kind of extraterritorial limbo that existed inside the United States in a literal sense but outside it for legal purposes. As such, migrants could be denied basic constitutional rights while detained.

The entry fiction meant that even though the Fifth Amendment guaranteed the right to due process when a person was deprived of liberty, an "entrant" stopped at the border did not have the right to contest their exclusion in court, even if they were incarcerated on American soil. Indeed, the 1891 law affirmed that "all decisions made by the inspection officers or their assistants touching the right of any alien to land, when adverse to such right, shall be final unless appeal be taken to the superintendent of immigration, whose action shall be subject to review by the Secretary of the Treasury."

In other words, the judiciary had no role to play in exclusion matters. While migrants who were apprehended inside the United States had to be afforded constitutional rights, "entrants" who were stopped at the border were only entitled to the procedures that Congress provided for them, whether or not that included a hearing. Accordingly, Chinese entrants had no right to contest their exclusion in court and could only appeal to the secretary of the Treasury, as had been established by Congress in the 1891 act.

AFTER LUELLA APPEALED TO THE SECRETARY OF THE TREASURY ON THE men's behalf, Chi Hao and Hsiang Hsi were informed that they would no longer be detained aboard the vessel on which they had arrived. Instead, they would now be held on the second floor of a wooden shed that the Pacific Mail Steamship Company had converted into detention quarters. It was there where they would await decisions on their cases. Because they were "entrants," however, they would not have the full protection of the law.

An officer ushered Chi Hao and Hsiang Hsi to the side of the large warehouse and up a dark, steep stairway. After their weeklong detention on the *Doric*—following their three weeks at sea—the friends were grateful to disembark. When the officer opened the door of the shed, however, they realized that being on land was the extent of their good fortune.

The stench hit Chi Hao like a punch. A nauseating combination of sweat, tobacco, and opium had soaked into the hall's bones. There were only six small windows—all covered with one-and-a-half-inch wire mesh screens—and they let through little air and light. Chi Hao looked around. The door to the narrow stairs was the only exit from this dungeon, and the officer locked it after they went through.

The friends followed the officer, their feet scuffing along the grimy floor. The space had been built for two hundred people but regularly housed twice as many. For the privilege of living in these cramped quarters, each person had to pay fifty cents a day (the equivalent of eighteen dollars in 2023). If they could not afford it, they were deported. It didn't matter if they had a legal right to enter the country.

The official pointed at the bunk beds where the men were expected to sleep. They were made of wood and rose four tiers high. There was less than two feet of space between each tier—not sufficient to sit upright. Each narrow bed generally held two men, as there were not enough beds for everyone. Women, Chi Hao soon learned, were held in another ward of the shed, behind another locked door.

The shed contradicted the very essence of what America represented to Chi Hao. Chinese people knew to expect harsh treatment upon arrival, but this went beyond anything Chi Hao could have imagined. America was supposed to be "the only free country in the world, the refuge of the oppressed and the champion of the weak." How could this happen in the country "which had sent their beloved pastors and teachers" to China? The contradiction pained him.

At dinnertime, the shed's door opened, and workers came in with rice and stewed meat from a nearby restaurant. By then, the detained men were hungry, and they rushed to get food. To Chi Hao's horror, they squatted or sat on the filthy floor to eat, having no other option. As he recalled years later: "There are no tables, no chairs. We were treated like a group of animals."

Chi Hao thought he had seen the worst of this place when, for no apparent reason, an officer kicked one of the detained men. More often than not, his jailers showed open contempt, and violence was a regular occurrence. Chi Hao did not want to believe that he had escaped the Boxers only to experience abuse at the gates of Christian America.

AND SO THE DAYS PASSED. CHI HAO AND HSIANG HSI BECAME JUST TWO MORE bodies in the crowded hall. There was no news from the outside. Officials forbade visitors or outside correspondence in order to prevent those held from being coached on how to pass the interrogations that would determine their fate.

Because Chinese exclusion barred most Chinese people from entering the country, those who sought to migrate, or their children—known as "paper sons"—had to falsely claim that they were American citizens or that they belonged to one of the exempt categories: merchants, teachers, students, diplomats, or travelers. Knowing that Chinese migrants often tried to circumvent exclusion through such claims, immigration officials would question Chinese arrivals in great detail and then try to verify their claims by separately interviewing witnesses who supposedly knew them. The inspectors would then cross-check the answers, interpreting any inconsistencies that arose between the two sets of interrogations as evidence that the migrants were lying.

What is the nature of your father's business?

Have you been living in that store ever since you went back to China?

Is the store to the right of you in the next building?

What comes next to the vacant place?

Because the questions were often impossible to answer, even for migrants who were, in fact, telling the truth, Chinese entrants came to rely on a sophisticated black market that sold "coaching books" in China containing the same answers as those their witnesses received in the United States. At times, however, Chinese entrants detained in the shed had not been properly coached or had forgotten the answers they were supposed to provide and needed to get such information from the outside. It was the guards' responsibility to ensure they didn't.

THE CHINESE COMMUNITY IN SAN FRANCISCO ROUTINELY LIKENED THE SHED to a prison, even referring to it as the "Chinese jail." One man explained that while detained there, he felt as if he were "a prisoner expiating a crime." Chinese people were not alone in making this comparison. One reverend maintained that in the shed "a man is often imprisoned as a criminal who has committed no crime."

The implication that those who committed crimes ought to be imprisoned overlooked that the legal categories of "innocent" and "criminal" were based on racial and social prejudices rather than on individuals' actions. Indeed, many Americans considered being Chinese in the United States a crime in and of itself. In the popular imagination, Chinese migrants were involved in the businesses of prostitution, opium, or gambling.

Stays in the shed tended to be lengthy: Chinese entrants were regularly locked in there for four or five months, and at times for almost a year—it was long enough to kill some of them. One morning, a detained migrant with whom Chi Hao was speaking pointed to a place where a man had hanged himself. After four months of imprisonment, the man had sought "to end his agony and the shameful outrage." Chi Hao could still see the rope. Although infuriated, he was not surprised that some people could not endure the cruelty of this dreadful dungeon. After just a few days in the shed, Chi Hao was experiencing suffering "too great for physical endurance."

While some migrants took their lives, others tried to escape. Breakouts from the shed occurred on a monthly, or even weekly, basis. A few weeks after Chi Hao and Hsiang Hsi arrived, a group of migrants managed to smuggle a cleaver into the detention hall and used it to cut a hole in the side of the building so that they could crawl out onto the shed's roof. They then hung a rope from a water pipe and lowered themselves down to street level. Five men escaped before the guards noticed what was happening.

There were other, less vigorous ways to escape. Six months earlier, fifteen-year-old Chan Yit had arrived from China on the *Coptic*. The officers in San Francisco denied him permission to land and sent him to the detention shed to await deportation. But when customs officials went to retrieve him, they found in his place a fifty-year-old man who claimed to be him. The boy wanted to enter America and had friends who were willing to help him; the elder man wanted a free ticket back to China. All it took to swap places was the bribing of a watchman at the door.

If Chi Hao and Hsiang Hsi ever considered escaping or withdrawing their appeals and returning to China, their sense of obligation to the families of their murdered friends stopped them. They had to enter the country legally and make it to Oberlin. They still held the letters that their missionary brethren had written before dying, their teachers' clothes, their books, their photographs. They could not leave America without returning these possessions to their owners' families. Still, they were not sure how long they could last in the shed.

6

ELLIS ISLAND WAS A PRISON

Ellen Knauff

AUGUST 14, 1948

The Statue of Liberty passed unnoticed, just another shimmering green wave in the endless green ocean. After yelling at Ellen, the inspector aboard the *Comfort* had ordered the boat's crew members to send her to Ellis Island on a US Army tugboat. As she sped toward her new destination, her fantasies of being welcomed to the "land of opportunity" by the tall copper sculpture no longer seemed relevant. Instead, her eyes fell on the barbed wire that surrounded the island and on a group of people standing on the lawn behind fences—or were those women locked in kennels?

No. They couldn't be. After all, this was America.

Before she could think much about it, the tugboat reached shore, dropped her off, and turned around. With that, Ellen's only means of departing the island sputtered away.

The immigration officer who took Ellen in ensured that she had eaten before leading her to her room. She followed him through a maze of grim corridors, noting how at each turn he had to stop to unlock a gate for them to go through and then quickly lock it behind them. "At each gate," Ellen wrote years later, "I felt more cut off from life."

Six beds and a few chairs furnished her new bedroom. Its small windows, laced with thick iron bars, were perched so high up that she could not reach them. Ellen's stomach churned. She had a "terrible feeling" that she "would never leave the place again."

THOUGH AMERICANS BLITHELY REFERRED TO ELLIS ISLAND AS THE "GATEway to America," the facility was also used to imprison immigrants. The Ellis Island reception center opened its doors in 1892 with the intent of screening out "undesirable" foreigners. Following the passage of the Chinese Exclusion Act, which provided a legal framework for excluding "unwanted" aliens from all over the world, legislators extended the idea to deny admission to immigrants who were sick, suspicious, "likely to become a public charge," or who partook in "criminal" or "immoral" activities. Ellis Island was created to weed out arriving migrants who belonged to any of these unwanted categories.

Most immigrants managed to quickly pass through the sieve: over 80 percent of the twelve million immigrants inspected at Ellis Island made it through to the US mainland in less than a day. But 2 percent were denied entry, and between 13 and 20 percent were held on the island for some time. The majority of those detained had to wait for relatives or funds to arrive before they were allowed in; others were detained because they were deemed unqualified for entry and had to appear before a special inquiry board that evaluated their cases. Still others were sick and had to be hospitalized before being released into the country.

Migrants detained on Ellis Island lived in dreadful conditions, as was the case for Joseph Haas, who, at fourteen, came from Germany by himself in 1922. His uncle, who already lived in the United States, had sponsored his immigration after the First World War left Joseph's family in ruins. A starving teen before his voyage began, Joseph endured nearly two weeks of seasickness aboard the ship before making landfall at Ellis Island; by the time he arrived, he weighed only eighty pounds. During the interrogation process, Joseph queued up in line, saw the doctor, and showed his papers, just like everybody else around him. Out of nowhere, however, an officer grabbed him by the shoulder, opened a door, and shoved him into a cell.

Eleven days passed. During the daytime, the officers allowed him to roam the building but did not let him go outside. Even the windows were boarded shut. At night, he and the other migrants slept in overcrowded, lice-infested compartments that had wire for walls, as if they were kennels. Or, in Joseph's words, "chicken crates."

No one explained why they were holding him, when they would release him, or whether they would deport him. They didn't need to: stopped at Ellis Island, Joseph had fallen prey to the entry fiction. He was not legally considered to be in the country and could thus be denied basic rights.

Joseph did not learn why he had been detained until he was eventually released and arrived at his uncle's home in Wisconsin. His uncle, it turned out, had made a mistake when filling out the affidavit stating that he would financially support Joseph. As soon as the Immigration Service informed him of his mistake, he sent a new affidavit, but the process took almost two weeks—a period during which Joseph remained behind bars.

Immigrants detained longer than Joseph recalled their time on Ellis Island as imprisonment. In 1922, thirteen-year-old Ruth Metzger arrived in the United States with her mother after escaping the violence that enfolded Russia after the revolution, which had already killed Ruth's father. As often happened to women arriving without male companions, Ruth and her mother were deemed "likely to become a public charge" by immigration officers at Ellis Island and ordered to appear before a special inquiry board. Until then, they were remanded to Ellis Island. The two were caged for eight bleak weeks. They were not allowed outside the building and had to sleep in small bunk beds without pillows. "I say that a jail is much nicer," Ruth later recalled.

Detained migrants were not alone in comparing Ellis Island with prison. During the nineteenth and early twentieth centuries, Sing Sing prison in New York was known for its harsh conditions and severe discipline. Nevertheless, after touring Ellis Island in 1922, the British ambassador to the United States exclaimed, "I should prefer imprisonment in Sing Sing to incarceration on Ellis Island awaiting deportation."

Even the island's immigration commissioner equated the facility to a prison. In his memoir, he wrote: "I became a jailer instead of a commissioner of immigration; a jailer not of convicted offenders but of suspected persons who had been arrested and railroaded to Ellis Island as the most available dumping ground under the successive waves of hysteria which swept the country."

The commissioner was not exaggerating: during that period, the Immigration Service not only detained new arrivals on Ellis Island but also used the facility to imprison immigrants already residing in America whom it deemed dangerous. In 1917, when the United States entered the First World War, 1,170 German "enemy aliens" were held there solely because they had worked on German or Austrian ships. The following year, the government used Ellis Island to confine immigrants it believed to be too radical, particularly anarchists, before deporting them. Well-known anarchist Emma Goldman described how during her detention on Ellis Island, the "quarters were congested, the food was abominable, and they [the detained immigrants] were treated like felons."

By the Second World War, there could no longer be any doubt: immigration detention officially became a law enforcement issue when the Immigration Service moved from the Department of Labor to the Department of Justice. As happened during the First World War, the Immigration Service detained "enemy aliens" believed to be subversives. It incarcerated approximately 8,000 Japanese, 2,300 Germans, and a few hundred Italians, many of them on Ellis Island.

The Immigration Service's detention of these "enemy aliens" should not be confused with the War Relocation Authority's mass incarceration of Japanese immigrants and Japanese Americans on the West Coast. After the attack on Pearl Harbor in 1941, President Roosevelt signed Executive Order 9066, which cleared the way for the imprisonment of 120,000 people of Japanese ancestry. While the Immigration Service primarily detained "enemy aliens" it deemed to have committed subversive acts—however inaccurate it was—the War Relocation Authority imprisoned ethnic Japanese people based solely on their ancestry and residence on the West Coast.

By the time Ellen arrived on Ellis Island in August 1948, only one German "enemy alien" remained there. The Second World War had already ended. The Cold War, however, was just beginning. And thus, as she quickly found out, America would continue its history of running prisons disguised as detention centers.

AFTER A MONTH OF LIVING BEHIND BARRED WINDOWS, ELLEN STILL KNEW neither why she was being held nor how long she would be locked up. She had not been charged with breaking the law, but she was nonetheless a prisoner of the state.

By then, she had grown accustomed to the place's rhythms. At seven in the morning, a loud handbell woke everyone up. It chimed again at eight for breakfast; an hour later for sick call; at nine thirty for children's milk time; at ten thirty, baggage time; at eleven for the Kosher meal; and so on throughout the day. Each chime was a reminder of time robbed.

Ellen's spirits sank. She found the food at the dining hall "fit for pigs." To supplement her diet, she frequented the island's canteen, which functioned like a prison commissary. And, like in prisons, some detainees took on jobs—such as sweeping halls or working in the kitchen—to be able to buy goods at the canteen. These jobs, which Ellis Island officials called "recreation work," paid ten cents an hour at a time when the minimum wage was seventy-five cents per hour.

As days and weeks passed, Ellen began to make friends with those who, like her, were facing lengthy confinements on the island. There was the refugee who had fled his country during the Second World War only to arrive in the United States and find that Congress had limited the number of displaced people who could enter—and that the ceiling had already been surpassed.

There was also the woman who was detained for having refused a man's advances. A Swedish professional dancer, she had embarked for the United States with the hope of getting discovered in Hollywood. During the trip, the ship's doctor tried to court her, but she turned him down. The day before the ship reached New York, she experienced a brutal bout of seasickness, and the doctor medicated her. She awoke at the Ellis Island Immigrant Hospital, in Ward 13, known as the "mental ward" for "acutely disturbed patients." The doctors kept her there for two months until they decided that she was "mentally deficient" but not dangerous and sent her to the big detention hall while she appealed her deportation.

And then there was Wilma, a small woman in her early thirties who soon became Ellen's closest confidante. Born in the small town of Rockville, Indiana, Wilma was a US citizen. She was only there to accompany her husband, Frederick Bauer—the last German "enemy alien" detained on Ellis Island.

The War Department had accused Frederick of being a German spy and sought to deport him. But Frederick refused to accept this decree. Although he had been born in Alsace, then a part of the German Empire, he had naturalized as a US citizen. He had never carried out a spying mission, which the War Department admitted even while insisting that he should be thrown out of the country. He and Wilma spent all of their savings fighting his deportation in the courts. While appeals came and went, and years passed, Frederick was detained with Wilma by his side.

By the time Ellen arrived on Ellis Island, Frederick and Wilma had been imprisoned for almost three years. Ellen refused to be stuck there indefinitely, but she also needed to become an American citizen.

ELLEN WAS IN FACT A STATELESS PERSON, A CITIZEN OF NOWHERE. AT THE time, when women from European countries married men of different nationalities, they automatically lost their natural-born citizenship and acquired their husband's citizenship. Thus, when Ellen married her first husband, who was Czech, she forsook her German citizenship and became Czech. Then, when she married Kurt, she lost her Czech citizenship—but she did not acquire US citizenship. In the United States, feminists had successfully fought to break away from Europe's citizenship rules by disentangling women's citizenship status from that of their husband.

Immigrating to America was the only way for Ellen to become a citizen of somewhere. Settling in Germany—the nation responsible for her family's fate—seemed impossible, especially without the protection that citizenship offered. As Ellen later explained, if she returned, Germans could do with her as they willed and "owe no explanation to any country." She was not the only refugee with this thought. As Ellen withered away on Ellis Island, the renowned philosopher Hannah Arendt, who was also a stateless Jewish refugee from Germany, published an article explaining that the "right to have rights" stems directly from citizenship.

While Ellen was fully aware of the benefits that US citizenship offered, her experience in detention had made her question America's very meaning. Before her arrival, she would have expected the treatment she was receiving on Ellis Island to occur in any place behind the Iron Curtain but not in the country that everyone believed to be the cradle of democracy.

Ellen tried to convey these thoughts to Kurt via letter. Even the act of doing so, however, reminded her of the island's repressive nature: a censor read all the correspondence that detained people composed and could block it from reaching the post office.

No matter. Ellen would not censor herself. Squeezing her pen, she told Kurt about her "bitter disappointment in the Ellis Island version of American freedom."

Even these words did not seem strong enough.

"Ellis Island is a concentration camp with steam heat and running water," she wrote.

7

OUT ON BOND

Fu Chi Hao

AUTUMN 1901

Chi Hao looked at Hsiang Hsi's pallid face, not knowing what to do. His friend had become ill while at sea and had then dramatically deteriorated in the squalid atmosphere of the shed, where medical attention was nonexistent. Some migrants died because of the dire conditions inside the warehouse; such was the case for Chun Dow, who arrived in the port of San Francisco in 1902. During his interrogation, Dow claimed that he did not plan to stay in America: upon arrival, he would transfer to a boat bound for Mexico, where he had a job waiting. The officials who heard his story suspected that Dow was going to Mexico only to then cross the border illegally and reenter the United States without having to navigate the interrogation process. They refused him permission to land and took him to the detention shed instead. Dow arrived at the facility in perfect physical condition but became deathly ill after six months. He constantly begged his jailers for medical attention but received none until it was too late. He died a few hours after he was finally taken to the hospital.

Dow's story would repeat itself over the ensuing years. In 1909, a young boy named Low Suey Sing arrived in San Francisco on the steamer *Siberia.* When the inspector of the port denied him permission to land, his father appealed, claiming that his son was an American citizen. He asked the authorities to release the child on bond, but the inspector refused. In the shed, the boy became seriously ill. Once again, officials rejected requests for medical attention until there was little doctors could do. Low Suey Sing died a few days after arriving at the hospital.

Like detained migrants before and after him, Chi Hao repeatedly requested a doctor for his companion, but his petitions went unheeded. As the days passed, Hsiang Hsi became increasingly pale, until he was "looking like a ghost." Still, no doctor came.

Luella Miner, however, managed to visit. Using all her connections and her status as a white missionary woman, she was able to get permission from the Chinese Bureau to enter the shed, as long as an interpreter went with her to ensure she did not provide the men with information that could help them pass their interviews.

Luella was appalled by the smell, the putrid conditions, the dirt. But above all, by the faces of her friends. One glance confirmed that she had been right to worry about them. Hsiang Hsi, she noticed, "especially was in a critical condition physically, and a few more days in that vitiated atmosphere would undoubtedly sow the seeds of incurable disease."

She needed to get them out. The only way to do so without agreeing to their deportation was for a doctor to certify that the men would die if they remained in detention. If she obtained such a certificate, her friends could be released on bond.

While Chi Hao's and Hsiang Hsi's requests had been ignored, Luella was able to cut through the red tape and get a physician to visit the shed. She also reached out to the Chinese consul general, who assured her that he would be willing to post bond for the students. By the end of the week, Luella was successful: a doctor had visited the shed and written the necessary certificate, which allowed the men to be released.

CHI HAO AND HSIANG HSI WERE PRIVILEGED IN HAVING BEEN GRANTED BAIL. From the earliest years of the republic, the criminal justice system had considered bail a fundamental right for all noncapital offenses. After all, bail was seen as a guarantee of the presumption of innocence before individuals appeared in court. In 1789, the first United States Congress passed the Judiciary Act, which held that "bail shall be admitted, except where the punishment may be death." And in 1895, six years before Chi Hao and Hsiang Hsi's detention, the Supreme Court reaffirmed the importance of bail in *Hudson v. Parker*, avowing: "'Bail may be admitted' upon all arrests in capital cases, and 'shall be admitted' upon all arrests in other criminal cases." Since Chinese entrants were not being held in capital cases or even accused of committing crimes, under the bail practices of the time, they should have been allowed to post bond while waiting.

The champions of exclusion, however, ardently opposed letting Chinese migrants out on bail, arguing that this practice would allow the new arrivals to mingle with Americans and take jobs that belonged to citizens. An article in San Francisco's *Daily Examiner*, for instance, claimed that, if released, Chinese migrants would "come ashore as native-born 'citizens' and 'merchants,' and remain here for six or eight months, or longer, on bonds, until their cases are tried. During that time, they may engage in any occupation they please." Releasing these migrants on bond defeated the purpose of Chinese exclusion, which was to purge Chinese people from US society.

It was easy for authorities to heed these calls. Even if offering bail was the standard, Chinese migrants were stopped at the border and thus considered to be outside the country, in a place where the Constitution did not apply. Once the shed opened in 1898 as a detention site, the government stopped offering bail to most Chinese entrants, even though it was routine practice in the prison system.

Chi Hao and Hsiang Hsi were also lucky because Luella convinced the Chinese consul to pay their bond, which amounted to $2,000 ($71,559 in 2023 dollars). Few migrants could have disbursed such a large sum, even though this, too, went counter to the law. The Eighth Amendment states: "Excessive bail shall not be required, nor excessive fines imposed." Policymakers knew that high bail was the functional equivalent of denying bail.

Few other Chinese migrants had been offered bail and could get it paid; Chi Hao and Hsiang Hsi's connections helped them become exceptions to this reality. Their experience reflects a two-tiered system in which the poor or poorly connected are held behind bars before appearing in court, while the rich or well-connected are often released pending trial.

As Chi Hao and Hsiang Hsi found out, however, even those released on bail were by no means free. By law, bondsmen became the custodians of those whose bail they had paid—the prisoners' new jailers. At any time and for any reason, bondsmen could surrender back to jail those whose bond they had paid. As one lawyer explained, "Truly, a prisoner released on bail may accurately express both his position and the principle involved in the cases by saying: 'I am out on bail; I am still in jail.'"

Perhaps most important of all, though, was that Chi Hao and Hsiang Hsi were still not free, even though they were no longer detained, because of the entry fiction. Their status as "entrants" meant that they lacked constitutional rights everywhere in the United States—not only in detention. State officials could order them detained once again at any point without needing to tell them why. The edict that they were "not in the country" had followed them from the ship to the shed and now to the interior of the country.

BY THE TIME CHI HAO AND HSIANG HSI WERE RELEASED ON BOND, IT WAS too late for them to make it to Oberlin in time for the start of the academic year, as classes had already started. Given this, the Chinese consul insisted that the two men remain in San Francisco until their corrected paperwork arrived from China. This way, he could ensure that they were nearby if the government sought to deport them.

To pass the time, the two men began to study under the tutelage of Jee Gam, a minister of the Congregational church and a fervent critic of Chinese exclusion. Chi Hao enjoyed his studies, but as the "weary months rolled on," he became increasingly frustrated. As he later explained, it was as if he and Hsiang Hsi had been "left suspended, as it were, 'twixt heaven and earth," with no place to call home.

After Chi Hao and Hsiang Hsi spent eight months in San Francisco, the consul agreed to let them move to Tacoma, Washington, to live in a missionary's home. Despite the clear water of the Puget Sound and the idyllic backdrop of Mount Rainier, Chi Hao still could not relax. He and Hsiang Hsi could be deported at any moment, and if they were, they would first be sent to the shed, where conditions continued to deteriorate and were turning violent.

Almost twelve months after being released, Chi Hao and Hsiang Hsi received good news: the missionaries had convinced the Chinese consul to allow the men to go to Oberlin for the start of the school year, with the understanding that they would return to San Francisco if needed. It seemed their dreams were finally coming true.

Chi Hao and Hsiang Hsi planned their trip meticulously. They would take the railroad to Milwaukee, where they would meet the mother of a deceased missionary, and then head on to Oberlin. They intended to arrive there by October 16, when the American Board of Commissioners for Foreign Missions would lay the cornerstone of a monument to commemorate the missionaries who had lost their lives in the Boxer Uprising. Chi Hao and Hsiang Hsi had "known and loved" each one of those individuals.

On the day of their departure, the students eagerly boarded a train on the Canadian Pacific Railway, which they had heard offered magnificent scenery. The route was, indeed, dazzling. It went north along the salt waters of Bellingham Bay, crossed the border into Canada, and then headed east past blue creeks and calm lakes. The friends marveled every day at what they saw, even as they anxiously awaited their arrival in Milwaukee.

After three days of travel, the train headed back south, reentering the United States in the dead of night through Portal, North Dakota. Chi Hao was fast asleep when he was awoken by a roaring voice: "Get out of here, you fellows!" It was "spoken in a tone which a self-respecting dog would resent," he later recalled.

It turned out that because Chi Hao and Hsiang Hsi were out on bond, they did not have the right to reenter the United States if they left. It did not matter that they had boarded the train in the United States and were going to disembark in the United States.

In that instance, the two friends encountered another fundamental problem with the bail system: its regulations are so hard to comply with that many of those released end up breaking the rules, often accidentally, and are thus reincarcerated.

Once off the train, the two men considered their options. They clearly needed help, and Toronto was the nearest city where they were likely to get it. But no sooner had they arrived there than they received a telegram from the Chinese consul in San Francisco, urging them to return immediately to the Bay Area. Officials from the Treasury Department in Washington had learned that Chi Hao and Hsiang Hsi were outside the country and had contacted the collector of the port in San Francisco, who claimed that the Chinese Bureau had only permitted the men to be out on bond while they were sick. According to the collector, he had never been informed that Hsiang Hsi had been released from the hospital. Upon hearing this, the Treasury Department sent out an order to arrest and deport the two men, since they had broken the conditions of their bond. Newspapers throughout California latched on to the story, publishing articles that portrayed the missing Chinese students as "fugitives."

Chi Hao and Hsiang Hsi had no option but to return. If they did not do so immediately, the Chinese consul would lose his bond money. Resigned at last to their deportation, the men went to buy train tickets back to San Francisco. But at the station they encountered yet another obstacle: train companies in Canada, they were told, could not sell tickets to the United States to Chinese people who did not possess proper certificates of entry.

Chi Hao could not believe the absurdity of what he was hearing. "The law required us to return to San Francisco; the law refused us permission to travel on the American soil; and, again, the law forbade us to secure tickets," he wrote years later, noting the irony of the situation.

In the end, he and Hsiang Hsi were once again rescued by the American Christian community, which mounted yet another defense in their names. Missionaries who had known Chi Hao or Hsiang Hsi in China sent dozens of telegrams and letters to Washington. A well-known Oberlin professor personally appealed to the Treasury Department on the men's behalf. A Washington lawyer volunteered his services. Under such pressure, the attorney general relented. The students could remain in Canada for three months while waiting for the revised documents to arrive from China.

But the victory was bittersweet: Chi Hao and Hsiang Hsi had to remain in Toronto during the memorial of their slain friends.

"I WOULD LIKE TO TRY AND TELL YOU SOMETHING TONIGHT ABOUT 'THE yellow skin,'" Chi Hao told the crowd. He was speaking at a Sunday school gathering in Toronto about the prejudice he and Hsiang Hsi had faced.

By this point, Chi Hao was all too familiar with anti-Chinese sentiment in the United States. He and his friend had not only been denied entry but also experienced much discrimination while they were out on bond. In the streets of San Francisco, people had sometimes laughed, made fun of them, or thrown things at them. On one occasion, Chi Hao and a group of friends were out exploring when they saw a public bathhouse. The group headed to the entrance and inquired how much tickets to the facility cost.

"We do not want you to take a bath here, even if you pay me a hundred dollars," came the reply.

"Why?" Chi Hao asked.

"Because you have yellow skin."

Now stranded in Canada, Chi Hao sought to combat the racism he had encountered. "Friends, you know our aim is to go to the United States and get our education there," he told the crowd. "But we are kept out from that country because our passports were not quite right, because we are Chinese, and we have yellow skin."

Then, Chi Hao uttered a radical message.

God, he said, "does not care where you come from, and what country you belong to, nor what color you are, and He does not care that you are white, I am yellow, or he is black. The Father will open the door and receive us just the same."

In the United States, people who had experienced discrimination on the basis of their class, gender, race, or ethnicity had regularly resorted to shunning other marginalized groups to defend their own. But Chi Hao refused to do that. At a time when few people spoke out for the rights of Black people, he did.

A few months later, the seminal African American scholar and civil rights activist W. E. B. Du Bois also linked the struggles of Black people to those of other ethnic groups, writing, "The problem of the twentieth century is the problem of the color-line,—the relation of the darker to the lighter races of men in Asia and Africa, in America and the islands of the sea." One way forward, Du Bois noted, was to forge "a new human unity, pulling the ends of earth nearer, and all men, black, yellow, and white."

Chi Hao's time in detention and on bail had transformed him. While he had once seen the United States as a Christian land of freedom, he was now among the voices demanding racial equity in the country.

SIXTEEN MONTHS AFTER CHI HAO AND HSIANG HSI HAD ARRIVED AT THE Golden Gate on the *Doric*, they finally received their corrected papers from China and at last made it to Oberlin College.

After everything he had been through, Chi Hao was determined to change the way Chinese immigrants were treated. So was Luella. She had brought him and Hsiang Hsi to America only to see them suffer for no reason. And so Chi Hao and Luella began to speak out against Chinese exclusion and detention, publishing articles in the top-ranking magazines of the time about what the two friends had experienced. In 1903, Chi Hao also published his autobiography, *Two Heroes of Cathay*, which Luella edited. His chronicle was powerful, and reporters covered his story in newspapers throughout the country, including *The Pacific Commercial Advertiser*, the *Boston Evening Transcript*, the *Joliet Evening Herald*, and the *Santa Cruz Weekly Sentinel*. Chi Hao and Hsiang Hsi's story also reached China, where people were becoming increasingly upset by the treatment of Chinese migrants. In 1905, merchants in China even began a boycott of American goods to protest this discrimination.

Congress also started to take notice of the negative coverage of the detention shed. The year after Chi Hao and Luella published *Two Heroes of Cathay*, legislators appropriated $250,000 to construct an immigration facility in San Francisco similar to the one that existed on Ellis Island. The following year, the Department of Commerce and Labor requested twenty acres of land on Angel Island to build a new detention center that would replace the shed. Like its counterpart on the East Coast, this new facility would be located on a remote island, away from the public eye and where it was harder for Chinese detainees to flee.

The Angel Island Immigration Station opened its doors in January 1910, showing the malleability of detention facilities. Since the 1800s, migrants had been imprisoned in vessels, jails, missions, and dock sheds across San Francisco.

Although Angel Island soon came to be referred to as the "Ellis Island of the West," the purpose of the two isles was entirely different. Ellis Island certainly functioned as a detention center, but it was primarily used to process the entrance of European immigrants—especially during its early years. In contrast, the central objective of Angel Island was to enforce the nation's exclusionary policies and particularly to keep Chinese immigrants out of the United States. Approximately 70 percent of all passengers who arrived in San Francisco ended up on Angel Island, 60 percent of whom were detained for up to three days. By comparison, only 20 percent of arrivals were detained on Ellis Island—half for legal reasons and the other half for medical treatment.

While the detention facilities on Angel Island were a vast improvement over the shed, they were nonetheless abysmal: noisy, dirty, overcrowded, and packed with rows of double- or triple-deck steel bunks. As at a prison, a fence surrounded the barracks and recreation yard. Iron bars enclosed the windows. Lights were turned off early. Guards performed daily counts. Individuals were escorted from their dormitories to the dining hall by armed guards.

Over the years, immigrants who came from Europe, Latin America, and Asia were also held on Angel Island, but Chinese people still constituted 70 percent of all migrants held there. They also had the longest stays, averaging two to three weeks, with some housed for months or years. The facility itself was segregated by race. Those labeled "Occidentals" were detained on the second floor of the administration building, while those classified as "Orientals" were held in less comfortable quarters within a two-story building on a hillside above the administration building. Even the food was regulated by race. The government subcontracted meals from private firms and paid less for the repasts of Asian arrivals than for those of Europeans.

Chinese migrants also had to face ruthless interrogations, as immigration officials attempted to determine whether they belonged to one of the exempt classes or were native-born American citizens or the children of such citizens. Like the interrogations that had taken place when Chinese migrants were held on vessels and in the shed, the questioning that occurred in Angel Island was anxiety-inducing and opaque enough that even those telling the truth had difficulty answering.

Migrants held in Angel Island conveyed their despair by writing or carving poems on the walls that told of their incarceration, homesickness, and loneliness. One such poem read:

> Imprisoned in the wooden building day after day
> My freedom withheld; how can I bear to talk about it?

A sense of hopelessness pervaded the detention facility. In October 1919, Fong Fook, a thirty-two-year-old migrant, hanged himself with a towel tied to a gas fixture. Another, Soto Shee, attempted suicide in 1924 by hanging herself in the women's bathroom after her son died at the immigration station.

IN THE END, IT WAS A FREAK ACCIDENT—NOT THE WEIGHT OF HUMAN PAIN, discrimination, and death—that closed Angel Island. On the night of August 12, 1940, an overloaded circuit in the basement of the administration building ignited a fire in the immigration station. Shortly after midnight, guards noticed smoke coming out of the women's dining room. They immediately rang the fire alarm and cleared the building. Twelve hours later, the fire was under control, but the administration building and the stairway that connected it to the Chinese men's barracks had been destroyed.

While the fire shuttered the immigration station at Angel Island—the symbol of detention on the West Coast—it would take more than a decade for Ellis Island, and the government's detention policy as a whole, to follow suit.

8

THE CONSTITUTION DOES NOT APPLY

Ellen Knauff

OCTOBER 1948

Ellen walked into the dark visiting room. It had been two and a half months since she had last kissed Kurt, but her detention on Ellis Island made it seem like an eternity. Yet there he was now. He had come from Germany to see her and figure out how to release her from this prison. In his arms, Ellen felt a sense of safety she had not experienced since her arrival. Even the guard who interrupted their embrace failed to erase the smile from her face. "So this is the mess you get yourself into the moment you get away from me!" Kurt joked.

In the past few hours, Ellen's life had changed dramatically. Up until then, immigration officials had not allowed her to have visitors or to hire an attorney to represent her. But that very day, after Kurt informed officials that he was in America to see his wife, the island's assistant director had told Ellen that Washington had revised its position on visitation and that immigration officials would allow her to access a lawyer. Kurt's return had clearly put pressure on the agency to provide her with some fundamental rights.

Visitations could only last two hours, but before he left, Kurt promised Ellen that he would go straight to Washington to secure her release. When he returned a few days later, however, he seemed frustrated rather than happy. In Washington, officials from the Immigration Service had sent him from one office to the next, but no one could explain why Ellen was being detained or how she could attain her freedom. From then on, Kurt's visits began to mark Ellen's time. Every few days, he would shuttle between Ellis Island and the nation's capital. With every visit, he grew less cheerful and more evasive and exasperated.

Amid these now disquieting comings and goings, Ellen's cousin showed up at the island with important news. Her husband, who knew high-ranking government officials, had found out that Attorney General Tom Clark had acquired information that Ellen was allegedly a former "paid agent of the Czechoslovak Government." According to Clark's sources, Ellen had reported on the activities of the American Civil Censorship Division in Germany, where she had worked. Ellen's entry into the country thus represented "a hazard to internal security."

Ellen immediately had an inkling about how this "information" had spread. Back in Germany, one of Kurt's ex-girlfriends had started this very rumor, accusing Ellen of being a spy of the Czech government while working for the US Army's Civil Censorship Division.

Ellen would not let her win. The spurious nature of the allegations would help her gain her freedom in court.

ON DECEMBER 9, 1949, ELLEN ASCENDED THE LONG FLIGHT OF STEPS TO THE Supreme Court. Its soaring Corinthian columns made her feel small. Everyone around her spoke in hushed voices, as if the marble palace demanded silence.

As soon as immigration officials had allowed it, Ellen had hired a lawyer to represent her. Gunther Jacobson was a smart man who had kind, probing eyes that always led Ellen to trust him. And that trust had only increased over time. Gunther had first brought her case to the district court and then to the court of appeals. Through his relentless efforts, it had now reached the nation's highest court.

Because Ellen had been stopped at the border, she lacked the constitutional right to contest her exclusion proceedings. To get around this, Gunther had sought a writ of habeas corpus to "test the right of the Attorney General to exclude from the United States, without a hearing, the alien wife of a citizen who had served honorably in the armed forces during World War II." Gunther was not trying to prove in court that Ellen ought to be admitted to the country but only that she deserved the right to a hearing before being detained and expelled.

Chief Justice Frederick Vinson led the rest of the judges into the courtroom. Ellen had studied their pictures in the newspapers and could recognize each of them as they presided behind the raised mahogany bench. She looked directly at Justice Tom Clark. This was the very man who had until recently been the attorney general and who had received "information" that Ellen had been a spy. He would most definitely vote against her, Ellen thought.

She tried to focus, to hear everything being said, but it was impossible. The justices repeatedly interrupted Gunther and the government's attorney. Gunther supplied the court with documents substantiating that Ellen had been a trustworthy employee, including excellent character references written for her by her superiors in the US Army, and showing that she had twice passed the army's security clearance. In contrast, the government's attorney provided no evidence against Ellen; he did not even say what the charges against her were. All he maintained was that she was a security risk whose admittance would gravely endanger the safety of the United States.

After two days of back-and-forth, Ellen had no idea how the vote would go, but her lawyer's arguments had at least illuminated the significance of her case. She was not just fighting for herself, she realized. Her intimate struggle was a struggle for freedom. Back in her hotel room, she wrote a long letter to Kurt. "I have developed a soapbox," she said. "I don't know what to do with it or where it's going to take me."

FOR OVER A MONTH, ELLEN FRETTED ABOUT HER FUTURE. THE SUPREME Court released its opinions on Mondays, and so every Monday she would call Gunther to check on her case. On a cold January day in 1950, his dejected voice said it all.

"We've lost?" she asked.

"Yes," came the answer. "I am very disappointed."

Justice Sherman Minton had delivered the opinion of the court, affirming that the nineteenth-century entry fiction doctrine continued to be the law of the land. "At the outset," it held, "we wish to point out that an alien who seeks admission to this country may not do so under any claim of right." Minton backed this decision by citing a case from the era of Chinese exclusion that held that the Bill of Rights did not protect those stopped at the border in immigration proceedings.

Three justices disagreed. In his dissenting opinion, Justice Robert Jackson noted that this was an affront to Kurt, a US citizen: "I do not question the constitutional power of Congress to authorize immigration authorities to turn back from our gates any alien or class of aliens. But I do not find that Congress has authorized an abrupt and brutal exclusion of the wife of an American citizen without a hearing," he wrote.

Jackson's scathing dissent also noted the importance of ensuring habeas corpus. The government, it stated, "says we must find that Congress authorized this treatment of war brides and, even if we cannot get any reasons for it, we must say it is legal; security requires it. Security is like liberty in that many are the crimes committed in its name."

FIVE DAYS AFTER THE SUPREME COURT RULED ON ELLEN'S CASE, ALGER HISS sat stoically in court, looking from one juror to the next, head held high.

Silence fell when the clerk asked if the jury had reached a verdict. Hiss swallowed once. "Guilty," he heard.

The slender, Harvard-trained government lawyer had become an unlikely character in an equally improbable plot. Until recently, Hiss had been an American exemplar: he had clerked for Supreme Court Justice Oliver Wendell Holmes, served in Roosevelt's New Deal administration, helped found the United Nations, and even been a US adviser at the Yalta Conference, where Roosevelt, Churchill, and Stalin redrew the map of postwar Europe.

His fortunes had changed on August 3, 1948, eleven days before Ellen was first detained on Ellis Island. That day, Whittaker Chambers, a stout, disheveled editor for *Time* magazine, testified before the House Committee on Un-American Activities that he had been part of a Communist organization in the 1930s—as had Hiss.

At risk of losing his reputation, Hiss sued Chambers for slander, which in turn led Chambers to broaden his allegations. In the 1930s, he now claimed, Hiss had stolen State Department files for the Soviet Union. To prove this, Chambers led federal agents to his farm in Maryland, where, inside a hollowed-out pumpkin, he had hidden film that contained classified documents. These "Pumpkin Papers," as they were soon dubbed, had been typed on Hiss's old Woodstock typewriter. Hiss, Chambers held, had reproduced them for the Soviet Union.

The nation followed each new farcical twist and tangle, accusation, and vindication in the case. Throughout it all, Hiss insisted he was no traitor.

The statute of limitations for espionage had passed, but on January 21, 1950, the government indicted Hiss on two counts of perjury for lying under oath. The judge sentenced him to five years in prison.

The nation, however, was not ready to move on. Joseph McCarthy, then a little-known Republican senator, was determined to use the case's infamy to place himself at center stage. With bombastic enthusiasm, he declared that the Hiss case demonstrated that the entire State Department was "thoroughly infested" with Communists. Yes, Hiss was now locked up, but Americans could still see his visage in the watchful and duplicitous eyes of other state officials.

McCarthy's accusations were outlandish, but he was nonetheless able to tap into the deep fears Americans held about Russian access to the atomic bomb and the unexpected victory of Chinese Communists under Mao Zedong. Secret conspiracies, long shadows, treason—the dangers of espionage proliferated everywhere. Nine months after Hiss's imprisonment, Congress passed the Internal Security Act of 1950, over President Harry Truman's veto. The act required Communist organizations to register with the Justice Department; authorized the exclusion and deportation of Communists and those who advocated for totalitarian doctrines; and provided that if the president proclaimed an "internal security emergency," the attorney general could detain anyone likely to engage in espionage or sabotage.

Fears of espionage had placed Hiss and Ellen behind bars; the Internal Security Act led hundreds of others to face the same fate. Within ninety days of the law's passage, the population on Ellis Island shot from approximately four hundred to twelve hundred, even though the dining hall could seat only three hundred. The misery inside intensified. As Ellen later recounted: "The noise became unbearable, and the establishment was a complete madhouse. Men slept two hundred fifty to three hundred in one dormitory; women were only slightly more comfortable," and fleas feasted on everyone.

ELLEN FLIPPED THROUGH THE PAGES OF THE *ST. LOUIS POST-DISPATCH.* EDWARD Harris, a muckraker who had received the Pulitzer Prize, had recently interviewed her, and she was anxious to see what he had written. "The *Post-Dispatch* is willing to risk the prediction that this ruling will be reversed, even though not in time to do Mr. and Mrs. Knauff any good. Such injustice cannot stand always," she read.

Looking at those words, Ellen realized that the media was her key out of this prison. For so long, she had been disconnected from the world, stuck on an island, voiceless. But with Harris on her side, she could finally reach people.

After Harris's piece came out, reporters ate her story up, emphasizing in their articles how Ellen measured up to the nation's idealized gendered norms and stereotypes: she was a beautiful woman and the adoring wife of a former American GI who had saved her from a wretched past. Her troubles, the reporters asserted, could all be pinned on her husband's ex-girlfriend. Detaining her went against the nation's principles of freedom and justice.

Between 1950 and 1954, newspapers and magazines published over two thousand articles on her case, with the *St. Louis Post-Dispatch* and the *New York Post* leading the crusade. Although Ellen never gained as much attention as Hiss, she nonetheless became a household name. People throughout the country clamored for her release, writing impassioned letters to the *St. Louis Post-Dispatch* thanking its reporters for going "to work on behalf of justice for her."

Soon after the media frenzy began, William Langer, a bull-voiced, cigar-chewing senator from North Dakota, decided to dig deeper into Ellen's case. In 1947, he had fought for the rights of the German "enemy aliens" detained on Ellis Island, and Ellen's situation seemed even more meritorious. On February 3, 1950, he introduced a bill in the Senate directing the attorney general to discontinue Ellen's exclusion and grant her "immediate entry" into the United States. Seeing the popularity of this campaign, Congressman Francis Walter introduced a comparable bill in the House. As chair of the House Judiciary Subcommittee on Immigration, Walter could push the bill forward with exceptional speed, and on May 2, 1950, the House of Representatives voted to admit Ellen to the United States.

IRATE AT THE HOUSE'S DECISION, THE NEW ATTORNEY GENERAL, JAMES McGrath, concluded that he had to deport Ellen as quickly as possible, before her case garnered even more attention and support. On May 16, 1950, the US Court of Appeals for the Second Circuit ruled that the government could deport Ellen, even though there were pending bills in Congress to permit her admission. McGrath lost no time: Ellen would be deported the following day, he ordered.

That night, Ellen packed her belongings, feeling miserable about the turn of events. She set aside an elegant suit, a black beret, and tan shoes to wear on her way out. If she had to leave the country, she would do it in style.

The following morning, Ellis Island officials lined up to say their goodbyes. Ellen had been detained for nearly two years, during which time the island's staff had come to root for her success. Now they were eager to wish her well.

Ellen arrived at Idlewild Airport shortly before ten in the morning. A friendly guard took her baggage to the plane's loading area while another rushed her to the customs room to keep her away from the scrum of reporters who had flocked to catch a glimpse of her. Through the window, she could see the American Airlines plane that would take her back to Europe. It was scheduled to take off at eleven. At least this plane would "take her back to freedom, back to Kurt," she thought.

AT ROUGHLY THE SAME TIME THAT ELLEN WAS HEADING FOR THE AIRPORT, Gunther's colleague, Armand Grégoire, was rushing from New York to Washington. Like Ellen, her lawyer had only found out that she was to be deported the previous evening. He had mailed a special-delivery letter to the Supreme Court petitioning Justice Jackson to issue an order to stay her deportation. But Gunther was not about to take chances. He also instructed Armand to hand-deliver a duplicate letter to the justice.

By the time Justice Jackson arrived at his office, both Armand and the mailed letter awaited him. Jackson had little time to deliberate. Ellen's plane was set to depart less than two hours later. He thought about what he should do. He almost always refused stays that the court of appeals had denied, but this case, he concluded, was different.

Together with the court clerk, he rushed to draft the stay. "Bundling this woman onto an airplane to get her out of this country within hours after the decision of the Court of Appeals," the justice wrote, "would defeat this court's jurisdiction to consider her petition for review." It would also "circumvent any action by Congress . . . to cancel her exclusion, already unanimously taken by the House of Representatives." He continued: "If the Department had at any time shown even probable grounds to believe that [the] presence of this woman a few days more in this country might jeopardize national security, even infinitesimally, I should refuse the stay. But the Department of Justice has not only had the opportunity, it has been importuned to show courts or Congress any reason for its exclusion order."

By 10:00 a.m., the justice and the clerk were almost done; only a few more details needed to be ironed out. At 10:18 a.m., the clerk telephoned Edward Shaughnessy, the district director of immigration and naturalization for the District of New York. "This is to inform you that Justice Jackson has just signed a stay of deportation," the clerk said. "We want to officially request you to do everything in your power to carry the order out."

Shaughnessy, who like McGrath had been trying to deport Ellen for months, replied only, "I was afraid of that."

At 10:40 a.m., Ellen, unaware of what was transpiring, readied to embark.

The telephone rang. The deportation was off. Ellen did not board the plane, but by then it was too late to retrieve her bags.

The following day, the *Daily News* printed: "After 22 months of effort to ship German war bride Mrs. Ellen Knauff bag and baggage back where she came from, the Government scored a moral victory yesterday. It shipped the baggage."

BACK ON THE ISLAND, THOUGH, ELLEN CONTINUED TO DESPAIR. ALTHOUGH Justice Jackson had prevented her deportation, she was now stuck on Ellis Island once again. Days had turned into months, which had turned into years, and still no resolution had come. To make matters worse, she soon learned that Gunther, who had fought indefatigably for her, was dying of cancer and had to step down from her case.

Seeing Ellen's increasing anguish, Kurt, who had kept working in Germany to help defray the case's legal costs, decided that it was time to visit his wife once more. And as it turned out, his return to America proved to be even more propitious than either he or Ellen could have foreseen. On January 30, 1951, they learned that Ellen's new lawyer, Alfred "Al" Feingold, had petitioned for her to be released "on parole"—the term used for pretrial release in immigration cases. The attorney general had agreed.

The next day, the *Daily News* reported the story by publishing a picture of Ellen and Kurt holding each other tightly, eyes closed. Ellen, the paper stated, was "so happy at her unexpected release that she could scarcely speak coherently."

For the next three weeks, Ellen and Kurt lived together for the first time since she had arrived in the United States. "We were flat broke, living on whatever we were able to sell," Ellen wrote in her memoir. "We had to live in a hotel while longing for a home. Yet, despite all these handicaps, we found that we were still as much in love."

Unfortunately, their time together could not go on forever, as Kurt had to return to Germany. In his absence, the attorney general agreed to transfer Ellen's custody to her lawyer while her case was reevaluated. On February 23, Kurt set sail while Ellen remained in New York. She missed her husband terribly but was nonetheless delighted to be out under Al's custody and was determined to thrive.

Then, that March, an immigration official called her on the phone.

The attorney general had granted her a hearing, he told her. Ellen immediately realized the magnitude of his words: this was exactly what she, Gunther, Al, and everyone in the press had been fighting for all these long years.

ON THE STAND, ELLEN KEPT PERFECTLY COMPOSED AS MARIO T. NOTO, THE examining officer for the government, fired questions at her.

Had she given a true and correct testimony when she was first interrogated on Ellis Island?

Had she ever corresponded or been in contact with Czechs who might be doing espionage work?

Was she a spy?

Calmly, Ellen answered. *Yes,* she had always given officials a true and correct testimony; *no*, she had never been in contact with Czechs involved in espionage; and *no*, she had definitely never been a spy.

Noto's interrogation became more intricate. *Why had she visited the Czechoslovak consulate in Frankfurt while working for the Civil Censorship Division?*

Unflustered, Ellen explained that her Czech passport had expired while she was in Germany, and she had to visit the consulate—known as the mission—every three months to extend it.

Noto excused Ellen and called his first witness. Dressed in a sharp brown suit, Anna Lavickova walked toward the stand. She was apprehensive and spoke with a heavy Czech accent that was hard to understand. But little by little, her story came through. She had worked at the Czech mission in Frankfurt as a typist and telephone operator from January 1947 to April 1948. During this period, she had seen Ellen visit the mission three times.

This seemed straightforward enough; Ellen had already referred to such visits.

Lavickova proceeded. During these calls, she claimed, Ellen had personally met Colonel Podhora, the mission's chief, and Major Vecerek. These officials, she said, speaking even more hesitantly than before, had no responsibilities in passport matters. They engaged in espionage.

Ellen could not believe what she was hearing. Her official Czech documents contradicted Lavickova's statements. Al, who continued to represent her, immediately introduced them as evidence. The board asked Ellen to translate the first document. It was a letter.

"Dated January 3, 1947," Ellen said with a steady voice. "On account of the fact that the Ministry of the Interior agrees to the prolongation of your passport for the time of three months, we sent it through the Czechoslovak mission in Frankfurt." The note was signed by Major Vecerek.

Lavickova looked at the letter. *Yes, the translation was correct*, she admitted. *And yes, it was Vecerek's signature.*

The board did not react.

Noto moved on quickly, calling his star witness to the stand. Major Vaclav Kadane had worked for the Czech government at the mission in Frankfurt. In contrast to Lavickova, Kadane looked poised and self-assured as he took the stand and related that intelligence reports had passed through his hands often. Many of these reports, he claimed, had been written by an agent he believed to be Ellen.

"Objection," roared Al every time Kadane backed his words with rumors he had heard. These claims were nothing more than hearsay. The board's chairman, however, overruled each of these objections, noting that the board was "not bound by the rules of evidence."

Finally, Noto called the government's third witness, William C. Hacker, a US captain who had been stationed in Frankfurt from April 1946 until August 1948, when he was investigating espionage activities against the United States. Dressed in uniform, Hacker told the board that "in late 1947" he had received "from a reliable and confidential source which cannot be disclosed" information that Ellen was "dealing and associating with" Colonel Podhora, who was known to be engaged in espionage.

Ellen wanted to pound the table over the inconsistency of this testimony. She was being accused of distributing information while she worked for the Civil Censorship Division, but by 1947, that division no longer existed.

When the hearing ended, Ellen waited nervously for the ruling—but not for long. After less than an hour, the board returned to court. The board members had clearly not dwelled on her case; they had not even had time to read all the documentary evidence that Al had submitted.

The room went silent as the board's chairman read the decision. "Testimony has been offered that you served the Czech liaison mission as an espionage agent." Ellen knew where this was going. "There is reason to believe that you would be likely to engage in activities which would be prohibited by the laws of the United States relating to espionage, sabotage, public disorder, or in other activity subversive to the national security."

Ellen wanted to scream but remained sitting, posture dignified. She still had one last chance: she could appeal the decision. That, however, was her last recourse. If she lost, she would be deported.

AFTER THE MARCH HEARING, THE ATTORNEY GENERAL REVOKED ELLEN'S parole and ordered her back to Ellis Island. Since then, she had once again lived in the monotony of captivity. But June 29, 1951, was different.

Al was arguing her case before the Board of Immigration Appeals. Ellen had not been allowed to attend, so she spent the day imagining what might be happening.

When she finally got her hands on the *St. Louis Post-Dispatch* that evening, she flicked quickly to the second page to find the story.

"The lawyer, Alfred Feingold, told the board that 'not a shred of legal evidence' had been brought forward" against her, she read. "'The Knauff case,'" the newspaper quoted him, "'is just another manifestation of the hysteria that is sweeping the country.'"

The board now had to assess the case and declare its position. Then, Attorney General McGrath would decide whether or not to follow suit. He had the final word. This was it, Ellen thought. The end of her struggle was in sight. She would either win and stay in America as a free woman, or she would lose and be deported to a stateless fate. Either way, after three years, her fight would soon be over.

But days and then months ticked by without updates. July, August, September. Finally, on October 30, Ellen received a telegram from Al: "Board of Immigration Appeals has decided case. Decision unknown. McGrath informed me that he is making a final review and hopes to be able to reach a final decision soon."

On November 2, *The Christian Science Monitor* reported that Representative Walter had heard that the board had voted in Ellen's favor while also quoting the board's chairman, stating that no one other than the attorney general knew what the board had recommended.

What was it?

Determined to clear her mind, Ellen headed to the big hall to play chess but was interrupted by one of the matrons. The night supervisor needed her to go to the main office.

"Well, Ellen," the supervisor said as soon as she entered, "I've always promised you I'd give you some good news one day." The Board of Immigration Appeals had ruled in her favor.

"All of the testimony" against her "is hearsay," the board had determined. McGrath had upheld its decision; the case was simply not worth the negative publicity it attracted.

ELLEN STOOD IN THE FERRY'S CABIN DRESSED IN HER FAVORITE SUIT—POWDER blue, the color of an endless clear sky. Her hair trailed easily in the wind as the ship surged forward. Feeling the breeze on her face, she took a deep breath. It was "the air of free America."

The right to a hearing had set Ellen free. As soon as she was able to learn the exact nature of the charges against her and defend herself before an unbiased tribunal, it had become clear that there was no real evidence against her. The entry fiction had cost her years of her life.

Tonight, November 2, 1951, she thought, *is my August 14, 1948*—the day that she had initially arrived in the United States.

She could already see the coastline. It was now time to move on and rebuild her life.

9

"AN ENLIGHTENED CIVILIZATION"

1954–1980

It was not just Ellen who felt the "air of free America" as she sailed toward Manhattan—it was America itself. Her very public case and victory would soon help dismantle the long-held principle that new arrivals ought to be detained while authorities determined their right to enter the country. In 1954, only four years after Ellen's release, government officials would conclude that there were more compassionate and effective ways to deal with the migrants who were coming to America. Detention, Ellen had shown the world, was not necessary.

Like Chi Hao, Ellen continued to speak out against detention even after she was released. By then she had learned the importance of liberty and the grievances immigrants faced. Only four months after being released from Ellis Island, she published a popular memoir about her three-year-long confinement. Public libraries throughout the United States—from North Adams, Massachusetts, to Kalispell, Montana, to Corvallis, Oregon, and Auburn, California—rushed to buy copies. Newspapers big and small covered the book breathlessly. *The Knoxville Journal*, a newspaper from Tennessee, claimed, "The story told in this book is one of the most shocking perversions of justice in American history." The Los Angeles *Daily News* showed a photograph of Ellen with the caption "free at last." *The New York Times* issued a story with the haunting title "It Happened Here," noting that Ellen's incarceration illustrated "how far we have strayed from the democratic process when it comes to granting foreigners permission to step upon our shores."

The national interest surrounding Ellen's case inspired the media to tell the stories of other detained migrants. "A single red rose can be more exquisite than a whole hedge of roses. An injustice involving one human being can arouse more sympathy than the suffering of thousands, perhaps because it is within the frame of understanding of fellow humans," began an article in *The Salt Lake Tribune*. It continued: "The case of Ellen Knauff . . . dramatized bureaucratic stupidity more than hundreds of other cases of more outrageous discrimination."

One of the most reported cases alongside Ellen's was that of Ignatz Mezei, who had been held on Ellis Island with Ellen but would remain caged there until 1954—the year in which government policy turned against detention. Upon his arrival to America in 1950, Ignatz was shuttled to Ellis Island, where he, too, fell prey to the entry fiction. As with Ellen, the attorney general neither disclosed why the government was detaining him nor provided him the right to a hearing. Following its decision on Ellen's fate, the Supreme Court ruled in Ignatz's case that the attorney general's actions did "not amount to an unlawful detention." Desperate for freedom, Ignatz tried to leave the United States, but France, Great Britain, Hungary, and a dozen Latin American nations refused to permit him entry. With no country willing to take him, Ignatz could do nothing to escape Ellis Island.

The media's fixation on immigrant detention infuriated government officials. In an interview conducted in 1967, General Joseph Swing, who was the commissioner of the Immigration Service in 1954, said that his policy had always been to try to keep the Immigration Service "out of the news any way you can." As he explained, "The news media today wants something startling. . . . If they can make an underdog out of somebody, they're going to make an underdog out of him and blow it up."

Beyond the negative attention that immigration detention was receiving in America, the issue was also casting a shadow over America's image abroad. At the beginning of 1954, for example, Canadian students picketed outside the US consulate in Toronto after American immigration officials detained two students from the University of Toronto. Then, that August, an Australian newspaper published an article calling Ellis Island "the most dreaded 27 acres of American soil" and "a place where some have been told daily to remember they are not in prison—that they have freedom to say what they will, think what they will, freedom to do anything but leave the place."

The international repercussions of detention should not have been surprising to those paying attention: as early as 1902, Luella Miner, the missionary who had helped Chi Hao and Hsiang Hsi come to the United States, had warned that America's detention practices and Chinese exclusion more broadly would eventually cause international problems for the United States. In an article she published in *The Independent*, she described how Chi Hao and Hsiang Hsi had risked their lives for Americans in China only to end up at the detention shed in San Francisco and cautioned: "America has weighty reasons just now for seeking to win the favor of Chinese, especially of the merchants, literati, and official class. Commerce has spread wide wings, and far-visioned prophets speak of the day when the Pacific will be an American lake."

Time had proved her right: Chi Hao had become an ardent advocate against American detention before becoming an important politician in Beijing; for his part, Hsiang Hsi had come to be known as Dr. H. H. Kung and had served as the premier of the Republic of China between 1938 and 1939. While Hsiang Hsi had not retaliated against America for having detained him, and few even knew about his history in the shed, his story was still indicative of the potential international repercussions that America could face because of its detention practices.

With so much opposition against immigration detention both inside and outside the United States, Attorney General Herbert Brownell began to wonder whether the government ought to discontinue this practice. History had already shown that detention was gratuitous. Just like Chi Hao, Hsiang Hsi, and Ellen, most of those detained had eventually made their way into the country. For instance, in 1907, the year of peak immigration, nearly 200,000 foreign nationals were detained. Despite these detentions, however, only 6,752 were deported. In other words, the government had imprisoned tens of thousands of people for no reason.

Detention had also failed in its purported goal of ensuring that migrants from excluded categories did not enter the country. The case of Chinese arrivals made this clear. According to both Chinese migrants and immigration officials, an estimated 90 percent of all Chinese people who arrived in the years between 1875 and 1940 had false papers, yet only 7 percent of all Chinese applicants caged at Angel Island were ultimately denied entrance to the country.

Detention was also financially costly, especially given that the nation no longer needed large detention centers like the one that existed on Ellis Island. During the height of European migration, thousands of immigrants had arrived at Ellis Island every day. In 1907, for instance, 1,004,756 immigrants had been inspected there. In contrast, by 1954, most arriving migrants never set foot on the island, and the immigration station only housed two or three hundred at a time. Migration to the United States had fallen dramatically since Congress had passed the Immigration Act of 1924, which excluded most Asians from immigrating and limited the number of European immigrants—primarily from Southern and Eastern Europe—who were allowed to enter the United States. Additionally, fewer European immigrants were being detained because American consuls had started issuing visas abroad, which meant that excludable migrants were now being barred from the country before they even arrived at America's shores.

While detention was unpopular, expensive, and ineffective, the parole system, by which migrants were released while their cases were being adjudicated, had long been shown to work. Even though granting bail to arriving migrants had not been standard practice before 1954, the government had tried and tested doing so over the years, including with Chi Hao, Hsiang Hsi, and Ellen. Chi Hao and Hsiang Hsi had been released from the Pacific Mail detention shed and had never tried to abscond. When they made a mistake and briefly left the country, they were willing to return to San Francisco immediately, even though they knew that this would mean detainment and deportation. The same was true for Ellen, who was twice released on bond and both times returned to Ellis Island without trying to flee. By 1954, there was a long history of paroled migrants appearing before the government when required to do so.

The criminal justice system offered the attorney general a model for releasing migrants on bail. In the immigration context, the government detained entrants while it reviewed their cases, but in the criminal justice system, it was supposed to offer defendants charged with noncapital crimes the right to post bond while they awaited trial. As the Supreme Court said in 1951, "Unless this right to bail before trial is preserved, the presumption of innocence, secured only after centuries of struggle, would lose its meaning."

This did not necessarily mean that all defendants in the criminal justice system had access to pretrial release. A seminal study published in 1954 found that in Philadelphia, 75 percent of defendants charged with noncapital crimes defined as "serious"—including arson, rape, and "sodomy"—were held in jail between arrest and trial because they could not hire attorneys, had not been informed that they had the right to bail, or simply could not afford to post bond. Another 27 percent of defendants who had been charged with "less serious" crimes also failed to obtain release because they could not afford to pay bail.

Still, there remained the ideal that noncapital offenders deserved a right to bail while awaiting trial. Perhaps, Brownell pondered, the government should also offer most foreign entrants the possibility of release while their cases were being adjudicated.

On November 11, 1954, Brownell announced that the administration was introducing a new detention policy. He emphasized the importance of the change in a dramatic speech he gave during the first mass naturalization ceremonies the government had ever held. That day, from coast to coast, nearly fifty thousand new citizens pledged their allegiance to the United States of America. Approximately sixteen thousand took their oaths during swearing-in ceremonies held in Brooklyn and Manhattan. There, Brownell announced that the government had brought the country "one more step forward toward humane administration of the immigration laws." From then on, he stated, "in all but a few cases, those aliens whose admissibility or deportation is under study will no longer be detained. Only those deemed likely to abscond or those whose freedom of movement could be adverse to the national security or the public safety will be detained." All others would be released on parole while their cases were being reviewed.

Because the new policy would dramatically decrease the number of migrants in detention, the attorney general told his audiences that the Department of Justice was going to discontinue six seaport detention facilities in New York, Boston, Seattle, San Francisco, San Pedro, and Honolulu. The facility in New York was, of course, Ellis Island. Its closure was in great part a result of the publicity that Ellen's story had generated.

At around 10:00 a.m. on November 12, 1954, Arne Pettersen, a Norwegian seaman who had overstayed his shore leave, walked across the platform at Ellis Island and boarded a Manhattan-bound ferry. He was the last foreign national to leave the island before the facility closed its doors. Once in Manhattan, Arne strode to freedom: he had been paroled under the administration's new detention procedures.

The government's new antidetention policy represented a massive change from the one it had held since 1891. And it was hailed by citizens and government officials alike. In 1958, the Supreme Court stated in *Leng May Ma v. Barber*: "Physical detention of aliens is now the exception, not the rule." It then concluded that "certainly this policy reflects the humane qualities of an enlightened civilization."

IT WAS A NEW ERA. THE EVOLVING VIEWS ON DETENTION COULD PUT AN END to much unnecessary suffering: no more detained people wondering when they would be let out, no more fear upon arrival, no more suicides and deaths inside migrant prisons.

Chi Hao's, Hsiang Hsi's, and Ellen's experiences shine light on the significance of releasing migrants on parole rather than incarcerating them. For Hsiang Hsi, leaving the shed meant, above all, ensuring that he could obtain the medical attention he desperately needed. It also allowed him and Chi Hao to escape a mercilessly cramped and unsanitary facility where those held inside could barely see daylight and where their very humanity was denied.

Parole was life-giving. On the outside, Chi Hao and Hsiang Hsi were able to explore San Francisco and see Tacoma. They were able to study under Jee Gam, one of the earliest Chinese people to be baptized and admitted into the First Congregational Church of Oakland. They could breathe fresh air.

For Ellen, being paroled from Ellis Island primarily meant that when her husband visited from Germany, she was able to see him, touch him, sleep next to him. Ellen thrived outside Ellis Island even when Kurt was not in America. She got a job selling junior girdles at Macy's, rented a furnished room, and found joy in life. Ellis Island's plain, white-tiled building had starved her of color; upon her parole, she went to New York's art museums to admire their vibrant paintings and spent hours outside florists' windows looking at each bouquet in detail.

Still, the system of parole was far from perfect or emancipatory. To be let out, Ellen, Chi Hao, and Hsiang Hsi had to pay exorbitant bond fees. Even after their release, they were not fully free but remained captives of the state and of those who had paid their bond. Chi Hao and Hsiang Hsi experienced terrible frustration when they were not allowed to be with their community in Oberlin. They had to ask for permission from the Chinese consul before relocating and were required to follow stringent parole rules. When they inadvertently broke them, government officials demanded their renewed detainment. For her part, Ellen felt as if she lived under the gaze of the attorney general and always feared being sent back to Ellis Island. She could not change residence or leave New York City without "prior written notice delivered in person" to the Immigration Service's New York office.

Still, while Chi Hao, Hsiang Hsi, and Ellen had to endure the continued limitations on their freedom and opposed the state's intrusion into their lives, they were nonetheless relieved to be out of detention. To roam beyond padlocks.

ON JANUARY 26, 1955, AT THE TOWN HALL CLUB IN NEW YORK CITY, ATTORney General Herbert Brownell delivered a speech hailing the success of the new antidetention policy, which was "giving both heart and conscience to the administration of the immigration laws." According to him, the Immigration and Naturalization Service had essentially stopped holding any migrants who were seeking entry to the country. As of January 21, he said, the agency had slashed the detention of migrants who were under deportation proceedings—which included not only new arrivals but also migrants apprehended within the country—to only seventy-three individuals. Brownell did add a caveat to this statistic, however, noting that it did not include "the aliens collected in the wetback 'staging' operations conducted in the Southwest."

By this, Brownell meant that he was not counting the detention of unauthorized Mexican migrants, who at the time were referred to by the derogatory term "wetbacks" because they had to wade or swim across the Rio Grande to get into the United States. Brownell's failure to include undocumented Mexicans in his detention count made the story he offered much more spectacular than it was. By the end of 1955, the government had detained 184,000 people, 94 percent of whom were Mexican nationals.

There was, however, a reason why Brownell did not factor Mexican migrants into his detention count: the confinement of Mexican nationals did not fit with the government's purported goal of immigrant detention. According to the Immigration and Naturalization Service, detention served to hold foreigners while their immigration claims were adjudicated or while they were awaiting deportation. But Mexican nationals were very rarely "deported," and few contested their removal.

To formally deport migrants, the government had to first arraign and try them in court. Given the sheer number of Mexicans apprehended, this would have entailed a huge expense. To get around this, immigration officials offered apprehended Mexicans voluntary departure, by which the migrants were returned to their home country without first going to court. Because most apprehended Mexican migrants agreed to go back to Mexico "voluntarily," the government did not consider them detained.

According to officials, the goal of holding Mexican nationals was different than that of detention: when apprehended, these migrants were taken to "staging areas" while officials arranged for their transportation back home. These areas were only holding grounds for migrants before they were tossed back across the border.

Mexican migrants agreed to voluntary departure because immigration officials told them that if their cases went to court, they would be detained for weeks or months while the proceedings took place. By using these threats, the government effectively diminished the rights of those apprehended within the country to those of entrants. Because of the entry fiction, undocumented migrants caught in the country's interior had more rights than "entrants" stopped at the border. Although they were undocumented, they were entitled to many constitutional protections. The Fifth Amendment, for instance, does not speak in terms of "citizens" but holds that no "person" can "be deprived of life, liberty, or property, without due process of law." When these migrants signed voluntary departure forms, they in effect signed away their right to hearings, and to all procedural protections the Constitution might provide in those hearings.

Significantly, in his 1955 speech, Brownell could have also shown that the Immigration and Naturalization Service had dramatically curtailed the confinement of Mexican nationals. The source of this decline, however, undermined Brownell's story about the growing "heart and conscience" of the nation's detention practices.

In June 1954, six months before announcing that immigration officials would no longer detain new arrivals, the attorney general had launched another initiative: a massive expulsion campaign against Mexicans known as Operation Wetback. He had done so in part to quiet the constant stream of newspaper articles that portrayed Mexican migrants not as sympathetic victims of the system, as Ellen and other detained Europeans were depicted, but as throngs of dangerous border crossers who had no faces or names.

Operation Wetback was led by General Joseph Swing, who long before becoming commissioner of the Immigration Service had participated in the 1916 Pershing expedition that sought to capture Mexican revolutionary Pancho Villa. During Operation Wetback, he went after another type of "enemy." The Immigration and Naturalization Service conducted a military-style attack, apprehending about 170,000 undocumented migrants within three months.

The operation had a massive effect on detention rates. By forcing unauthorized Mexican migrants out of the country, it reduced the number of people who could end up in detention. The violence of the operation itself made many Mexicans afraid of returning to the United States without papers. But equally important, when implementing Operation Wetback, government officials also increased the number of Mexican migrants who could come to the country legally. In 1942, the United States and Mexico had launched the Bracero Program, through which Mexican "guest workers," known as braceros, could migrate legally to labor in the United States for short periods of time. At the same time that the government was removing migrants through Operation Wetback, it was also expanding the number of braceros who could come to the country, thus replacing unauthorized migrants with guest workers. Through this substitution, the government could claim that it had curbed illegal border crossings while still keeping the farmers who hired the expelled workers content. And, unlike unauthorized migrants, braceros were not apprehended because of their status, which meant that fewer individuals were detained.

In 1953, the year before Operation Wetback began, the Immigration Service detained a total of 195,000 foreigners, most of whom were unauthorized Mexican workers. By 1959, the number of detained Mexican migrants had fallen to approximately 10,000.

THIS STATE OF AFFAIRS DID NOT LAST LONG, HOWEVER. IN 1964, CONGRESS terminated the Bracero Program to satisfy Mexican American organizations and labor unions, which accused braceros of taking jobs away from US citizens and residents and acting as strikebreakers. For the Mexican men who had worked as braceros, the end of the program was disastrous. During its twenty-two years in operation, the Bracero Program had issued over four and a half million guest-worker contracts. Now, without warning, braceros found themselves out of their traditional source of employment.

For most of them, remaining in their home country was not a viable solution. Mexico's Green Revolution—an economic strategy carried out jointly by the Rockefeller Foundation and the Mexican government—had introduced modern agrarian techniques, which had benefited large, commercial agricultural proprietors with irrigated lands but ruined small agricultural landholders with rain-fed parcels. Those who worked on these lands came to face unemployment and underemployment.

With little work available, thousands of Mexican men found that they had no option but to migrate; if they could not do so legally through the Bracero Program, they would do so without papers. One of these men was Clemente Lomelí. In the early 1960s, Clemente had worked in the fields of Salinas, California, as a bracero. When the program ended, he was unable to find work in his hometown in Mexico. After almost a year, he decided to return to the fields of Salinas by crossing the border illegally.

As the number of Mexicans who migrated without authorization grew, so did the number of migrants apprehended. In 1962, immigration officials caught about 30,000 migrants. That number rose to approximately 55,000 in 1965, before climbing dramatically to over 277,000 in 1970, and to almost a million by 1979.

The striking rise in apprehensions led to a concomitant increase in detention. In 1964, 31,000 migrants were detained; by 1965, after the Bracero Program had officially ended, the number rose to 44,000. That year, the Immigration and Naturalization Service's annual report explained that this 43 percent increase was "largely the result of the illegal influx of Mexican laborers seeking work after the 'Bracero' law expired." In the years that followed, the number of detentions mushroomed, reaching 340,300 in 1978.

Once again, immigrant detention centers became packed. In 1972, journalist Jesús Saldaña got himself detained inside a facility in El Centro, California, to witness what happened at these sites. He described how the food provided was inadequate and how the place was so overcrowded that some men had to sleep on the floor. That same year, San

Ysidro activists denounced the detention center in their town as being run like a concentration camp.

To quell criticism, immigration officials requested money from Congress to build new detention centers and expand existing ones. After Brownell's announcement in 1954, the Immigration and Naturalization Service had closed the facilities in New York, Boston, San Francisco, and San Pedro. In 1973, however, it reversed course, opening a new detention center in Indio, California. The following year, it expanded the facility in El Centro. Then, in 1979, Congress approved a request to expand and renovate the detention center in Port Isabel, Texas.

The expanded facilities did not make them any more humane, as Manuel Jiménez's experience demonstrates. One day, after finishing work, Manuel found immigration officials waiting outside, ready to catch all workers who were in the country illegally. Upon apprehending him, the officials sent Manuel to the detention center in El Centro. He was there for only a couple of days, but they were unbearable. The guards forced him and the other men to stay outside all day long under the broiling sun.

By 1970, the Immigration Service was detaining more migrants than it had before 1954, when Swing implemented Operation Wetback and Brownell announced the move away from detention. But immigration officials still argued that they were abiding by the 1954 policy of only detaining migrants who were under "deportation proceedings" if they posed a threat to public safety or were likely to abscond. To do so, they continued to disregard the incarceration of Mexican nationals, most of whom were still forgoing deportation proceedings.

The detainment of Mexican migrants blemishes the story of detention that the government put forward, but it does not do away with the significance of the move from detention to parole that occurred during this period. Before 1954, the government did not even consider that there were options other than detention for dealing with arriving migrants.

And although it never removed its blinders to the detention of Mexican nationals, in the years and decades that followed, it did come to conceive and even implement the notion of parole as an effective and humane alternative to detention.

Then came 1980, when Gerardo Mansur and 124,000 other Cubans set sail from the port of Mariel.

Part III

DETERRENCE

10

BACK TO THE DARK

GERARDO MANSUR

AUTUMN 1980

A forty-foot neon cowboy atop a rearing yellow horse beckoned Gerardo into the Hacienda Resort Hotel and Casino. He had been in the United States since the summer, when he had arrived in the Mariel boatlift, but he had spent most of that time held at Fort Chaffee. A few weeks earlier, however, he and Julia had finally been released after two of Julia's friends who lived in Las Vegas sponsored the couple. Now, after having faced down the Ku Klux Klan at the naval base, Gerardo was ready to start a new life in this vibrant city. And that meant getting a job. He had heard that the Hacienda, located on the far south end of the Las Vegas Strip, had a job opening, and he had reason to be hopeful. Other Mariel Cubans were working on the Strip, including Julia, who had already landed a job as a room attendant at Circus Circus.

Gerardo stepped into the personnel manager's office, where he was offered a temporary job as a laundry attendant. The manager, who was also Cuban, promised that if Gerardo learned English, he would hire him on a more permanent basis.

Gainfully employed, Gerardo and Julia could finally rent their own place. For days, they scoured the city until they came across the perfect home: a two-bedroom, ground-floor apartment on a sidewalk lined with palm trees, near where all their Cuban friends lived. The couple soon purchased their first car. They were making it in America.

Every morning, they fortified themselves with strong, sugary Cuban coffee, smoked a cigarette, and then headed out to work. Gerardo drove Julia to Circus Circus, where she vacuumed floors and changed linens. Meanwhile, at the Hacienda, Gerardo loaded and unloaded washers and dryers, then ironed and folded linens to welcome the next guests.

Because immigrant life could be lonely, the couple hosted regular dinner parties. After eating, the revelers would play dominoes or put on music and dance, occasionally drawing complaints from neighbors unaccustomed to the boisterousness of Cuban parties. They were all Mariel Cubans, and their friendships helped them feel at home in their new land.

One evening at dinner, their friend Avelino Rodríguez, whom everyone knew as Macho for his brawniness, confessed that he had been unable to pay rent and would soon lose his home. This did not surprise anyone. Always joking around and smoking weed, Macho was, according to Julia, as lazy as Gerardo was diligent. But Gerardo had known Macho since they were children playing with marbles in Havana. It had seemed like a miracle that the two ended up in Las Vegas. Julia and Gerardo immediately invited their friend to move in with them until he got back on his feet.

Macho brought much mirth to the household. One day, Gerardo and Julia arrived home, drained from work, to find that their houseguest had cooked dinner. Pots and pans were full of meat, potatoes, rice, and noodles, with the tangy aroma of cumin wafting through the kitchen.

"Let's dig into it," Gerardo said as he set the table. He leaned down to grab the silverware from the drawer. Then he spotted the empty cans in the trash. Cans of dog food.

"Macho, is this the food that you cooked?"

"Yes, I bought those cans of meat and made them."

"Macho! This is dog food!"

None of them could read English, Gerardo recalled years later with a grin, but even Macho should have noticed the large picture of a dog in the center of the cans.

On special occasions, Julia and Gerardo strolled down the Strip after work, sitting under the umbrellas of the hotels and catching up on their days. When night fell, they admired the neon lights illuminating the desert. Sometimes, they ventured into the casinos and gambled, but never enough to lose real money. Once, Gerardo even won a tidy pile.

Then, on September 5, 1981, almost a year and a half after they had landed in Florida, the couple had their first child together. They named him Ulises, as if he were a symbol that their odyssey had ended at last.

Both Julia and Gerardo had left children behind in Cuba. The decision still tormented them. They promised themselves that they would take care of this child together, raise him with love, and see him into adulthood. Every morning, before dropping him off at daycare, they told him stories and made sure he felt loved. After their shifts ended, they rushed home to see their boy laugh.

A year later, Julia was pregnant again. "We were happy," recalled Julia of that time. "Gerardo was a good father, a good man, very hardworking. . . . And he was also a good dad . . . very tender." That is, of course, until that fateful day in 1983 when the police barged into their home.

WHY THE POLICE SHOWED UP AT GERARDO AND JULIA'S SMALL GROUND-floor apartment is unclear. An *Orlando Sentinel* article published seven years after the fact reported that the cops were responding to a noise complaint from a neighbor. Thirty-six years after the event, Gerardo told a very different story, one in which the police targeted him because he had reported an extortion attempt to their superiors. He insisted that he had not been entertaining friends that day. The only person in the house other than the family and Macho was Gerardo's barber, who had come to cut his hair.

While the reasons why the police showed up are impossible to corroborate, what happened next is not. Once inside, the officers discovered a small plastic bag of marijuana. Less than an ounce. Gerardo explained that the weed belonged to Macho. It did not matter, the officer said as he handcuffed him and Julia—this was their house. They were charged with possession of a controlled substance and with intent to sell. The cops called social workers to transport Ulises to a foster home.

Terrified and confused, the couple spent the night behind bars. Questions swirled through their minds: Who was taking care of Ulises? Were the people imprisoned with them dangerous? How long would they be held?

The next morning's sunlight, however, renewed their optimism. They were released with instructions to show up in court at a later date, and social workers returned their son. The couple was not afraid to start over. They kicked Macho out, moved homes, and threw themselves back into their work. Gerardo secured a new job building swimming pools, which paid twice as much as his old job at the hotel.

Still, Julia worried. What would happen in court? Gerardo tried to reassure her, pointing out that their neighborhood was infested with drug dealers and nothing ever seemed to happen to any of them. Besides, she was pregnant. She should not worry so much. On May 4, 1983, Gerry came into the world. He was named after his father.

Julia promised herself she'd stop worrying.

As Gerardo had suspected, the court-appointed lawyer assured the couple that "it is not a problem; a little bit of marijuana is nothing." In fact, shortly after they spoke, the court dropped the charge of intent to sell. Now Gerardo and Julia were only accused of possessing a controlled substance. "You should plead guilty," the attorney recommended. Even though the weed was not theirs, this was their best strategy. With their clean records, the lawyer held, "they would simply be released on probation, and nothing would happen." To Gerardo, this suggestion seemed ideal—he just wanted the ordeal to be over.

The strategy seemed to work. On January 4, 1984, the court agreed that their offense was minor and that it merited only probation. The judge ordered them to see a probation officer—a man by the last name of Caballero—once a month for the next five years and set them free.

On the morning Gerardo was to meet with his probation officer, he put on his best pants and shirt. Julia wore her finest dress. Even though her appointment was on a different day than Gerardo's, she insisted on coming along to support him.

A smiling Mr. Caballero welcomed them into the office, telling them, "Just wait for me here—I will be with you in a few minutes." The couple did as they were told.

Suddenly, two immigration agents barged into the office. "Are you Gerardo Mansur?" one demanded. When Gerardo confirmed his identity, they handcuffed him.

Julia cried out in confusion. "What is happening?" she pleaded.

"Who is this woman?" one of the agents barked.

"She is his wife," Mr. Caballero answered.

Figuring that Julia was in the same situation as Gerardo—a Mariel Cuban under probation—the agents arrested her as well.

"WELCOME TO ATLANTA," THE OFFICERS SAID AS THE BUS ENTERED THE maximum-security federal prison in Georgia.

Immediately after his arrest, Gerardo was sent to an immigration center in North Las Vegas. A handful of other Mariel Cubans were locked inside with him. One had failed to pay traffic tickets; another had stolen a book. Gerardo could not leave his cell, which lacked natural light. Whenever he asked the officers why he was there or what was happening to his wife and children, they gave him no answers. "Inside there, it looked like the anteroom of hell. And it was, because from there they took me to Atlanta," Gerardo recalled.

An imposing, fortresslike structure, the United States Penitentiary (USP) in Atlanta had first opened its gates in 1902. Eleven guard towers along the walled perimeter loomed over twenty-eight acres of barren scrubland and derelict buildings. In 1980, Congress had directed the Bureau of Prisons to close the penitentiary because it was so dilapidated that the costs of renovation seemed prohibitive. This order was never followed, however, as officials from the Department of Justice soon realized that they needed somewhere to hold the growing number of detained Mariel Cubans. On February 4, 1982, they informed Congress that the facility would continue to operate.

Gerardo found the Atlanta penitentiary horrifying and bewildering. Most men were locked in Cellhouse A, a five-story building where each cell was meant to hold only four individuals but typically housed six to eight. Across the corridor was Cellhouse B, and in front of it lay Cellhouse C, where those with mental health conditions were confined. There was also the dreaded segregation unit, Cellhouse E, whose four floors held 182 single cells. A few dormitories in better condition held approximately two hundred imprisoned American citizens and a few Cubans who had "demonstrated good institutional adjustment." Altogether, the decaying walls of USP Atlanta caged 1,869 Mariel Cubans, each with his own story.

Nearly four hundred of them had never been released. Instead, they had languished at Fort Chaffee until 1982, when the federal government relocated them directly to the penitentiary. The government refused to release 191 of these individuals because it considered them a potential threat to society, but it was willing to release the remaining 209 as long as they—like all other Mariel Cubans—were sponsored by someone or some institution willing to assume responsibility for their supervision. But no one had sponsored these people. Now, rather than awaiting sponsorship at an interim location, they were housed in a prison.

Some of the men inside USP Atlanta who had never been allowed to live freely in the United States had been deemed dangerous because they had committed crimes in Cuba. Alberto Herrera was one of them. Born in Havana in 1952, Alberto was the eldest of seven children. At the age of eighteen, in an effort to feed his hungry family, he walked into a government grocery store, hid two pounds of goat cheese under his jacket, and fled. He was arrested and imprisoned for seven years. Upon release, he was even less prepared to find a job than before, and so, five months later, he stole two pairs of pants. He received a sentence of thirteen years. Then, on June 24, 1980, midway through his sentence, a guard came to his cell and told him that he was going to be placed on a boat headed to the United States as part of the Mariel boatlift.

While Alberto sailed across the Florida Straits, he heard other passengers talking about expensive cars and trips to Disney World. He pictured himself holding a job and living as a free man. When Alberto's boat anchored in Florida, however, his dreams of liberty sank. Upon questioning him and learning about his past, US officials sent Alberto, along with other exiles suspected of criminality, to the Federal Correctional Institution at Talladega, Alabama, and then to the Atlanta penitentiary.

Other Mariel Cubans ended up in Atlanta because they lacked the means to support themselves. Such was the case for Pedro Prior Rodriguez. Soon after his arrival, Pedro was mugged and severely beaten on the streets of Rochester, New York. He ended up being unable to pay his hospital bill, and when immigration officials learned of his debt, they sent him to prison.

Some exiles confined at USP Atlanta had, in fact, committed serious crimes in the United States and had been sent to prison. Once they finished their terms, however, they were not afforded the constitutional right of only being punished once for a criminal offense. Instead, they were sent to the Atlanta penitentiary on an indefinite basis: punished again, and now more severely.

This happened to a man who went by the name El Pintor, or the Painter. Born in Havana in 1959, El Pintor grew up surrounded by people who dreamed that the Cuban Revolution would bring justice and economic prosperity. His family did not share these dreams. "My youth was not that good," he said years later, recalling how his mother raised seven children alone. "The seven of us slept on a bed, and my mother slept sitting down on the sofa." They did not always have enough to eat, and they rarely saw ways to improve their situation.

When El Pintor heard about the Mariel boatlift, he applied to leave Cuba, thinking that the United States might offer him better prospects. Instead, he found himself living in dire poverty in Miami. In desperation, he and a friend started breaking into houses, but they were soon caught. El Pintor was sentenced to nearly two years, which he spent at the Glades Correctional Institution in Belle Glade. Once he completed his sentence, however, he was transferred to various other prisons and ultimately sent to Atlanta.

What brought all of these men together was the fact that when Mariel Cubans first arrived in Key West in 1980, they had been classified as "entrants." The Carter administration had provided "parole" to all those who found sponsors, but it had neither changed their legal status nor formally granted them admission to the United States. Mariel Cubans caught committing any infraction, large or small, had their parole revoked and were supposed to be deported.

But there was a snag: the Cuban government was unwilling to take them back. Not wanting to release the parole violators into society and unable to repatriate them, US officials imprisoned them on an indefinite basis while they waited for the Cuban government to agree to accept them.

Just like Chi Hao and Ellen before them, these Mariel Cubans possessed few rights in the United States. Under the entry fiction, US officials could deny them basic constitutional rights. As it had with El

Pintor, the US government could make them serve the same sentences twice. It could also cage them permanently without trial.

This was Gerardo now. For an offense that merited only probation, he had tumbled into a legal void with no end date.

LOCKED INSIDE A MAXIMUM-SECURITY PENITENTIARY INTENDED FOR THE most dangerous individuals, Gerardo was doing serious time in a serious place. Despite this, the government refused to call him an "inmate." Like the other incarcerated Cubans, he was officially classified as a "detainee," even though convicted American citizens were being held alongside him.

This is not to say that there were no significant differences. Incarcerated Americans had gone to trial and knew how long they would have to stay in prison. In contrast, the five thousand Mariel Cubans who were locked up at USP Atlanta and other prisons, jails, and processing centers throughout the country had not been sentenced by a judge. On the basis of the *Knauff v. Shaughnessy* ruling, Mariel Cubans, who were considered entrants, did not have the right to proper hearings. This meant that they had no idea when, or even if, they would ever be released. The Mariel Cubans had nothing to look forward to—no visible end, no calendars on the walls to count down their remaining days.

Every so often, seemingly randomly chosen men would be taken to a special room to meet with representatives from the Immigration and Naturalization Service, the Parole Commission, and the Department of Justice. If they could show that they were no longer a threat to society, the panel would supposedly set them free. The first time Gerardo went to meet with the panel, he was convinced that he would be let out, since he knew he never should have been imprisoned in the first place. To his dismay, the representatives informed him that he continued to pose a threat to society and would remain behind bars.

The panel's decision was not surprising. After all, the Immigration and Naturalization Service had little interest in setting Mariel Cubans free, especially since imprisoning them was good for business. Even though most Cubans were held in facilities run by the Bureau of Prisons, Congress gave the Immigration and Naturalization Service not only $350,000 annually for hiring employees to work at USP Atlanta but also funds for hiring agents to transport detained individuals to prison. The detention of Cubans also improved the agency's reputation and prominence. Americans knew that it was protecting the country against Mariel criminals sent by Castro himself.

THE INCARCERATION OF MARIEL CUBANS IN THE ATLANTA PENITENTIARY was only one piece of the government's broader strategy on refugee arrivals. When President Reagan took office in 1981, he vowed that he would never allow anything like the Mariel boatlift—which had contributed to Carter's electoral loss—to happen again. With this goal in mind, he created a task force that February to deal with immigration and refugee matters. The task force's official report noted that while Cuban migration had come to a halt the previous September, when the Cuban government closed the port of Mariel, the CIA still worried that "an additional 200,000 Cubans could come to the U.S. if Castro reopened the port of Mariel for this purpose." Furthermore, the report noted, Haitian migration was still underway. There were already thirty-five thousand Haitians in Florida and one thousand to fifteen hundred more came every month. It was these migrants, the task force suggested, that now needed to be stopped.

The task force proposed two possible "enforcement options" to preempt another Mariel boatlift and to stop Haitian migration. The first mandated that the US Coast Guard board vessels suspected of carrying undocumented migrants or refugees, question the passengers, and send back anyone who did not have valid entry documents or a "proper" claim to refugee status. The task force noted that "liberals, blacks, and church and human rights groups would strongly oppose" this measure but that it would deter at least eighteen hundred Caribbean migrants per year from ever setting sail.

Anyone whom the Coast Guard failed to interdict at sea would face the second option: detention. The task force advised the White House that instead of paroling excludable aliens as previous administrations had done, it should order the "detention upon arrival of those apprehended pending deportation or asylum." This measure would further dissuade asylum seekers and unauthorized migrants from leaving their home countries in the first place.

In 1954, the attorney general had spoken of immigrant detention as unrighteous and had tried to curtail it. Four years later, the Supreme Court had even held that immigrant detention had come to constitute "the exception, not the rule," reflecting the nation's "humane" and "enlightened" policies.

In 1981, the Reagan administration resolved to change course: it would reintroduce detention. It would also mutate its goal. Up to that point, detention had been conceived as a holding place for migrants pending deportation and other proceedings; now it was also understood as an intimidation tactic designed to discourage foreigners from migrating to the United States. That May, immigration officials began detaining all Haitian refugees without offering them the possibility of parole.

Maxine Petit-Frère was one among hundreds of Haitians ensnared in the tentacles of this new system. Twenty-four years old, Maxine had previously made his living as a builder in Port-au-Prince. Back home, he had refused to construct a house for a Tonton Macoute, a member of the dreaded Haitian paramilitary force. A few days later, the militia came looking for him, machine guns in hand. Maxine barely managed to evade them, dashing to a remote area along the Haitian coastline where he knew vessels sometimes departed for the United States. Seventeen days later, he arrived in Florida and pled for asylum. Had he disembarked a year earlier and managed to secure sponsorship, as most Haitians had,

Maxine would have been given parole while awaiting the decision on his case. Instead, he spent his days behind bars at a federal prison in Ray Brook, New York.

Other Haitians were held at Krome. Like Maxine, few understood English or the reasons for their detention. Between April and June 1982, twenty-nine people detained at Krome attempted suicide. Officials there noted that the most common method was "attempted hanging," but other methods included "ingestion of crushed glass," "ingestion of toxic liquid," and "self-laceration." Nevertheless, a spokesperson from the Immigration and Naturalization Service stressed that this was not the agency's fault. After all, he insisted, Haitians "don't have to be detained; they can go back to Haiti."

Attorneys behind the Political Asylum Project of the Lawyers Committee for International Human Rights and other advocates worked tirelessly to protest the new procedures. The denial of parole to Haitians, the lawyers argued, was "intended as an 'invidious discrimination' against the plaintiffs, as blacks and Haitians, to punish them for seeking political refuge and to deter other Haitians from seeking such refuge."

In June 1982, it seemed as if they had won: a federal district judge ordered that Haitians be tendered parole. But the judge who delivered this ruling did so not because the program was discriminatory toward Haitians but because of a procedural error—the Immigration and Naturalization Service had not advertised its intention to detain Haitian refugees in the Federal Register.

The agency refused to back down. The following month, the service published an interim rule in the Federal Register to formalize the policy of detention. Even though the judge had not cited discrimination, the Immigration and Naturalization Service used the new interim rule to extend the procedure to *all* migrants who arrived without proper travel documents. From then on, parole would only be available to children and pregnant women.

With that, America's brief brush with "enlightenment" faltered. As

Ira Kurzban, the primary attorney who aided Haitians, argued, the harsh new rules were "a throwback to a policy the US government abandoned in 1954." Now, detention would be the norm.

LESS THAN A YEAR LATER, CONGRESS AND THE REAGAN ADMINISTRATION pushed the nation further down the benighted path of pretrial detention without bail. This time, however, they had American citizens in mind. As fears about crime and drugs increased in the early 1980s, politicians argued that ensuring public safety was more important than ensuring the presumption of innocence. Judges, they claimed, should be able to deny bail to defendants they deemed dangerous.

This argument was not new. The idea of denying bail to a defendant who was presumed to be "dangerous" had been introduced in Congress as early as 1969 but had been turned down. In a 1970 hearing on "preventive detention," for instance, the chairman of the Senate Judiciary Subcommittee on Constitutional Rights rejected the concept of pretrial detention by stating: "To deny reasonable bail, and thus imprison without conviction or trial, represents a radical departure from traditions of law and justice and from constitutional principles held sacred in this country for nearly 200 years." By the 1980s, this argument had lost its weight.

In 1983, President Reagan requested that Congress introduce a bill calling for "reform of the bail laws to permit pretrial detention of dangerous defendants." Senator Edward "Ted" Kennedy, who had introduced similar bills in the past, voiced his support for the measure by noting that times had changed. "We face a serious problem of crime in America," he said. "Our outdated bail laws fail to protect the safety of the community and permit violent offenders to return to the streets to commit new crimes while awaiting trial." This time, most congresspeople agreed with this stance.

During the congressional hearings, the Department of Justice—run by Attorney General William French Smith, who also controlled the Immigration and Naturalization Service—issued a formal statement in favor of President Reagan's proposed changes. It held that in South Florida, the average bond for drug dealers was $75,000, yet 17 percent of all drug defendants never appeared for trial, as they could afford forfeiting such huge money bonds.

In the popular imagination, South Florida was already seen as a place infested with drugs, crime, and Mariel migrants. Only a few months after the hearings, *Scarface*, which told the story of a Mariel Cuban who settled in Miami and became a violent drug lord, premiered in US theaters. Fear of Mariel Cubans had already contributed to the new detention policy; it was now fomenting a broader antibail logic.

In fact, the pretrial detention policy that Congress enacted at the behest of President Reagan effectively mirrored the policy the government had applied to "entrants" between 1954 and 1982. During those years, immigration officials were supposed to parole unadmitted entrants unless they deemed that the migrants were likely to abscond or that their "freedom of movement could be adverse to the national security or the public safety." Now, the Reagan administration was urging Congress to allow judges to deny bail to not only those who might fail to show up for their trials but also those who were likely to "endanger the safety of any other person or the community."

In the end, the Comprehensive Crime Control Act of 1984, which restricted Americans' right to bail, breezed through. Even the Democratic-majority House voted in favor of the bill by a 406–16 vote. Incarceration rates would soon skyrocket.

ATTORNEY GENERAL FRENCH SMITH, WHO HAD FERVENTLY ADVOCATED FOR the permanent detention of Mariel Cubans, as well as for the denial of bail to residents and citizens who were deemed dangerous, realized that the Department of Justice needed more space to hold all these potential new people. As it was, the nation's prison and immigration detention centers—which were both under his charge—were already jam-packed. Indeed, Gerardo's prison experience at USP Atlanta, where he lived among six other men in a cell designed for four, was not unusual.

French Smith quickly realized that Mariel Cubans, who were already associated with criminality, were the perfect vehicle through which to make the case that the nation needed new prisons and detention centers for holding both incarcerated Americans and detained migrants. When transferring the last remaining Cubans from Fort Chaffee to USP Atlanta in 1982, Deputy Attorney General Edward C. Schmults demanded the construction of both a new immigration detention center and a new penitentiary, stating that Cubans "put great additional pressure on our already overcrowded federal prison system." The Department of Justice also issued a report explaining that prisons were overcrowded "due to several factors, including more vigorous prosecution policies and longer sentences and the current detention of approximately 2,000 Cubans and Haitians." In Congress, legislators upheld the idea that more facilities were needed because of Mariel Cubans. In a 1983 hearing on the status of the nation's prisons, for instance, Senator Alfonse D'Amato told Congress: "The already crippled prison systems of this land are in danger of total breakdown as a result of the influx of illegal aliens in recent years, especially since the Mariel boatlift in 1980."

While members of Congress voiced their support for French Smith's proposal to build more prisons, another opportunity presented itself to the attorney general, this time in the form of private capital. In January 1983, Tom Beasley, a West Point graduate and former chairman of the Tennessee Republican Party, struck up a cocktail-party conversation about creating for-profit private prisons with a Magic Chef executive. Beasley soon pitched the idea to venture capitalist Jack Massey, whose investment group had also funded Kentucky Fried Chicken and the Hospital Corporation of America. After a fifteen-minute discussion, Massey was convinced by Beasley's innovative proposition. He committed half a million dollars to the project. Beasley was ready to launch the Corrections Corporation of America, or CCA.

When Beasley proposed his idea to the Department of Justice, French Smith recognized its promise. Not only would private prisons reduce overcrowding, but private capital would be responsible for the construction costs of the new facilities. Given the novelty of the idea, it made sense to start with a minimum-security prison—an immigration detention center would be ideal.

By the end of the year, CCA had a contract. Within ninety days, it would build a three-hundred-bed institution in Houston, Texas, for the short-term confinement of unauthorized migrants. For its services, the Immigration and Naturalization Service would pay the company $23.50 a day for every individual who was imprisoned.

With only three months to build a detention center, Beasley and his partners did not have much time to celebrate. Together, they roamed the streets of Houston searching for potential sites. An old motel seemed to be the best potential fit. When the facility opened, "Olympic Motel" and "Color TV, Radio, Telephone" signs still hung next to a newly erected twelve-foot fence topped with coiled barbed wire.

CCA's immigration detention facility was the nation's first for-profit prison contracted by the federal government. For sure, profits had already been made from incarceration. The convict leasing system had laid the foundations for private contractors to make money from the labor of imprisoned Black people. Other forms of profiting off prison had also existed before the 1980s: the government used private community treatment centers to house some incarcerated people and contracted out specific prison services to private companies, such as the provision of food. But CCA's facility represented something entirely new: for the first time, the government could incarcerate people in a facility expressly built to generate money and entirely run by private interests. It is a model that continues to thrive. Today, CCA, now rebranded as CoreCivic, is the largest private prison contractor in the United States.

ALONG WITH 450 OTHER MARIEL CUBANS, GERARDO WORKED AT USP ATLANTA's factory, known as UNICOR, the name given to the quasi-public for-profit corporation operated by the Bureau of Prisons. In the penitentiary, the UNICOR jobs were the hardest ones, but Gerardo appreciated that they paid better than kitchen work or cleaning hallways. Gerardo helped make mail carts for the Postal Service, while other men manufactured military gloves and brooms. He worked hard enough that he quickly rose up the ranks, going from the lowest pay grade (which was twenty-two cents an hour) to the highest (which got him $1.10 an hour). Despite his raise, Gerardo's earnings paled by comparison with the $7 per hour he had made building pools and fell far short of the federal minimum wage of $3.35.

Congress had mandated the creation of UNICOR in 1934 to offset the costs of the prison system. As a result, UNICOR did not have to comply with federal or state minimum wage requirements. Nor did it need to provide its workers with basic benefits, such as health care, the right to unionize, and workers' compensation. While Gerardo made $1.10 per hour, the UNICOR plant at USP Atlanta earned $14 million in gross income and profits of $1.5 million.

Gerardo never complained about his wages. At least the work provided a respite from the torment of life behind bars. He had begged the corrections officers in his building for updates about his family, but they told him that there was no way to find out what had happened to his wife and two boys. Perhaps Julia had been freed and was taking care of the children, Gerardo thought. Perhaps the two boys—one a toddler and the other barely a baby—were back in foster care. Were they hungry? Were they scared? Did they remember him? When would he get to see them again? The humming of the machines, the exactness of the work, the notion that he was doing something useful—all distracted him from the uncertainty of his situation.

While Gerardo developed a rapport with some of the factory's officials, most guards outside the factory would insult and harass the detained men to no end, Gerardo recalled. "They would act like gang members rather than prison guards—they would shove you, they would throw you to the ground, they would humiliate you," he said. According to Gerardo, in the guards' eyes, "you were trash, simply trash. You weren't a human being."

Those who protested or seemed to cause problems suffered more. Guards regularly punished even minor infractions with solitary confinement in Cellhouse E and sometimes reclassified individuals as having mental health issues in order to send them to Cellhouse C. This was what detained Cubans feared most. People sent to Cellhouse C were often forcibly administered psychotropic medications, such as lithium and Haldol, which could have terrible side effects. Throughout the prison, men regularly talked about friends who had been sent to Cellhouse C and were now medicated into automatons, zombies who had no energy or personality.

In particular, the men feared the prison's psychiatrist, Dr. Bolivar Martineau, whom they believed performed medical experiments on his patients. Years later, Martineau denied such claims, insisting that "no medication that was given there was for experimental purpose[s]." Still, the men's fears were not unfounded: during the 1960s and '70s, several studies were, in fact, conducted on the prison population of USP Atlanta to determine if it was possible to infect humans with various strains of wild-monkey malaria.

AFTER HIS SHIFT AT UNICOR, GERARDO WOULD TAKE CLASSES OFFERED BY the prison. Along with 274 of his fellow Mariel Cubans, he studied English as a second language; he also enrolled in social education classes with 80 other Cubans, and he was one of the 74 Cubans who took adult secondary education classes to attain a GED, a high school equivalency certification, which he proudly did in 1985.

Those who did not want to work or take classes would spend their days hanging out in the yard, going to the gym and lifting weights, or playing Ping-Pong, basketball, baseball, or football. All housing units had cards, table games, chess, and checkers available. On weekends, Gerardo would run in the yard for exercise and then watch movies that the guards played on Saturdays or listen to musical groups they brought in from the outside. But even while he and the other men laughed, learned, played, or exercised, they never forgot they were behind bars.

At night, after they had returned to their cells, they would supplement their dinners with makeshift picnics from the goods they had bought at the commissary. Gerardo was in charge of heating up cans of soup over a small fire he created with matches and toilet paper. Miguelito, who slept in the bunk bed next to Gerardo's, would make peanut-butter-and-jelly sandwiches. Raúl prepared the coffee. Others were responsible for getting cigarettes and desserts.

When it came time for bed, the mood would shift. Sleeping was almost impossible. Late at night, as most men grew tired, some would begin to yell. Others sang. On the floor above Gerardo's, the voices of a handful of would-be vocalists reverberated through the prison every night until two or three in the morning. Some appreciated the entertainment and would clap and holler for more, while others shouted for them to shut up. All of this made it impossible for Gerardo to get a good night's sleep before he was woken up again at dawn.

GERARDO STOOD IN FRONT OF JUAN ALERS, A FORTY-ONE-YEAR-OLD PUERTO Rican priest who worked at USP Atlanta, and told the cleric his story. Although Gerardo was not Catholic, he figured that Father Alers might have a way to find his family. He was right. A few days later, Father Alers flew to Las Vegas, where he found the welfare agency that had taken in Gerry and Ulises. He then figured out that Julia was imprisoned at the Lexington Federal Correctional Institution, a prison in Kentucky that held both men and women—including detained Mariel Cubans—who required medical or mental health care. Upon his return to Atlanta, the priest handed Gerardo photos of his children, as well as addresses he could use to communicate with the welfare agency and with Julia.

Located on a bluegrass hilltop surrounded by Thoroughbred horse farms, the minimum-security prison in Lexington was more pleasant than the Atlanta penitentiary. Yet inside it, all Julia did was despair over her children. The other detained women around her had even nicknamed her Mommy, because while they gossiped about men, Julia only talked about her two young sons.

Once Father Alers put them in touch, Julia and Gerardo wrote daily letters to one another. They communicated their love, their desire to be with their children, their prayers to be reunited as a family, their fears that they would not be. Though almost four hundred miles apart, they told of their parallel lives: After breakfast, Julia also went to work for UNICOR, at a steel factory where she welded cables for the military. Like Gerardo, she attended classes and studied English. On the weekends, she exercised in the gym and watched the movies that the prison guards played. Unlike Gerardo's, Julia's prison did not seem to be overcrowded. She went to Mass several times a week, interacted with the other women who were being held, and read romance novels to pass the time.

But, mostly, Julia lived in fear. Guards had told her that she would remain in prison until she was deported. Since then, all she could think about was what this meant for her children. As she told a reporter who interviewed her in Lexington, "How could they deport me without my kids? They are US citizens. I want to stay here with them."

Julia sent regular postcards to the welfare agency in Las Vegas to try to get news about her sons, but they went unanswered. Then, in the summer of 1986, after having spent two and a half years in Lexington,

Julia received a letter from the social workers in Nevada. As she began reading, however, the blood drained from her face. The social workers had written to inquire if Julia and Gerardo would allow their boys to be adopted by a foster family. No one knew when, or if, Julia or Gerardo would be able to see Gerry and Ulises again—and the social workers assured her that the foster family, whose name was not provided, already loved the children. This would be best for them.

The suggestion went beyond Julia's worst fears. "I am their mother," she thought. "I will never let my children be adopted by anyone." She immediately wrote to Gerardo, and he replied with a plan. They would not only reject the offer but would also send the welfare agency as much of their UNICOR earnings as they could to support their children. They wanted to make sure that neither the government nor the foster parents would have to contribute a dime to the care of Gerry and Ulises.

Soon, Julia took on more overtime and started earning $198 per month. In October 1985, she was even named "employee of the month." She and Gerardo limited themselves to buying only the most basic necessities at the commissary. The rest of the money they saved to send to their children, in a desperate bid to keep them under their care after the government had ripped them away.

11

FAMILY SEPARATION

Fernando Arredondo

MAY 16, 2018

There was no way Fernando was going to allow the agents to take his twelve-year-old daughter away from him. A few days earlier, he and Andrea had been separated from the rest of the family by Mexican immigration officials before they even reached the US-Mexico border. Now, it seemed, US immigration officials at the Laredo Processing Center wanted to separate him from his child.

"She is my daughter; she is staying with me," Fernando insisted to the officer who ordered Andrea over to the children's area. She refused to go, clutching on to her dad more tightly than ever. But not tightly enough to prevent the now agitated officer from gruffly pulling her away from her father. There was nothing Fernando could do. His best option now, he thought, was to follow the official's orders and try to keep his daughter calm. She might even be safer there at night, surrounded only by other children. And, Fernando imagined, he would only be separated from his daughter until the next morning or, at worst, until the officials finished their paperwork.

What the agents did not tell Fernando or the other migrants detained with him was that a month earlier, President Trump's attorney general, Jeff Sessions, had introduced a zero-tolerance policy, by which all migrants who crossed the border without permission were to be prosecuted. Because adult migrants were to be imprisoned during their prosecution, any minors with them would be taken away and sent to one of the dozens of shelters run by the Office of Refugee Resettlement, an operational division of the US Department of Health and Human Services.

Fernando recalled: "When I left Guatemala, I had not heard about Trump's policy of separating immigrant children from their parents. Had I known that Andrea would be taken away from me and that I risked never seeing my family again, I would have never headed north."

The Trump administration had quietly begun separating children from their parents at the border in July 2017, before announcing the zero-tolerance policy on April 6, 2018. Since his son's murder in April 2017, Fernando and his family had lived in hiding in Guatemala and Mexico—not ideal conditions for learning about new US policies.

But even if Fernando had heard about the new policy, why would he have thought it concerned him? Zero tolerance was supposedly directed at individuals who crossed the border illegally, and he and Andrea had not. They legally presented themselves at a port of entry and asked for asylum. This was allowed by law. In fact, members of the Trump administration insisted that the Department of Homeland Security (DHS) was *not* separating asylum seekers from their children. On June 17, 2018, a month after Customs and Border Protection officials ripped Andrea from Fernando's arms, Secretary of Homeland Security Kirstjen Nielsen tweeted: "For those seeking asylum at ports of entry, we have continued the policy from previous administrations and will only separate if the child is in danger, there is no custodial relationship between 'family' members, or if the adult has broken a law." Nielsen's tweet came not only after Fernando and Andrea had been separated but also after the American Civil Liberties Union (ACLU) had brought a class-action lawsuit against Nielsen on behalf of multiple parents who'd sought asylum at ports of entry and had their children taken away.

The Trump administration's aim in implementing such a draconian policy was to make Central Americans fear coming to the United States. On March 3, 2017, before the family separation program began, DHS officials told Reuters that the administration was considering instituting a policy "to deter mothers from migrating to the United States with their children." Only a few days later, John Kelly, then Trump's secretary of homeland security, confirmed that he was contemplating separating children from their parents "in order to deter more movement along this terribly dangerous network."

Creating pain and chaos was, in fact, the goal. When separating children from their parents, the government didn't care how young they were, even if they were infants. No thought was given to ensuring that children could communicate with their parents, and no protocols were established to keep track of where children were sent. No plans were drafted on how to eventually reunite families. Reporters, immigrant advocates, and lawyers all struggled to understand the new system. Sometimes figuring out where a particular child or parent was seemed impossible. As one immigrant advocate told *The New Yorker*: "I have a master's degree, and I'm fluent in English. And it takes me days to figure one of these cases out." Migrants had no chance.

Trump's zero-tolerance policy stemmed directly from the nation's deep-rooted detention history. Rather than being exceptional, it heightened the inhumanity of existing practices, making an already cruel system even more vicious. In the 1980s, when the practice of detention became more punitive, US policymakers began to use incarceration as a means of deterring potential migrants from heading to the United States. Since then, punishing apprehended migrants has been the goal; the more pain inflicted, the logic goes, the less likely other migrants are to make the journey. Trump's policy of using family separation as a deterrence method simply extended a strategy that had been the norm for decades.

Moreover, while the Trump administration was the first to use family separation as a way of dissuading migrants from setting out for the United States, immigrant detention has long resulted in the separation of families. As Gerardo and Julia's case demonstrates, during the 1980s, government officials did not shy away from ripping children from their parents, even when that wasn't the government's explicit goal. As early as Fu Chi Hao's time, when the government was not using detention for deterrence purposes, children were regularly torn from their caretakers.

Zero tolerance and child separation have plenty of other antecedents in American history: During the era of slavery, children were regularly snatched from their parents' arms at auction blocks. Government-backed boarding schools forcibly took Native American kids away from their families. In fact, the practice of removing Native children from what the government deemed to be "unfit" households only ended in 1978, after Congress passed the Indian Child Welfare Act. Prior to that, 25 to 35 percent of all Native children were taken from their homes.

Family separation has also long been part and parcel of the country's prison system. During the 1970s, politicians vowed to get "tough on crime," which led to a dramatic increase in the prison population. Black children were the most likely to be separated from their parents, and especially from their fathers, because the booming rates of incarceration primarily targeted African Americans. Between 1979 and 1999, imprisonment increased by 430 percent, and Black people were eight times more likely to be imprisoned than white people. By the end of the 1990s, one in ten Black children under the age of ten had a father in prison or jail.

Juvenile incarceration further contributed to family separation. Between 1979 and 1999, the country's incarcerated juvenile population rose by about 50 percent, from 71,922 to 108,931. Placing kids behind bars meant separating them from their parents and family members, as well as from their communities and schools. But for policymakers, this form of family separation was inconsequential when compared with the need to curtail crime.

Given this context, it is unsurprising that the Trump administration did not find fault with tearing children from their parents while they were in immigration detention. After all, this was a world in which family separation was already occurring.

ON MAY 17, 2018, FERNANDO STEPPED OFF THE IMMIGRATION ENFORCEMENT van clutching Andrea's backpack. The night before, officials at the immigration station in Laredo had taken Andrea and the other children away, and now those same officials had informed the parents that they were being transferred. To Fernando, "it seemed obvious" that the officials would bring them to their children.

But when his eyes fell upon the barbed wire that surrounded the new facility, he hoped that Andrea wasn't there. Between the vastness of the place and the sight of the guards who policed it, he could only conclude that this was a prison.

He was right. He had been transferred to the Rio Grande Detention Center, a penitentiary facility for men run by the GEO Group, a private prison corporation. The women who had been held with Fernando the previous night had already been taken elsewhere.

"Form a line," a guard demanded. When the guard approached, Fernando called out, "Excuse me, sir, I came to the United States with my daughter, but they took her away."

"We know nothing about that here," the official said flatly.

The guards ignored Fernando's tears as they led him and the other men into a freezing room. He was handed lightweight blue shirts and pants, orange Crocs, and basic toiletries. Later he learned that blue uniforms were given to people who had no criminal convictions and were being held only because of immigration-related issues. Orange uniforms were given to migrants classified as having committed nonfelony crimes; red uniforms, to those who had "spent time in state or federal prison" and were deemed to be "high risk."

Fernando followed a guard through the thick metal door. His assigned chamber was a big room, illuminated solely by overhead fluorescent lights and packed with rickety bunk beds and metal tables and chairs. A short half wall separated the dormitory from the bathrooms, but it was not high enough to keep out smells or noises.

As the days passed, Fernando reflected upon every action he had taken, blaming himself for every choice, every decision. Most of those detained with him were from Central America and spoke Spanish, so he was able to ask them questions: *How long have you been detained? Did they also take your kids away from you? Why are we in prison?*

The answers were never satisfactory. Most had come without children. Some had only been there for a few weeks, but others had been detained for over a year. Some had been caught in the United States after having crossed the border illegally, while others were also asylum seekers who had presented themselves at a port of entry. They did not know much else. The guards never gave them any information.

But they did explain how they believed the asylum process worked. To be allowed to leave the detention center and enter the United States, the men told Fernando, asylum seekers had to undergo a "credible-fear" interview, in which they had to establish to an officer's satisfaction that they had a credible fear of returning to their country of origin. Individuals could be locked up for months before they were granted such interviews, and most failed it.

The credible-fear interview was supposed to ensure that the government did not summarily deport bona fide asylum seekers. If migrants managed to convince the officers who interviewed them that they had a credible fear of persecution in their home country based on their race, religion, nationality, political opinion, or membership in a particular social group, they were then allowed to seek asylum in immigration court.

FERNANDO'S PREDICAMENT, AS WELL AS THAT OF THE 38,398 INDIVIDUALS who arrived at ports of entry and asked for asylum in 2018, was determined by the entry fiction, a precedent well over a century old. According to the government, asylum seekers had never actually entered the country—even when it was holding them at detention centers deep in the heartland. As such, asylum seekers who had presented themselves at ports of entry could be detained indefinitely without basic constitutional due-process rights.

The persistence of the entry fiction in detention cases is particularly striking. Two decades before Fernando asked for asylum, Congress had eliminated the dual track in immigration court proceedings that gave preferential treatment to migrants apprehended inside the nation over those stopped at the border. The Illegal Immigration Reform and Immigrant Responsibility Act of 1996 had placed the two categories of migrants on the same legal footing, one that was based on legal admission rather than entry. This meant that undocumented migrants apprehended in the United States and inadmissible migrants stopped at ports of entry faced the same immigration adjudication process.

But they did not face the same detention prospects. In January 1999, the Code of Federal Regulations introduced a clause stating that immigration judges could not review the detainments of individuals stopped at the border. In contrast, migrants caught inside the country could receive bond hearings before immigration judges. In other words, "unentered" refugees were still subjected to the entry fiction when it came to their detention. This meant that asylum seekers who presented themselves at ports of entry, such as Fernando, could be held in indefinite civil detention with no recourse to procedural protections—just like thousands of other migrants stopped at the border before them, including Chi Hao, Ellen, and Gerardo.

All Fernando could do was wait. Once he had his interview, he thought, he would be released. After all, he had evidence to show the officers that he and his family would be in real danger if they returned to Guatemala. As soon as they heard his story, they would let him out, he was sure.

CLEIVI HELD HER YOUNGEST DAUGHTER TIGHTLY, TRYING TO STOP ALISON'S little body from shivering. She had no idea where her husband and middle child were. All she knew was that after gang members in Guatemala had killed her son and the family had fled, immigration officials at Mexico's Checkpoint 26 had ordered Fernando and Andrea to disembark from the bus. As she and Fernando had agreed before they departed, Cleivi carried on north with her two other daughters. And just like Fernando and Andrea would do four days later, when Cleivi, Keyli, and Alison reached Nuevo Laredo, they crossed the international bridge and asked for asylum. But unlike what happened to Fernando and Andrea, no one came to separate Cleivi from her children.

After a few hours inside the cold detention room, Alison's body turned into a furnace. The child continued to shiver, and Cleivi realized that her daughter was running a high fever. Desperate, she ran to the bathroom, grabbed an industrial roll of toilet paper, and used it to swaddle her youngest daughter to warm her up. Eventually, an official brought them some Mylar blankets.

Cleivi wondered how anyone could be so cruel to a child. What she didn't know was that at that very same facility, Customs and Border Protection agents were separating other young children from their parents. She could not imagine that in a few days' time, these very agents would drag her middle daughter from her husband's arms. Despite the ill-treatment that Cleivi and her daughters were experiencing, immigration advocates referred to people like them as "lucky," because they weren't separated. Border agents could not separate *all* adults from their children, as there simply was not enough space to hold them all.

The next morning, the officers took Alison to the hospital and then informed Cleivi that all of them would be transferred to another facility. Cleivi was delighted to leave the freezing room where they had been held. Before departing, however, she made sure to tell the agents to look out for her husband and other daughter, who were probably on their way to Laredo.

FROM WHAT SHE COULD SEE OUT OF THE SMALL, BARRED WINDOWS OF THE immigration enforcement van, Cleivi, who was handcuffed, thought they were being transferred to the most barren of regions, a flat and featureless landscape that resembled a hostile planet. She and her daughters were being taken to the South Texas Family Residential Center, an hour's drive away from San Antonio.

Although it was called a residential center, the fifty-acre facility in Dilley, Texas, designed to hold up to 2,400 people, was undoubtedly a detention center. Not only was it surrounded by high walls to prevent escape, but it was also run like a prison. And it was managed by CoreCivic, the for-profit prison company formerly known as Corrections Corporation of America. This was the very corporation that had built the first for-profit prison following the Mariel boatlift. It would now hold Cleivi and two of her daughters.

Compared with the Laredo Processing Center, the South Texas Family Residential Center felt almost luxurious to Cleivi. "They give you your own bed; you have air conditioning, your food, three meals per day. There I finally showered," she recalled. Upon their arrival, a short, gracious man welcomed Cleivi and her daughters and showed them their new home: a trailer that they would share with a Honduran mother and her children. The trailer had a room for each family and a living room for the two households to share. It even had a television. The man who greeted them explained that there was a school for the girls to attend, a library, a gym, and a dining hall where meals were served at regular times. For Cleivi, these homey touches diluted the horror of incarceration.

Most important, the man told Cleivi how she could contact a pro bono lawyer who worked inside the compound. The next morning, she hurried toward the office where the lawyers were headquartered. The detention facility was so immense that it felt like a city; it was certainly bigger than El Mirador, the suburb where they had lived in Guatemala. At the office, she was welcomed by a lawyer named Evelyn who appeared to be in her twenties. Cleivi explained what had happened and left the lawyer's office feeling hopeful.

But as the days passed without an update, dread began to consume her. Every morning, Keyli and Alison headed to school, and Cleivi stayed in the trailer waiting. She tried to distract herself by watching the Mexican TV show *La rosa de Guadalupe*, but her anxiety about her husband and middle daughter's fate kept taking over. She was well aware that the Nuevo Laredo region where Fernando and Andrea had been stopped was overrun with drug cartels that regularly extorted and even killed Central Americans.

Then, after about a week of waiting, Cleivi received a letter from Evelyn saying that Fernando and Andrea had entered the country, asked for asylum, and been separated from each other. She didn't know what to make of that.

"What does this mean? What can we do?" Cleivi asked her lawyer. There was no way for her to contact Fernando. But Evelyn had tracked down a phone number to reach Andrea.

"MOM! I THOUGHT THAT I WOULD NEVER SEE YOU AGAIN," ANDREA WEPT through the phone. She had just turned twelve, but she revealed a bravery beyond her years, trying to reassure her mother she was okay, despite everything that had happened. Even now, years after her May 2018 detention, Andrea still cannot bring herself to share her experience with

Fernando or Cleivi. She can only say that she was scared and that she regularly wanted to cry but tried to hold in her emotions as much as she could. In her declaration for asylum, Andrea provided a few more details, stating: "I was sent to a detention place for kids. I didn't know where my father was or if I would ever see him again. I didn't know anyone in this place. I didn't know where my mother and sisters were. This was the most painful time of my life."

Given how reserved Andrea has been about her experiences, it is difficult to know what, exactly, she went through while in detention—especially because questioning her carries the risk of retraumatizing her. But eyewitnesses who managed to gain entry to detention sites have described the horrors that children lived through. Like Andrea, most children were separated from their caregivers at the Border Patrol facility where they were first detained. Legally, children were not supposed to be held there for more than seventy-two hours before being sent into the care of the Office of Refugee Resettlement. In Andrea's case, the Customs and Border Protection agents in Laredo respected the law. She was only in their custody for one night. But that was not the experience of hundreds of other children who were held for days and sometimes weeks. In these facilities, children had no or limited access to clean clothes, toothbrushes, and regular showers.

Michelle Brané, who worked for the Women's Refugee Commission, an advocacy organization, was able to visit the holding facilities in McAllen, Texas, in June 2018. She later testified: "It is impossible to overstate the impact of seeing Government officials performing as part of their daily job functions what can only be described as cruelty. Families were separated before my eyes with no explanation, no opportunity for goodbyes, no humanity." According to Michelle, at the McAllen Station, "no official took responsibility. No one admitted to what was happening in that facility. No one told the parents or the kids what was going to happen to them, but everyone detained there knew to be afraid."

Michelle also visited the Ursula Processing Center, a nondescript seventy-seven-thousand-square-foot facility that became the epicenter of the zero-tolerance policy. Michelle described it as "a giant warehouse divided into what can only be referred to as cages." In the back of the windowless facility were "over 500 children who had been separated from a parent who were being held in cages." The children slept on thin mats with only Mylar blankets, despite the chilly temperature inside Ursula. They had nothing to do. They were not given toys or books, and the televisions that hung from some of the fences had been turned off. If the children ran or tried to play, guards scolded them.

Michelle was struck by how young some of the children were, noting that several of them "were listed as being 1 or 2 or 0 years old." When she asked the guards who was taking care of these babies and toddlers, they replied that they didn't know. Incredulous, Michelle demanded to see some of those babies and speak to their caregivers. An officer returned a few minutes later and told her: "I can't find them, ma'am. I called their name, but they did not answer."

Michelle could not believe what she was hearing. "Of course they did not answer. They were babies." Trying to control her anger, she asked again: "Who is taking care of these babies?"

Eventually, the officer came back with a sixteen-year-old girl carrying a child. The detained teenager told Michelle that this toddler was not hers. She had "found the child there in her cage" with no adult supervision and noted that the diapered little one needed to be changed and fed. The toddler did not know Spanish but tried to make herself understood in the indigenous K'iche' language while pointing and crying. No official or anyone else had come to take care of her, so the teenage girl, who had herself been separated from her mother, had decided to look after her, comforting her when she cried, changing her diapers, helping her to get in line for food, giving her bottles, and singing to her at night so that she could fall asleep.

Only after Michelle complained did the officials track down the toddler's caregiver. The child had entered the United States with her aunt, and the Border Patrol had separated them four days earlier. Because Michelle had witnessed this atrocity, the officials agreed to reunite the child with her aunt. But as Michelle later wondered, "What would have happened to this child if I had not been there that day, or if a 16-year-old girl had never met nor cared for her?" And how many other babies, toddlers, and children were lost in this nightmare?

All the children inside Ursula were scared and traumatized, living through unimaginable torment. A nine-year-old girl was unable to describe how she was doing; all she could say was that she needed to find her mother: "I have to hug her and tell her I love her. I need her to know I love her very, very much." A five-year-old boy grabbed Michelle's hand as soon as he saw her, and when she lifted him, he began to shake inconsolably before hugging her and crying for his mother. A boy in his cage had been taunting him, saying that he would never see his mother again.

After being separated from their parents in Border Patrol stations, children were transferred to the custody of the Office of Refugee Resettlement and placed in facilities across the country. Andrea was sent from the Laredo station to a shelter in San Antonio run by BCFS Health and Human Services (formerly known as Baptist Child and Family Services). In general, the shelters were run by nonprofit organizations and segregated by sex. Babies, toddlers, and children who were twelve years old or younger, such as Andrea, were held in "tender-age" facilities. According to an August 2018 study conducted by the Washington Office on Latin America, children were detained in shelters for an average of fifty-seven days.

The shelters varied. The thirty-three-acre youth shelter in Yonkers, New York, featured picnic tables, sports fields, and an outdoor pool. A shelter in Tucson, Arizona, consisted of a converted motel in a strip of discount stores and gas stations, where children had to play in a grassless compound. As the Trump administration demanded that more children be detained, the detention spaces and conditions deteriorated. In June 2018, for example, BCFS opened a "tent city" in Tornillo, Texas, that at one point held more than twenty-five hundred minors who were seeking asylum.

Where children were sent depended solely on luck. Still, the shelters were notably more comfortable and better suited to detain children than the Customs and Border Protection facilities. Instead of sleeping on mattresses on the floor—or on the floor itself—inside freezing rooms or fenced cages, children had their own assigned beds in the shelters.

"Better suited," however, still did not mean that these shelters were fit for children. Even before the Trump administration implemented its zero-tolerance policy, the Department of Health and Human Services documented high levels of abuse at these facilities. Between October 2014 and July 2018, it received 4,556 allegations of sexual abuse or sexual harassment in these shelters; 178 of those cases involved accusations that adult staff members had sexually assaulted immigrant children. The rest were accusations of minors assaulting other minors.

The San Antonio BCFS facility where Andrea was held had seen its own set of abuses over the years. In April 2017, an employee had arranged for a child's family to send money for their kid but had then kept the cash rather than passing it on. The year before, a staff member had given "inappropriate pornographic magazines" to minors, and a few months before that, employees had failed to prevent one child from "inappropriately" touching others.

But even when employees behaved as they should, these facilities were, by their very nature, inhumane. In a strongly worded statement against the US government's detention policy, the UN's high commissioner for human rights said: "Children should never be detained for reasons related to their own or their parents' migration status. Detention is never in the best interests of the child and always constitutes a child rights violation."

In the shelters, the children led lives governed by pitiless rules: they could not share food, use nicknames, or hug anyone—not even their siblings for comfort. Lights were out by 9:00 p.m. and on by dawn, at which time they had to make their beds according to detailed posted instructions. They had to mop the bathrooms and scrub the toilets. They had to line up for all their meals. If they misbehaved, consequences could be severe. Adonias, a small boy from Guatemala who was sent to a facility in Chicago, could not cope with being detained by himself. He had fits and would throw things around. The staff dealt with his despair by injecting him with sedatives that put him to sleep almost immediately.

Of course, for the children, the ache of being separated from their parents, not knowing when or if they would ever see them again, and not understanding why this was happening, was the most painful aspect of detention. Leticia, a little Guatemalan girl who had been separated from her mother and sent to a shelter in South Texas, wrote letters telling her mother how much she missed her. "Mommy, I love you and adore you and miss you so much," the twelve-year-old wrote in one. "Please, Mom, communicate. Please, Mom. I hope that you're OK, and remember, you are the best thing in my life." The children could not send outgoing mail, so Leticia kept the stack of missives she wrote.

Being separated from their parents inflicted a profound and enduring trauma on the children. An investigation by Physicians for Human Rights (PHR) found that both parents and children who were separated in detention met diagnostic criteria for at least one mental health condition, such as post-traumatic stress disorder, major depressive disorder, or generalized anxiety disorder, that was likely linked to that separation. Psychologists also found that for children under the age of five, being separated from their parents could lead to physical changes in their brains, and that all children could experience "cognitive delays, impairments in executive functioning, and disruptions of the body's stress response" as a result. For children, psychologists concluded in an amicus curiae brief supporting the asylum seekers, the family separation policy amounted to nothing less than torture.

AFTER HEARING FROM HER MOTHER, ANDREA FELT IMMENSE RELIEF. IT IS hard to call her "lucky," but at least she knew that her mother was still in the United States. Not all children were as fortunate. The parents of over 470 children were deported while they remained in detention, and unless they had other parental figures or family members in America who were willing to take care of them, they had to remain in detention.

This is what happened to eight-year-old Byron after his father, David Xol-Cholom, was deported.

David had fled Guatemala with Byron after some ex-coworkers who belonged to M-18 punished him for belonging to an evangelical community that tried to dissuade youths from joining gangs. On October 15, 2017, he was driving his motorcycle when a car intercepted him, and four men forced him into a vehicle. They drove him to an empty street, tied him to a utility pole, and violently beat him with a baseball bat while telling him that Byron was next. They cut his feet, arms, stomach, and neck with a knife.

On May 18, 2018, two days after Fernando and Andrea crossed the international bridge and asked for asylum, David and Byron illegally crossed the US-Mexico border through the Rio Grande. Border Patrol officers apprehended them. Immediately, David asked for asylum, and the officers sent him and Byron to the McAllen Station.

They waited three days in mesh cages until an official asked David to sign a document that would allow him and his son to be deported. David refused, saying he was asking for asylum. Another officer responded that if he did not sign the paperwork, he would remain in custody for at least two years, and Byron would be placed in the system for adoption. David could not allow that to happen. How could they simply give Byron away to another family when he was there?

Ultimately, David acquiesced and agreed to sign. As he later explained: "Fearing the permanent loss of [Byron] in a foreign land to an unknown American family was too much for me to bear. As a result, I was forced to sign the paper in front of me that I could not read, and agreed to be deported in order not to lose my eight-year-old son to adoption."

To his distress, the opposite happened. Immediately after David signed the paperwork, the officers shackled his hands and feet and took Byron away.

David was brought to the federal courthouse in McAllen to be prosecuted for illegal entry in a mass trial. "Sir, do you have anything to say on your behalf?" asked US Magistrate Judge Juan Alanis after David pleaded guilty.

David knew he had to act. He would be sent back to Guatemala soon. He answered: "If you are going to deport me, I want you to deport me with my son."

The judge replied, "It is a policy of the US government at this time to separate minors from adults. We understand it puts you in a hard situation. . . . Unfortunately for you, I'm not in a position to give you other answers in regards to you being separated from your minors."

In late May 2018, the government deported David to Guatemala without allowing him to say goodbye to his son. Like other youths who had been separated from their caregivers, Byron was designated an unaccompanied minor—as if he had entered the country by himself—and placed in the custody of the Office of Refugee Resettlement. The agency was supposed to find family members or other adults who could care for the separated children, but Byron had no family in the United States. As such, the agency held, he had to stay in detention. For the next ten months, it transferred Byron between different facilities in Texas, including the BCFS facilities in Baytown, Driscoll, San Antonio, and Raymondville.

Byron could make weekly calls home, but those calls were hard. Every time he heard his parents' voices, he begged them to bring him back to Guatemala. He didn't understand why his father had left him in detention. At times, he was so angry that he refused to speak with David, who now worked chopping trees an hour's drive away from his old town so that his former coworkers would not learn of his whereabouts.

On April 9, 2019, at the BCFS facility in Raymondville, Byron suffered a serious injury while playing soccer. Instead of taking him to an emergency room to be properly evaluated, a nurse practitioner misdiagnosed the wound and bandaged the lower part of his leg. It was later found that he had broken his distal femur. By the time Byron got injured, human rights lawyer Ricardo de Anda had learned about David and Byron's case and decided to help. Upon hearing that Byron was hurt, Ricardo contacted Amy J. Cohen, a Harvard-trained doctor who determined that the treatment the child was receiving constituted "extraordinary medical negligence" and could leave him at "ongoing risk of further injury, deformity, and disability."

Determined to get Byron out of detention, Ricardo found a caring couple who agreed to host the boy until he was returned to his parents: Matthew and Holly Sewell. The Sewells had never been involved in refugee issues before, but they were horrified by the zero-tolerance policy and wanted to help. They told each other, "We have enough room, we have enough love, we have enough time." They could foster a child in need. A friend put them in touch with Ricardo.

The Sewells did not want to act without consent, so they called David and his wife in Guatemala. Byron's parents readily agreed that Byron would be better off with them than in detention. But the Department of Health and Human Services refused to let Matthew and Holly sponsor Byron because the child was not related to them and they had no prior relationship.

Ricardo took the case to court, showing how the government's actions went against the law. In 1997, a federal court had approved what came to be known as the Flores settlement, which required the government to "place each detained minor in the least restrictive setting appropriate to the minor's age and special needs." Ricardo was successful: the court ascertained that the government was required to "release [the] minor from its custody without unnecessary delay."

Holly and Matthew did everything they could to welcome Byron, greeting him with a wheelchair for his broken leg, showering him with toys, and hanging pictures of his parents on the walls. The Sewells knew that it was important for Byron to remain in touch with his family, so they encouraged him to talk to them daily over video calls.

While Byron tried to adjust to this new life—playing around with his foster siblings in the pool and grimacing at Holly's cooking—he remained deeply traumatized by his experience. He had trouble processing his own emotions, so he became irritable and would lash out. At first, he couldn't sleep with the lights off, and then he had nightmares about monsters putting him in a cage or being reunited with his parents only to find that they no longer looked like his mother and father. He also completely forgot how to speak his native language, K'iche', which made it impossible for him to communicate with his own mother.

It was clear that he could not comprehend the fullness of what had happened. He had no concept of the government and blamed his father for abandoning him at the detention facility. Holly and Matthew hired a therapist to work with him. They tried to explain that his father had not wanted to leave. But what can a child understand of such cruelty?

CLEIVI ENTERED THE DARK ROOM. A BLOND ASYLUM OFFICER SAT BEHIND metal bars. Cleivi knew what to do and say, as Evelyn, her pro bono lawyer, had spent countless hours preparing her. This credible-fear interview would determine whether she could pursue a formal asylum claim or whether she and her two daughters who were with her would be deported.

The asylum officer did not speak Spanish, but there was an interpreter who translated all questions and answers.

"Were you threatened or harmed in your country?"

"My son was killed by the gangs," Cleivi said. "My daughter Keyli witnessed the killing. So now the gang members are targeting Keyli and our family."

"What was the name of the gang who murdered your son?"

"Gang 18."

"If you had to move to another area of your country, would Gang 18 be able to find you?"

"Yes, the Gang 18 is everywhere."

After hearing Cleivi's testimony, the officer informed her that she could leave. The agency would examine her case and let her know its decision.

Cleivi returned to the trailer to wait. Days passed without an answer. She tried to appear strong before her girls, but she was consumed by anxiety. After several days, she finally received a response in the mail. Her fear, the officer had written, was credible. Cleivi, Alison, and Keyli would be able to leave the detention center that very week. They would present their case for asylum before an immigration judge at a later date. Then Cleivi received even better news: with Evelyn's continued help, and after four weeks of separation, Andrea would soon be released into her care.

12

UPRISING

Gerardo Mansur

OCTOBER 1984

Atlanta was sweltering in October 1984, regularly surpassing eighty degrees, and the Mariel Cubans detained in the penitentiary were beginning to fume. The government was never going to set them free. They needed another way out. "We have to do something," they began murmuring in their cells. "We have to show the world that we are here, that they are abusing us." So they hatched a plan.

At approximately 1:15 p.m. on October 14, seventy men gathered in the recreation yard. Slowly, they pulled out handmade signs that read "Liberty Now" and "Strike for Dignity Now."

An insurrection. The guards could not allow it. Dressed in riot gear and clutching batons, the officials swarmed the sign-waving protesters. The Cubans had no way to defend themselves. They immediately put their placards down and followed orders. The guards led them to Cellhouse E, the dreaded segregation unit.

After the men were safely locked behind bars, the warden decided to send an even stronger message. He ordered a prison lockdown. No one would be allowed to leave their cells, including those like Gerardo who had not participated in the protest. At lunch and dinnertime, the guards brought bagged food to the men's cells. They did not, however, bring toilet paper. That should teach the Cubans a lesson, the warden thought. In case it did not, he also cut off the prison's water.

The men put up with these conditions for three days. Then they decided to revolt. Under a scream of "Freedom!" that carried well beyond the prison walls, some men started pounding their fists against the cells. Others followed. Together, they shattered the windows of the prison's two five-story cellblocks. Before long, the entire prison mutinied. The men lit fires with matches, burning their towels, sheets, and clothing.

The uprising only increased the warden's ire. Once the fires had burned out and the men had quieted, he ordered guards to enter each cell and throw away all personal property: photographs, Bibles, letters, and other mementos of their previous lives. In an instant, Gerardo lost the prized photos of his children that Father Alers had managed to get him, as well as Julia's letters.

If the warden thought he had broken the men's will, he was gravely mistaken. Not two weeks passed before the Cubans protested again. This time, the warden decided, he would *really* teach them a lesson.

Gerardo first felt the tear gas. His eyes stung as he choked. Panic overtook the prison. "The guards came with their rifles, those enormous helmets, the stairs, people asphyxiating, nearly two thousand people asphyxiating," recalled Gerardo. The officers ordered the incapacitated men into the recreation yard. There, the guards beat them up and then left them outside all night long.

That was only the beginning. The following morning, guards took everyone back inside. As they entered, the men noticed that there were no linens in their cells, only mattresses. They then learned that the lockdown would resume. This time, they had running water and were allowed out of their cells for one hour per day. But the lockdown would not end after a few weeks. Cellhouse A remained this way for nearly a year, while Cellhouses B, C, and E were on lockdown for more than three.

"Those were the saddest and darkest days of my life," Gerardo recalled decades later. The guards "left us there as if we were dogs in those cells," he explained. "You had a headache: there was no medicine. You were sick: you did not get to go to the doctor. You were cold: there was nothing with which to cover yourself." Because the prison staff never fixed the windows that the protesters had broken, freezing winds would gust into the cells. "There were no visits; there was no sun. That was a wasteland, everyone shut away."

Some men could not handle it. By 1986, there were over four thousand cases of "self-mutilation" at USP Atlanta, and eight men had died by suicide—including one of Gerardo's friends, who went by the name of Papito Guzmán. Many others had attempted to take their own lives without success. Between 1983 and 1987, Alberto Herrera tried to strangle himself with a rope, drank gasoline, violently beat his head against the wall until he bled from his ears, overdosed on pharmaceutical drugs twice, and, on his last suicide attempt, refused to eat for thirteen days.

Locked up in Cellhouse A, Gerardo was one of the fortunate ones. On September 1, 1985, ten months after the lockdown was imposed, the guards announced that those held in his building would be able to eat hot food in the dining hall again. Soon after that, the guards allowed them to resume work at UNICOR—even as other buildings remained under full lockdown.

For the next year and a half, Gerardo counted his blessings for having avoided the worst of the warden's punishment. Still, every day he would look out through his window and long to be free. He yearned to see his children and his wife.

IF GERARDO SOUGHT TO FORGET ABOUT HIS WOES, SALLY SANDIDGE AND Carla Dudeck, two American women who believed deeply in social justice and had little patience for social norms, decided that they could no longer turn a blind eye to what was happening on the inside. After years of reading stories about the unfair imprisonment of Cubans and the terrible conditions there, they knew that they could not continue to drive by the penitentiary—located on the same street as Atlanta's zoo—without doing anything for the caged men inside. They created a group to fight for detained Mariel Cubans.

By writing opinion pieces in the local newspaper and holding events that attracted concerned citizens, they recruited dozens of members to their new organization, which they eventually called the Coalition to Support Cuban Detainees. The coalition met at the Presbyterian Publishing House where Sally worked and organized regular marches and vigils outside the penitentiary on the last Sunday of every month. These events drew media attention and, with it, more participants—including the family members of those being held.

Jane Ochoa was one of those who joined the group. Her husband, Mario Ochoa, had been an auto mechanic in Cuba who fled the island during the Mariel boatlift. Three years after arriving in the United States, Mario was out drinking with a female friend at a bar in New York City's Washington Heights when a man approached and, for no reason, started attacking his companion with a barstool. Without thinking, Mario drew a gun and fired. Screams rang through the bar. The bullet grazed a bystander. Minutes later, the police arrived and arrested Mario.

Mario was not scared. Not only was he quickly released on bail, but all the witnesses were willing to testify that he was only defending his friend. With little to no fear, Mario continued to live life to the fullest. He went to work in the morning and partied at night. On one of those nights, as he danced at a local club, he met Jane. She knew little Spanish. He knew little English. It did not matter—they fell in love.

Their time together, however, did not last long. At his trial, Mario was found guilty and sent to the Fishkill Correctional Facility. At least the prison was located in New York State, where Jane could visit on a regular basis. As she came and went, their connection grew, as did their love. They married while Mario was still behind bars. Now all they had to do was count down the days until he got out.

They did not know what it meant to be a Mariel Cuban, an excludable "entrant."

Immigration authorities were waiting for Mario on the day he was released from prison. They first sent him to the Varick Street Detention Center in Lower Manhattan and then to USP Atlanta. Now Jane could no longer visit whenever she had a day off. She quit her job in Manhattan and relocated to Atlanta. She could not believe what had happened. Of course, as soon as she heard about the Coalition to Support Cuban Detainees in her new city, she became one of its most active members.

Gary Leshaw, a young and energetic attorney at the Atlanta Legal Aid Society, also threw himself into the fight. Almost a year before Carla and Sally organized the coalition, the US Court of Appeals for the Eleventh Circuit had held that the government could keep Mariel Cubans in indefinite detention. The Supreme Court had upheld this ruling. As Gary explained years later, his organization had long pursued "a lot of the litigation over the status of the detainees." But, by 1985, "we'd lost most of it."

Gary decided to focus on a different strategy: improving conditions in the penitentiary. Day after day, he hunted for evidence that he could present in court about what was happening inside, while other members of the coalition sent letters to government officials describing the inhumane conditions.

Their efforts paid off. On February 3, 1986, Representative Robert Kastenmeier, head of the Subcommittee on Courts, Civil Liberties, and the Administration of Justice, headed to Atlanta to examine the prison's conditions in person. This was the moment that the coalition had been working toward. Now all its members had to do was draw the public's attention to what was happening while they waited for Kastenmeier to issue a congressional report.

Less than a week after the representative's visit, sixty group members amassed outside the prison, carrying candles and signs that read "Release the Captives" and "With Liberty and Justice for All?" A three-year-old girl held her mother's hand and, with the other hand, a sign that asked "Why Is My Papa Still in Prison?"

The sound of the crowd's chants carried all the way to the prison's cells. The detained men stood by their windows, gazed down at the streets, and prayed for rescue.

The coalition's actions sparked conversations in Atlanta, but they did not reverberate nationally. Despite their best efforts, the coalition's members were unable to garner the support of the broader Cuban American community in Miami, whose social network and political power would have proved helpful. Cuban exiles who arrived in the United States before 1980 had long reproached Mariel Cubans for their association with criminality, lower economic status, and blacker skin. As a result, most Cubans in Miami refused to defend their incarcerated compatriots, even though they were constantly up in arms about prison conditions in Cuba. They cared so little about the fates of detained Mariel Cubans that they even declined to follow the example of their bishop, Agustín Román, who was one of the few members of their community to speak out against the abuses happening in Atlanta.

The congressional report that Kastenmeier issued in early April 1986 was damning. It asserted that Cubans at the penitentiary lived in conditions "worse than those which exist for the most dangerous convicted felons." The very "warehousing" of these individuals who had no legal rights was both "brutal and dehumanizing." The report recommended improving the prison's conditions, transferring some men to different facilities, releasing others, and reopening negotiations with the Cuban government so that the rest of those detained could be sent back to the island.

AS GERARDO STOOD BY HIS WINDOW WATCHING THE COALITION'S VIGILS, HE could feel that the times were changing. He had heard rumors that congresspeople were speaking out against the imprisonment of Mariel Cubans. On the night of Monday, April 28, 1986, he sat down on his bed and carefully penned a letter to Carla—that fearless woman whom he had heard at the rallies. In it, he described what had happened to him, Julia, and his children, who by then were two and four years old. As best he could, Gerardo tried to convey his and Julia's pain from being separated from their boys. "Today our distraught hearts cry because we have not been permitted to see them for all this time and we don't know their fate," he wrote. It was this pain, more than imprisonment, that was unbearable. He then pleaded for help publicizing his case, and for Carla to let other Americans know about "the crying of a hopeless father." He also asked her to visit him in prison. She would be his first visitor.

Carla received Gerardo's letter among dozens of others. Hundreds of detained Cubans had written to the coalition describing their histories and asking for help. Most did not expect much. They wanted human connection; they wanted to thank the few people who took an interest in them and might respond to their letters. One man wrote to Sally: "It's been four years that I am in captivity. It is killing me slowly." He begged her to write back and thanked the coalition for fighting "every day to achieve our liberation from this valley of tears." Another man wanted to tell Sally that he had been baptized Yet another sent her a postcard wishing her a happy Mother's Day. A detained Cuban named Tito drew her flowers and wrote: "I thank you a thousand times and beg that you do not forget this banished man who will be grateful to you for an entire lifetime even though he has not seen your face. You cannot imagine the happiness one feels when he receives a letter."

Among the hundreds of letters that Sally and Carla received, few touched them more than Gerardo's. The coalition investigated the case and reached out to Julia and to the kids' foster parents. Then they contacted reporters. On July 13, 1986, *The Atlanta Journal and Constitution* published an article about Julia and Gerardo's predicament.

After Kastenmeier's report, an exposé condemning the detention of Mariel Cubans was the last thing immigration officials needed. They resolved to contain the story. Julia was incarcerated in Lexington, Kentucky, far from coalition members who might try to approach her. But in the Atlanta penitentiary, Gerardo was at the epicenter of the protests. Not for long, officials decided. The following month, they quietly transferred Gerardo to a detention center in Florence, Arizona.

The move ended up being a blessing. As Gerardo recalled years later: "In Atlanta, there was a rule for everything: how you could move, how you could express yourself, when you could talk to a guard. . . . In Florence, it wasn't like that. You could move more freely; you could talk to guards if you needed something."

Rather than being locked up in a maximum-security federal penitentiary, he was now in a detention center, otherwise known as a "service processing center." But he was still locked up.

"WE DARED TO DREAM WE COULD DO SOMETHING ABOUT IT. WE DARED TO dream, and we didn't have to give up," proclaimed George Mowad, the mayor of Oakdale, Louisiana, on Saturday, March 22, 1986. A sense of confidence and pride filled the room—emotions that had been absent among the city's residents since those despairing days three years back when many of the area's factories shut down, leaving behind a 31 percent unemployment rate, the highest in the nation.

Behind Mowad, Norman Carlson, director of the Federal Bureau of Prisons, and Alan C. Nelson, commissioner of the Immigration and Naturalization Service, also beamed. This was their victory as well: the opening of the then largest federal detention center in the United States and the first Bureau of Prisons facility built specifically to detain migrants and asylum seekers.

The links between the nation's prison and immigrant detention systems were now out in the open. Each supported and reinforced the other. To symbolize their agencies' joint effort, both Nelson and Carlson (along with the prison's new warden and the deputy attorney general) cut a red ribbon to mark the opening of the new center.

Later that year, in its annual report, the Immigration and Naturalization Service explained the need for the Oakdale center, stating: "The primary reason for the continued shortage of bedspace is the detention of Mariel Cuban criminals." Carlson, a fifty-two-year-old man with a razor-shaved head, announced that the prison would be "a functional and attractive, yet very secure institution." He even joked that some people were criticizing the new facility for being "too plush."

Still, no one gloated more than Mowad. And for good reason. Fourteen years earlier, at the age of thirty-nine, Mowad had quit his job as a physician after winning Oakdale's mayoral race. He was determined to see his small city succeed. But if anything, Oakdale—a city of seven thousand people, located in the dusty, flat center of Louisiana by the edge of Cajun Country—had experienced a deep decline since Mowad had become mayor. Since 1975, the community had lost more than a thousand jobs.

When Mowad heard that the government was planning to build a new immigration detention center, he decided that this could be the solution to his city's problems. He knew that other locales were also pursuing this strategy. During the 1980s, rural towns and small cities throughout America started to court prisons in order to reduce unemployment. The California Department of Corrections had even hired marketing professionals to promote the economic development associated with their construction.

Mowad resolved that the new detention center would be erected in

Oakdale. He flew to Washington, lobbied the Justice Department, wrote to Congress, and organized his community. Residents of Oakdale sent hundreds of letters and telegrams to Reagan administration officials insisting that the prison be built in the small Louisiana city. Oakdale's Sacred Heart of Jesus Catholic Church even held all-night prayer vigils calling for the federal detention center.

Their efforts worked.

A "recession-proof industry" is coming to Oakdale, Mowad declared in 1983—the same year that the attorney general approved the facility and the administration appropriated $17 million for its construction. Mowad's promise: "With all the jobs it's going to create and the spinoff, it's going to turn this place around."

Nothing could stop him now, Mowad believed, not even the prison's opponents. In July 1984, a group of attorneys from the ACLU and the Lawyers Committee for International Human Rights mounted an effort to prevent the facility from being built by arguing that the "remote," rural location would make it hard for those detained to acquire legal representation. But the judge in charge of the case summarily dismissed it. The prison would be built in Oakdale.

The facility opened in April 1986. A few months later, the Immigration and Naturalization Service announced that it would transfer to Oakdale the men who were still under lockdown in the overcrowded Atlanta penitentiary. Gerardo, who always tried to avoid trouble, did not know how lucky he was to have been transferred to Florence rather than to Oakdale.

ONLY SEVEN MONTHS AFTER THE OAKDALE DETENTION CENTER'S OPENING ceremony, disenchantment shrouded the small city. Even Mayor Mowad felt gloomy, admitting in the local newspaper: "We have not had the dramatic improvement in business that I had expected." The reason behind this letdown was clear: the detention center's officials believed that

Oakdale's residents were not qualified to work at the facility and had brought in staff from other communities instead of hiring locals.

Oakdale's experience echoed that of other rural communities that had courted prisons to reduce local unemployment. Most public prison jobs required education and experience that rural residents did not have. In addition, seniority rules, and in some cases union rules, led prisons to hire veteran correctional personnel from other facilities. The government of Corcoran, California, for instance, was shocked to find out that even after it organized workshops to teach residents how to apply for prison work, only 20 percent of the jobs in the city's new facility had gone to locals.

In Oakdale, the disillusionment portended worse things to come.

Shortly after 7:00 p.m. on November 20, 1987, some of the Mariel Cubans held in Oakdale were watching NBC's *Nightly News* when its host, Tom Brokaw, announced that Cuba had agreed to take back approximately twenty-five hundred Mariel exiles who were mentally ill or who had broken laws in the United States.

The Cubans could not believe what they were hearing. Tom Brokaw was talking about them, and they did not like what he was saying. Many of them had wives in the United States who had not been arrested and who regularly visited them. Others had children who had been born in the land of Uncle Sam. They wanted to be near them. Moreover, the men believed that, for them, life in Cuba would be an even worse hell. Castro's government hated Mariel Cubans. If they were sent back, they would end up in Cuban prisons—if they were lucky.

Perhaps even more important, the men inside Oakdale had started dreaming about being set free. Not only had they been transferred out of the maximum-security penitentiary in Atlanta, but they had heard that the Reagan administration was considering letting many of them go. They were right. After Kastenmeier's report, the government had instituted the Cuban Review Plan, which held that two immigration agents would interview each man to determine whether he could be released. By the time of the *Nightly News* broadcast, a handful of detained

Cubans had already been freed, and most others imagined every day that they would be next.

Twenty-four hours after the broadcast, 250 men gathered in the prison's yard, pulled homemade machetes and clubs from underneath their coats in perfect unison, and began chanting "Somos los abandonados!" (We are the abandoned ones!) Many of the men had been in the 1984 protests at USP Atlanta. They knew what was coming next. This time, they were prepared.

As soon as the prison guards threw volleys of tear gas, the men split into two groups. One group started breaking windows and setting fires to distract the officials. The men in the other group broke into the mechanical service building. They armed themselves with fire axes, picks, shovels, saw blades, and gasoline, which they used to disarm twenty-eight correctional officers, whom they held as hostages. When the other officers realized what was happening, they escaped the facility. Mariel Cubans were now in control of the prison.

Within fifteen minutes, the FBI and the National Guard were on their way to the penitentiary. By then, local police officers had already positioned themselves around the prison's perimeter fence, but they did not dare go inside. They watched as eleven of the fourteen prison buildings were set aflame.

At around 2:00 p.m. the following day, the prison's administrators cut the facility's electricity and water. The prison, already destroyed by the previous day's fires, looked like a war zone. Inside, the men remained resolute. They would win this battle.

Attorney General Edwin Meese III considered his options. Given that those imprisoned were holding hostages, he did not want to send in troops. He decided to negotiate. A radio message boomed inside the prison asking one of the detained Cubans to come to the front gate to receive a message. At the entrance, officers handed the man a three-sentence letter signed by the attorney general. It offered the men an indefinite moratorium on repatriation in exchange for the hostages.

The group considered the offer. Why should they trust Meese? Once they returned the hostages, they would lose their bargaining chips. They had to negotiate with someone they could trust. They would continue the revolt.

BY SUNDAY, NOVEMBER 23, NEWS OF WHAT HAD BEEN HAPPENING FOR THE past two days in Oakdale had reached USP Atlanta. In the yards, in the cells, in the halls, the men inside the maximum-security penitentiary started to talk. They started to plan. "Tomorrow," they concluded, "this explodes."

A portentous silence fell over the usually raucous dining hall in the Atlanta penitentiary as the men sat down to breakfast at 5:30 a.m. on the following day. One of the migrants, who clearly feared what was about to happen, handed an officer a note warning that there would be "a lot of problems today; a lot of killing." Another Mariel Cuban called the chief dental officer and told him, "Doc, we have had our differences in the past, but I like you. Things are going to blow at 10:30 or 11:00; watch your ass." Another told a female employee at UNICOR that she should go home. Upon hearing this, the warden asked all of the prison's female staff members to leave the buildings and requested help from the National Guard.

The revolt began at 10:20 a.m., as planned. A group of men set the UNICOR building ablaze. Alarms rang throughout the penitentiary like air-raid sirens warning of impending danger. The migrants pulled out homemade machetes and started taking hostages. Tower guards shot at the protesting Cubans. José Peña Pérez, who had been chasing a staff member with a knife, fell to the floor dead. Five other detained men were wounded. Ammunition continued to fly until a group of Mariel Cubans held a knife to the throat of one of their hostages. The gunfire ceased.

Like in Oakdale, Mariel Cubans now controlled the prison—this time, a maximum-security penitentiary. As the prison's buildings burned, the men—who had gone from being captives to captors—counted their hostages. Seventy-nine.

Hundreds of Cuban men dashed to the roof to see what was happening outside. Tanks and SWAT teams surrounded the facility. Soon, helicopters started flying overhead. Rafael Quintana, who had been locked in Atlanta for years, concluded: "This is war."

Less than three hours later, the migrants received a xeroxed letter from Meese similar to the one that the men at Oakdale had received. It offered them an indefinite moratorium on repatriation and a review of each of their cases in exchange for the hostages. But like the men in Oakdale, the men in Atlanta had little reason to trust Meese. The US government had kept them locked up for years without reviewing their cases while waiting to send them back to Cuba. Nothing had changed. They rejected the offer and insisted on negotiating with someone they could trust. They wanted their lawyer, Gary Leshaw, who had long been working to improve the prison's conditions. They wanted Bishop Agustín Román, who had been speaking out for them, ignoring the wishes of Miami's Cuban community.

Despite their show of force, the men were scared. Rafael thought he would die in there that day. But they also knew that they couldn't show their fear to the outside world. They needed to act strong.

The following day, a group constructed a small platform near the administration building and surrounded it with rags and mattresses that had been soaked in gasoline. They placed a chair on top of the stage and issued a threat to the guards stationed at the front of the gate: if the helicopters did not cease flying over them, they would strap hostages to the chair and burn them to death. The flyovers continued but much less frequently.

During the next eight days, the protesters performed similar theatrical maneuvers with their hostages. Meanwhile, the buildings around them continued to smolder from the fires, and the facility had no water or electricity. Tensions mounted.

Finally, Meese relented. Neither the men in Oakdale nor those in Atlanta seemed like they would capitulate. It was time to ask Bishop Agustín Román for help, just as the incarcerated Cubans had demanded.

On the morning of Sunday, November 29, armed officials set up televisions all around the perimeter fence of the Oakdale facility. At 8:00 a.m., the slender cleric with disproportionately large glasses appeared on the screens. He implored the Cubans to release the hostages and accept the attorney general's proposal of indefinite moratorium on deportations and a review of each man's case.

The men in Oakdale conferred. Less than half an hour later, a group walked outside the entrance building with a sign that said: "We want the Bishop, our lawyer, and national press inside before we sign the agreement or no agreement."

By 1:50 p.m., the bishop had arrived in the city of Oakdale. He climbed atop a pickup truck outside the detention center and spoke over the loudspeaker through the razor-wire fence. Incarcerated Cubans should accept the agreement, he said in Spanish. "We have reviewed the document in detail, and I can tell you there is nothing missing in it. It is my great desire that this matter end this evening and that a new life will begin for you," the bishop said. The men cheered. "I want you to release the prisoners who are in your custody," the bishop continued before asking them to pray. Almost immediately, the men's homemade knives, machetes, and clubs fell to the ground as they lifted their hands in prayer. They signed the agreement.

As the hostages walked out of the prison amid cheers from their waiting family members, some of the detained migrants offered them flowers from the grounds of the burned prison. Once the hostages were gone, the bishop held Mass, and the Mariel Cubans sang. They were then taken to prisons throughout the nation to wait for the individual hearings the attorney general had promised.

The men at USP Atlanta heard about the agreement at Oakdale within hours. They, too, demanded that Bishop Román come to see them. Instead, Meese sent FBI agent Diader Rosario along with three leaders of the Cuban community in Miami: Jorge Mas Canosa, chairman of the Cuban American National Foundation, and Cuban political prisoners Roberto Martin Perez Rodriguez and Armando Valladares.

When the men walked into the prison, the detained migrants could scarcely believe their eyes. Why would the government send *them*? Valladares had joined President Reagan to condemn prisons in Cuba but had never spoken out against the imprisonment of Mariel Cubans in the United States. Neither had the other two men. The protesters angrily booed at them. The siege continued.

On December 3, Meese succumbed to the detainees' demand. At 9:45 p.m., Meese, Rosario, Gary Leshaw, and Bishop Román entered the prison. They met with a group of eight men who had helped lead the revolt. By the following morning, they had reached an eight-point accord similar to the one that ended the protest in Oakdale: detained Cubans would have individual hearings, all of which would happen by June 30, 1988. In the meantime, none would be deported to Cuba.

The rebellion had been successful. The Mariel Cubans, who had long been detained without hope, had won.

13

GUANTÁNAMO

Yolande Jean

1991

What lessons can we learn from the past? When should we imitate those who have preceded us, and when should we recoil?

These were the questions that George H. W. Bush's cabinet faced in November 1991, as hundreds of makeshift vessels—if they could even be called that—sailed through the Caribbean toward Florida. The rafts were fewer and ricketier, and they carried a different group of people than those ships that had come eleven years earlier, but all the president saw in those turquoise waters was the reflection of the Mariel boatlift. He saw not the faces and lives of those who had embarked upon it, such as Gerardo and Julia, but the fear that the boatlift had wrought among US voters.

It was through this prism that the Bush administration decided what measures to implement. Its decision not only came to affect the lives of thousands of Haitian refugees but also changed the course of US history.

IT ALL BEGAN A FEW MONTHS EARLIER, IN FEBRUARY 1991, WHEN A ROMAN Catholic priest who had practiced liberation theology was inaugurated as Haiti's first democratically elected president after winning two-thirds of the vote. Upon taking office, Jean-Bertrand Aristide worked to normalize Afro-Creole practices, initiated a literacy program, and championed the rights of the poor. Most Haitians were elated, but the country's army and elites refused to sit quietly and see their power dwindle. On September 29, a group of soldiers seized the National Palace, captured Aristide, and took him to army quarters. The army's leaders spared his life only because of Venezuelan, French, and US pressure, but they exiled him from the country.

Aristide's followers—a vast network of peasants, workers, students, priests, and the urban poor—were not so lucky. After the coup, the military and the police tortured and killed the president's supporters. Amnesty International reported that within a year, "hundreds of people" had been "extrajudicially executed or detained without warrant and tortured." The army did not limit its bloodshed to those who belonged to Aristide's party—it targeted any Haitian who had supported him, which placed most citizens in danger.

Fearing for their lives, tens of thousands of Haitians fled the country. Some crossed the border to the Dominican Republic, while others set sail to seek refuge in Florida or on any other shore where they could find safety.

Twenty-eight-year-old Yolande Jean was one of those refugees. She and her husband, Antenor Joseph, had been members of a political party that supported Aristide. Before the coup, the two had celebrated the birth of democracy in their country and had come to believe that perhaps change was possible—that perhaps their six- and eleven-year-old sons could grow up with hope.

The coup shattered their dreams. As soon as it happened, they knew that Antenor's life was at risk. All the members of their organization were in danger, but as one of the party's key figures, Antenor would be among the army's most prized targets. That very day, he said goodbye to Yolande and fled to one of Port-au-Prince's suburbs to go into hiding.

Yolande was terrified, but she did not let fear stop her. Instead, she set out "to mobilize the people" by typewriting political flyers inside the tin shanty where she lived with her mother and children. After writing the flyers, Yolande handed them to trusted connections for distribution.

The operation did not last long: after a few months, police officers found out what one of Yolande's connections was up to and killed him.

They then went after Yolande.

The day it happened, Yolande could hear the military truck approaching her house. She heard the warning gunfire. The angry voices. The nearing footsteps. There was nothing she could do.

Yolande's mother, Thérèse, rushed to the door to protect her daughter, but the soldiers cracked it open and barged inside.

"Is this where Elsie lives?" one of the soldiers demanded. That was Yolande's nickname, but Thérèse pretended not to know. "I don't know anybody named Elsie," she said. A soldier punched her, and she collapsed.

The men then went after Yolande. One of them threw her to the floor; the others then dug their boots into her spine.

"I am pregnant," Yolande cried.

The men stopped hitting her and lifted her up to handcuff her. But they then kicked her again as they dragged her outside.

Inside the house, Yolande's two boys screamed as the soldiers drove off with their mother. The truck stopped outside a nondescript concrete building that most Haitians knew was the Criminal Investigation Unit of the Port-au-Prince Police Department, where those imprisoned were regularly tortured and killed.

During the interrogation, a police officer ordered Yolande to tell him where her husband was hiding. Yolande said she didn't know. It was a costly response: another officer took the cigarette he was smoking and put it out on her arm, twisting the stub into her skin. Still, Yolande did not reveal where her husband was hiding, so the officers beat her with the butts of their rifles. The pain was unbearable, but she remained resolute.

Then Yolande felt blood streaming out of her. She was having a miscarriage.

The police regularly killed those they arrested, but this time they chose not to. Instead, they took Yolande to a military hospital and then released her on a provisional basis. They were probably hoping that she would lead them to Antenor.

Yolande had survived but knew that she had to flee. Staying at home put her sons and mother at risk and would most likely end in her death. She soon said goodbye to all of them and fled to where her uncle lived in the southwest of the country. But even there she was not safe, she quickly realized. Police officers in the region were suspicious of all newcomers. There was only one way out, one way to remain alive: to escape the country.

She made arrangements. Then, in the second week of May 1992, she headed out in the dead of night to a beach where a small, rattletrap boat packed with other refugees awaited. She did not know where it was headed, only that it was sailing out of Haiti.

BACK IN THE US, PRESIDENT BUSH'S AIDES ONLY SAW THE POTENTIAL EFfects of Haitian migration on the polls. Elections were coming up the following year, and the president was after a second term.

The Mariel boatlift had left such a mark on the country that it was still the primary frame of reference most Americans had when they heard that Haitian refugees were heading to their country by boat. And, as Bush's cabinet members saw it, the boatlift had not earned any points for the country's leaders at the time. Indeed, just a month earlier, in October 1991, the governor of Arkansas, Bill Clinton, had announced that he would be bidding for the Democratic nomination for president. When reporting on his candidacy, the media had immediately fixated on the Fort Chaffee fiasco, reminding readers of the riots and explaining that Clinton had lost the governorship in 1980 because he had allowed President Carter to detain Mariel Cubans in the state. *The Wall Street Journal* told its readers that Clinton's "Little Rock idyll was ruined both by what he has come to call 'a young man's mistakes' and the rioting of Cuban refugees at Fort Chaffee, which occurred during his tenure."

The incumbent president's cabinet members were not about to follow the young governor's miscalculations from 1980. The administration decided to quell Haitian migration at its root, fearing that allowing a few Haitians into the country would encourage more refugees to set sail. As an official from the Department of Defense told the media: "You've got a potential for a Mariel boatlift operation, once the Haitians hear that they'll be taken care of as soon as they get into international waters. Once it starts, we're all concerned—the Justice Department, too—with how many will come out and whether we'll have the facilities and care they'll need."

There was another issue at play beyond capacity: even though the Mariel boatlift came to everyone's mind, government officials knew that Americans feared Haitians much more than they ever did Cubans. Haitians were blacker. The Haitian American community in the United States was much smaller and weaker than the Cuban American one. And Haitians were associated with—and even blamed for—the AIDS epidemic. When AIDS first emerged as a new enigmatic yet fatal disease, the Centers for Disease Control (CDC) had identified four high-risk groups: gay men, heroin users, hemophiliacs, and Haitians. Since then, Haitians had been equated with the disease. Given how poorly Americans had reacted to the Mariel boatlift, it seemed clear that letting Haitians into the country would be terribly unpopular.

There was an easy way for the Bush administration to stop Haitian refugees from ever reaching America's shores. In 1981, the Reagan administration had signed an agreement with Haiti's then dictator, "Baby Doc" Duvalier, by which US Coast Guard cutters stationed near the Haitian coast could stop Haitian vessels and forcibly return those on board to their home country. To give the impression that the United

States was still complying with its international obligations toward asylum seekers, the Reagan administration had ordered US officials to interview the intercepted Haitians and bring to the United States all those who had a credible fear of persecution if deported back to Haiti. In practice, however, immigration officials were more interested in preventing Haitian migration to the United States than on checking asylum seekers' claims. According to the chief of the US Immigration and Naturalization Service interdiction program in Miami, only twenty-eight Haitians out of the twenty-four thousand picked up at sea between 1981 and 1991 had been brought back to the United States for asylum hearings. The rest had been sent back to Port-au-Prince.

The Bush administration feared that sending coup-fleeing refugees back to Haiti would provoke international condemnation and so decided to modify the "screen and return" practice implemented during Reagan's governance. According to the revised procedures, the Coast Guard continued to intercept Haitian vessels, but rather than sending the migrants back to Haiti, it began to hold them aboard its cutters while US diplomats pressured other countries into admitting the fleeing refugees.

Days passed as the US negotiated with other countries, none of which agreed to accept a significant number of Haitians. In the meantime, the number of Haitians aboard US vessels exploded. On November 8, Coast Guard vessels held two hundred refugees. By November 16, the number had climbed past one thousand, and three days later, the figure doubled to surpass two thousand. The Coast Guard set up tents on the ships' decks for the refugees to sleep in, and helicopters dropped food supplies. Eventually, some of the Coast Guard ships anchored at the US naval base in Guantánamo Bay, Cuba, to refuel, reduce exposure to the elements, and disembark some of the sick refugees who needed medical care.

Just as it had done during the late 1800s, the US government was once again detaining foreigners aboard ships. In the nineteenth century, migrants were held on commercial steamers rather than Coast Guard cutters, but the purpose remained the same: to keep foreigners from entering the United States while the government figured out what to do with them. As the media noted, the Haitian refugees had effectively become prisoners. "Floating U.S. Jails Hold Haitian Refugees" read one *Orlando Sentinel* headline; "Haitian Refugees Held, for Now, in Floating Jails" proclaimed *The Sun* of Baltimore.

With the number of confined Haitians rising by the day, the conditions aboard the ships deteriorating, and no countries willing to accept a substantial number of refugees, the Bush administration concluded that it had to change course. On November 13, the National Security Council issued a memorandum outlining the potential options available to the government in order of preference. The most desirable option was to simply deport the intercepted Haitians, just like the Reagan administration had done. The next best option was to use the naval base at Guantánamo "as temporary safe haven" in which to detain the exiles. All other alternatives, the memorandum stated, were too impractical and potentially counterproductive.

Five days after the council issued the memorandum, Attorney General William Barr implemented the most preferable option and announced that the government would reintroduce the "screen and return" practice. The administration presented this decision as the only moral choice available, noting: "We hope this return of boat people to Haiti will deter others from risking their lives by taking to the sea in unseaworthy boats." The government was about to deport Haitians back to a country where they were at risk of being tortured or killed, but it insisted that it was doing so for Haitians' well-being. By the following day, the government had deported over five hundred refugees.

Although the administration acted fast, its new plan was halted almost immediately. The Haitian community in the United States might not have been as big as the Cuban one, but it did have a strong organization in South Florida to support its needs: the Haitian Refugee Center, which filed a suit to stop the deportations. It argued that immigration officials were unable to conduct proper credible-fear interviews aboard the overcrowded Coast Guard ships, increasing the likelihood that refugees who deserved asylum would be deported. Donald Graham, a US district judge, agreed with the center's lawyers and issued a temporary restraining order preventing the government from returning the refugees back to Haiti.

Stymied by this order, the administration moved on to the next best option proposed by the National Security Council: detaining Haitians at the naval base in Guantánamo.

GUANTÁNAMO BAY IS AN INLET IN SOUTHEASTERN CUBA WHERE THE CARIBbean Sea indents the coast. Its waters are well sheltered, allowing for a wide and long harbor. Its position near the Windward Passage, which separates Cuba and Haiti and links the Atlantic Ocean to the Caribbean Sea and Panama, has long made it both a strategically important site and a contested one. In 1898, the same year that the Pacific Mail Steamship Company opened its detention shed in San Francisco, US Marines stormed into Cuba to support the island's war of independence against Spain. Once victory was secured, the US government forced Cubans to accept the terms of the Platt Amendment, which recognized Cuban independence but, among other clauses, established that the United States had the right to buy or lease land in Cuba for coaling or naval stations. Two years later, the US government established a forty-five-square-mile naval base on the shore of Guantánamo Bay and has kept it ever since, despite protests from the Cuban government.

The National Security Council was not the first to suggest using the naval base in Guantánamo for detaining migrants. During the Mariel boatlift, Bill Clinton had unsuccessfully tried to convince the White House to detain the arriving Cubans at Guantánamo rather than at Fort Chaffee. Then, during the 1980s, the Reagan administration considered transferring the "excludable" Mariel Cubans from Fort Chaffee to Guantánamo, although in the end it decided not to do so.

Under Reagan, the Department of Defense issued various secret memorandums detailing the pros and cons of "using Guantánamo to hold the undesirables who arrived in the Mariel boatlift." The advantages were clear. Transferring this population to the base in Cuba "would avoid the domestic political costs of continuing to hold them within the United States" and would be viewed as a victory for the administration. But the disadvantages—which were the same ones that Carter's aides had noted—were too costly. As the memorandums noted, the treaty with Cuba under which the United States occupied the base in Guantánamo provided that the area could only be used as a coaling or naval station. If the US breached the treaty, Castro would have "legal cover for breaching it himself" and could try to expel American forces. Additionally, Guantánamo did not have proper facilities to house a large group of migrants; the operational costs of opening a detention center in Guantánamo were tremendous, as the base's water had to be derived from desalinization and food had to be brought in.

Faced with the Haitian crisis, the Bush administration made a different calculation and did not consider Guantánamo's lack of appropriate facilities to be a deal-breaker. In fact, detaining migrants in poor conditions would simply extend the policy of deterrence that the government had adopted since 1981, by which detention served to warn other potential migrants not to set sail. Housing the refugees in terrible conditions at Guantánamo Bay had the potential to amplify the deterrent effects of detention.

Detaining Haitians there had other advantages. Because the naval base was outside the United States, the government could argue that the refugees had no legal rights there. The US Constitution did not protect foreign nationals who were outside the country; at Guantánamo Bay, the Bush administration could argue, Haitians were just that:

foreigners outside the United States. Furthermore, because access to Guantánamo required the permission of the US military, the government could prevent reporters and human rights lawyers from getting to the refugees.

It was then, in the final weeks of 1991, under the administration of George H. W. Bush, that Guantánamo first became a detention site where people could be imprisoned without constitutional rights. It wasn't suspected terrorists who were first held there but Haitian refugees escaping torture and death.

The establishment of Guantánamo as a site off US soil where those held lacked rights was, in fact, an extension of the entry fiction. The Bush administration simply broadened the logic of the entry fiction by classifying Guantánamo—and, respectively, all refugees detained there—as also being outside the United States, even though the area was under US control.

Lawyers from the Haitian Refugee Center immediately contested the notion that Guantánamo was outside the United States, but the US District Court of Southern Florida and the US Court of Appeals for the Eleventh Circuit agreed with the government. The courts even used the entry fiction as precedent to rule that Haitians held no constitutional rights while detained aboard US cutters or at Guantánamo.

To the government's dismay, however, connecting Haitians' detention at Guantánamo with the entry fiction led the US Court of Appeals for the Second Circuit to rule that Haitians ought to have access to legal counsel. In Ellen Knauff's case, which the court cited, the Supreme Court had ruled that "whatever the procedure authorized by Congress is, it is due process as far as an alien denied entry is concerned." This meant that while "entrants" had no guaranteed protections under the Constitution, they had to be afforded the rights that the legislative branch of the government had provided them. And in the Immigration and Nationality Act, Congress had affirmed that "entrants" had the right to access lawyers at no expense to the government.

YOLANDE WALKED AROUND IN A DAZE. A FEW DAYS EARLIER SHE HAD MANaged to escape Haiti on a small boat, but she and the other passengers on board had almost died after getting lost at sea for two days. She had been scared and cold as her clothes clung to her, soaked with salt water and vomit. A young mother who had been sitting near her had fallen so ill that Yolande had taken the woman's baby in her arms and tried to comfort it. A last act of humanity.

But Yolande had not died on that boat. At dusk, she and the other passengers spotted a ship out on the horizon, and soon enough they were all safely aboard a Coast Guard cutter that was carrying hundreds of other Haitian refugees. It was taking them to Guantánamo.

At the base, refugees slept inside olive-green tents that offered little protection from the blazing sun or pouring rain. By the time Yolande arrived, the place was already over capacity, housing more than twelve thousand Haitians. To gain some semblance of privacy inside the overcrowded tents, the refugees hung sheets between their cots.

Yolande lived in waiting. There were long lines for identification bracelets and cards, for soap, for the latrines, for food, for flip-flops. But above all, she waited for her credible-fear interview. As she had learned, all the refugees at Guantánamo were to be interviewed. Those who passed the interviews were taken to the United States, and the rest were deported back to Haiti. The problem was that no one knew what criteria were being used to determine who "passed." Some of those around her insisted that anyone who had supported Aristide would never be allowed into the United States; others held that the only way to pass was by claiming to have been an Aristide supporter.

On the morning of her interview, Yolande was escorted to a hangar where a tall Haitian man introduced himself and told her that he would be translating for the government official. Yolande looked at her compatriot, who gave her an encouraging nod, so she decided to tell her story:

how she had belonged to a group that supported Aristide, how she had been kidnapped by soldiers and tortured by the police. It was too hard to speak of her miscarriage, so instead she raised her sleeve to show them the fresh scar left by the policeman's cigarette.

A few days later, Yolande learned that she had been "screened in." Finally, she thought, she would be safe. She would rebuild. She had no idea how she would get her husband, children, and mother out of Haiti—she didn't even know if they were all still alive—but she would work as hard as possible to reunite with them. As Yolande waited to be taken to the United States, the number of refugees in the camp began to dwindle. On May 24, ten days after she arrived at Guantánamo, President Bush issued Executive Order 12807, which instructed the Coast Guard to send all refugees interdicted at sea back to Haiti without conducting credible-fear interviews. The administration defended its decision by claiming that Guantánamo was at capacity. It did not acknowledge that returning the refugees to Haiti could result in their deaths. Because of the executive order, the Coast Guard ceased bringing new refugees to Guantánamo while immigration officials continued emptying the camp. As a result, between May 24 and June 3, the refugee population at Guantánamo fell from over twelve thousand to around nine thousand and would continue to decrease dramatically thereafter.

Despite having passed her credible-fear interview, Yolande had reason to worry. US officials were known to have mistakenly deported Haitian refugees who had been screened in, as had happened with Marie Zette. Marie had arrived at Guantánamo long before Yolande and passed her credible-fear interview. Immigration officials had told her that she would be going to the United States, but then, in February 1992, the officials seemingly changed their minds and said that she was heading back to Haiti. Marie could not believe what she was hearing. Her life would surely be in danger, but there was nothing she could do about it. Right before she was deported, she chanted a song to the other refugees conveying her fears. Then, the day after she had been taken to Haiti, officials called her name: she was supposed to leave for Miami. The officials had made a mistake and deported someone who would be at risk in Haiti. A few weeks later, some of Marie's relatives were intercepted by the Coast Guard and sent to Guantánamo, where they told the detained refugees that their returned friend had been killed by Haiti's military police.

After waiting for what seemed like an eternity, Yolande finally heard her name called. It was time for her to leave this place, to head to the United States, she thought. Instead, an official told her that the government needed to get another blood sample. When refugees first arrived at Guantánamo, their blood was drawn and tested; according to the official, the government had lost Yolande's test results. After drawing her blood, the official sent her away with no information.

For twelve more nail-biting days, Yolande waited. When the results came in, she was told that she had "some germs" in her blood and that she would have to see a specialist. But her care would take years. She had two options: she could stay at Guantánamo for ten more years, or she could sign a paper saying that she wanted to be sent back to Haiti.

Yolande was shocked. If they returned her to Haiti, she would certainly be killed. "Send me to the specialist," she pleaded, begging to know her diagnosis. The nurse simply said she had a virus. Then two soldiers marched her off to a waiting bus.

The bus took Yolande to another part of the naval base called Camp Bulkeley. It was surrounded by razor wire and guard towers. As she descended from the bus, Yolande observed dozens of plywood huts in the camp's main area. Plastic bags hung from the buildings to keep the rain out. This, she quickly realized, would be her new home.

After several days of living with uncertainty about her health, she was told by a military man who called himself Dr. Malone that she was HIV-positive and had a low T-cell count. Yolande didn't really understand what HIV or T cells were, and the doctor didn't really explain. Instead, he gave her AZT, a medication to slow the reproduction of the virus, a drug called isoniazid to prevent her from contracting tuberculosis, and an antibiotic so that she would not get pneumonia as a result of her impaired immune system.

Yolande was being detained in the first HIV detention camp.

Since 1987, the United States had barred HIV-positive people from entering the United States. The Bush administration argued that HIV-positive Haitian refugees who had been screened in were in legal limbo: the government could not deport them without breaking international and domestic laws on refugee rights, but it also could not admit them into the United States without a waiver. This was why, the government argued, it was keeping them at Camp Bulkeley, an indeterminate place that was neither in Cuba nor in the United States.

If it had wanted to, the Bush administration could have let HIV-positive refugees into the country by offering them waivers. But it didn't even need to do that: according to the law, HIV-positive people who were already in the United States could be admitted to the country without waivers. Restrictions only applied to those immigrants seeking asylum from third countries, meaning that they were trying to enter the United States from countries that were not their nations of origin. And, indeed, these Haitians were not applying from third countries: the Coast Guard had interdicted them at sea and placed them under the custody of the US government at a US military base. But Bush's cabinet members knew that bringing HIV-positive Haitians into the United States was politically unwise and continued to insist that Guantánamo was outside the United States, so they therefore could not bring the refugees to the mainland.

Attorney General William Barr even refused to guarantee that refugees who had developed full-blown AIDS could be brought to the United States, despite knowing that Guantánamo did not have adequate facilities to care for such patients. Joel Saintil, a detained refugee with AIDS, lost thirty pounds, and his T-cell count became dangerously low. His doctors could not treat him at the naval base and requested that the Department of Justice allow him to get medical care in the United States. The department denied the request three times. It soon did the same with Yolande, who went from being HIV-positive to actually having AIDS.

Significantly, the administration's policies toward HIV-positive Haitians paralleled government practices that drove the incarceration of a significant proportion of HIV-positive citizens on the US mainland. Unlike in Guantánamo, the administration did not implement an explicit policy of imprisoning citizens who tested positive for HIV, but by not distributing more information about how the virus spread among populations already more likely to be incarcerated, such as poor Americans and racial minorities; by not giving these communities proper access to medical care; and by incarcerating drug users instead of helping them, the government contributed to the likelihood that HIV-positive people ended up behind bars. In 1989, the state and federal prison systems reported that 202 out of every 100,000 incarcerated individuals had AIDS, a rate that far exceeded the rate of AIDS among the general US population, which was 14.7 cases per 100,000 people. In some areas of the country, the rates of HIV and AIDS among the prison population were even higher. In 1992, an estimated 17 to 20 percent of all imprisoned people in New York State prisons were HIV-positive. They, too, were basically living in HIV-positive detention facilities.

THE REFUGEES AT GUANTÁNAMO HAD TROUBLE TRUSTING THE MEDICAL STAFF at the base. Although the doctors provided their patients with life-prolonging AZT and fought for them to be given access to care in the United States, they also transgressed basic medical norms, knowing that the refugees had no rights. Yolande experienced this denial of medical rights firsthand. One day, she attended a meeting for refugee women in which one of the camp doctors said that too many of them were getting pregnant. He then told them there was a shot they could get that would prevent them from getting pregnant and also improve their T-cell counts. At first, Yolande, like most of the women, was not interested in the injection, but every time she went to the hospital for her recurring headaches, the doctors insisted that the shot would be good for her. Knowing that it was important for her to raise her T-cell count, Yolande eventually agreed. The injection she got was Depo-Provera, a birth control method that has no beneficial effect on people's T-cell counts.

The medical staff pushed the women to get the injection by lying to them and playing on their fears about their declining health. The legal and ethical doctrine of informed consent, it seemed, could be ignored when dealing with Haitian refugees at Guantánamo. The doctors also failed to tell Yolande and the other women who agreed to get the shot about the side effects that they might experience, including terrible headaches, acute menstrual cramps, and heavy bleeding. For Yolande, these effects were excruciating. She bled heavily for a month and continued to have pelvic pain four months later.

These lies and omissions, the constant surveillance, and the limited flow of information from camp officials led to mounting frustration. In the summer of 1992, Yolande and the rest of the refugees decided that they had had enough. By then there were just under three hundred Haitians left at Guantánamo, and they were all either HIV-positive or the family members of HIV-positive people. Many of them had been activists in Haiti and decided to organize themselves.

During the first protest, a small group of refugees dressed in white marched throughout the camp. The army stood by. During the second protest, however, soldiers used a fire hose to blast them to the ground and ransacked their huts, ostensibly to search for weapons. They then sent the protest's leaders to Camp Seven, the segregation unit, where people were confined to outdoor cells surrounded by barbed wire and slept on cardboard rather than mattresses.

But the camp refused to be subdued. After the protest leaders had been detained for six weeks, the rest of the refugees decided to act against what they considered to be a terrible injustice. If peaceful protests did not work, then perhaps violence would. In an act of defiance, they took their belongings from the huts and set them on fire.

The military's response was immediate and brutal. As Yolande later described: "They came with three tanks. They came with police dogs. They came with trucks and fire trucks, approximately 5,000 military personnel against 295 people who were here." They beat the refugees to the ground with sticks and then continued to kick them.

After that, protesting seemed futile. To the detained Haitians, it now seemed that their best option lay with external forces. There was a looming presidential election in the United States, and Bill Clinton, the Democratic candidate facing off against George H. W. Bush, had decried the treatment of Haitians. If he were to become president, he promised, he would "give fleeing Haitians refuge and consideration for political asylum" and "lift the current ban on travel and immigration to the United States by foreign nationals with HIV." With no HIV ban, Guantánamo's very raison d'être would disappear.

On November 3, 1992, Yolande and the other refugees assembled in front of a television to wait for the results. Every time CNN's map of the United States turned a state blue for Clinton, the Haitians would cheer. Every time it turned red for Bush, they cursed and jeered.

At around 9:00 p.m., the CNN anchor suggested that the results would come in soon and that Clinton would probably win. The camp erupted. "Clin-tawn! Clin-tawn!" some of the refugees screamed as others tried to silence them, warning them not to celebrate too early.

Almost two hours later, the final results were called. Ohio had gone blue. Clinton would be the next president.

BUSH HAD LEARNED FROM CARTER AND CLINTON THE POLITICAL COSTS OF letting a large group of refugees into the country, and he took from Reagan the ability to interdict Haitian ships. As a presidential candidate,

Clinton had good reason to oppose Bush's measures toward Haitians, especially given his support among Black voters and the gay and lesbian community, which wanted to see an end to the exclusion of HIV-positive immigrants.

As president, however, Clinton had different concerns. Three days before he assumed office, the media published article after article examining his stated position on Haitians in the context of his history with Mariel Cubans. *The New York Times* reported that "mass arrivals would, of course, create huge logistical problems. When similar numbers arrived from Cuba in 1980, rioting broke out among a group waiting to be processed at Fort Chaffee in Arkansas. Then-Governor Clinton surely remembers the experience." The *Sun-Sentinel* held that "Clinton has acknowledged that riots by Cubans who came in on the Mariel boatlift and who were jailed by the government at Fort Chaffee, Ark., in 1980 were a factor in Clinton's losing his first bid for re-election, given that he had invited the government to bring the Cubans to Arkansas in the first place." Now that he had been elected, Clinton realized that welcoming Haitians and HIV-positive people into the country would be deeply unpopular. A week into his presidency, he had already stated that he would continue to intercept and deport all Haitians fleeing by boat without providing them with asylum interviews.

Yolande and the other refugees at Guantánamo despaired over Clinton's about-face. Their captors seemed intent on keeping them locked up forever. Being imprisoned at Guantánamo meant being held in an indeterminate place that was neither Haiti nor the United States, neither life nor death. If they could not be free, Yolande thought, they might as well not be "alive" in this place.

She approached the other refugees with an idea. "We have to go on a hunger strike," she said. "If we are going to get out of here, we've got to put real pressure on Clinton. But we have to be prepared to die." At first, the other refugees were uncomfortable with the idea. They had already attempted peaceful and violent protests to no avail. Going on a hunger strike would be terribly hard on their undernourished bodies. But those thoughts dissipated quickly.

"We would prefer to die than stay here in Guantánamo," one of the refugees said, reflecting a widespread sentiment.

Already, some of them had attempted suicide. One tried to hang herself with a shoelace. Another used a parachute cord. And then there was Robert Henry, who woke up one morning after having attempted suicide the night before and jumped into the barbed-wire fence that surrounded the camp in a desperate effort to slash his throat.

The refugees figured they had little left to lose. They headed out to the soccer field under the blazing tropical sun and from then on denied themselves all provisions from the US government. They refused to eat food. They slept outside rather than on the cots in the huts. Days passed. Some of the refugees began to faint, but the strike continued. *There is no life for me here anymore, considering the treatments here and what I've been going through*, Yolande thought. *There is nothing left of me.*

As the days passed, the strike began to make a difference. The press and famous activists such as Jesse Jackson gained permission to visit the naval base and returned home with horror stories of the mistreatment that the refugees faced. Some Black clergy and members of civil rights organizations even organized their own hunger strikes to stand in solidarity with the detained Haitians. Amid this onslaught of negative publicity, the military clamped down on the refugees' hunger strike, beating the captives into submission with nightsticks. But by then the Haitians at Guantánamo had succeeded in making their cause a public issue.

The hunger strike even catalyzed the refugees' lawyers to accelerate their efforts. As one of the lawyers later said, the strike "made us, the lawyers, pay a lot more attention to our clients. From the strike forward, we were a continuous presence in the camp." Shortly thereafter, the lawyers decided that they had to go to trial to challenge the legality of the detention facility at Guantánamo.

The trial began on March 8, 1993. When the government's lawyers arrived at the Brooklyn courthouse, dozens of protesters, including Jesse Jackson, confronted them with shouts and chants. The protesters filled the courtroom, murmuring their opinions. At the end of the day, they headed to the streets to demonstrate. For their part, the refugees' lawyers made their case strongly: at Guantánamo, refugees who had already passed credible-fear interviews were being detained indefinitely without basic constitutional rights and without adequate medical care.

Judge Sterling Johnson issued his ruling a month later. The Guantánamo operation, the judge held, was "nothing more than an HIV prison camp." He ordered the government to release those detained, stating that it could send them "to anywhere but Haiti." The refugees would finally be free.

The ruling forced the US government to accept the refugees, as no other country would take them. By the end of June, the last Haitians held at Camp Bulkeley were brought to the US mainland.

Yolande resettled in a small apartment in Queens, New York. In January 1994, she drove to LaGuardia Airport to pick up her parents, children, brother, and sister, whom she had managed to bring to the United States. The only person absent was her husband, Antenor. He had been killed in Haiti.

JUDGE JOHNSON'S ORDER COULD HAVE CHANGED THE COURSE OF GUANTÁnamo's history. In his final ruling, the judge wrote: "The U.S. Naval Base at Guantánamo Bay, Cuba, is subject to the exclusive jurisdiction and control of the United States where the criminal and civil laws of the United States apply." According to this ruling, Guantánamo was juridically equivalent to the continental United States, which meant that the rights provided by the US Constitution had to be respected there.

This part of the ruling especially bothered Clinton's cabinet members. In August 1993, the Department of Justice appealed Judge Johnson's decision. By then all the Haitian refugees who had been held captive at Guantánamo were in the United States, but the Clinton administration did not want to have a legal precedent establishing that the Constitution's due-process clause applied on the naval base. One government official maintained that Clinton's aides were "confident that they would do the right thing" but did not want "to be forced by the law to have to do so."

The administration's appeal was a big blow to the lawyers who had fought for the refugees. They were convinced that if the case reached the Supreme Court, which had been unsympathetic to the refugees' cause from the start, they would lose. Distressed by the possibility of losing at trial, the lawyers ended up settling with the Department of Justice. As part of the settlement, Judge Johnson vacated his final opinion, which meant that there would be no legal precedent and that Guantánamo could again be used in the future as an extraterritorial site to hold foreigners without rights.

If Clinton administration officials ever intended to "do the right thing" at Guantánamo, they most definitely forgot their lofty goal as soon as they were no longer legally mandated to respect it. In June 1994, Clinton's White House opened Guantánamo's detention facilities once again. This time, the government detained twenty thousand Haitian refugees who were escaping violence, as well as thirty thousand Cubans who had fled the island after Castro once more opened the door to emigration. As before, the detention of these refugees seemed interminable. It was not until the end of 1995 that the last Haitians were taken out of Guantánamo—most of them deported back to Haiti. The last set of Cuban balseros (rafters) were allowed to leave in early 1996—most of them for the United States. The Clinton administration then continued to use the naval base to detain refugees when it considered detainment necessary. In 1997 and 1999, the Coast Guard intercepted various groups of Cubans and sent them to Guantánamo.

ON JANUARY 20, 2001, BILL CLINTON'S SUCCESSOR AND GEORGE H. W. BUSH'S son, George W. Bush, became the forty-third president of the United States. His victory had been highly contested, but after September 11, 2001, the country rallied around the new commander in chief. That day, nineteen militants associated with the Islamic extremist group al-Qaeda hijacked and crashed four planes, killing nearly three thousand people. They were the deadliest attacks on American soil since Pearl Harbor. Americans were outraged and terrified at the prospect that they might again be attacked without warning.

That night, Bush addressed the nation. "Terrorist attacks can shake the foundations of our biggest buildings, but they cannot touch the foundation of America. These acts shattered steel, but they cannot dent the steel of American resolve," he said. Part of that resolve was to apprehend those responsible, as well as those who aided them. "I've directed the full resources of our intelligence and law enforcement communities to find those responsible and to bring them to justice. We will make no distinction between the terrorists who committed these acts and those who harbor them."

Weeks later, the United States launched a war in Afghanistan to topple the Taliban, an ultraconservative political faction that ruled the country and was providing sanctuary to the organizers of the 9/11 attacks. The government wanted to ensure that it could interrogate anyone the US Army captured using whatever means it saw fit. For this, the Bush administration needed to find detention sites that were beyond the reach of US courts. On December 27, 2001, Defense Secretary Donald Rumsfeld announced that the administration would send those it captured to the naval base on Guantánamo Bay.

It is not surprising that George W. Bush chose Guantánamo as a site to hold detained foreign nationals without having to grant them rights. His father was the first president to use the naval base for such a purpose, and the practice had persisted.

To head off legal challenges, the administration asked John Yoo and Patrick Philbin from the Office of Legal Counsel to look into whether foreign nationals held at Guantánamo had the right to habeas corpus, which would give them the right to challenge the legality of their detention in the courts. On December 28, the two lawyers issued a classified memorandum on the question, which was later leaked to the press. "The great weight of legal authority," they wrote, "indicates that a federal district court could not properly exercise habeas jurisdiction over an alien detained at GBC [Guantánamo Bay, Cuba]." The lawyers reached the desired conclusion by using the same logic that the George H. W. Bush administration had used: although Guantánamo was under the full control and jurisdiction of the United States, it was still outside the country, which meant that US laws did not apply there. The memorandum's authors even addressed the case of Haitian detention, claiming that any wins the refugees' lawyers had achieved were inconsequential. "We believe that these precedents are not good law," the memo stated.

The administration also tried to work around the Geneva Conventions, which consist of a series of international treaties intended to ameliorate the effects of war on soldiers and civilians. According to the conventions, which the United States had signed and ratified, prisoners of war cannot be tortured. On January 9, 2002, two days before the first individuals arrived at Guantánamo, Yoo issued another memorandum arguing that the Geneva Conventions did not apply to members of al-Qaeda or the Taliban. His argument was that terrorist organizations were not state actors and thus could not be parties to international agreements. That same week, Rumsfeld publicly labeled those it captured as "unlawful combatants" rather than prisoners of war and declared that "unlawful combatants do not have any rights under the Geneva Convention."

The government would do as it willed with the people whom it imprisoned. In total, the Bush administration caged 780 Muslim men and boys at Guantánamo. They didn't know when or even if they would be released. Most of them were never charged with any crimes.

Such practices were not new. They built on the ignoble legacy from the days of Chi Hao and Ellen, Gerardo and Yolande, and thousands of other migrants who had experienced indefinite detention without being charged with any crimes or having received prison sentences. Those classified as "entrants" because they had been stopped at the border had regularly been prevented from contesting their detentions in court. And many, including Ellen, were held without being informed why. The government's treatment of detained migrants and refugees had been brutal. Individuals had regularly been beaten, denied medical attention, separated from their children, and deprived of proper food while in detention. These measures constituted nothing less than torture. The cruelty of the system was intentional, designed as a deterrent for future migrants, long before Bush became president.

But there was a big difference: while previous administrations had used Guantánamo as a detention site where incarcerated migrants held no rights and could be abused, the George W. Bush administration understood it as a site of torture, where the government could extract information from captured subjects using any means it desired. The Bush administration even euphemistically referred to torturing detainees as using "enhanced interrogation techniques." These "techniques" included waterboarding, sleep deprivation, solitary confinement, exposure to extreme temperatures and loud noises, stress positions, forced nudity, rectal feeding, sexual assault, threats against family members, beatings, and strangulation.

One of the most powerful accounts of torture inside Guantánamo comes from Mohamedou Ould Slahi, who wrote letters to his lawyers about what was being done to him. His account can be corroborated through the plans that the Joint Task Force Guantánamo crafted to "interrogate" him, which closely match Mohamedou's own report of what happened. Mohamedou was subjected to around-the-clock interrogations, which lasted twenty hours and continued for days. During that period, he was not allowed to sleep or rest at all. He was not allowed to shower for weeks and was kept in stress positions that exacerbated his sciatic nerve issues. He would sometimes not be allowed to sit or lie down for days on end. His interrogators deprived him of his medication. They kept him in a freezing cell and poured cold water on him. They sometimes blasted loud music or continuously banged on his door. They deprived him of food. Female interrogators sexually abused him.

On August 13, 2003, Defense Secretary Donald Rumsfeld himself approved the escalation of Mohamedou's torture. Less than two weeks later, masked men charged into the room where Mohamedou was being interrogated and beat him up, punching him in his face and ribs. They then covered his eyes with goggles, put a bag over his head, and drove him off toward the sea. There, the interrogators forced Mohamedou onto a watercraft, which quickly sped away so that he would think he was being kidnapped and taken to another country in order to "replicate and exploit the 'Stockholm Syndrome' between detainee and his interrogators." After the trip, the interrogators took Mohamedou to another part of Guantánamo, where he was kept for a month in a small cell in total darkness.

Although the government never intended to transfer Mohamedou, the CIA had, indeed, begun to operate undisclosed prisons in countries outside the United States, including Afghanistan, Lithuania, Romania, Poland, Thailand, and nations across the Middle East. It used these so-called black sites to torture detained individuals and keep them out of the reach of US courts. Though many people had heard of Guantánamo Bay, very few knew about the existence of such prisons, much less who was detained in them. In 2003, the CIA reproduced this model at Guantánamo by opening a secret compound inside the naval base, which it dubbed Strawberry Fields after the Beatles song. Just like in the song's lyrics, officials joked, those held there would be at the compound "forever."

"OBAMA! OBAMA! OBAMA!" THE CHANTS OF THE DETAINED MUSLIMS REVERberated from the concrete buildings of the detention camp at Guantánamo Bay. It was the night of November 4, 2008, and those who were allowed to were watching the returns come in through the television. They were delighted by the results: Barack Obama would be the next president of the United States.

Their chants echoed those of "Clin-tawn! Clin-tawn!" that Haitian refugees had hollered sixteen years earlier almost to the day, inside a tent located in that very place. While campaigning for the presidency, Clinton had pledged to end the HIV ban, which would have allowed all refugees who remained at the naval base to enter the United States. Obama similarly promised to close Guantánamo: "In the dark halls of Abu Ghraib and the detention cells of Guantánamo, we have compromised our most precious values. . . . It is time to turn the page."

There were good reasons to trust him. Obama desperately wanted to break away from Bush's policies, and by now it had become clear that the vast majority of those held at Guantánamo were not terrorist leaders. Some were extremists who had little power, while many others were simply men who had been in the wrong place at the wrong time. After it invaded Afghanistan, the US Army had paid local warlords significant bounties for suspected terrorists. It had also distributed leaflets throughout Afghanistan and Pakistan promising to pay those who handed over "Arab terrorists" enough money that they would be able to feed their families for life. Unsurprisingly, the army had been handed not just members of terrorist organizations but hundreds of men who had simply been turned in for the monetary reward.

On his second day in office, Obama issued an executive order directing the detention facility in Guantánamo to be shut down within a year. By then, over five hundred individuals had already been transferred to other countries, but 242 remained at the naval base.

The Obama administration's first serious effort to transfer a group of people out of Guantánamo revolved around seventeen Uyghurs, mostly Chinese Muslims who had fled persecution from the Chinese government by heading to Afghanistan. They had been among the individuals turned in to the US military for no reason other than the promised bounty. The Bush administration had previously tried to transfer the Uyghurs out of Guantánamo without success; in China they would probably be tortured or executed, so the government couldn't send them there, but no other country was willing to take them. In April 2009, the Obama administration designed a plan to bring them to Northern Virginia, which had one of the country's largest Uyghur communities. But when the idea leaked, the Republican congressman from the area and the Senate Democratic leader refused to accept them, claiming that they didn't want "terrorists" in their neighborhoods. The White House did not force the issue.

The Uyghurs thus found themselves in the same situation as thousands of detained migrants before them: the US government was willing to release them but wouldn't allow them in the United States, and no other country was willing to take them, so they remained in indefinite detention.

The case of the Uyghurs broadcast that Obama was unwilling to use the political capital needed to close Guantánamo—and such capital was truly needed if the goal was to succeed. After all, the plan had many opponents. The Department of Defense considered it indispensable to have a site where the government could detain people without rights, and many in the Department of Justice supported that position, even though the attorney general did not. Similarly, most legislators had no interest in bringing those held at Guantánamo to the United States. As the months and years went by, Obama focused on other priorities, such as passing the Affordable Care Act. Without a strong push from the White House and amid so much opposition, closing Guantánamo became a distant dream.

Obama finally put the nail in the coffin when he concluded that it was too dangerous to transfer some of the detained men to other countries but that they could not be legally prosecuted either. During Obama's eight years in office, his administration transferred, repatriated, or resettled 197 captives from Guantánamo. By the end of his tenure, forty-one Muslim men were still imprisoned there. Guantánamo remained a site where people could be incarcerated indefinitely without rights.

WHILE THE PUBLICITY THAT ELLEN HAD RECEIVED DURING HER INCARCERATION on Ellis Island had led policymakers to rethink the nation's detention practices and to support parole, the same was not true of Americans' response to the so-called enemy combatants held at Guantánamo. Newspaper articles, television shows, and radio programs all broadcast the treatment of Muslim men and boys at the detention camp. Citizens were forced to acknowledge the abuses enacted in the name of American values. And, on the whole, they supported them. In 2002, a Gallup survey revealed that 72 percent of Americans considered the treatment of those held at Guantánamo acceptable, and in 2016, 56 percent of Americans opposed closing the facility.

The new president was prepared to give these Americans what they so craved.

During the 2016 presidential campaign, Donald Trump vowed to keep Guantánamo open and even to increase its population. "We're gonna load it up with some bad dudes, believe me, we're gonna load it up," he said.

But as president, he would focus his energy on another set of people whom many Americans considered foreign enemies: immigrants and refugees. They, Trump would come to argue, belonged in prison. His administration would soon implement draconian measures to deter those hoping for a better life in America from crossing the border.

Part IV

WHERE WE ARE, WHERE WE'RE GOING

14

LAW AND TORTURE

Fernando Arredondo

JUNE 2018

Voices reverberated across the cold room as Fernando tossed and turned in his bunk bed. He had thought he could not fall lower than the Rio Grande Detention Center, yet here he was at the Stewart Detention Center, located in a place he had never heard of before: Lumpkin, Georgia.

A few days earlier, Immigration and Customs Enforcement (ICE) officers at the detention center in Texas had informed Fernando that they were going to transfer him, without providing any explanation. After he had spent two and a half weeks in that facility, the officers had put him and the other transferees in shackles, cuffing their legs and wrists as if they were dangerous. They placed the cuffs so tightly around Fernando's wrists that the restraints hurt, making it nearly impossible for him to eat the lunch they gave him.

If the Rio Grande Detention Center had seemed big, Stewart was monstrous. The hulking penitentiary, one of the most notorious for-profit prisons in the country, jolted Fernando as soon as he saw its scope. The infrastructure was no less forbidding, with its cold rooms, booming sounds, and artificial lights.

The lack of information and the stress of being separated from Andrea and not knowing what had happened to Cleivi and his other two daughters was starting to take a physical toll: Clumps of hair fell from his head in the shower. Then came the stomach pain, which persisted no matter what he ate. Then hives, which he desperately tried to hide, covered his body. Fernando knew that if he scratched himself in front of the guards, they might place him in solitary confinement to prevent contagion. Those thought to have dengue fever from mosquito bites were quarantined in "the hole": single cells, generally used for punishment, in which individuals had no contact with anyone. To hide the marks, Fernando borrowed a long-sleeved shirt from a fellow Central American detained at the facility.

ON JUNE 19, 2018, AS FERNANDO WAS TRYING TO CONCEAL HIS HIVES TO AVOID solitary confinement, another man detained at Stewart, Efraín Romero de la Rosa, was sent to the hole. Efraín, a Mexican migrant, was first apprehended in the United States in February 2018, charged with larceny, and sent to jail in Raleigh, North Carolina. ICE showed up to deport him, first sending him to Stewart. During his intake screening, a registered nurse reported that Efraín had schizophrenia and suffered from auditory hallucinations. This should have alerted the guards to be wary of sending Efraín to the hole, as it is well known that solitary confinement can exacerbate existing mental health conditions.

Stewart's guards nonetheless sent Efraín to the hole twice. The first time he was there for fifteen days. Six days after his release from solitary, he was placed on one-on-one suicide watch and then sent for a month to a mental health hospital because he insisted that "God was trying to kill him."

Upon his return to Stewart following his hospitalization, Efraín reported to a nurse that he believed he would "suffer three terrible deaths." Despite this report, as well as ICE's own detention standards, which classify schizophrenia as a special vulnerability, and the fact that he had just returned from a mental hospital, the correctional staff marked that he had no "Special Vulnerability." Six days after Efraín returned to Stewart, a social worker did note that he "met the criteria for serious mental illness." But that very evening at around 4:44 p.m., Efraín tried to touch a female correctional officer and was once again sent to the hole—this time for thirty days. He only lasted twenty-one.

At Stewart, solitary confinement consists of a small cell with a chrome toilet and sink, a seat, a table, and a bunk bed. Sometimes Efraín seemed like he was coping; other times he screamed that he was a prophet, or that he missed his family, or that he was the Antichrist. Dressed in a red jumpsuit, he would push against the cell door and weep.

On the night of July 10, Efraín constructed a noose out of his orange socks, attached it to his bunk bed, and hung himself.

This was not the first time that someone with mental health issues had died by suicide in the hole at Stewart. Only a year earlier, twenty-seven-year-old JeanCarlo Jimenez-Joseph, who had also been diagnosed with schizophrenia, killed himself after nineteen days in solitary confinement.

FERNANDO HAD TO TRY. THE ONLY PERSON WHO MIGHT BE ABLE TO GIVE HIM information about his family was Marleny, Cleivi's niece. The family's original plan had been to stay with her in Los Angeles until they got settled. But Fernando could not remember her phone number. He had written it on a piece of paper, but the officers at the Laredo station had thrown the scrap away. Since his detention, he had tried to remember it to no avail.

He knew the Los Angeles area code and remembered most of the numbers. But he wasn't sure about one of the digits and couldn't recall the order of the last four. He couldn't simply try all combinations, because dialing from the detention center was expensive, and he had no money. Whenever he could, he would borrow credit for a three-minute call from someone in his cellblock and try variations on the number.

One day, Fernando finally got it right. When he heard his wife's voice, he became so flooded with emotions that he found it hard to speak. "I am so glad you are safe," he managed to utter. "Are the girls with you? Do you know what happened to Andrea?"

"Yes. Alison and Keyli are with me, and I managed to get a social worker to bring Andrea with me too. She is here with me in Los Angeles and safe," Cleivi said.

Once their time elapsed, Fernando allowed himself to weep with relief.

Fernando spent two weeks at Stewart before officials informed him that they were transferring him again, this time to the Folkston Detention Center in Georgia, about four hours away. Transfer meant being placed in full chains once more. Being sent to a freezing room for a night while going through registration. Enduring another body search. Being separated from all the acquaintances he had made. Starting in a new place. It even made it harder to acquire a pro bono lawyer. These hardships meant nothing to ICE officials, who once again did not tell him why they were relocating him.

The three facilities where Fernando was detained were each run by for-profit corporations. The Rio Grande and Folkston Detention Centers were run by the GEO Group, one of the country's largest private, for-profit prison operators. The Stewart Detention Center—as well as the South Texas Family Residential Center, where Cleivi, Keyli, and Alison had been detained—was operated by CoreCivic, previously known as Corrections Corporation of America.

The use of private prisons had skyrocketed in the years since Corrections Corporation of America had launched the nation's first fully privatized prison in 1983, transforming an old motel into a three-hundred-bed facility in response to the Mariel boatlift. By 2018, the year Fernando was detained, approximately 8 percent of *all* people held in US state and federal prisons—118,400 individuals—were held in private prisons. This proportion was particularly stark when it came to immigration detention. In 2020, 81 percent of those in the custody of ICE, or 148,123 individuals, were held in privately owned or managed facilities. The corporations that ran these prisons made huge profits. In 2019, the GEO Group made $708 million in revenue from ICE detention contracts alone, while CoreCivic made $574 million. These amounts represented approximately 29 percent of each company's total revenue.

But private prisons were not alone in profiting from incarceration; public prisons and jails did so as well. With the dramatic growth of incarceration in the United States and the increasing overcapacity in most federal and state prisons, counties across the nation built new jails or expanded old ones to secure contracts from state and federal agencies, particularly from ICE. By incarcerating people, these counties hoped to make a profit. The profit motive did not end there. Counties regularly funded the construction and expansion of jails by issuing municipal bonds. The private holders of these bonds profited when individuals were locked up in the public jail.

Whether prisons are run by private companies or not, many of the services provided within them are handled by private contractors. Phone companies are the classic example. In 2016, a ten-minute long-distance call out of immigrant detention facilities in California cost $9.50, a prohibitive amount for most migrants, who were thus left incommunicado. For Cleivi to stay in touch with Fernando, she had to deposit money to Talton Communications, one of the largest telephone service providers for detention centers. Similarly, both private and public prisons have regularly outsourced health care, drug testing, food servicing, transportation, and other goods and services to for-profit companies.

Caging people like Fernando, Cleivi, Keyli, and Alison was, and continues to be, big business.

FERNANDO ENTERED THE SMALL OFFICE, FEARFUL AND EXCITED. THE DAY had finally come for his credible-fear interview. A monitor and a telephone sat atop a brown desk. Fernando held the handset tightly as he looked into a blank one-way monitor through which an asylum officer could see him. She first certified his details: Name. Date of birth. Nationality. It was clear that the officer could not speak or understand Spanish fully and that she was in a rush. She often interrupted him and didn't allow him to ask for clarification. The officer asked Fernando to explain why he had left his country. He told her about Marco, about how Keyli had witnessed the murder, about how gang members had followed and threatened his family after Marco's killing.

Once Fernando finished the story, the woman began to interrogate him, asking him information he had already provided, as if to corroborate it. "When did you say that happened? You said Marco was murdered in May?"

"No," Fernando answered, "I told you he was murdered in April."

"On April 16?"

"No, as I said, it was on April 28." That date was seared into his memory.

The officer asked him to repeat the names of the people involved and to once again describe how certain events had happened. Despite his trauma, Fernando told his story as cogently as he could, corroborating all the details he had provided earlier.

"Are you afraid of returning to your country?"

"Yes, of course," Fernando replied. "The gangs will try to kill me and my family once again."

After about an hour, the officer concluded the interview, telling him that he would be notified of the decision at a later date. Fernando left the room feeling good. He had proved that he needed to escape his country beyond doubt, he thought; his fear was credible. Now all he had to do was wait.

That night when he talked with Cleivi, she tried to reassure him that it would be okay. After all, her asylum officer had believed her. She had relayed the same story, and now she was out on parole.

Several days passed before the results came in: Fernando had failed his credible-fear interview. The government had decided that claims pertaining to domestic or gang violence no longer qualified for asylum.

Fernando held his breath. "What will happen now?" he asked an officer. "Is there anything I can do?"

Now he would be deported, the officer replied.

CLEIVI AND FERNANDO HAD ARRIVED AT THE SAME BORDER STATION ONLY A few days apart. They both asked for asylum by telling the same story about their son's murder. Only one was released into the United States and given the chance to ask for asylum; the other was to be deported. What made such a stark difference?

The distinct outcomes in Cleivi's and Fernando's cases highlight the arbitrariness of the immigration system.

First, inside the South Texas Family Residential Center, Cleivi had access to a pro bono lawyer who met with her regularly and explained which experiences were pertinent to tell the asylum officer and which were not. By contrast, Fernando, detained at the Rio Grande Detention Center, then at the Stewart Detention Center, and then at the Folkston Detention Center, had no access to legal counsel. He went into the interview not knowing what to expect.

In the United States, asylum seekers are not guaranteed access to a lawyer. Since most cannot afford one, they must resort to pro bono legal services. However, the organizations that provide such services have limited resources and are overstretched; they also tend to be concentrated in cities, while detention centers are generally located in demographically sparse areas. As a result, from 2014 onward, when Central Americans started fleeing their countries in greater numbers, over 20 percent of all asylum seekers have had no legal representation, even though counsel is vital to their success. Without legal representation, only one out of every ten asylum seekers wins their case; with legal counsel, nearly half do.

Cleivi also had a different experience during her interview because a translator was present and the interview took place in person. This allowed her to feel comfortable while telling her story. In contrast, Fernando only spoke on the phone to his interrogator while looking at a blank screen. He also had trouble communicating with the officer, who was not fluent in Spanish.

The timing of their detention also mattered. Although Cleivi and Fernando arrived at the border a few days apart, Cleivi had her credible-fear interview in May and received parole on June 1, 2018. At that time, Fernando was still languishing at the Stewart Detention Center. Fifteen days later, on June 15, he was sent to Folkston. In between these two dates, on June 11, 2018, Attorney General Jeff Sessions severely limited the availability of asylum for survivors of domestic and gang violence. This meant that Cleivi's asylum officer could consider having to escape gangs a reason to ask for asylum, while Fernando's officer could not.

Still, because of the government's murky actions, it is hard to know how much the timing mattered. Even before Sessions issued the new decision, agents were denying asylum to victims of domestic and gang violence. As one lawyer explained, "You know, [asylum officers] weren't like, 'Now we have a lawful basis to turn people around.' They were already doing it" before June 11.

But something even more troubling might have occurred to Fernando. Unlike Cleivi's files, which contain records and a transcript of her credible-fear interview, Fernando's files have no such documents. Even after the US district judge for the Southern District of California ordered the government to produce every document it had on Fernando's case, officials could not supply any proof substantiating that he ever had a credible-fear interview. While Fernando was told that he was undergoing a credible-fear interview during the phone call, attorneys who have since reviewed his case maintain that it is not clear that such an interview took place, much less that it was appropriately conducted.

After Fernando heard that he had failed the interview, he immediately asked an ICE agent if there was any way to appeal the decision. By law, asylum seekers who do not pass their credible-fear interviews have the right to request a review from an immigration judge. But the agent told Fernando that there was nothing he could do, as immigration judges always sided with ICE. "The U.S. government doesn't care; it doesn't care about your case or whatever you went through in your country," the agent told him. "There are thousands of cases like yours."

The agent handed Fernando a sheet of paper to sign. The form was in English and had no Spanish translation. It had two boxes: one with a "Yes," offering Fernando exactly what he had asked for—the opportunity to have the decision revisited—and one with a "No," indicating that he did not want his case reviewed by an immigration judge. Before signing the paper, Fernando had to tick one of the two boxes. He did not understand the form, but the agent told him that if he did not check the "No" box, he would be detained indefinitely and eventually deported.

ON JUNE 20, 2018, FIVE DAYS AFTER ICE TRANSFERRED FERNANDO TO THE Folkston Detention Center, President Trump issued an executive order to stop family separation, following huge demonstrations throughout the country. Most protesters claimed victory, but Lee Gelernt, the deputy director of the ACLU's Immigrants' Rights Project, knew better. He recognized that the new order did not address the fate of families who had already been separated and contained plenty of exceptions that allowed the government to continue taking children away from their parents.

Lee, a generous man with a receding hairline and a warm smile, had been fighting family separation before the Trump administration even announced its zero-tolerance policy. His first case was that of a Congolese woman, known in court papers as Ms. L. to preserve her privacy. Ms. L. had feared for her and her daughter's lives in the Democratic Republic of the Congo. They had fled the country with the help of the Catholic Church. The two traveled through ten countries over four months before legally presenting themselves at the port of entry near San Diego and requesting asylum. Immigration officials first detained mother and daughter together for four days, but then they seized Ms. L.'s daughter. Ms. L. heard her child screaming "Don't take me away from my mommy!" as they bore her away. The daughter was flown to Chicago and, like Andrea, placed in a facility for unaccompanied minors.

Upon hearing about her case, Lee filed a suit in support of Ms. L. in the district court in San Diego before Judge Dana Sabraw. On March 6, 2018, soon after the first hearing, ICE abruptly released Ms. L. and allowed her to pick up her daughter at the shelter in Chicago a few days later.

For Lee, this victory did not suffice. Hundreds of other children had also been separated from their parents. Three days later, he expanded the case to a national class-action suit, asking Judge Sabraw to issue an injunction to stop family separation and reunite children and parents who had already been separated. That June, three days after Trump issued the executive order to stop family separation, Lee told the judge in an emergency hearing, "At this point, you are the only one who can really stop the suffering of these little children." He classified the suffering of those who had already been separated as "a humanitarian crisis of the utmost proportions."

On June 26, 2018, Judge Sabraw stated that the government's practice "shocks the conscience" and granted a nationwide injunction ordering the government to reunite all children under five with their parents within fourteen days and all other children within thirty days.

At that point, Fernando was still behind bars at the Folkston Detention Center. Andrea had been released five days earlier and joined her mother and sisters in Los Angeles. Fernando had not heard of Judge Sabraw's order, but by its mandate, the government had to reunite him with Andrea within the next thirty days. Instead, two days later, Fernando was sent back to the Stewart Detention Center to await deportation.

The government had until July 26 to reunite all parents and children whom it had separated. This was a formidable task, as officials had not kept track of where they had sent each respective child and parent. To make matters worse, the government had already deported almost four hundred parents without their children. As a result, by the time July 26 came, the government had only reunited a little over half of the families.

On August 3, 2018, Judge Sabraw issued a follow-up order reiterating that the government must reunite the separated children from their parents. "The reality is that for every parent who is not located, there will be a permanently orphaned child, and that is 100 percent the responsibility of the administration," he stated.

The argument that the government could not track down some parents or children did not apply to Fernando and Andrea: the government knew exactly where each were. But officials did not reunite Fernando with his daughter by July 26, or even after August 3. Instead, two months after Judge Sabraw's first order and less than three weeks after his second one, the government deported Fernando to Guatemala.

Before sending him back, the guards returned his clothes and Andrea's small backpack—the items with which he had entered the US almost four months earlier. As he changed out of his prison garb, he noted how his old clothes hung loosely from his gaunt body.

For months behind bars, he had feared this very moment. Now the worst had happened, and Fernando felt a kind of relief.

15

INTERGENERATIONAL TRAUMA

Gerardo Mansur

1988–2020

Gerardo waited, tapping his left foot on the worn carpet. *Tap, tap, tap, tap*, an urgent bloodbeat. He thought he had learned something about patience in prison, but sitting on that small gray chair at the Las Vegas child welfare agency was excruciating. He hadn't seen his sons since his arrest four years earlier. Ulises had been two years old; Gerry was just a newborn. Not a day had passed since then that Gerardo didn't think about his children, and yet he knew almost nothing about them. How they looked, what they liked, how their personalities had developed. Nothing.

It was 1988, a few months after the rebellions at the Oakdale and Atlanta penitentiaries had ended, and the Department of Justice had agreed to review the case of each incarcerated Mariel Cuban on a fair and speedy basis. Probably because Gerardo's case had garnered so much media attention, government officials quickly approved his release. Still, to be set free, he—like all approved Mariel Cubans—needed an organization or person to assume responsibility for him. Gerardo wrote to

Father Alers, the priest at the Atlanta prison who had helped him find Julia and the children. Father Alers immediately offered support and, with that, the last barrier to Gerardo's freedom fell. Upon his release, Gerardo headed to Kissimmee, Florida, where the priest now lived.

While Gerardo was lucky to have befriended a person like Father Alers, not all Mariel Cubans knew someone who could sponsor them, and halfway houses were already full. By early February 1988, of the 1,300 individuals eligible for freedom, only 280 had been released; the rest had found no sponsors and remained behind bars. While they waited for spaces in halfway houses to become available, they underwent such terrible treatment in prison that they believed the guards were retaliating for the uprising. Years later, one man held at the penitentiary in Marion, Illinois, described the experience: "That was hell. Worse than anything I had ever lived through. We slept on the floor. We were not allowed outside. We were given cold meals day and night. The guards beat us up. It was as if they hated us for what we had done but also feared us for it. Because of this, they kept us in the worst and most isolated conditions. I heard of people being killed there." Another man imprisoned at Fort Leavenworth Penitentiary wrote to his lawyer that Atlanta was a "palace compared to the roughness" he was now experiencing. By the year's end, twenty-five hundred people, or approximately 60 percent of the thirty-eight hundred Cubans incarcerated during the protests, had been released. The others were declared threats to society and not offered parole.

When Gerardo arrived in Kissimmee, he found that Father Alers had lined up a dishwashing job for him at a restaurant. The priest had also arranged for Gerardo to live rent-free in an apartment owned by the church while he looked for a more permanent place to live. With this support, Gerardo was able to land on his feet, and Kissimmee ended up being the perfect place for him: nearby Disney World meant jobs were plentiful; the weather was hot and humid, like in Cuba; and there were Cubans everywhere.

A day after he arrived in Florida, Gerardo dressed in clothes the priest had given him and went to work. He was a free man. In the evening, he wanted to explore his new town, to walk its streets and feel the fresh air. But first he had to figure out how to get his children back and free Julia from prison. After he submitted much paperwork and showed the caseworker who visited his apartment that he was ready, Nevada's child welfare services agreed to return his boys to him. He could now pick up his children in Las Vegas whenever he wanted. The very next day, Gerardo flew to the city where he had begun his life in the United States.

The door of the child welfare agency opened, and two little boys walked through. If Gerardo had bumped into them on the street, he might not have recognized them. Ulises was six, and Gerry was four—so different from the toddler and newborn whom Gerardo had left behind. They could both walk and talk now, but their foster parents had only spoken English, so the children knew no Spanish. They were thin and tall. And then Gerardo saw what hurt him most: the boys were terrified.

For the next two days, Gerardo didn't let his sons leave his side. He told them everything he could about himself and their mother. Back home in Kissimmee, however, he had another problem. The children needed supervision while he was at work, but his job did not pay enough for childcare, in addition to everything else the little family needed.

The only solution came at a tremendous cost. For the next month, Gerardo woke up at 5:00 a.m., dressed the two boys, and dropped them off with a babysitter. He worked as a dishwasher until 3:00 p.m., then rushed to a second full-time job at a hotel, where he worked the four-to-midnight shift. By the time he picked up his children at the babysitter's house, they were both fast asleep.

Life was exhausting, but there was nothing else Gerardo could do. After several weeks of this, an immigration agent called the restaurant where Gerardo worked. They were freeing Julia. She would arrive at the Orlando airport the following day.

Gerardo spotted Julia as she came out of the terminal. He had not seen his wife in four years. The boys did not remember her. Her years in prison had profoundly changed her appearance. But none of that mattered at this moment. Julia saw her Gerardo. She saw her two babies. She ran to them with a long, inconsolable cry.

WITH JULIA HOME TAKING CARE OF THE BOYS, GERARDO QUIT HIS SECOND job and soon moved up from dishwasher to morning cook, doubling his pay. But he wanted more.

One day, he passed by a small hotel advertising a position for a mechanic who could fix air conditioners. Gerardo didn't have any relevant experience, but he applied for the job anyway. His buoyant confidence won him the position, and he soon made himself indispensable, disassembling the machines, studying their manuals, and memorizing their pieces. He painted a wall when painters failed to show up, fixed a drain that the owner told him was broken, and enlisted a friend to fix the building's erratic wiring. After he became certified as an air conditioner, pool, and Jacuzzi technician, the owner tripled his wages and made him the maintenance manager.

While Gerardo was moving up, Julia remained stuck. Unlike Gerardo, she could not compartmentalize all the things she had lived through. The trauma of the arrest and separation consumed her. For months after she arrived, her sons had trouble connecting with her and did not see her as their mother. She could hardly communicate with them because she had not learned English, and they knew little Spanish. It was devastating. These were her kids—they were supposed to know and trust her more than anyone else.

Over time, the boys became fluent in Spanish and grew more accustomed to living with their parents. Eventually, they went off to school, and Julia took a housekeeping job at a hotel. But she remained broken. As she later described: "I felt so strange. Like a zombie. Everything was so weird. . . . The kids gave me happiness, but I was doing poorly, so, so poorly." The pain felt almost physical.

At other times, she seethed with anger. "They treated us like dogs, like we aren't worth anything," she recalled. "They took them from me while I was still breastfeeding." For that, she never forgave America.

As the years passed, the gap between Julia and Gerardo grew. He was happy, successful, and adventurous. She was depressed and lethargic. He did not see her sadness and couldn't understand why she did not have more energy. He found adventure elsewhere, cheating on her with other women. When Julia found out, she cried and screamed. He promised he would never to do it again. But he did—multiple times. And so, almost a decade after they had left prison, she separated from him.

Ulises and Gerry, teenagers now, did not handle the separation well. After the trauma of being taken from their parents as children, the divorce hit hard. They lived with Julia, and Gerardo visited almost every day, but it did not help. They felt stranded and abandoned. To make matters worse, Julia constantly bad-mouthed Gerardo, telling the boys how she had suffered in prison and how he should have been faithful. She was so hurt—and wanted her kids to take her side so badly—that she stopped putting limits on them.

The boys began acting up and dropped out of school. They were furious at the world, and their only balm was stealing cigarettes from local stores or smoking marijuana. The police soon apprehended them. In a more caring and effective social system, their behavior would have been understood as a cry for help. They obviously needed to process their grief and trauma. But that was not the system in America. Instead of receiving mental health care in a warm and supportive atmosphere, they were dumped at the Manatee Regional Juvenile Detention Center, a medium- to low-security prison.

The trip behind bars did not prevent recidivism. A few months after their release, they were back in the system. After that, they were incarcerated again. And again. And again. Between the two of them, they were arrested more than a dozen times between 2000 and 2017 for charges such as armed burglary, possession of cocaine, and theft of a motor vehicle.

It is unsurprising that Gerry and Ulises found themselves in and out of prison from their early teens onward. Existing research shows that the children of parents who have been incarcerated are three to six times more likely to end up in prison themselves. Prison leads to prison, across generations.

This cycle damaged the whole family. Julia could neither bear seeing her beloved sons engage in such antisocial behavior nor imagine them in prison. She tried to subdue the pain with alcohol. Then with cocaine. Then with heroin. Eventually she lost her job.

Gerardo still cared deeply about Julia. At times he tried to reason with her; other times he would show up at her house screaming, ordering her to get back on track. Nothing worked until she hit rock bottom.

After losing her job, Julia wasn't able to pay rent and had to move in with some friends who had severe drug problems. When Gerardo heard about this, he drove to the house. "Pack up your stuff—I am going to take you to my house," he said. "At my place, I am going to treat you well. You are going to have your own room. The only thing is that if I ever catch you or believe that you are using something illegal in my house, I swear on the health of your own children that that is the last day you live with me."

At Gerardo's house, Julia recovered. Although she was still too weak to work, she quit using drugs and instead spent her days chatting with her new neighbors, cooking meals, and cleaning the house. She and Gerardo were no longer in love, but they still cared for each other. And they lived comfortably. Gerardo had recently opened his own company fixing pools and air conditioners and was making more than enough money.

In 2009, Gerardo met Irania Sori González. She was a sensual, smart, and kind Cuban woman who flirted and laughed her way through life. She and her daughter, Jennifer, had recently arrived in the United

States and would soon become permanent residents through the "wet foot, dry foot" policy, which at the time allowed any Cuban who touched American soil to pursue residency a year later. Irania had chosen to live in Kissimmee because it was calmer than Miami and close to Disney World, which she thought Jennifer would love.

Gerardo was immediately struck by Irania. He offered her work, promising to teach her how to fix air conditioners. She agreed. From then on, Gerardo did his best to seduce her. He brought her flowers, fixed anything that broke in her apartment, and regularly took her and Jennifer out. He even shaved his head after Irania teased that his receding hairline made him look eighty years old. It took almost a year, but one day Irania realized that she, too, was in love. She kissed him. Gerardo responded by asking her to move in with him and Julia, which she did.

Life in Gerardo's house was delightful. "I never had a bad moment with him," Irania recalled years later. She was never jealous or resentful of Julia for her past with Gerardo or for living in the house. On the contrary, the two of them truly liked and cherished each other. For her part, Jennifer soon saw Gerardo as a father and Julia as an aunt. In 2012, Irania and Gerardo married. That same year, they had a beautiful baby girl: Aisha.

Between a growing household and Gerardo's thriving business, the family bought a new house. It was massive, modern, and even had its own pool. For the first five years of her life, Aisha knew nothing of the horrors of family separation that Gerry and Ulises had lived through. She was so attached to Gerardo, and he to her, that everyone called her "Daddy's girl."

IT WAS 5:30 A.M. ON JANUARY 6, 2017, AND SOMEONE WAS KNOCKING SO HARD on the front door that Jennifer thought they might bust it down. Rushing past the dining table, where wrapped presents with colorful bows lay on that Three Kings Day morning, she peeked through a window to see about eight armed, uniformed men with flashlights.

"What do you need?" she asked through the door, thinking they were police officers.

"I need to speak to the person that owns the vehicle parked outside," one of them replied. "We just need to ask a couple of questions."

Gerardo came out of his room, still in boxers.

"What do you need?" he asked sleepily through the door.

One of the men informed him that they were ICE agents.

"What's happening?" a terrified Irania yelled as she came into the living room.

Gerardo's stomach tightened. It was as if his past were a relentless hunter, pursuing him even now, even here. He could not endure being detained once more. He needed to escape. He turned around and headed quickly toward the back of the house, where he could leave through the patio. Jennifer stopped him. She had seen agents on that side of the house as well.

The banging on the door grew louder.

"Do you have a search warrant?" Gerardo hollered. He knew that he did not have to open the door otherwise.

"We just want to talk to you. If you don't come out and talk to us, you are going to give us no choice but to come in."

"You guys don't have a warrant. Let me see the warrant. Slip it under the door," he said.

Now the commotion woke Julia. The last time Gerardo was arrested, she had started crying and had been identified as someone who should also be held. This time, she would not make the same mistake. She hid in her room.

"We have a warrant," one of the agents eventually said, pushing a piece of paper through the crack underneath the door.

Gerardo picked it up. It was a handwritten note that said he should come out. "This is a lie. This is not a warrant, so I am not going to open the door," Gerardo yelled.

Irania looked through the windows in a panic. So many men. So many lights. "It was as if they were looking for Osama bin Laden," she later described. All she could do was weep and holler.

Gerardo prepared himself a cup of coffee. He couldn't stand seeing Jennifer and Irania like this, so he hugged them and opened the door.

He was immediately handcuffed and shoved into the back of a vehicle.

Neither he nor his family understood how this could be happening. He was a successful man who had built a legal business, owned a house, paid taxes, and even donated money to organizations—including to the local police department. Why had they come after him?

Gerardo was being arrested—once again—because of that single ounce of marijuana that police officers had found in his house more than thirty-three years earlier. The same crime for which he had been given probation and ended up losing years to prison.

In 1984, while Gerardo was still at USP Atlanta, the Cuban government had agreed to take back 2,746 Mariel Cubans who had criminal convictions. Out of those, the US government had deported 2,022; another 246 had died, and 478 were considered too old or sick to be returned. Since no one else could be sent back, the list ceased to matter. But on January 12, 2017, six days after Gerardo's arrest, the Obama administration issued a joint statement with the Cuban government that said the US could replace people from the original list of 2,746 with other Mariel Cubans who had broken the law.

With this agreement, the US government went after Mariel Cubans who had been detained. Most were impossible to find. Many were homeless; some had died, while others had changed their names and created new identities. But because of Gerardo's success, authorities could easily locate him. He had a house, a telephone number, a car, and a business all in his name. He had done everything legally, never expecting to be punished again.

The authorities took Gerardo to the Krome Service Processing Center in Miami, where he was held for the next four months. Inside this facility, memories of Atlanta came flooding back: the beatings, the lockdown, the poor food, the years of waiting without knowing about his children or when he would get out. All he could do was cry and plead to see his daughter.

One day, a friendly Cuban immigration officer pulled him aside and warned him: "Look, I can't tell you anything, but if you have a good lawyer, get him, because you are on the list of the excludable folks who are to be sent to Cuba."

Through friends in Miami, Irania hired an expensive lawyer and tried to reassure Gerardo. But she was falling apart.

There were also money problems. Even though Irania never questioned paying for the best lawyer she could find, she could not afford it. Without Gerardo's income, she had to pay the mortgage on the house and the payments on the luxury car—a BMW that Gerardo had bought before his arrest—by herself. She dug into their savings. She sold all her jewelry, including her engagement ring. She went back to work for the first time since Aisha was born. Every morning before dawn, she stood alongside other day workers outside a Home Depot, hoping to get hired carrying furniture for customers. She developed a hernia but had to continue working through it. She was now the sole provider for the family.

Despite her efforts, Irania fell behind on the mortgage. Gerardo had only been able to afford it because his business had been doing so well—there was no way for Irania, alone, to make as much money as he could.

Irania, Julia, and the two girls were evicted on Aisha's birthday. Irania bought her a cake with the little money she had left, and they ate it using the car's trunk as a table. It was the very car in which they would sleep for the next few weeks. They were homeless but owned a BMW. It made no sense. Irania continued going to the Home Depot every morning and finally accumulated enough money to rent a small apartment in Kissimmee. It was dirty and full of cockroaches, but at least they had a roof over their heads.

Even through this torment, Irania visited Gerardo at Krome every other week. She brought Jennifer and Aisha the first few times but quickly realized that it was too hard for the girls, so she would visit Gerardo by herself.

One day, however, Irania arrived at Krome only to find out that Gerardo was not there. No one seemed to know where he had gone. She should call the facility's phone number to find out more information, an officer told her. During the next few days, she spent hours on the phone but always got the same answer: "No, he is not here anymore; we don't know where he was taken."

About a week later, Irania received word from a friend of Gerardo's that he had been deported. She couldn't believe that she was hearing about his deportation days after it had happened—and from another detained Cuban rather than an official source or their expensive lawyer.

Gerardo had been just as surprised. One day, after having been imprisoned for almost five months, he was informed by an immigration officer that he was going to be transferred to a prison in Louisiana that night, together with a few other Cubans. None of them doubted the line they were fed about the transfer. None protested. They all marched willingly onto the plane, where they were then told that they were headed to Cuba. At the last moment before takeoff, the agents pulled one of the men from the plane—it was this very man who informed Irania that Gerardo had been deported.

EVEN IN CUBA, GERARDO AND THE OTHER DEPORTEES WERE NOT FREE. AS soon as they disembarked in Havana, officials drove them to El Combinado del Este, Cuba's maximum-security prison.

Gerardo was once again surrounded by watchtowers and layers of barbed wire. Migration had connected the American and Cuban prison systems: some Mariel Cubans had gone directly from Cuba's penitentiaries to America's and then back to Cuba's.

Gerardo was locked in a cramped and unbearably hot cell, bewildered that he had been deported and was now back in Cuba. And yet here he was. Every day, Cuban officials pulled him out of his cell to interview him, probably to ensure that he was not a spy. They also tested him for all sorts of communicable diseases. After about a month, they released him onto the streets.

Gerardo had no money. No job. Nowhere to live. The family members he had left in Cuba took him in for short periods. He shuttled from house to house until he was able to find a few odd jobs and rent a small room. He couldn't afford much food, and in his first year back, he lost over thirty pounds, even though he was never a heavy man. After having worked all his life in the United States, he had always expected to spend his retirement in comfort. But all the money he had made was gone, and he had no way to claim the Social Security benefits owed to him.

All he could think about was returning to the United States or at least moving to northern Mexico, where Irania, Aisha, and Jennifer could come visit.

It would remain a dream. Gerardo had risen with tremendous vitality every time life had knocked him down, but he could not recover from this final injustice. In 2018, he was diagnosed with cancer, and although he had access to doctors, he could not afford the medicine he needed.

On September 7, 2020, he passed away, far from his loved ones and everything he had built in America.

16

DREAMS DEFERRED

Fernando Arredondo

2019

After being deported, Fernando could not return to Peronia, the place where he had grown up and then raised his children. It was too dangerous. A relative of his closest friend who lived far from his old community rented him a room. No one knew he was there. No one could find him. He regularly changed jobs, going from sewing shoes in a small workshop inside someone's home, to working in a factory, to driving an ice cream truck. Every time a motorcycle went by, he jumped with fear. He longed to visit Marco's grave but was too scared of bumping into a gang member who might recognize him.

His life lacked meaning. He could not see any of his old friends, and he missed his family terribly. There was seemingly no end to his situation: he could not return to America, and his family should not return to Guatemala. He only looked forward to his daily video calls with Cleivi and the girls. Through his phone, he could play games with his youngest daughter, counsel Andrea and Keyli about the importance of doing well in school and helping their mother, and tell Cleivi how much he loved and missed her.

Cleivi was not having an easy time either. She and her daughters were still staying with her niece Marleny. Cleivi could not work until her asylum case had been pending for six months. When it became legal, she worked nights so that she could care for her daughters during the day. She was always exhausted, but they needed money. There was also the trauma. She had never processed her son's murder, her family's escape from Guatemala, her daughter's forceful separation from Fernando while in detention, her husband's deportation. As Cleivi described, "I felt like I couldn't do it anymore; I just couldn't."

One evening, Marleny had news: "A lawyer called me today. She said she wanted to talk to you because she wants to take up your case and help you for free if you are interested. She said she heard about your case through Andrea, because she was one of the kids who was separated from their parents."

Cleivi agreed, but she wasn't optimistic. She felt lost in the system.

The lawyer was Linda Dakin-Grimm, a pious and successful Catholic lawyer who had represented dozens of unaccompanied migrant children since 2014. She had learned of Andrea's case through Kids in Need of Defense—the leading organization protecting unaccompanied children entering the United States—and although Andrea had entered with her father, she had been classified as an "unaccompanied minor."

It did not take long for Linda to realize that Cleivi and the girls needed more than legal aid. They were clearly falling apart. Linda reached out to her large Catholic network. The Archdiocese of Los Angeles helped Cleivi find a place to live; a donor subsidized her rent; well-meaning citizens showered her and the girls with so much furniture, clothing, and household supplies that they were able to sell extra items at a yard sale.

In the meantime, Linda threw herself into the case's legal work. With the help of translators, she interviewed Fernando over the phone for hours and regularly spoke with Cleivi at her office in Los Angeles. She filed paperwork and got declarations from all of them.

Linda was hopeful that Cleivi and the girls would get asylum, but bringing Fernando back seemed almost impossible, even though the government had disobeyed Judge Sabraw's orders by deporting him. After all, Trump was still president, and his government remained extremely anti-immigrant. But Linda was ready to fight. As long as any avenues of possibility existed, she would do everything she could.

And there was a glimmer of hope. The ACLU had reached an agreement with the government by which parents who had already been deported without their children could return to the United States to pursue their claims to asylum if they had "rare and unusual" cases.

Linda reached out to Lee Gelernt, the head of the ACLU's Immigrants' Rights Project. He in turn connected her with other lawyers representing deported migrants who had experienced family separation. Together, this group came up with a list of individuals who had been deported under "rare and unusual" conditions. On July 12, 2019, the ACLU issued a motion demanding that the government allow twenty-one of the nearly five hundred parents who had been deported without their children back to the United States to seek asylum. Fernando was among them.

Cleivi heard the news in early September: Judge Sabraw had ruled that eleven parents could return to the country to reunite with their children and pursue their asylum cases. Fernando was among them. So was David Xol-Cholom, the father who had been separated from his then eight-year-old son, Byron. Their deportation, the court ruled, had been unlawful.

TO FERNANDO, THE FLIGHT BACK TO LOS ANGELES SEEMED AT ONCE SHORT and eternal. "It was only five hours from Guatemala. Five hours and that was it. The restlessness I felt. I was dying to get there immediately," he recalled.

As he and the other parents flew north, their family members headed to the airport to receive them. They had all been looking forward to this day for weeks. Some knew to be cautious, however. Holly Sewell, who was fostering Byron, feared that when David and the others arrived at the airport, ICE officers would take them away again—perhaps even in front of their children. She was not alone in this fear: the returnees' lawyers believed that this was a distinct possibility.

Once at the airport, Byron waited anxiously with Holly for his father to come out. He had brought with him David's belt and wallet, which officers had given to him after his father was taken away. To make his dad proud, Byron had filled the wallet with money, some of which he had made selling lemonade.

Next to Byron and Holly stood Keyli, Andrea, and Alison, who by then were seventeen, thirteen, and seven years old. They held a handmade blue poster that said "Welcome, Daddy" and a yellow one that read "Te Extrañamos" (We Miss You). Some of the other separated children were also at the airport, but not all: some remained in government custody.

The plane landed. Andrea had not seen Fernando since the day the official ripped her from his arms almost two years earlier. The same was true for Byron and the other children. They all shook with tension. As the minutes ticked by, Holly explained to Byron that his father needed to pass through immigration before being allowed in. They waited some more. Byron's stomach hurt from anxiety.

Then cheers erupted when the crowd spotted the parents making their way toward their children.

"Oh my God," Holly said when she saw David rushing toward them. When he reached his son, David dropped to one knee crying and held Byron as tightly as he could, not letting him go for minutes. The nine-year-old boy he had been forced to leave behind had grown taller over the past two years.

Like David, as soon as he saw his family, Fernando ran toward them. He hugged his three daughters first and then added Cleivi into the embrace. This was the moment he had prayed for. Reuniting with them felt "like a miracle." Now all he wanted was to spend time with his family, to "be with them, hug them, and kiss them." Alison cried inconsolably, relieved to see her father, clinging to him as if she would never let him go again.

"That was the last worst day of my life . . . or better said, the last worst day that ended and the best one that began," Fernando still says.

This was a new beginning. Now he and his family were finally in a place where they could all be safe. He had entered the United States, and the whole family would have a chance at an asylum hearing. No matter what happened, they were together now.

EPILOGUE

FREEDOM

Almost absolute silence on the issue. Silence outside the White House. Silence in Huntsville, Alabama, and in Columbus, Ohio. Silence in San Francisco, in Los Angeles, in New York City, in Atlanta, in Chicago. Silence in Bedminster, New Jersey, in Marquette, Michigan, in El Paso, Texas, in Salt Lake City, Utah. Almost no word about it in *The New York Times* and *The Washington Post*, or on CNN, Fox News, and MSNBC. Clearly, immigrant detention is not on people's radar.

What a contrast with June 2018, when on the last Saturday of the month, thousands of Americans in those towns and cities, as well as in hundreds of others, took to the streets to oppose President Trump's zero-tolerance policy. Demonstrators held large, colorful banners and chanted: "Families belong together" and "When children are under attack, what do we do? Stand up, fight back!"

Ironically, the protests' focus on family separation rather than on immigrant detention ensured the movement's quick death and failed to put an end to the separation of families or to the other abuses ingrained in the detention system. This trajectory was not obvious from the start.

At first, it seemed like the demonstrations had succeeded: they put enough pressure on the administration that President Trump signed an executive order to end family separation in detention, except in cases where the parent represented a risk to the child. Protesters immediately declared victory, and most Americans turned their attention elsewhere. Unbeknownst to them, however, the brutality of detention—including the practice of separating families—continued. As this book has shown, immigrant detention regularly rips parents away from their children, even when an intentional policy of family separation is absent. This is what occurred, for example, with many of those detained on Angel Island, as well as with Gerardo and his sons.

So, too, continued the separation of children from their parents even after Trump's executive order took effect. In November 2018, it came out that immigration officials were once again separating immigrant families at the border. The administration did so by alleging that the parents had committed some form of wrongdoing, such as crossing the border illegally, which made them unfit to take care of their children. This time, Americans barely protested.

A month later, in December 2018, the Trump administration introduced another measure that would ultimately lead to family separation: offshoring immigrant detention to Mexico. Under the Migrant Protection Protocols, best known as the Remain in Mexico policy, immigration officials could send non-Mexican asylum seekers to wait in northern Mexico while their claims to asylum were being adjudicated in US immigration courts. This policy was, in effect, a modified version of the strategy employed by previous administrations of detaining refugees at sites outside the country. In the past, the US government had held Haitian and Cuban nationals at the naval base on Guantánamo Bay, where it was responsible for them. Under Trump's policy, the Mexican government became responsible for the asylum seekers whom the United States sent south of the border. It only accepted this measure because Trump threatened to impose a tariff of up to 25 percent on all Mexican imports if Mexico did not cooperate.

While Central Americans waited in northern Mexico for their asylum cases to be adjudicated, they lived in makeshift tent camps where physical and sexual abuse, extortion, and murder were regular occurrences. But there was nothing they could do; they were trapped there. Returning to their home countries would have placed them at even greater risk, and most had nowhere else to go. They were effectively detained in the migrant encampments.

The Remain in Mexico policy also failed to capture Americans' attention, even though it, too, promoted the separation of parents from their children. Because unaccompanied minors were exempt from Trump's policy and could live in the United States during the duration of their asylum cases, parents sometimes made the heart-wrenching decision of sending their kids across the border by themselves to save them from having to live in the dangerous encampments of northern Mexico. Alexis Martinez, a Honduran man who sent his two children across the Gateway International Bridge into Texas to ask for asylum by themselves, explained: "These tents are not good for children because the cold goes right through them." He added: "Sometimes you do things not because you're a bad father, but because you want what's good for them, and you don't want to see them suffer." From October 1, 2019, to January 13, 2020, the US Department of Health and Human Services identified 350 children who had been sent alone to the United States while their families remained in northern Mexico.

Following the breakout of the COVID-19 pandemic, the Trump administration introduced an even more draconian measure against refugees. It ordered immigration authorities to expel most asylum seekers from El Salvador, Guatemala, Honduras, and Mexico without even allowing them to apply for asylum. It did so by invoking a little-known public health law from 1944 known as Title 42, which allows US officials to prevent migration when "there is serious danger of the introduction of [a communicable] disease into the United States."

Immigrant advocates hoped that Joe Biden's electoral victory would put an end to Trump's policies, but the changes they hoped for came slowly, if at all. While Biden suspended the Remain in Mexico policy on his first day in office, a federal judge in Texas managed to block its termination until the summer of 2022. And Biden did not seem much interested in ending Title 42. At first, his administration simply modified it so that children were exempt from expulsion. For refugee parents, this meant that they once again had to decide whether to send their children across the border by themselves to claim asylum or keep them living in dangerous conditions in Mexico.

Together, the Remain in Mexico policy and Title 42 came to constitute a new family separation practice. As Holly Sewell, who fostered Byron after he was separated from his father while in detention, said, "The separations are still happening [under President Biden]. They're just happening on the other side of the Mexican border." Parents, she said, send their children to the United States alone, believing that it is their best chance at a good life.

When Title 42 expired after the public health emergency order for COVID-19 was lifted, the situation at the border made some headlines. Fear that ending the pandemic-era policy "would set off a stampede from Mexico" was widespread. The Biden administration addressed this concern by announcing that it would penalize asylum seekers who didn't apply for protection in the countries through which they passed on their way to the United States unless they met a narrow set of exceptions or signed up for an appointment at an official port of entry using a mobile app called CBP One. The app opened up a thousand appointment slots each day and distributed them using a semirandom algorithm. Its effects thus mirrored those of the Remain in Mexico policy: asylum seekers still had to wait in refugee camps in northern Mexico while rolling the dice for an appointment that may never come. The offshoring of detention would continue unabated.

So would detention in the United States proper, with all its concomitant abuses. When Biden took office in January 2021, there were, on average, fifteen thousand migrants detained each day. That number was particularly low because Title 42 and the Remain in Mexico policy had kept asylum seekers out of the country. But detention rates quickly began to rise once more. By July 2023, ICE was detaining an average of thirty thousand people per day. The use of for-profit detention centers also grew during this period. At the start of the Biden administration, 81 percent of migrants were detained in such facilities; by July 2023, over 90 percent of people in ICE custody were being caged in private prisons.

Neglect and mistreatment also remained widespread well after Trump left office. On March 16, 2022, the inspector general from the Department of Homeland Security issued an alert calling for all migrants to be removed from the Torrance County Detention Facility in Estancia, New Mexico, because of safety issues. ICE refused to do so, and an immigrant from Brazil died a few months later. In a facility run by GEO, a man was denied medical care despite repeated pleas and then died after suffering a heart attack. The staff at a detention center in Florida engaged in sexual voyeurism, punished women by denying them sanitary napkins, and denied migrants medical assistance. The list goes on.

SINCE ITS INCEPTION, IMMIGRANT DETENTION HAS BEEN AN AFFRONT TO basic ideals of justice and compassion.

Between the end of the nineteenth century and the mid-1950s, detention was conceived as a means of enforcing the nation's exclusionary laws. The government caged foreigners while it determined whether they had the right to enter the country or not. During those years, the purpose of detention was not to hurt migrants, but the system nonetheless did. On Ellis Island, in the Pacific Mail's detention shed, on Angel Island, and in other such holding areas, "entrants" were incarcerated without knowing why or when they would be released. They were held in conditions so terrible that many died by suicide. Guards regularly beat them. Detained migrants lived in a world where spending time outside was rare, windows were barred, and quarters were overcrowded. At these sites, children were often separated from their parents and guardians.

After the Mariel boatlift of 1980, the Reagan administration changed course and came to explicitly conceive of detention as a means of deterrence. The more harshly that those detained were treated, government officials came to believe, the more effective detention would be at dissuading other individuals from immigrating. During this period, family separation was not used intentionally as a means of discouraging other migrants from attempting the journey, but it still occurred frequently.

Abuse and dehumanization occurred no matter when, how, or why detention was used—they are intrinsic to the system. This is not surprising. After all, immigrant detention facilities were originally conceived in 1891 as spaces where the Constitution did not reign.

The United States was founded on the notion that people have "certain unalienable Rights, that among these are Life, Liberty, and the pursuit of Happiness." The Fifth Amendment echoed this assertion, stating that "no person" should "be deprived of life, liberty, or property, without due process of law." The amendment did not speak in terms of citizens but in terms of persons, and it was unambiguous: people deserved due process before being deprived of liberty. In 1798, Thomas Jefferson explicitly wrote: "Habeas Corpus secures every man here, alien or citizen, against everything which is not law."

Jefferson was clear on his point that foreigners deserved due process, but perhaps he and the other Founding Fathers should have been more specific about what they meant by the seemingly unequivocal term "here." After all, slightly over a century later, Congress passed a law by which those stopped at the border were not considered to be "here." As such, these "entrants" had no rights beyond those expressly provided by Congress and the executive branch and could not claim any additional protections under the Constitution's guarantee of due process.

Immigrant detention centers, where individuals can be incarcerated without rights or legal protections, are nothing less than legal black sites. They function as spaces outside the law, similar to Guantánamo, where foreign "enemy combatants" have been detained indefinitely without trials. This, too, is not surprising: Guantánamo first functioned as an immigrant detention facility.

The existence of unknown legal black sites and of a legal category of people who are rightless by design not only stands at odds with basic ethical norms but also endangers the freedoms of all American citizens. By constructing Guantánamo as an immigrant detention site where the Constitution was ignored and abuse was rampant, the government forged a path for the naval base to become a site of torture. Even Americans were at risk of being sent there, and indeed, a US citizen was held at the naval base for a short period of time.

Immigrant detention also helped shape the nation's prison system, which deeply affects the lives of millions of US citizens. Even though Americans make up only 5 percent of the global population, the United States holds 20 percent of the world's prison population. According to the ACLU, one out of every three Black boys born today in the United States can expect to end up in prison during his lifetime. So can one of every six Latino boys, and one of every seventeen white boys. The massive US prison system, which like the detention system is the largest in the world, has made millions of citizens less safe.

Beyond the dangers it poses to foreigners and citizens, immigrant detention has also slashed America's global standing and reputation. The detention of foreigners overlooks how US intervention abroad regularly fomented the migration of many of those individuals. It also exposes the hypocrisy of America's role in the world: officials regularly defend the US government's actions abroad by portraying other countries as violent, but when such actions lead people from those regions to migrate to America, the government subjects them to the violence of immigrant detention. As we have seen, the migrants snared in detention had previously contended with America's imperialist actions in China, which were buttressed by the belief that Chinese people were "barbaric"; with the government's refusal to accept Jewish refugees during the Holocaust because of antisemitic beliefs; with an embargo against Cuba and promises that all those escaping Castro's regime would be welcome; and with America's violent intervention in Central America to topple "unfriendly" regimes.

Beyond its incalculable human costs, its erosion of our principles, and its inherent danger to the nation and its citizens, detention is also financially costly. Throughout America's history, the federal government has spent vast sums to keep migrants behind bars. In the 2018 fiscal year, when Fernando and Andrea were detained, the country spent over $3 billion on immigrant detention. That money could have been used for myriad other purposes. That very year, the enacted budget of the Environmental Protection Agency was $8.8 billion—only three times more than the amount the government used to detain nearly four hundred thousand migrants among a nation of over three hundred million people. If those immigrants had been freed into the custody of their families and friends, that money could have been used to further protect the nation's water, reduce pollution, clean up toxic lands, and safeguard human health.

Detaining migrants is pointless. The human pain it causes is unnecessary. The money used is wasted. Immigrant detention has never been effective in its intended goal, whether that goal is exclusion or deterrence.

Even today, many Americans believe that detaining foreign arrivals while the government determines if they have a right to enter the country is an indispensable practice. Otherwise, the thinking goes, unauthorized migrants will abscond and vanish among the American populace. This logic resembles the government's reasoning for detaining arrivals before 1954. But hard evidence in both our nation's history and our present shows that this reasoning is fallacious. In the years between 1954 and 1980, US officials released most non-Mexican entrants on parole instead of imprisoning them, knowing that the vast majority of released migrants would not flee. The same was true for migrants whom the government freed during other periods, when detention was still official policy. Chi Hao, Ellen, and Gerardo were all released on parole at one point or another and, like other parolees, did not attempt to escape.

Similarly, current data suggests that most migrants released today appear in court when required, which means that there is no need to detain them. Multiple studies have shown that approximately 88 percent of all nondetained individuals attended their court hearings in the past two decades, including in recent years. That percentage rose to 98 percent among those with legal representation or among asylum seekers regardless of whether they had access to legal counsel or not.

Another myth is that detention protects Americans from dangerous immigrants. If anything, the history of immigrant detention shows that at any given period, the incarceration of entrants was guided more by America's particular hysterias at the time than by migrants' potential or actual actions. Chi Hao risked his life for Americans during the Boxer Uprising but migrated during a period when US citizens feared that Chinese men were taking jobs that belonged to Americans. His actions did not matter; only his race did. Ellen supported the war efforts against the Nazis and then worked for the US army in Germany, but she came to America during the Cold War and, like many individuals at that time, was suspected of being a spy. A different form of hysteria affected Gerardo. Like other Mariel Cubans, he was stereotyped as a dangerous criminal who could not be released from prison even though according to the judge his offense merited only probation. As for Fernando, he arrived soon after the Trump administration classified Central American refugees as "criminals" and "MS-13 members." Fernando did not break the law in any way but rather asked for asylum, as was his right. He was nonetheless imprisoned for months and then deported.

Immigrant detention does not make us safer.

Detention is also useless as a means of deterrence. It never stopped foreign nationals from coming to the United States. No matter how long migrants were detained or how cruel the system was, they kept coming, because the situations in their home countries were even more dire. Europeans knew that they would have to pass through Ellis Island, but that did not dissuade them from migrating. Before departing, Chinese migrants had heard that they would be detained. They still boarded the ships. Haitian refugees were aware that the US government would incarcerate them if the Coast Guard caught them, but migrating was a matter of life and death. Central American asylum seekers fled to the United States even after hearing that they would be detained in freezing rooms under dehumanizing conditions. Even Trump's draconian family separation policy, which was intended to curtail migration, failed in its goal: the year after it was introduced, apprehensions along the US-Mexico border were 88 percent higher than the year before. Migrants had continued to come.

THANKFULLY, AMERICA'S HISTORY NOT ONLY SHOWS THE COSTS, VIOLENCE, and futility inherent in detention but also provides us with potential alternatives and suggests how we might avoid certain pitfalls.

Martin Luther King Jr. once claimed that the long arc of history bends toward justice, but when it comes to immigrant detention, America has moved backward. As we saw, in the years between 1954 and 1980, US government officials rejected the notion that detention is the best way to handle new arrivals. In 1958, the Supreme Court said that this position reflected "the humane qualities of an enlightened civilization." For us to move toward justice today, we must first return to that more humane position. Rather than caging migrants and refugees, the government should simply release them and allow them to reside with friends, family, or community members in the United States while it examines their cases.

The experiences of the four main people in this book show that parole does not come without problems—but these can be jettisoned if we understand them. Ellen's and Chi Hao's stories point to the inequities created by forcing released migrants to pay bonds for their freedom. The Eighth Amendment holds that "excessive bail shall not be required," and yet entrants, like incarcerated Americans, have regularly been unable to afford their bonds. Chi Hao was only released because the Chinese consul paid for his freedom; Ellen, because her lawyer paid for half of hers. Most arriving migrants do not have such connections—and should not have to.

Chi Hao's story also demonstrates that the rules of parole cannot be too convoluted. After all, he and Hsiang Hsi inadvertently broke the terms of their release by taking a train that passed through Canada; they did not know that leaving the country was prohibited. Similarly, today's post-confinement regulations are so demanding that many immigrants—like many US citizens released from prisons—break them without being aware.

Strict release rules can also defeat one of the main objectives of parole: providing migrants with freedom. Chi Hao and Hsiang Hsi couldn't go to Oberlin as they wished. While on parole, Ellen was always reminded that she was "the very special prisoner of the Attorney General." She could not change residences without informing her lawyers or the Immigration Service. In recent years, alternatives to detention programs have grown dramatically and are having a similar effect. These programs are meant to keep watch over released migrants and ensure compliance with release conditions. They include home visits, telephonic monitoring, facial recognition check-ins through smartphone apps, and the use of electronic ankle bracelets with GPS monitoring. People subjected to these programs feel as if they are under constant surveillance and have difficulty participating fully in their communities. Ankle bracelets, for instance, limit users' freedom of movement, stigmatize them, and make it harder for them to obtain jobs. Notably, these alternatives to detention programs are managed by the same for-profit corporations that run the nation's main prisons. Profit remains the motive, and released migrants continue to be deprived of full liberty.

America's detention history also cautions us to be vigilant of how race and other perceived differences affect the parole system. Even in the years when US officials turned against immigration detention, they continued to hold Mexicans while they arranged for their departures to their home country. Similarly, in the 1980s and '90s, Cubans were much more likely to be paroled than Haitians, both because Cubans were perceived as whiter and because the US government wanted to show the world that Communism was failing.

Parole offers the most viable alternative to the costly, inhumane, and ineffective system of detention, at least until there is a complete overhaul of the nation's immigration laws. For it to be fair and successful, however, it should be implemented without discrimination and without forcing released individuals to post bond, follow strict or convoluted rules, or live under surveillance—all of which we know is unnecessary.

These changes might seem hard to implement, but the history embedded in this book also suggests a path forward: it is time to listen to and support the demands of those held behind bars and walls. The four primary figures in this book managed to leave their cages because they were heard. Chi Hao, Ellen, Gerardo, and Fernando were all featured prominently in the media. The nation was aware of their cases, which put pressure on the government to release them and, in Fernando's case, to bring him back after he was deported. National pressure not only saved individual lives; it sometimes helped change the system as a whole. Ellen's case provoked such an outpouring of anger against detention that, a few years later, the attorney general moved away from detention to parole. Though comparatively less visible, the protests at the Atlanta and Oakdale penitentiaries caused enough consternation that the government released the vast majority of detained Mariel Cubans. And the national opposition to the Trump administration's zero-tolerance policy pushed the president to end it, even as family separation continued in another form.

Pressure matters. It is time that we follow the demands of detained people and voice our opposition to the nation's immigrant detention system. Several organizations are already doing that effectively, as well as fighting for the rights of detained migrants, refugees, and asylum seekers. (A list of such groups can be found in the resource guide that follows.)

Americans turned against detention once before. We can do it again.

ACKNOWLEDGMENTS

"He belongs in our history books." Those were the words Fernando's lawyer said before introducing me to him. She was right.

Above all, I want to thank the four individuals around whom this book revolves: Fu Chi Hao, Ellen Knauff, Gerardo Mansur, and Fernando Arredondo. Through their respective memoirs, Chi Hao and Ellen left us with some of the only glimpses we have into the practice of detention during their respective lifetimes, while Gerardo and Fernando spent days telling me their stories. I cannot thank them enough for the time and vulnerability it took to do so.

It wasn't only Gerardo and Fernando who shared their experiences with me but also their family members: Julia Martínez, Irania Sori González, and Cleivi Jerez. Their stories, and those of their children, were just as critical for me to write this book. I also want to thank the more than one hundred individuals with whom I conducted oral history interviews, some of which lasted multiple hours. I do not name them here because most of them requested anonymity.

It is an understatement to say that this book would not exist without the help of my brilliant editor, Ibrahim Ahmad. He read the manuscript multiple times, in each instance making it immeasurably stronger. He paid attention to issues big and small and always replied to my neurotic emails and calls no matter the time of day. Ibrahim, I cannot thank you enough for all your support, vision, and hard work on this project.

The same is true of my audacious and gifted agent, Amelia Atlas. When the world shut down during the pandemic and colleagues retreated in search of safety, Molly became my principal interlocutor. As she guided me through the ordeal of writing a proposal, she helped me clarify my thoughts and sharpen my arguments. I cannot imagine a better team than Ibrahim and Amelia.

I owe a huge debt to Jill Lepore, who suggested I write this book in the first place and taught me the importance of narrative.

Multiple scholars read all or part of the manuscript and provided invaluable feedback. They include Madeline Hsu, Gordon Chang, Mary Lui, Lucy Salyer, Matt Sommer, Tom Mullaney, Jennifer Chacón, Jayashri Srikantiah, Gabriel "Jack" Chin, and Hiroshi Motomura. I also received exceptional comments from the members of the Johns Hopkins Department of History seminar and the Modern America Workshop at Princeton University. In addition, I received extremely detailed feedback from Alexis Richland and Jessica Ryan. I also want to thank my students, whose thoughtful discussions in class strongly influenced my thoughts and forced me to ask hard questions.

Special thanks to Oscar Blanco and John Ermer for their assistance with the oral histories I conducted in Miami. I also am indebted to Gary Leshaw, the lawyer who helped Mariel Cubans at the Atlanta penitentiary; Sally Sandidge, who led the Coalition to Support Cuban Detainees; and Linda Dakin-Grimm, Fernando's lawyer. The three of them allowed me to conduct long oral history interviews with them; Gary and Sally granted me access to dozens of boxes of documents; and Linda introduced me to Fernando in the first place and shared important legal documents on his and his family's case. I also want to note the importance of scholarly collaboration when it comes to finding sources. Much of this work was written at the height of the pandemic when archives were closed. Historian Lucy Salyer scanned and gave me access to the photocopies of documents she had gathered in the archives years earlier. Once the archives opened, I was able to supplement this information, alongside the many other interview subjects who generously shared their personal collections. I am grateful for all the help I received from archivists at the National Archives in Washington, DC, the Atlanta History Center, the Jimmy Carter Presidential Library, the Ronald Reagan Presidential Library, the Special Collections and University Archives at Florida International University, and the University of Miami Cuban Heritage Collection.

This work received indispensable support from the Andrew Carnegie Fellows Program, Stanford University's School of Humanity and Sciences, and the Impact Labs Design Fellowship at Stanford.

I am forever grateful for the scholarship and mentorship of my colleagues and friends, including Monica Muñoz Martinez, Kelly Lytle Hernández, Naomi Paik, Kristina Shull, Natalia Molina, Adam Goodman, George Sanchez, David Gutiérrez, Torrie Hester, Erika Lee, María Cristina García, Judith Irangika Dingatantrige Perera, Jessica Ordaz, Sara Julia Kozameh, Priya Satia, Allyson Hobbs, Laura Stokes, Jonathan Gienapp, Ada Ferrer, Julio Capó, Steve Pitti, Mae Ngai, and Elliott Young.

Researching and writing this book was emotionally hard. The horrors it addresses regularly pummeled me. Sanno Zack, I am profoundly grateful for your brilliant insights, consistency, availability, and, above all, for teaching me the most important life lessons. There are no words adequate for that. Tiffany, thank you for the meals, workouts, laughter, and trips. But how can I truly express my gratitude: you always laughed at me when I feared falling down the mountain's ledge during our hikes and yet, when I actually fell, you helped pull me up. SAM, when the pandemic drained my energy, you helped me write again. I am blessed to have such a wonderful chosen family: Tiffany, Priya ("my favorite"), Silas, SLAM, Rae, Kendra, Emily, Ana Paola, Azeret, Pamela, Lizzette, Eva, Ximena, Elana, Ilana, Laura, Allyson, Kate, Ruby, Molly, Max, Zoe, Adam, and Julio. Thanks also to everyone in AIDS/LifeCycle.

I feel fortunate for my family. My sisters, Tamara and Nadia, shed light on how to live life. Their daughters—Reneé, Sarah, Batia, and Natasha—are my biggest joy. Thank you, too, to Moisés and Jim, as well as to my New Zealand family: Helen, Ed, Peter, Rachel, Nick, Adria, Toakahu, Jess, Mike, Mackenzie, and Juno.

And, of course, my parents. Dad: thank you for teaching me how to laugh and be silly (con tus "chistosadas") and, above all, thank you for your constant support and encouragement, without which nothing would have been possible. Mom: you are my best friend, my inspiration, the meaning of home. You taught me what it means to fight for justice and when to raise my voice. More important, you showed me the meaning of love, and for you I have only the purest love.

More than anyone, I thank Melanie, who saw me write this book from beginning to end and supported me as I processed the injustice of the system and the terrible suffering of those caught in its tentacles. Thank you.

RESOURCE GUIDE

The following organizations are fighting to support detained migrants, refugees, and asylum seekers, and they welcome donations and other support.

Capital Area Immigrants' Rights (CAIR) Coalition

CAIR Coalition promotes justice for individuals at risk of detention and deportation through direct legal representation, know-your-rights presentations, impact litigation, advocacy, and the enlistment and training of attorneys to defend immigrants. The organization provides information, support, and legal representation to detained children and adults in the Washington, DC, area. CAIR Coalition also promotes the rights of detained immigrants nationwide through impact litigation.

Detention Watch Network

Detention Watch Network (DWN) is a national coalition building power through collective advocacy, grassroots organizing, and strategic communications to abolish immigration detention in the United States. DWN's core purpose is to bring together complementary strategies for a multipronged approach to ending detention, including organizing, advocacy, litigation, direct service, research, and communications. DWN provides a space for networking and information-sharing as well as for sharing analysis and expertise on shifting government policies.

The Florence Immigrant and Refugee Rights Project

FIRRP provides free legal services and trauma-informed social services to immigrants facing detention and potential deportation in Arizona. FIRRP's advocacy team works to protect the rights of adults and children in immigration detention and advance systemic change.

Freedom for Immigrants

Freedom for Immigrants is devoted to abolishing immigration detention while ending the isolation of people currently suffering in this profit-driven system. Freedom for Immigrants monitors the human rights abuses faced by immigrants detained by ICE through a national hotline and network of volunteer detention visitors while also modeling a community-based alternative to detention that welcomes immigrants into the social fabric of the United States. Through these windows into the system, Freedom for Immigrants gathers data and stories to combat injustice at the individual level and push systemic change.

Mijente

Mijente is a Latinx- and Chicanx-led political organization working campaigns, building networks, and functioning as a hub for culture, education, and advocacy on racial, economic, gender, and climate justice issues. Mijente's work has involved investigating the inner workings of ICE's operations amid ongoing threats of mass deportation raids and bringing to light ICE's tactics to target and expel migrants from their communities. Mijente has also brought attention to the relationship between data broker companies and ICE, leading to a surge in organizing, lawsuits, and investor actions against Thomson Reuters, RELX, and other technology companies that support immigration enforcement.

National Bail Fund Network

The National Bail Fund Network is made up of over ninety community bail and bond funds across the country that regularly pay bail/bond within the immigration detention system for community members. The community bail and bond funds that are part of the network are dedicated to being an organizing tool aimed at ending pretrial and immigration detention.

National Immigrant Justice Center

The National Immigrant Justice Center (NIJC) combines individual client advocacy with broad-based systemic change through legal services, policy reform, impact litigation, and public education. NIJC provides legal representation and consultations to more than ten thousand low-income immigrants, refugees, and asylum seekers each year. NIJC works to expose system-wide deficiencies in the immigration detention system and end the use of immigration detention. Recent campaigns focus on reducing excessive funding to immigration enforcement and detention operations and promoting accountability for ICE's pervasive mistreatment of detained people with mental illness.

National Immigration Project

The National Immigration Project is a membership organization of attorneys, advocates, and community members who are driven by the belief that all people should be treated with dignity, live freely, and flourish. Through litigation, advocacy, and education campaigns, the organization aims to ensure that those who bear the brunt of racist criminal and immigration systems are uplifted and supported. NIP's litigation and policy campaigns include ending policies that criminalize immigration and promoting accountability for medical abuse in ICE detention.

Northwest Immigrant Rights Project

Northwest Immigrant Rights Project defends and advances the rights of immigrants through direct legal services, systemic advocacy, and community education. The organization's work centers on ending immigration detention and expanding access to legal representation. Their work spans diverse and challenging cases, representing recent arrivals and long-term residents. They assist survivors of domestic violence, trafficking, and torture, along with individuals with criminal convictions.

Project South

Project South monitors and exposes human rights violations in immigration detention centers with the goal of ending immigration detention. The organization conducts interviews in Georgia ICE detention centers, publishes reports, and engages in legal action to expose abuses and support advocacy efforts at international and national levels.

RAICES

RAICES provides free and low-cost legal services to underserved immigrant children, families, and refugees. RAICES promotes justice for immigrants and refugees through legal services, social programs, bond assistance, and advocacy initiatives focused on changing the narrative around immigration in the United States.

South Texas Pro Bono Asylum Representation Project (ProBAR)

ProBAR supports immigrants through legal education, representation, and connections to services. ProBAR serves immigrants in the Rio Grande Valley border region with a particular focus on the legal needs of adults and unaccompanied children in federal custody. ProBAR provided legal services to more than thirty-one thousand people during 2022.

NOTES ON SOURCES

I come from a family of migrants and refugees. I have studied immigration history for over two decades. And yet, when the Trump administration introduced its zero-tolerance policy, I was horrified. How had we arrived at a point where ripping children from their parents was official government policy? Equally important, what did this tell us about America? This book answers these questions by telling the story of those held in the federal immigrant detention system from its late-nineteenth-century inception to the present. It traces how policies and procedures evolved, shows the emotional and physical costs of detention, and, above all, reveals the interior lives and motivations of those held behind bars.

To tell the political, legal, and social history of detention while covering a span of nearly 150 years, I had to use a wide variety of sources. I also had to make difficult decisions about what stories to tell in order to document the experiences not just of the individuals I was to follow but of all migrants who have been incarcerated without access to basic rights. Here, I offer a brief description of the sources I used and the choices I made.

It was the summer of 2019, and I had gone to Havana, Cuba, to conduct an oral history interview with Gerardo Mansur, who had already been deported from the United States. We spent seven days together, beginning each morning with an early breakfast and continuing through dinner, talking about his life from his childhood to the present. I took notes on all these conversations, going through the most important parts of his story multiple times, and recorded over fifteen hours of a more traditional oral history.

Through these in-depth conversations and interviews, I learned new details about events that transpired in the detention facilities where Gerardo was held, but even more important, I became witness to his most intimate feelings, worries, joys, and ambitions. I grasped how he had experienced life behind bars, how he understood the injustice of his detention, and how he dealt—both emotionally and practically—with the effects that it had on him, Julia, their children, Irania, and his daughter with her.

I also spent a week in Kissimmee, Florida, talking with Julia and Irania, hearing about their lives and experiences through hours-long interviews and conversations. Similarly, I conducted oral histories with nearly a dozen other Mariel Cubans who had been held in the Atlanta or Oakdale penitentiaries and interviewed over a hundred other Mariel Cubans who had been released on parole soon after they arrived. I also conducted oral history interviews with Gary Leshaw, the lawyer who defended Mariel Cubans at the Atlanta penitentiary, and with Sally Sandidge, who coordinated the Coalition to Support Cuban Detainees. They both allowed me to review the dozens of boxes of documents they had kept.

It was hard to find Mariel Cubans who had been incarcerated in Atlanta or Oakdale. Many of them were traumatized by their time behind bars; upon their release, some lived on the streets or developed severe mental health conditions. Some had died; others had changed their names, seeking to leave their past behind. For the most part, I met those I interviewed by spending time in Domino Park, a place in Miami where hundreds of Cubans—many of whom arrived in the Mariel boatlift—gather every day, especially on weekends. At first people were scared to talk with me: not only do Mariel Cubans as a group have an ill reputation within the Cuban American community, but those gathered at the park knew that the government was deporting Cubans who had been detained in the 1980s. As the weeks went by, however, people came to trust me and introduced me to their friends who had been imprisoned.

I originally learned about Gerardo through newspaper articles that had been published about him and Julia, through the letters he had sent to Sally

Sandidge, and through internal documents of the Coalition to Support Cuban Detainees. By the time I was able to track him down, he had already been deported. As such, I met and interviewed Irania and Julia before heading to Cuba.

Focusing on Gerado's experience, rather than on those of the other Mariel Cubans whose stories I learned, was a hard choice, and I was well aware of the costs of this decision. Gerardo was a straight, cisgender, and white-appearing man, even though gay, gender-nonconforming, and Black individuals had arrived in disproportionately large numbers during the Mariel boatlift. Focusing on Gerardo could inadvertently erase the experiences of queer and nonwhite Cuban migrants. Equally important, Gerardo was a charismatic individual who had been arrested for possessing a small amount of marijuana. I thus feared that readers might interpret his detention as unjust because they viewed him as "innocent" rather than noting that, as this book shows, detention is inhumane and ineffective even for those who commit serious offenses. I tried to address the biases that my choice wrought by also telling the stories of Black, "mulatto"—as people self-identified—gay, and gender-nonconforming migrants. I also related the experiences of those who ended up behind bars after causing more serious harm.

The primary reason I decided to focus on Gerardo was because telling his story would not put him at risk. As I drafted these pages, the government was actively deporting many of the Mariel Cubans who had been incarcerated decades earlier, as had happened with Gerardo. But precisely because Gerardo had already been deported, recounting his experiences did not pose that danger. In addition, Gerardo had the time and inclination to tell me his story in detail, and he had an especially sharp memory. Gerardo's case had also garnered so much attention that there was an abundance of documentation about his ordeal, which allowed me to cross-check most of the details he told me.

Compared to researching the experiences of the Cuban migrants who were detained in the 1980s, investigating the government's policies during that period was relatively straightforward. To understand the latter, I examined official documents held at the Ronald Reagan Presidential Library and the Jimmy Carter Presidential Library, combed through newspapers of the time, analyzed transcripts of legislative hearings, studied court decisions, and read through lawyers' files, which are held at the Atlanta History Center as well as in Sally Sandidge's and Gary Leshaw's personal repositories. Together, these sources provided a comprehensive picture of the political and legal history of immigrant incarceration during the 1980s and underscored that it was during this decade that the government reintroduced detention and changed its goal toward deterrence.

I consciously decided to narrate the history of immigrant detention in the 1980s by focusing on Mariel Cubans rather than on Haitian refugees. Anthropologist Michel-Rolph Trouillot has shown how Haitian history has been consistently suppressed, and I did not want to reinforce this pattern.* In the end, however, I concluded that the Mariel boatlift, which was larger in scope and attracted much more attention than the arrival of Haitian migrants, was the primary catalyst for the government's changing position on detention. Thankfully, several books that document the detention of Haitians have been recently published.† Additionally, I was able to incorporate Haitian voices in the Guantánamo chapter by following Yolande Jean's experiences in detail.

It was for similar reasons that I decided to focus on Fernando Arredondo's story even while recognizing its drawbacks. In particular, Fernando is not indigenous, and indigenous Guatemalans have historically faced much violence and oppression, which forced them to flee their country. Again, concerns over safety took primacy: I did not feel confident that telling the stories of other individuals who had experienced family separation during the Trump administration would not jeopardize their asylum claims. Fernando's lawyer, Linda Dakin-Grimm, was able to assure me that this would

---

*Michel-Rolph Trouillot, *Silencing the Past: Power and the Production of History* (Boston: Beacon Press, 1995).

†See, for example: Carl Lindskoog, *Detain and Punish: Haitian Refugees and the Rise of the World's Largest Immigration Detention System* (Gainesville: University Press of Florida, 2018); Jenna M. Loyd and Alison Mountz, *Boats, Borders, and Bases: Race, the Cold War, and the Rise of Migration Detention in the United States* (Oakland: University of California Press, 2018); and A. Naomi Paik, *Rightlessness: Testimony and Redress in U.S. Prison Camps since World War II* (Chapel Hill: University of North Carolina Press, 2016).

not happen to Fernando or his family. Additionally, Fernando felt particularly empowered by sharing his experiences, which was important to me.

In total, I spent two weeks in Los Angeles conducting over twenty hours of interviews with Fernando and Cleivi. I intentionally did not interview Andrea to avoid retraumatizing her—the same is true for all other minors whose stories I tell in this book. Instead, I gathered children's experiences from the public record, including from the reports of individuals who had been able to visit the centers where children were held. I also interviewed Holly Sewell, who fostered a boy who had been separated from his father.

I corroborated the stories Fernando and Cleivi told me by conducting an oral history interview with their lawyer and examining legal documents pertaining to their case as well as relevant newspaper articles. To unpack the broader history of detention during the Trump administration, I supplemented these stories with additional oral history interviews, court records pertaining to the cases of numerous asylum seekers, transcripts of congressional hearings, and official government statements and orders.

I took other considerations into account when examining the history of Ellis Island. By the time I began the research for this book, most individuals who had been held there had already passed away. I thus had to rely on existing memoirs, letters, diaries, and interviews. I decided to center on Ellen's story because of its impact: the national media attention around her case played an essential role in the government's decision to move away from detention. But like in the other instances, this decision came at a cost. Most Europeans who were detained on Ellis Island arrived during the early 1900s, long before Ellen. As such, her case is not the most representative of the Ellis Island experience. I addressed this problem by also recounting the stories of those detained in earlier decades.

Ellen's memoir provides a detailed account of her thoughts, experiences, and feelings while she was held in the "gateway of opportunity." Because this work was motivated by her opposition to detention, however, I had to be careful about biases and one-sided impressions. I corroborated and supplemented Ellen's voice and story by examining the records of immigration authorities, legislative hearings, judicial proceedings, newspaper articles, and other migrants' narratives. I also placed an FOIA request and thus acquired internal immigration documents related to Ellen's case. These sources provided me with a comprehensive understanding of the social, legal, and political dimensions of immigrant detention on the island.

I also thought carefully before deciding to focus on the Pacific Mail detention shed and give prominence to Chi Hao's experiences. The primary and best-known site in which Chinese migrants were detained was not the shed but Angel Island. I nonetheless chose to concentrate on the shed both because the history of Angel Island is comparatively well known and because the shed is an integral part of the history of detention: it was one of the first sites where migrants were held on land and thus one of the first sites where the entry fiction was enacted. Given the importance of the entry fiction to this history, I paid close attention to its enactment, the legal challenges it faced in court, and the ways in which local officials interpreted it when dealing with those arriving on America's shores.

In important ways, Chi Hao's story is not representative. While most Chinese villagers headed to America to escape domestic turmoil or in search of economic opportunities, Chi Hao fled because of his religious beliefs and with the support of the missionary community. Unlike him, the vast majority of detained Chinese migrants did not have the connections needed to be paroled and had to remain in the shed while their cases were adjudicated. Despite these shortcomings, I decided to focus on Chi Hao because his memoir provides more insights into the thoughts and experiences of someone held in the shed than any other source I found. Indeed, there is a true scarcity of such accounts. And although Chi Hao's story is not typical, his memoir details the conditions experienced by everyone who was held in the shed. I complemented his narrative with the insights I gleaned about the experiences of other detained migrants, as documented in newspaper articles from that era. In addition, I found Chi Hao's story to be particularly significant because it shows the racism and absurdity of immigration rules and detention policies: even a man who had risked his life for Americans and was migrating legally could be locked up upon arrival.

Here, too, I had to be careful about biases. Historians of Chinese and Asian American history have documented how Chinese people in both China and the United States sought to gain the support of US missionary networks because of the educational, financial, and migratory advantages they provided.* It is likely that some of Chi Hao's descriptions about his experiences were a narrative device to gain missionaries' support. To minimize this issue, I fact-checked his story using as many sources as possible, including newspaper articles, the diaries and letters of missionaries, photographs, and reports from immigration inspectors.

The texture of the four stories I tell was primarily shaped by the availability of sources. For instance, while I couldn't conduct oral history interviews with Chi Hao or Ellen, I had the opportunity to interview Gerardo and Fernando. I also maintained regular contact with them to ask follow-up questions of varying importance. "Were you ever sick while you were detained?" "What color was your curtain in Cuba?" These details allowed me to provide richer stories. And yet, it is only by placing the narratives of these four individuals together that we can reckon with America's long history of immigrant detention and the crushing truth that our country has designed and expanded a system in which thousands of prisoners are meant to have no rights other than those given to them by their captors.

*Madeline Y. Hsu, *The Good Immigrants: How the Yellow Peril Became the Model Minority* (Princeton: Princeton University Press, 2015), 23–54; Jane Hunter, *The Gospel of Gentility: American Women Missionaries in Turn-of-the-Century China* (New Haven: Yale University Press, 1984); Peggy Pascoe, *Relations of Rescue: The Search for Female Moral Authority in the American West, 1874–1939* (New York: Oxford University Press, 1993), 73–176.

NOTES

PREFACE

ix **Ignoring his surroundings:** Fernando Arredondo, oral history interview by the author, August 21–28, 2021, Los Angeles, California, digital recording.

x **Her sequestered daughter:** Arredondo, oral history interview.

x **unusually hot summer:** National Oceanic and Atmospheric Administration, "Summer 2018 Ranked 4th Hottest on Record for U.S.," NOAA, September 6, 2018, https://www.noaa.gov/news/summer-2018-ranked-4th-hottest-on-record-for-us.

xi **The marches took place:** Phil McCausland, Patricia Guadalupe, and Kalhan Rosenblatt, "Thousands Across U.S. Join 'Keep Families Together' March to Protest Family Separation," *NBC News*, June 30, 2018, https://www.nbcnews.com/news/us-news/thousands-across-u-s-join-keep-families-together-march-protest-n888006.

xi **Zero tolerance was one of:** John Sides, "The Extraordinary Unpopularity of Trump's Family Separation Policy," *Washington Post*, June 19, 2018, https://www.washingtonpost.com/news/monkey-cage/wp/2018/06/19/the-extraordinary-unpopularity-of-trumps-family-separation-policy-in-one-graph/.

xi **Unaware of when:** Elliott Young, *Forever Prisoners: How the United States Made the World's Largest Immigration Detention System* (New York: Oxford University Press, 2021), 5. In this 2021 book on indefinite detention, Elliott Young notes: "The book's title, *Forever Prisoners*, takes its name from the term used by journalists and others to refer to the terrorist suspects being held at the US prison at the military base at Guantanamo Bay, Cuba."

xi **If our leadership perpetrates:** Black sites are often defined as secret sites outside the United States. Here, I'm using the term as it is more commonly understood—to mean places where the government ignores the rights of those it holds.

xi **To understand how America:** Ethan A. Klingsberg, "Penetrating the Entry

Doctrine: Excludable Aliens' Constitutional Rights in Immigration Processes," *Yale Law Journal* 98, no. 3 (January 1989): 639–58; Charles D. Weisselberg, "The Exclusion and Detention of Aliens: Lessons from the Lives of Ellen Knauff and Ignatz Mezei," *University of Pennsylvania Law Review* 143, no. 4 (April 1995): 933–1034; and Eunice Lee, "The End of Entry Fiction," *North Carolina Law Review* 99, no. 3 (March 2021): 565–642.

xii **When these "entrants":** The term "entrants" is not a defined legal term. In this book, like in much legal scholarship, it is used to refer to the category of people who are within the territorial jurisdiction of the United States but legally treated as if they are still seeking to come into the country, because they were stopped at or near the border. Additionally, it is important to note that the entry fiction functions in both detention and non-detained parole settings. In detention settings, the government takes advantage of the entry fiction when it lets a noncitizen onto US territory but holds them in an immigration prison with limited rights. In parole settings, the government takes advantage of the entry fiction when it lets a noncitizen onto US territory on the condition that the government doesn't expand the noncitizen's ability to claim rights.

xii **Unauthorized migrants who evade:** Zadvydas v. Davis, 533 U.S. 678 (2001), vacated and remanded; Zainab A. Cheema, "A Constitutional Case for Extending the Due Process Clause to Asylum Seekers: Revisiting the Entry Fiction after *Boumediene*," *Fordham Law Review* 87, no. 1 (2018): 295, 306–7; and Lee, "The End of the Entry Fiction," 571-76. In 1996, Congress enacted IIRIRA, which altered how the government classified foreigners. Up until then, immigration law distinguished between unauthorized migrants who had already effected an entry into US territory and those stopped at the border. IIRIRA did away with the line between exclusion and deportation that had been based on the distinctions between having entered and not having entered. IIRIRA sought to classify migrants who had not been "admitted" into the country as legally similar, whether they were truly outside the nation's borders, stopped at or near the border, or even living in the country after physical entry without formal admission. However, as legal scholars have noted, the entry fiction doctrine "continues to hold unabated force as far as nonresident arriving aliens are concerned." Indeed, in the 2001 landmark case *Zadvydas v. Davis*, the Supreme Court stated that the "distinction between an alien who has effected an entry into the United States and one who has never entered runs throughout immigration law," which meant that "certain constitutional protections available to persons inside the United States are unavailable to aliens outside of our geographic borders."

xiii **the Trump administration held:** Mark Noferi, "Immigration Detention: Behind the Record Numbers," Center for Migration Studies, February 13, 2014, https://cmsny.org/immigration-detention-behind-the-record-numbers/; and Immigration and Customs Enforcement, *U.S. Immigration and Customs Enforcement Fiscal Year 2019 Enforcement and Removal Operations Report*, https://

www.ice.gov/sites/default/files/documents/Document/2019/eroReportFY2019.pdf.

xiii **Because of the pandemic:** "FY 2021 Detention Statistics" and "FY 2022 Detention Statistics," Immigration and Customs Enforcement, accessed August 25, 2023, https://www.ice.gov/detain/detention-management.

xiii **existing statistics show:** Calculated from the corresponding yearly reports, the *Annual Report of the Immigration and Naturalization Service* and the *ICE Enforcement and Removal Operations Report.*

xiii **This means that more migrants:** The latest population count for Pennsylvania at the time of research was derived from "QuickFacts, Pennsylvania," United States Census Bureau, July 1, 2022, https://www.census.gov/quickfacts/fact/table/PA.

xiii **largest immigrant detention:** Carl Lindskoog, *Detain and Punish: Haitian Refugees and the Rise of the World's Largest Immigration Detention System* (Gainesville: University Press of Florida, 2018), 1.

xiii **originally a detention center:** Mark Dow, *American Gulag: Inside U.S. Immigration Prisons* (Berkeley: University of California Press, 2004), 97; and Kristina Shull, *Detention Empire: Reagan's War on Immigrants and the Seeds of Resistance* (Chapel Hill: University of North Carolina Press, 2022), 320. Note that profits had already been made from incarceration. For more on this, see chapters 10 and 14.

xiv **the nation's detention and prison:** Kelly Lytle Hernández, *City of Inmates: Conquest, Rebellion, and the Rise of Human Caging in Los Angeles, 1771–1965* (Chapel Hill: University of North Carolina Press, 2017), 90.

xiv **President George H. W. Bush:** Lindskoog, *Detain and Punish*, 105–111; A. Naomi Paik, *Rightlessness: Testimony and Redress in U.S. Prison Camps since World War II* (Chapel Hill: University of North Carolina Press, 2016), 87–113; Shull, *Detention Empire*, 64–103.

xv **"an enlightened civilization":** Leng May Ma v. Barber, 357 U.S. 185 (1958).

CHAPTER 1

3 **A horde of shirtless:** Note that most details of Chi Hao's experiences come from his autobiography, Fay Chi Ho and Luella Miner, *Two Heroes of Cathay: An Autobiography and a Sketch* (New York: Fleming H. Revell Company, 1903). All information without endnotes comes from this memoir. Similarly, all dialogue that is not cited relies on this memoir and thus on Chi Hao's memory and telling. The various Chinese dialects and multiple systems for transliteration made it hard to consistently render names and places. I used pinyin to transliterate Chinese places, so readers can better identify where events unfolded. However, I made the conscious decision to keep personal names in the way they were rendered in English-language sources as they were written at the time, since this book seeks to capture people's experiences and interiority. In his autobiography, Fu Chi Hao is spelled Fay Chi Ho. Here, I use Fu Chi Hao because that

is how he wrote it in the article "My Reception to America," published on August 10, 1907, in *Outlook*, which is the only piece of writing with which he was solely credited (Luella was credited as the coauthor of his memoir). Because this book refers to people by their given names after first mention of their full names, I often refer to him as Chi Hao.

3 **Fu Chi Hao had heard:** Henrietta Harrison, "Village Politics and National Politics: The Boxer Movement in Central Shanxi," in *The Boxers, China, and the World*, ed. Robert A. Bickers and R. G. Tiedemann (Lanham: Rowman & Littlefield, 2007). It was in the spring of 1900 that the first alarming reports of the Boxers and their affronts against Christians began to reach Shanxi Province. See the state of affairs at the time in Joseph W. Esherick, *The Origins of the Boxer Uprising* (Berkeley: University of California Press, 1988), 188, 258. According to Rev. Price's diary, the mission did not hear about them until the beginning of June. Esherick, *Origins of the Boxer Uprising*, 269–71.

4 **It began with an illness:** I was unable to find Fu Chi Hao's father's name. Fu is the family name.

4 **Mrs. Fu burned incense:** In China women didn't typically adopt their husband's surnames. I use Mrs. Fu only because I could not find her name in the sources.

4 **Mr. Fu solved this issue:** The city was known as Peking at the time. For an analysis of how Chinese people sought connections with missionaries for pragmatic reasons, see Jane Hunter, *The Gospel of Gentility: American Women Missionaries in Turn-of-the-Century China* (New Haven: Yale University Press, 1984); and Madeline Y. Hsu, *The Good Immigrants: How the Yellow Peril Became the Model Minority* (Princeton: Princeton University Press, 2015), 23–54.

5 **roving bands of Boxers:** Paul A. Cohen, *History in Three Keys: The Boxers as Event, Experience, and Myth* (New York: Columbia University Press, 1997), 47; and Nat Brandt, *Massacre in Shansi* (Bloomington: iUniverse, 1999), loc. 3046 of 6632, Kindle.

6 **for most Chinese people:** Esherick, *Origins of the Boxer Uprising*, chap. 3.

6 **Their very efforts:** Esherick, 75–86, 91–95; and Lindsay Schakenbach Regele, *Manufacturing Advantage: War, the State, and the Origins of American Industry, 1776–1848* (Baltimore: Johns Hopkins University Press, 2019), 142.

6 **Under the "unequal treaties":** Teemu Ruskola, *Legal Orientalism: China, the United States, and Modern Law* (Cambridge, MA: Harvard University Press, 2013), 25, 110, 12–130, 186–87. For more information on this, see Pär Kristoffer Cassel, *Grounds of Judgment: Extraterritoriality and Imperial Power in Nineteenth-Century China and Japan* (Oxford: Oxford University Press, 2012).

7 **As Chinese villagers' frustration:** Cohen, *History in Three Keys*, 23; and Esherick, *Origins of the Boxer Uprising*, 144–47.

7 **Two months later, an army:** Alfred Emile Cornebise, *The United States Army in China, 1900–1938: A History of the 9th, 14th, 15th and 31st Regiments in the East* (Jefferson, NC: McFarland, 2015), 30–32; and Esherick, *Origins of the Boxer Uprising*, 288, 302–3.

7 **The declaration of war:** Cohen, *History in Three Keys*, 51.

8 **their decision might cost them:** Excerpts from the diary of Reverend Price, in E. H. Edwards, *Fire and Sword in Shansi: The Story of the Martyrdom of Foreigners and Chinese Christians* (Edinburgh: Oliphant, Anderson & Ferrier, 1903), 285.

8 **two hundred Boxers:** Edwards, *Fire and Sword*, 288.

9 **Charles was handing over:** Belongings other than the ones Charles handed to Chi Hao also survived.

11 **A direct descendant:** K'ung Hsiang Hsi later went by H. H. Kung and is also known today as Kong Xiangxi. In the 1930s and '40s, he served as China's finance minister. He married Soong Ai-ling, Madame Chiang Kai-shek's older sister.

12 **from the Pearl River Delta:** Gordon H. Chang, *Ghosts of Gold Mountain: The Epic Story of the Chinese Who Built the Transcontinental Railroad* (New York: Mariner Books, 2019), 15–16; Mae Ngai, *The Chinese Question: The Gold Rushes and Global Politics* (New York: W. W. Norton, 2021), 32; and Erika Lee, *At America's Gates: Chinese Immigration during the Exclusion Era, 1882–1943* (Chapel Hill: University of North Carolina Press, 2003), 25.

12 **the Red Turban Rebellion**: Chang, *Ghosts of Gold Mountain*, 25.

13 **Pacific Mail Steamship Company began:** Chang, 28.

13 **Reports written by:** Lee, *At America's Gates*, 25, 27, 34, 169; John Kuo Wei Tchen, *New York before Chinatown: Orientalism and the Shaping of American Culture, 1776–1882* (Baltimore: Johns Hopkins University Press, 2001), 75, 90, 94; Chang, *Ghosts of Gold Mountain*, 60; Nayan Shah, *Contagious Divides: Epidemics and Race in San Francisco's Chinatown* (Berkeley: University of California Press, 2001), 77–104.

13 **"The Chinese Must Go!":** Lee, *At America's Gates*, 26; Beth Lew-Williams, *The Chinese Must Go: Violence, Exclusion, and the Making of the Alien in America* (Cambridge, MA: Harvard University Press, 2018).

13 **"We have a great right":** Lee, *At America's Gates*, 197.

13 **These calls altered the course:** Lee, 23–24.

13 **immigration at the national level:** Hidetaka Hirota, "The Moment of Transition: State Officials, the Federal Government, and the Formation of American Immigration Policy," *Journal of American History* 99, no. 4 (March 2013): 1092–108; Gerald L. Neuman, *Strangers to the Constitution: Immigrants, Borders, and Fundamental Law* (Princeton: Princeton University Press, 1996); Kunal M. Parker, "State, Citizenship, and Territory: The Legal Construction of Immigrants in Antebellum Massachusetts," *Law and History Review* 19, no. 3 (Autumn 2001): 583–643; Kevin Kenny, "Mobility and Sovereignty: The Nineteenth-Century Origins of Immigration Restriction," *Journal of American History* 109, no. 2 (September 2022): 286; and Gabriel J. Chin and Paul Finkelman, "Birthright Citizenship, Slave Trade Legislation, and the Origins of Federal Immigration Regulation," *UC Davis Law Review* 54 (July 2021): 2228. The Alien and Sedition Acts of 1798 had established the authority to expel or deport aliens. Before the passage of the Page Act, states had already been able to control

immigrant admissions, sometimes with the power of Congress. In the late eighteenth century, Atlantic Seaboard states had begun to prohibit the entrance of destitute foreigners and those likely to become public charges, but the federal government continued to endorse an open-door policy. Then, in 1803, Congress prohibited vessels from bringing "any negro, mulatto, or other person of colour, not being a native . . . into any port or place of the United States, which port or place shall be situated in any state which by law has prohibited or shall prohibit the admission or importation of such negro, mulatto, or other person of colour." See Act of Feb. 28, 1803, ch. 10, 2 Stat. 205. This law did not apply across the entire nation but banned the immigration of non-whites into states that prohibited them.

13 **"we have no treaty":** In re Kaine, 55 U.S. 103 (1852).

14 **Seven years later:** Beth Lew-Williams, "Before Restriction Became Exclusion: America's Experiment in Diplomatic Immigration Control," *Pacific Historical Review* 83, no. 1 (February 2014): 26. At the time, the Chinese Exclusion Act was known as the Chinese Restriction Act.

14 **This law barred Chinese laborers:** Lew-Williams, *Chinese Must Go*, 56.

14 **Crammed with cargo:** Wendy Rouse Jorae, *The Children of Chinatown: Growing Up Chinese American in San Francisco, 1850–1920* (Chapel Hill: University of North Carolina Press, 2009), 12; and Luella Miner, "Chinese Students and the Exclusion Laws," *Independent*, April 24, 1902.

14 **Most of the voyagers:** Miner, "Chinese Students and the Exclusion Laws."

14 **On these trips:** Robert Eric Barde, *Immigration at the Golden Gate: Passenger Ships, Exclusion, and Angel Island* (Westport, CT: Praeger, 2008), 84.

14 **"The peril of the water":** Fu, "My Reception in America."

14 **A smaller boat appeared:** "Landing Chinese," *San Francisco Chronicle*, April 18, 1887.

14 **If this man concluded that:** California Commissioners for the Revision and Reform of the Law, *Report of the Commissioners for the Revision and Reform of the Law: Recommendations Respecting the Political Code* (Sacramento: A. J. Johnston, Superintendent State Printing, 1902), 306–10; and California Senate Legislature, *The Journal of the Senate during the Thirty-Fourth Session of the Legislature of the State of California* (Sacramento: A. J. Johnston, Superintendent State Printing, 1901), 391, 394. For the earlier case of the *Doric* at Angel Island, see "One Transport and an Ocean Liner from the Orient Are in Quarantine," *San Francisco Call*, April 18, 1901. Angel Island opened as a quarantine station in 1891. For more on how Chinese people were regularly seen as carriers of disease, see Shah, *Contagious Divides*.

15 **Luella had warned him:** Miner, "Chinese Students and the Exclusion Laws."

15 **When they awoke:** Lucy E. Salyer, *Laws Harsh as Tigers: Chinese Immigrants and the Shaping of Modern Immigration Law* (Chapel Hill: University of North Carolina Press, 1995), 38.

15 **Inspectors from the Chinese Bureau had:** "Landing Chinese," *San Francisco*

Chronicle. These were immigrant inspectors from the Chinese Bureau, which was responsible for enforcing Chinese exclusion laws. In 1901, inspectors were still boarding the ships to conduct their initial assessments. See "Jackson's Plan Admits Coolies," *San Francisco Call*, May 8, 1900; and "Collector Jackson Must Aid the United States Courts," *San Francisco Call*, May 10, 1900.

16 **these purported mistakes:** "Departure of Steamship *Doric* for Japanese and Chinese Ports," *San Francisco Call*, September 21, 1901.

CHAPTER 2

17 **a realist to believe that:** Note that most details of Ellen's experiences come from her memoir, Ellen Raphael Knauff, *The Ellen Knauff Story* (New York: W. W. Norton, 1952). All information without endnotes comes from this source. Similarly, all dialogue that is not cited relies on her autobiography and thus on Ellen's memory and telling.

17 **Like thousands of immigrants:** Edward A. Harris, "The Perplexing Case of Ellen Knauff," *St. Louis Post-Dispatch*, February 5, 1950. For an idea of what German women often thought about in terms of the United States and its soldiers, see Bruce Haywood, *Bremerhaven: A Memoir of Germany, 1945–1947* (Morrisville, NC: Lulu, 2010), 205.

17 **she was coming:** "List of United States Citizens, SS USAT COMFORT sailing from Bremerhaven August 14, 1948," Ancestry.com; and "New York, U.S., Arriving Passenger and Crew Lists (including Castle Garden and Ellis Island), 1820–1957," Ancestry.com, accessed February 6, 2020.

18 **Among them was Rosi:** "Manifest of Alien Passengers," USAT *Comfort*, August 14, 1948; and Rosi Dyer, Petition for Naturalization, No. 2815, Waco, Texas, Ancestry.com.

18 **There was also Jadwiga Osowicz:** "Manifest of Alien Passengers," USAT *Comfort*; and "List of United States Citizens, SS USAT COMFORT."

18 **brides like Katherine Martinoff:** "Manifest of Alien Passengers," USAT *Comfort*; and "List of United States Citizens, SS USAT COMFORT." The fact that the two were married is drawn from Serge B. Martinoff's obituary.

19 **Edgar Boxhorn:** In her autobiography, Ellen refers to Edgar as "Eddie." His actual name is documented in official documents. See, for instance, "Mrs. Ellen Knauff," H. Rep. No. 1940, 81st Cong., 2nd Sess., 4 (1950).

19 **Edgar was Czech:** *Exclusion of Ellen Knauff: Hearings before Subcommittee No. 1, Committee on the Judiciary*, 81st Cong. 10 (1950) (statement of Ed Gossett, Texas); Knauff, *Ellen Knauff Story*, 11; and Harris, "The Perplexing Case of Ellen Knauff." Ellen's father was born in the small town of Buk, which was then part of Prussia; her mother was born in Dortmund, Germany.

19 **Hitler had only risen:** For a history of how life changed for Jews during the first years of the Nazi regime, see Marion A. Kaplan, *Between Dignity and Despair: Jewish Life in Nazi Germany* (New York: Oxford University Press, 1998).

19 **industrialized city of Dortmund:** Marta Appel, "Memoirs of a German Jewish Woman," in *Sources of European History since 1900*, eds. Marvin Perry, Matthew Berg, and James Krukones (Boston: Cengage, 2010), 170.

20 **At a time when almost:** Kryštof Zeman, "Divorce and Marital Dissolution in the Czech Republic and in Austria: The Role of Premarital Cohabitation" (PhD diss., Charles University, 2003), 23.

20 **the situation for Jews:** Saul Friedländer, *Nazi Germany and the Jews: The Years of Persecution, 1933–1939* (London: Phoenix Giant, 1998), 141–51.

20 **too young to be taken:** "The Central Database of Shoah Victims' Names: Hans Peter Raphael," Yad Vashem, the World Holocaust Remembrance Center, accessed April 15, 2020, https://yvng.yadvashem.org/nameDetails.html?language=en&itemId=11610645&ind=1; and "Dortmund Holocaust Victims: Raphael," JewishGen, accessed April 15, 2020, https://www.jewishgen.org/databases/jgdetail_2.php?df=JG0402&georegion=01holocaust&srch1=Raphael&srch1v=S&srch1t=Q&srchbool=AND&dates=all&newwindow=0&recstart=0&recjump=0. Details from Dortmund also found in Chris Webb, "Dortmund: The City and the Holocaust," Holocaust Education & Archive Research Team, accessed July 2, 2023, http://www.holocaustresearchproject.org/nazioccupation/dortmund.html.

20 **"Arbeit Macht Frei":** Mary Fulbrook, *Reckonings: Legacies of Nazi Persecution and the Quest for Justice* (New York: Oxford University Press, 2018), 165; and United States Holocaust Memorial Museum, "Sachsenhausen," Holocaust Encyclopedia, accessed July 2, 2023, https://encyclopedia.ushmm.org/content/en/article/sachsenhausen. The same motto hung on the gates of Dachau and other concentration camps and would later also hang outside Auschwitz.

20 **A three-meter-high wall:** "Sachsenhausen (Oranienburg): History & Overview," Jewish Virtual Library, accessed July 2, 2023, https://www.jewishvirtuallibrary.org/history-and-overview-of-sachsenhausen-oranienburg-concentration-camp.

20 **several weeks of this torture:** Webb, "Dortmund."

20 **guards at Sachsenhausen:** "Sachsenhausen (Oranienburg): History & Overview," Jewish Virtual Library; and Webb, "Dortmund."

21 **Between one-quarter:** Richard Bessel, *Germany 1945: From War to Peace* (New York: HarperCollins, 2009), 221–22; and Editors of Encyclopedia Britannica, "The Era of Partition," Britannica, accessed July 2, 2023, https://www.britannica.com/place/Germany/The-era-of-partition.

21 **During the workday:** *Exclusion of Ellen Knauff*, 16.

21 **extermination camp near Riga:** *Exclusion of Ellen Knauff*, 10.

21 **Like most German Jews:** Kaplan, *Between Dignity and Despair*, 129–31.

22 **Évian-les-Bains, France:** Daniel J. Tichenor, *Dividing Lines: The Politics of Immigration Control in America* (Princeton: Princeton University Press, 2002), 161.

22 **After March 1938:** *Admission of German Refugee Children: Joint Hearings before a Subcommittee of the Committee on Immigration, United States Senate, and a Subcommittee of the Committee on Immigration and Naturalization*, 76th Cong. 38 (1939).

22 **Yet between 1939:** United States Holocaust Memorial Museum, "The United States and the Refugee Crisis, 1938–41," Holocaust Encyclopedia, last updated September 12, 2022, https://encyclopedia.ushmm.org/content/en/article/the-united-states-and-the-refugee-crisis-1938-41.

22 **In February 1939:** Richard Breitman and Alan M. Kraut, *American Refugee Policy and European Jewry, 1933–1945* (Bloomington: Indiana University Press, 1987), 73.

22 **transatlantic liner *St. Louis*:** Laurel Leff, *Buried by the Times: The Holocaust and America's Most Important Newspaper* (New York: Cambridge University Press, 2005), 43.

23 **An estimated 254:** United States Holocaust Memorial Museum, "The United States and the Refugee Crisis, 1938–41."

23 **would be deported by train:** "The Central Database of Shoah Victims' Names: Gustav Raphael," Yad Vashem, the World Holocaust Remembrance Center, accessed July 2, 2023, https://yvng.yadvashem.org/nameDetails.html?language=en&itemId=11610644&ind=1. The other family members were also found on this website.

23 **The ghetto had been created:** Gertrude Schneider, *Journey into Terror: Story of the Riga Ghetto* (New York: Ark House, 1979), 11.

23 **graves had already been dug:** Schneider, *Journey into Terror*, 12.

23 **"Don't forget us":** Schneider, 12.

23 **they murdered between:** Schneider, 14.

24 **"frozen in glasses of water":** Schneider, 27.

24 **the one from Dortmund:** Schneider, 39.

24 **responded the kid gleefully:** Schneider, 56.

24 **not miss their truck:** Schneider, 56.

24 **stories they had heard:** Schneider, 58.

25 **he was killed in Riga:** "The Central Database of Shoah Victims' Names: Gustav Raphael," Yad Vashem.

25 **Virtually all of its horrors:** Christian Hartmann, *Operation Barbarossa: Nazi Germany's War in the East, 1941–1945* (Oxford: Oxford University Press, 2013), 135–39; Samuel W. Mitcham Jr., *The German Defeat in the East: 1944–45* (Mechanicsburg, PA: Stackpole Books, 2007), 3–20; "Majdanek," Yad Vashem, the World Holocaust Remembrance Center, accessed July 2, 2023, https://www.yadvashem.org/odot_pdf/microsoft%20word%20-%206622.pdf; United States Holocaust Memorial Museum, "Liberation of Nazi Camps: Majdanek and Auschwitz," Holocaust Encyclopedia, last updated February 12, 2021, https://encyclopedia.ushmm.org/content/en/article/liberation-of-nazi-camps; and Anita Kondoyanidi, "The Liberating Experience: War Correspondents, Red Army Soldiers, and the Nazi Extermination Camps," *Russian Review* 69, no. 3 (July 2010): 444–49. On June 22, 1944, the Soviet Army launched Operation Bagration. Within days, 2.5 million troops, supported by forty-five thousand mortars and heavy guns, six thousand tanks, and eight thousand airplanes

had destroyed the German Army on the Eastern Front and shattered the German front line. A month later, the Red Army reached the Majdanek extermination camp near Lublin.

25 **the Soviet Army's reach:** Daniel Blatman, *The Death Marches: The Final Phase of Nazi Genocide* (Cambridge, MA: Harvard University Press, 2011), 45–59.

25 **the Nazis transferred Elisabeth:** Tracing the Past, "Elisabeth Raphael née Steinweg," Mapping the Past, accessed June 9, 2020, https://www.mappingthelives.org; and "The Central Database of Shoah Victims' Names: Raphael [Last / Maiden Name], Riga [Place]," Yad Vashem, the World Holocaust Remembrance Center, accessed July 2, 2023, https://yvng.yadvashem.org/index.html?language=en&s_id=&s_lastName=Raphael&s_firstName=&s_place=Riga&s_dateOfBirth.

25 **Twelve days later:** United States Holocaust Memorial Museum, "Riga," Holocaust Encyclopedia, accessed April 15, 2020, https://encyclopedia.ushmm.org/content/en/article/riga. It is likely that Elisabeth and Peter Hans were first sent to the Kaiserwald concentration camp or one of its subcamps. See Kaplan, *Between Dignity and Despair*, 115, 134.

25 **gas chamber and crematorium:** Schneider, *Journey into Terror*, 421.

25 **second week in Stutthof:** "Hans Peter Raphael," Geni, accessed June 21, 2020, https://www.geni.com/people/Hans-Raphael/6000000076713156822. Peter Hans died on October 10, 1944, at the age of twenty-two.

25 **the camp that winter:** "The Central Database of Shoah Victims' Names: Elisabeth Raphael," Yad Vashem, the World Holocaust Remembrance Center, accessed July 13, 2020, https://yvng.yadvashem.org/nameDetails.html?language=en&itemId=11610633&ind=2/.

26 **"When a hand trembled":** Rivah Hirurg, as cited in Dan Stone, *The Liberation of the Camps: The End of the Holocaust and Its Aftermath* (New Haven: Yale University Press, 2015), 49. Her name appears as Riva Chirurg in the book.

26 **had opposed the Nazis:** South Carolina, U.S., Naturalization Records, 1868–1991, for Kurt Walter Knauff, Columbia, Columbia Petitions 1943 Mar–1943 Jul (Box 2); and Harris, "The Perplexing Case of Ellen Knauff."

26 **After the war broke out:** South Carolina, U.S., Naturalization Records, 1868–1991, for Kurt Walter Knauff.

26 **He had been awarded:** *Exclusion of Ellen Knauff*, 7; Knauff, *Ellen Knauff Story*, 62.

26 **images of courageous heroism:** South Carolina, U.S., Naturalization Records, 1868–1991, for Kurt Walter Knauff.

26 **When Ellen first met him:** Harris, "The Perplexing Case of Ellen Knauff."

26 **single German women:** Susan Zeiger, *Entangling Alliances: Foreign War Brides and American Soldiers in the Twentieth Century* (New York: New York University Press, 2010), 72; Maria Höhn, *Gis and Fräuleins: The German-American Encounter in 1950s West Germany* (Chapel Hill: University of North Carolina Press, 2002), 124–25. The same was true for other foreign women. See Jenel Virden, *Good-Bye, Piccadilly: British War Brides in America* (Urbana: University of Illinois Press, 1996).

27 **the onerous visa process:** War Brides Act, 59 Stat. 659 (1945). According to the 1924 Immigration and Naturalization Act, the European wives of US citizens were exempt from the quotas imposed on other immigrants. They were allowed to enter the country unless they were unable to pass the required mental and medical checks. But they had to obtain a visa first. The War Brides Act held that spouses of service members were to be allowed in even if they were considered "physically and mentally defective," and it exempted them from the visa requirement.

CHAPTER 3

29 **Gerardo Mansur observed:** Gerardo Mansur, oral history interview by the author, June 28–July 4, 2019, Havana, Cuba, digital recording; follow-up questions and interview via phone on August 25–28, 2019. All uncited information comes from these interviews. Similarly, all dialogue that is not cited relies on these interviews and thus on Gerardo's memory and telling.

30 **Rafael was one:** María Cristina García, *Havana USA: Cuban Exiles and Cuban Americans in South Florida, 1959–1994* (Berkeley: University of California Press, 1996), 51–53.

30 **These were luxuries:** García, *Havana USA*, 51–53.

32 **regime they abhorred:** Mirta Ojito, *Finding Mañana: A Memoir of a Cuban Exodus* (New York: Penguin Press, 2005), 85.

32 **who surrounded the compound:** Ojito, *Finding Mañana*, 86.

32 **Pedro Ortiz Cabrera:** García, *Havana USA*, 56.

33 **"his face turned deep red":** William M. LeoGrande and Peter Kornbluh, *Back Channel to Cuba: The Hidden History of Negotiations between Washington and Havana* (Chapel Hill: University of North Carolina Press, 2014), 216.

33 **pulling out all guards:** "Declaración del gobierno revolucionario de Cuba," *Granma*, April 4, 1980.

33 **flocked to the embassy:** García, *Havana USA*, 54–57.

33 **refuge in the Peruvian embassy:** García, 57.

34 **"It was depressing":** Carlos Pardon, oral history interview by the author, December 27, 2017, Miami, Florida, digital recording.

34 **the ambassador's pet parrot:** García, *Havana USA*, 56.

34 **"Cuba for the workers!":** "¡Que se vayan!," *Bohemia*, April 18, 1980; "Una batalla por la dignidad," *Granma*, April 17, 1980; and "¡Todos mañana a la marcha del pueblo combatiente!," *Granma*, April 18, 1980. All from Biblioteca Nacional, Hemeroteca, José Martí, Havana, Cuba.

34 **crowds enveloped the plaza:** "¡Este sí es pueblo!," *Granma*, April 20, 1980; and "Y el pueblo entro en acción," *Bohemia*, April 25, 1980. Both from Biblioteca Nacional, Hemeroteca, José Martí, Havana, Cuba.

34 **collect their relatives and friends:** "Hay que mostrarle al imperialismo Yanqui que es Cuba," *Granma*, April 21, 1980.

35 **"an open heart and open arms":** García, *Havana USA*, 65.

36 **as a daily occurrence:** Nara Roza, oral history interview by the author, January 5, 2018, Miami, Florida, digital recording.

37 **"spiritual and moral development":** Lillian Guerra, *Visions of Power in Cuba: Revolution, Redemption, and Resistance, 1959–1971* (Chapel Hill: University of North Carolina Press, 2012), 221.

37 **"the woman has to stay":** Roza, oral history interview.

38 **no relatives at all:** García, *Havana USA*, 61.

39 **the week Gerardo did:** Memorandum by Frederick M. Bohen to Eugene Eidenberg, "Monthly Entrant Report for October," November 6, 1980, Folder: Data Processing, Box 2, Records of the Cuban-Haitian Task Force, Record Group 220, Jimmy Carter Presidential Library. Date Gerardo traveled found in "El Mariel, Boat and Passengers Records," accessed January 22, 2020, http://pubsys.miamiherald.com/cgi-bin/mariel/people/search.

39 **miles north of Havana:** Jeff Prugh, "10 Die, 4 Missing as Boat Carrying Cubans Capsizes," *Los Angeles Times*, May 18, 1980.

39 **died on the journey:** García, *Havana USA*, 61.

39 **"rougher in appearance":** Mark S. Hamm, *The Abandoned Ones: The Imprisonment and Uprising of the Mariel Boat People* (Boston: Northeastern University Press, 1995), 51.

40 **"We will not permit":** Edward Walsh, "17 Americans Summoned Home: Carter Moves to Stop Cuban Boatlift," *Washington Post*, May 15, 1980.

40 **"petty theft to murder":** Dan Sewell, "Convicts among the Refugees," *Boston Globe*, April 30, 1980.

40 **These stories ignored:** García, *Havana USA*, 65.

40 **Although 26,000 of those:** García, 64.

40 **"perverts on American shores":** Steven V. Roberts, "Economic Woes Strain Feelings in U.S. Toward Refugees," *New York Times*, October 19, 1980.

40 **A poll conducted:** García, *Havana USA*, 66.

41 **released from the camps:** Cuban/Haitian Task Force, Data System and Analysis Division, "Entrant Data Report, October 31, 1980," Folder: Data Processing, Box 2, Records of the Cuban-Haitian Task Force, Record Group 220, Jimmy Carter Presidential Library.

42 **only watched baseball games:** Luis de la Paz, oral history interview by the author, December 18, 2017, and December 20, 2017, Miami, Florida, digital recording.

42 **"most American girls have":** *La Libertad* newsletter from the personal archives of Luis de la Paz.

42 **ex-husband had prevented:** Julia Martínez, oral history interview by the author, February 22–24, 2019, Kissimmee, Florida, digital recording.

43 **Whenever a beautiful woman:** George de Lama, "Life in U.S. for Two Refugees: To One Horror, the Other Hope," *Chicago Tribune*, October 6, 1980.

43 **"Different in language":** de Lama, "Life in U.S. for Two Refugees."

43 **Haitian refugees had embarked:** For more on the migration and detention of Haitians in the 1980s, see Carl Lindskoog, *Detain and Punish: Haitian Refugees and the Rise of the World's Largest Immigration Detention System* (Gainesville: University Press of Florida, 2018), 12–70; Kristina Shull, *Detention Empire: Reagan's War on Immigrants and the Seeds of Resistance* (Chapel Hill: University of North Carolina Press, 2022), 64–103; and A. Naomi Paik, *Rightlessness: Testimony and Redress in U.S. Prison Camps since World War II* (Chapel Hill: University of North Carolina Press, 2016), 87–113.

43 **Haitians landed in Florida:** Department of Human Services, "Entrant Data Report, Appendix A: Haitian Arrivals and Resettlements," Folder: Miscellaneous Informative Materials [1], Box 15, Records of the Cuban-Haitian Task Force, Record Group 220, Jimmy Carter Presidential Library.

44 **wild stretch of Everglades:** Jana K. Lipman, "'The Fish Trusts the Water, and It Is in the Water That It Is Cooked': The Caribbean Origins of the Krome Detention Center," *Radical History Review* 2013, no. 115 (Winter 2013): 115–41.

44 **"made it here alive":** Lipman, "'The Fish Trusts the Water, and It Is in the Water That It Is Cooked,'" 123.

44 **"I saw women sleeping":** Lindskoog, *Detain and Punish*, 43; Lindskoog, 12–70; and Shull, *Detention Empire*, 43–50.

45 **92 percent of all Haitians:** Memorandum for Eugene Eidenberg from Frederick M. Bohen, "Daily Executive Summary," November 28, 1980, Folder: Executive Summary 11/80, Box 3, Records of the Cuban-Haitian Task Force, Record Group 220, Jimmy Carter Presidential Library.

45 **the sun's rays glistened:** "Klansmen Picket Ft. Chaffee Gate," *Galveston Daily News*, May 25, 1980.

45 **"Imagine my fear":** Martínez, oral history interview.

45 **antagonize thousands of Cubans:** Jim Etter, "Klan Calls at Chaffee," *Sunday Oklahoman*, May 25, 1980.

45 **Klansmen's English-language signs:** Etter, "Klan Calls at Chaffee"; and "Klan Urges Overthrow of Castro Government," *Hawaii Tribune-Herald*, May 25, 1980.

46 **"take their cigarettes":** Etter, "Klan Calls at Chaffee."

47 **Once they reached the edge:** "Cubans Riot at Center in Arkansas," *Washington Post*, June 2, 1980.

47 **State troopers amassed:** "Cubans Riot at Center in Arkansas."

47 **President Carter announced:** "Draft Statement of President Carter on Consolidation at Ft. Chaffee," Folder: Consolidation [1], Box 1, Records of the Cuban-Haitian Task Force, Record Group 220, Jimmy Carter Presidential Library.

47 **"It is no longer reasonable":** "Draft Statement of President Carter on Consolidation at Ft. Chaffee," Jimmy Carter Presidential Library.

48 **Eglin Air Force Base facility:** "Consolidation Q & A, August 1, 1980," Folder: Consolidation [2], Box 1, Records of the Cuban-Haitian Task Force, Record Group 220, Jimmy Carter Presidential Library.

48 **"a favorable economic impact":** "Consolidation Q & A, August 1, 1980," Jimmy Carter Presidential Library.

48 **A Barling weapons store:** Karen de Witt, "New Cuban Influx at Fort Chaffee Arouses Hostility," *New York Times*, August 11, 1980.

48 **scared "is an understatement":** Bill Clinton, *My Life* (New York: Vintage Books, 2005), 275.

48 **"The use of Ft. Chaffee":** Memorandum for James Baker and Edwin Meese from Lyn Nofziger and Richard Williamson, "Political Implications of the Ft. Chaffee, Arkansas Refugee Situation," June 11, 1981, Folder: Detention Center and Chaffee Working Files (2), Box 8, Francis S. M. (Frank) Hodsoll Files, Ronald Reagan Presidential Library. See also Shull, *Detention Empire*, 53–54.

48 **one of those exiles:** Karla Bausman and Bridget Bigatel, "Cubans Fear Another Move to 'Dead End,'" *Boston Globe*, October 5, 1980.

49 **"Chaffee has had":** Letter from Tom Casey to Russell Dynes, "Consolidation of Refugees at Fort Chaffee," August 18, 1980, Folder: Consolidation [2], Box 1, Records of the Cuban-Haitian Task Force, Record Group 220, Jimmy Carter Presidential Library.

49 **"They will have to drag":** Bausman and Bigatel, "Cubans Fear Another Move to 'Dead End.'"

49 **"security of the enclave":** "Report of the Subcommittee on Security and Law Enforcement," Folder: Consolidation [1], Box 1, Records of the Cuban-Haitian Task Force, Record Group 220, Jimmy Carter Presidential Library.

49 **they would be "physically searched":** Joan Higgins, "Telegraphic Message, 9/241980," Folder: Consolidation [2], Box 35, Records of the Cuban-Haitian Task Force, Record Group 220, Jimmy Carter Presidential Library.

49 **Once within Fort Chaffee:** Memorandum from Acting INS Commissioner David Crosland to Associate Deputy Attorney General Paul R. Michel, "INS's Enforcement Plan for Consolidation of Cuban Refugees at Fort Chaffee, Arkansas," Folder: Consolidation [1], Box 1, Records of the Cuban-Haitian Task Force, Record Group 220, Jimmy Carter Presidential Library.

49 **The refugees who were moved:** Office of the Federal Protective Service, draft, "Operational Plan in Support of Cuban Refugee Processing Centers," Folder: Consolidation [1], Box 1, Records of the Cuban-Haitian Task Force, Record Group 220, Jimmy Carter Presidential Library.

CHAPTER 4

51 **Every evening at eight:** Fernando Arredondo, oral history interview by the author, August 21–28, 2021, Los Angeles, California, digital recording. All uncited information on Fernando's story comes from this days-long interview. Similarly, all dialogue that is not cited relies on this oral history interview and thus on Fernando's memory and telling.

51 **a charismatic forty-one-year-old:** Fernando's birthday confirmed in "Declara-

tion of Fernando Arredondo Rodriguez in Support of Request to Be Returned to U.S. to Apply for Asylum," provided by his lawyer, Linda Dakin-Grimm.

52 **While vigilantes had existed:** See also Anthony W. Fontes, *Mortal Doubt: Transnational Gangs and Social Order in Guatemala City* (Berkeley: University of California Press, 2018), 69–71; Deborah Levenson-Estrada, *Por sí mismos: Un estudio preliminar de las "maras" en la Ciudad de Guatemala* (Guatemala: Asociación para el Avance de las Ciencias Sociales en Guatemala, 1989); and Deborah Levenson, *Adiós Niño: The Gangs of Guatemala City and the Politics of Death* (Durham: Duke University Press, 2013), 21–52.

52 **a small flip phone:** Other than via oral history interviews, I was not able to confirm that this occurred in 2015; it is notoriously hard to remember exact dates.

53 **Marco had been receiving:** Anthony W. Fontes, "Declaration in the Matter of Cleivi Marilu Jerez Lara, A# 216-590-956; Keyli Yetsari Arredondo Jerez, A# 216-590-957; Andrea Fernanda Arredondo Jerez, A# 216-591-337; Esvin Fernando Arredondo Rodriguez, A# 216-591-336; and Alison Samanta Arredondo Jerez, A# 216-590-958," provided by his lawyer, Linda Dakin-Grimm.

53 **mareros recruited youths:** Levenson, *Adiós Niño*, 98–104; Fontes, *Mortal Doubt*, 8, 43–45, 69–71.

54 **"Guatemalan national police":** Edwin Felipe Escobar, "Declaration in the Matter of Fernando Arredondo," provided to the author by Fernando's lawyer, Linda Dakin-Grimm. Escobar is the former mayor of Villa Nueva, where the suburb of Peronia is located.

55 **Most Guatemalans viewed:** Mario Avalos Quispal et al., *Historias y relato de vida de pandilleros y expandilleros de Guatemala, El Salvador y Honduras: Inicio de diálogo desde su realidad y percepciones* (Guatemala: Instituto de Estudios Comparados en Ciencias Penales de Guatemala, 2012), https://idl-bnc-idrc.dspacedirect.org/bitstream/handle/10625/50609/IDL-50609.pdf. Miguel Martínez is a pseudonym.

55 **Jacobo Árbenz became the president:** Stephen Schlesinger and Stephen Kinzer, *Bitter Fruit: The Story of the American Coup in Guatemala*, rev. ed. (Cambridge, MA: Harvard University Press, 2005); and Kirsten Weld, *Paper Cadavers: The Archives of Dictatorship in Guatemala* (Durham: Duke University Press, 2014), 8.

55 **A brutal civil war:** Weld, *Paper Cadavers*, 2.

55 **Soldiers entered towns:** Levenson, *Adiós Niño*, 25, 34–38.

56 **"We were forced to":** "Sepur Zarco Case: The Guatemalan Women Who Rose for Justice in a War-Torn Nation," UN Women, October 19, 2018, https://www.unwomen.org/en/news/stories/2018/10/feature-sepur-zarco-case; Jeff Abbott and Julia Hartviksen, "Justice for the Women of Sepur Zarco," North American Congress on Latin America (NACLA), March 11, 2016, https://nacla.org/news/2016/03/11/justice-women-sepur-zarco; and Borgen Project, "Justice for the Abuelas of Sepur Zarco, Guatemala," *Borgen Magazine*, May 28, 2021, https://www.borgenmagazine.com/abuelas-of-sepur-zarco/.

56 **one-fifth came from Guatemala:** Nora Hamilton and Norma Stoltz Chinchilla,

"Central American Migration: A Framework for Analysis," *Latin American Research Review* 26, no. 1 (1991): 99.

56 **M-18 and Barrio-18:** Fontes, *Mortal Doubt*, 80.

56 **Over 1.5 million people:** Levenson, *Adiós Niño*, 34.

57 **meant to be a gang member:** Quispal et al., "Historias y relato de vida de pandilleros y expandilleros de Guatemala, El Salvador y Honduras," 95.

58 **As he drove away:** Linda Dakin-Grimm, *Dignity and Justice: Welcoming the Stranger at Our Border* (Maryknoll, NY: Orbis Books, 2020), 106.

58 **standing up to M-18:** Anthony W. Fontes, "Declaration in the Matter of Cleivi Marilu Jerez Lara"; and "Respondent Family's Brief in Support of Claim for Asylum, Withholding of Removal, and Relief Under the Convention Against Torture in the Matter of Cleivi Marilu Jerez Lara et al.," July 30, 2020, 2–3.

58 **the neighborhood watch program:** "Respondent Family's Brief in Support of Claim for Asylum," 2–3; Escobar, "Declaration in the Matter of Fernando Arredondo."

59 **A neighbor told him:** Dakin-Grimm, *Dignity and Justice*, 88.

59 **died in her arms:** Martínez, oral history interview.

60 **"If someone betrays you":** Fontes, "Declaration in the Matter of Cleivi Marilu Jerez Lara."

60 **"After they killed Marco":** Fontes, "Declaration in the Matter of Cleivi Marilu Jerez Lara."

60 **arrived at the crime scene:** "Respondent Family's Brief in Support of Claim for Asylum."

60 **The flash of a camera:** Dakin-Grimm, *Dignity and Justice*, 88.

61 **Fernando stood there in silent:** Dakin-Grimm, 91.

63 **When Fernando left to get:** Dakin-Grimm, 93.

64 **began with a Faustian bargain:** Ana Raquel Minian, "Offshoring Migration Control: Guatemalan Transmigrants and the Construction of Mexico as a Buffer Zone," *American Historical Review* 125, no. 1 (February 2020): 89–111.

64 **deportations of Central Americans:** Rodolfo Casillas, "The Dark Side of Globalized Migration: The Rise and Peak of Criminal Networks—the Case of Central Americans in Mexico," *Globalizations* 8, no. 3 (June 2011): 298.

64 **removed 5,000 Central Americans:** Immigration and Naturalization Service, *Statistical Yearbook of the Immigration and Naturalization Service* (Washington, DC: Government Printing Office, 1991), 144.

64 **Mexico deported 1.7 million:** David J. Bier, "Mexico Deported More Central Americans than the U.S. in 2018," CATO Institute, June 12, 2019, https://www.cato.org/blog/mexico-deported-more-central-americans-us-did-2018.

65 **When Fernando and Cleivi decided:** Victoria A. Greenfield et al., *Human Smuggling and Associated Revenues: What Do or Can We Know about Routes from Central America to the United States?* (Santa Monica: Homeland Security Operational Analysis Center, 2019), https://www.rand.org/pubs/research_reports/RR2852.html. During that period, coyotes' fees generally ranged between $6,000 and $10,000 per person.

65 **boarded la Bestia:** María García (pseudonym), oral history interview by the author, June 24, 2013, San Francisco, California, digital recording.

65 **Although she recovered:** García, oral history interview; Cassandra Ogren, "Migration and Human Rights on the Mexico-Guatemala Border," *International Migration* 45, no. 4 (October 2007): 203–43; and Jacqueline Maria Hagan, *Migration Miracle: Faith, Hope, and Meaning on the Undocumented Journey* (Cambridge, MA: Harvard University Press, 2008), 75.

65 **end of February 2018:** Dakin-Grimm, *Dignity and Justice*, 93.

66 **total amounted to $250:** "El Instituto Nacional de Migración convoca," Gobierno de México, accessed March 13, 2023, https://www.gob.mx/cms/uploads/attachment/file/463175/3_CONVOCATORIA_OPIS.pdf. The salary offered in 2019 to immigration agents in Mexican pesos was $11,425. The average exchange rate in 2019 was 1 MXN per 0.052 USD (https://www.exchangerates.org.uk/MXN-USD-spot-exchange-rates-history-2019.html).

71 **The minutes it took:** Texas Department of Transportation, "Texas-Mexico International Bridges and Border Crossings: Existing and Proposed 2015," 35, accessed August 18, 2023, https://ftp.dot.state.tx.us/pub/txdot-info/iro/international-bridges.pdf.

71 **The 1951 UN Convention:** "Convention Relating to the Status of Refugees," Article 1, A (2).

72 **principle of the 1967 Protocol:** "The 1951 Refugee Convention," UN Refugee Agency (UNHCR), accessed August 15, 2023, https://www.unhcr.org/media/convention-and-protocol-relating-status-refugees.

72 **passed the Refugee Act:** Deborah Anker, "U.S. Immigration and Asylum Policy: A Brief Historical Perspective," *In Defense of the Alien* 13 (1990): 74–85, https://www.jstor.org/stable/23143024.

CHAPTER 5

77 **a thick layer of dust:** We know it was coaling from Luella Miner, "Chinese Students and the Exclusion Laws," *Independent*, April 24, 1902. For accounts about the experience of coaling, see David Colamaria, "A Sailor's Life in the New Steel Navy," Steel Navy, 2010, http://www.steelnavy.org/history/exhibits/show/steelnavy/hardlife/coal; and Allen G. Nichols, "Oil Fuel in the Navy," in *Out West: A Magazine of the Old Pacific and the New*, ed. Charles Fletcher Lummis (Los Angeles: Land of Sunshine Publishing Company, 1910), 208.

77 **With feverish energy:** Miner, "Chinese Students and the Exclusion Laws."

78 **The absurdity of it all:** Madeline Y. Hsu, *The Good Immigrants: How the Yellow Peril Became the Model Minority* (Princeton: Princeton University Press, 2015), 35; and Mae Ngai, *The Chinese Question: The Gold Rushes and Global Politics* (New York: W. W. Norton, 2021), 293.

78 **"suffering in a hell":** Miner, "Chinese Students and the Exclusion Laws."

78 **passed the Page Act in 1875:** Page Act of 1875 (Immigration Act), 18 Stat. 477 (1875).

79 **frequently filed habeas petitions:** Christian G. Fritz, "A Nineteenth-Century 'Habeas Corpus Mill': The Chinese Before the Federal Courts in California," *American Journal of Legal History* 32, no. 4 (1988): 347–72.

79 **steamship companies would shift:** Lucy Salyer, "Captives of Law: Judicial Enforcement of the Chinese Exclusion Laws, 1891–1905," *Journal of American History* 76, no. 1 (June 1989): 92–93. This was a particular problem when dealing with Chinese immigrants. Between 1894 and 1901, the percentage of Chinese people denied entrance to the United States fluctuated between 5 percent and 34 percent because of Chinese exclusion laws. In contrast, the rate of rejection of non-Chinese applicants never surpassed 1.3 percent. More important, Chinese migrants arriving to the West Coast contested their exclusion at a much higher rate than Europeans arriving to the East Coast, a process that delayed their deportation. As such, Chinese migrants' detention rates were higher.

79 **no other vessels in port:** See, for instance, the case of the *Gaelic* in "Along the Water Front," *San Francisco Call*, October 2, 1895.

79 **immigration inspectors would:** Robert Eric Barde, *Immigration at the Golden Gate: Passenger Ships, Exclusion, and Angel Island* (Westport, CT: Praeger, 2008), 57–59; Daniel Wilsher, *Immigration Detention: Law, History, Politics* (Cambridge, UK: Cambridge University Press, 2011), 14–19; and "Along the Water Front." After Angel Island opened in 1891 as a quarantine station, detained migrants were sometimes stationed there as well.

79 **built for 140 individuals:** "A City Black Hole: Shameful State of the County Jail," *San Francisco Chronicle*, November 19, 1890; and "Prison and Jail: Inspecting Tour of the Health Board," *San Francisco Chronicle*, August 1, 1889.

79 **roofs of their cells:** "Chinese Prisoners: Marshal Long Inspects the County Jail," *San Francisco Chronicle*, November 16, 1891. See also Barde, *Immigration at the Golden Gate*, 58.

79 **The jailing of these early:** See also Kelly Lytle Hernández, *City of Inmates: Conquest, Rebellion, and the Rise of Human Caging in Los Angeles, 1771–1965* (Chapel Hill: University of North Carolina Press, 2017), 64–90; and Elliott Young, *Forever Prisoners: How the United States Made the World's Largest Immigration Detention System* (New York: Oxford University Press, 2021), 23–53.

80 **the system of convict leasing:** Douglas Blackmon, *Slavery by Another Name: The Re-enslavement of Black Americans from the Civil War to World War II* (New York: Doubleday, 2008); Mary Ellen Curtin, *Black Prisoners and Their World, Alabama, 1865–1900* (Charlottesville: University Press of Virginia, 2000); Talitha LeFlouria, *Chained in Silence: Black Women and Convict Labor in the New South* (Chapel Hill: University of North Carolina Press, 2015); Alex Lichtenstein, *Twice the Work of Free Labor: The Political Economy of Convict Labor in the New South* (New York: Verso, 1996); and David M. Oshinsky, *Worse Than Slavery: Parchman Farm and the Ordeal of Jim Crow Justice* (New York: Free Press, 1996).

80 **"imprisoned at hard labor":** Act of May 5, 1892 ("Geary Act"), 27 Stat. 25 (1892). See also Hernández, *City of Inmates*, 69–72.

80 **"aliens to infamous punishment":** Wong Wing v. United States, 163 U.S. 228 (1896). See also Young, *Forever Prisoners*, 33–34; and Hernández, *City of Inmates*, 87–90.

80 **In 1891, Congress had passed:** Immigration Act of 1891, 26 Stat. 1084 (1891). By the time Congress passed the 1891 law, makeshift detention centers had already cropped up on American soil when immigration agents did not know where else to place those they detained. In San Francisco, for example, migrants had already been detained in jails and missions, and in Washington State, migrants had been held on McNeil Island. The law formally authorized these "impromptu" sites to exist. See also Young, *Forever Prisoners*, 23–53.

81 **"Such removal shall not":** Immigration Act of 1891.

81 **the 1891 law affirmed:** Immigration Act of 1891.

81 **apprehended inside the United States:** Yamataya v. Fisher, 189 U.S. 86, 100-01 (1903). At first, the Supreme Court wavered on whether deportable migrants—or those who were already inside the country—deserved constitutional rights. In *Fong Yue Ting v. United States*, an 1893 case involving a Chinese migrant who lived in New York, the Supreme Court ruled that "the right of a nation to expel or deport foreigners" was "as absolute and unqualified as the right to prohibit and prevent their entrance into the country." Soon after this ruling, however, the court ruled in *Yamataya v. Fisher* that unlike "entrants," unauthorized migrants caught inside the country were, indeed, protected by the due-process clause.

81 **they would now be held:** Barde, *Immigration at the Golden Gate*, 59–60. Pacific Mail had opened the shed in 1898, following the outbreak of the Spanish-American War. The shed complied with the provision of the 1891 law that migrants could be held on land.

82 **An officer ushered Chi Hao:** Oscar Greenhalgh, "Illustrated Report Showing Southern Pacific Steamships and Whorf [*sic*], also, Views in Chinatown," Photographs, March 19, 1899, File 52730/84, INS Subject Correspondence, Central Office, Records of the Immigration and Naturalization Service, RG 85, National Archives.

82 **extent of their good fortune:** Fu Chi Hao, "My Reception in America," *Outlook*, August 10, 1907. As Chi Hao wrote years later: "Fortunately, or, if you please, unfortunately, our friends in this country did their best to have us stay."

82 **nauseating combination of sweat:** Miner, "Chinese Students and the Exclusion Laws."

82 **only six small windows:** Miner, "Chinese Students and the Exclusion Laws."

82 **The space had been built:** "Chinese Complain of Detention Sheds," *San Francisco Examiner*, September 22, 1901. Based on descriptions from Luella and Chi Hao, we can estimate that there were approximately two hundred people detained in the shed during Chi Hao's time; the fact that sometimes more than four hundred individuals were locked up there comes from "Chinese in Bond," *San Francisco Call*, November 6, 1898; and "Detention Sheds of the Pacific Mail

Dock Swarm with Chinese from the Streamer *Coptic*," *San Francisco Call*, May 12, 1900.

82 **privilege of living:** "Chinese Complain of Detention Sheds"; and calculated based on data from August 2023 (which will continue to change over time) using CPI Inflation Calculator, accessed August 15, 2023, https://www.in2013dollars.com/us/inflation/1901?amount=0.50.

82 **pointed at the bunk beds:** Description of what officials said when detained migrants entered the shed from Lucy E. Salyer, *Laws Harsh as Tigers: Chinese Immigrants and the Shaping of Modern Immigration Law* (Chapel Hill: University of North Carolina Press, 1995), 63.

82 **Each narrow bed:** Miner, "Chinese Students and the Exclusion Laws."

82 **behind another locked door:** Miner, "Chinese Students and the Exclusion Laws"; and "Chinese in Bond."

82 **"the only free country":** Fu, "My Reception in America."

83 **The contradiction pained him:** Chi Hao's descriptions of his surprise at America might have been in part shaped by his aim to maintain support from US missionary networks. For more on this, see Madeline Y. Hsu, *The Good Immigrants.*

83 **the shed's door opened:** "Chinese Complain of Detention Sheds."

83 **detained men were hungry:** "Chinese in Bond."

83 **Knowing that Chinese migrants:** Official records of Chinese births, marriages, and divorces were nonexistent.

84 ***What is the nature*:** Although the questions asked on Angel Island are well known, the questions asked during this earlier period in the shed can be glimpsed from articles such as "The Chinese Bureau Is Suspected," *San Francisco Call*, September 3, 1898; and "Making Chinese Citizens by Wholesale," *San Francisco Call*, April 13, 1900. See also Salyer, *Laws Harsh as Tigers*, 59.

84 **not been properly coached:** Erika Lee, *At America's Gates: Chinese Immigration during the Exclusion Era, 1882–1943* (Chapel Hill: University of North Carolina Press, 2003), 216.

84 **the "Chinese jail":** Lee, *At America's Gates*, 124.

84 **"a prisoner expiating a crime":** Quoted in Lee, *At America's Gates*, 124.

84 **One reverend maintained:** Ira M. Condit, "John Chinaman in America," in *The Missionary Review of the World*, ed. Arthur T. Pierson et al. (New York: Funk & Wagnalls Company, 1902), 98.

84 **In the popular imagination, Chinese migrants:** Mary Ting Yi Lui, *The Chinatown Trunk Mystery: Murder, Miscegenation, and Other Dangerous Encounters in Turn-of-the-Century New York City* (Princeton: Princeton University Press, 2007), 2; Wendy Rouse Jorae, *The Children of Chinatown: Growing Up Chinese American in San Francisco, 1850–1920* (Chapel Hill: University of North Carolina Press, 2009), 164; and "Moving on Their Works," *San Francisco Examiner*, February 24, 1880.

84 **Stays in the shed:** Miner, "Chinese Students and the Exclusion Laws"; Lee, *At America's Gates*, 125.

85 **"to end his agony":** Fu, "My Reception in America."
85 **still see the rope:** Jorae, *Children of Chinatown*, 18.
85 **Five men escaped:** "Chinese Escape from the Sheds," *San Francisco Examiner*, October 28, 1901.
85 **bribing of a watchman:** "Chinese Trick of Substitution Played," *San Francisco Call*, March 8, 1901; and "Crooked Work at Mail Dock," *San Francisco Call*, March 9, 1901.

CHAPTER 6

87 **only means of departing:** See Knauff v. Shaughnessy, 88 F. Supp. 607 (1949). Ellen arrived in New York City aboard the *Comfort* on August 14, 1948.
88 **Following the passage:** Erika Lee, *At America's Gates: Chinese Immigration during the Exclusion Era, 1882–1943* (Chapel Hill: University of North Carolina Press, 2003), 30.
88 **immigrants managed to quickly:** Daniel Wilsher, *Immigration Detention: Law, History, Politics* (Cambridge, UK: Cambridge University Press, 2011), 17; and United States Industrial Commission, *Reports of the Industrial Commission on Immigration and on Education* (Washington, DC: US Government Printing Office, 1901), xcix. Most immigrants escaped.
88 **majority of those detained:** Industrial Commission, *Reports of the Industrial Commission on Immigration and on Education*, xcix.
88 **Migrants detained on Ellis Island:** Joseph Haas, oral history interview by Nancy Dallett, November 4, 1989, West Allis, Wisconsin, Oral History Library, The Statue of Liberty–Ellis Island Foundation, Inc., https://heritage.statueofliberty.org/oral-history-library; and Elliott Young, *Forever Prisoners: How the United States Made the World's Largest Immigration Detention System* (New York: Oxford University Press, 2021), 8.
89 **"chicken crates":** Haas, oral history interview.
89 **thirteen-year-old Ruth Metzger:** Ruth Metzger, oral history interview by Debby Dane, December 17, 1985, Chicago, Illinois, Oral History Library, The Statue of Liberty–Ellis Island Foundation, Inc., https://heritage.statueofliberty.org/oral-history-library.
89 **women arriving without male companions:** Sam Erman, *Almost Citizens: Puerto Rico, the U.S. Constitution, and Empire* (New York: Cambridge University Press, 2018), 76; and Industrial Commission, *Reports of the Industrial Commission on Immigration and on Education*, 145–46.
90 **Sing Sing prison:** David Rothman, "Perfecting the Prison," in *The Oxford History of the Prison: The Practice of Punishment in Western Society*, eds. Norval Morris and David J. Rothman (New York: Oxford University Press, 1997). For reforms at Sing Sing, see Denis Brian, *Sing Sing: The Inside Story of a Notorious Prison* (Amherst, NY: Prometheus, 2005).
90 **"I should prefer imprisonment":** Quoted in Vincent J. Cannato, *American Passage:*

The History of Ellis Island (New York: HarperCollins, 2009), 340. The ambassador's view on Ellis Island was informed by his racist notion that British immigrants should not be detained alongside Eastern European and especially Jewish immigrants. Still, it is significant that the comparison he made was with a prison.

90 **"I became a jailer":** Frederic C. Howe, *The Confessions of a Reformer* (New York: Charles Scribner's Sons, 1925), 267.

90 **entered the First World War:** Harlan D. Unrau, *Ellis Island, Statue of Liberty National Monument, New York–New Jersey* (Washington, DC: U.S. Department of the Interior, National Park Service, 1984), 773; Cannato, *American Passage*, 295.

90 **Well-known anarchist Emma Goldman:** Emma Goldman, *Living My Life: Two Volumes in One* (New York: Cosimo Classics, 2011), 713.

90 **detained "enemy aliens" believed:** See Presidential Proclamations No. 2525, 2526, and 2527, December 7–8, 1941; Roger Daniels, "Incarceration of the Japanese Americans: A Sixty-Year Perspective," *History Teacher* 35, no. 3 (May 2002): 300; and Cannato, *American Passage*, 352.

91 **Japanese Americans on the West Coast:** Daniels, "Incarceration of the Japanese Americans," 302.

91 **committed subversive acts:** Daniels, 300–302.

91 **To supplement her diet:** Fiduciary Obligations Regarding Bureau of Prisons Commissary Fund, 19 Op. O.L.C. 127 (1995), https://www.justice.gov/file/20216/download. Eighteen years earlier, the Department of Justice had established the commissary system to sell goods that prisons did not provide to inmates, including certain foods, toothpaste, stamps, soap, and newspapers.

91 **officials called "recreation work":** The ten-cents figure was taken from Ellen Raphael Knauff, *The Ellen Knauff Story* (New York: W. W. Norton, 1952). Additionally, A. H. Raskin, "New Role for Ellis Island," *New York Times*, November 12, 1950, documented that ten cents was the nominal wage paid in 1950 for work on Ellis Island. For minimum wage in the United States in 1950, see "History of Federal Minimum Wage Rates under the Fair Labor Standards Act, 1938–2009," U.S. Department of Labor," accessed May 25, 2020, https://www.dol.gov/agencies/whd/minimum-wage/history/chart.

92 **refugee who had fled:** Robert L. Fleegler, *Ellis Island Nation: Immigration Policy and American Identity in the Twentieth Century* (Philadelphia: University of Pennsylvania Press, 2013), 92.

92 **discovered in Hollywood:** Beyer Blinder Belle, *Ellis Island, Statue of Liberty National Monument* (Washington, DC: U.S. Department of the Interior, National Park Service, 1988), 4:294.

92 **then there was Wilma:** William M. Farrell, "Ex-G.I. May Give Up Deportation Fight," *New York Times*, May 11, 1950. In Ellen's memoir, Wilma appears by the name of Clara, but all other sources make it clear that Clara is a pseudonym for Wilma Bauer.

92 **War Department had accused:** "Army Recommends Suspected Spy Be Returned to Germany," *Daily Press*, November 22, 1945.

92 **He and Wilma spent:** "Wife to Fight Move to Deport Bauer as Undesirable Alien," *Palladium-Item*, November 22, 1945.

93 **feminists had successfully:** Jane Perry Clark Carey, "Some Aspects of Statelessness since World War I," *American Political Science Review* 40, no. 1 (1946): 113–23. Even if she had not married Edgar, Ellen would have lost her German citizenship, because she was a Jewish woman who had left Germany. In 1935, the Nazis had passed the Reich Citizenship Law, which stated that Jews could not be German citizens—only nationals, who did not have full political rights. Then, a 1941 order jettisoned "German national" status from all Jewish people who lived abroad.

93 **"owe no explanation":** Edward A. Harris, "The Perplexing Case of Ellen Knauff," *St. Louis Post-Dispatch*, February 5, 1950.

93 **also a stateless Jewish refugee:** Jordan David Thomas Walters, "On the Right to Have Rights," *Human Rights Quarterly* 43, no. 2 (2021): 398–403.

94 **"Ellis Island is a concentration":** I could not find the letters in any existing archives. The quotes from the letters come from Knauff, *Ellen Knauff Story*.

CHAPTER 7

95 **dire conditions inside the warehouse:** "Loud Complaints among Chinese," *San Francisco Chronicle*, August 30, 1909; "Pacific Mail Prisoner Dies: Another Victim Is Added to the Detention Shed Record," *San Francisco Chronicle*, May 8, 1902.

95 **He constantly begged:** "Pacific Mail Prisoner Dies," *San Francisco Chronicle*, May 8, 1902.

95 **Dow's story would repeat:** See, for instance, the case of Ho Mun in "Death of a Chinese," *San Francisco Examiner*, November 22, 1899; and Erika Lee, *At America's Gates: Chinese Immigration during the Exclusion Era, 1882–1943* (Chapel Hill: University of North Carolina Press, 2003), 56.

96 **Low Suey Sing died:** "Loud Complaints among Chinese."

96 **"in a critical condition":** Luella Miner, "Chinese Students and the Exclusion Laws," *Independent*, April 24, 1902.

97 **earliest years of the republic:** Shima Baradaran Baughman, *The Bail Book: A Comprehensive Look at Bail in America's Criminal Justice System* (New York: Cambridge University Press, 2018), 19–21.

97 **"bail shall be admitted":** Judiciary Act, 1 Stat. 73 (1789).

97 **And in 1895:** Hudson v. Parker, 156 U.S. 277 (1895).

97 **"any occupation they please":** "Chinese in Transit," *San Francisco Examiner*, October 16, 1888.

98 **amounted to $2,000:** Calculated based on data from August 2023 (which will continue to change over time) using CPI Inflation Calculator, accessed August 15, 2023, https://www.in2013dollars.com/us/inflation/1901?amount=2000.

98 **Policymakers knew that:** Baughman, *Bail Book*, 33.

98 **Few other Chinese migrants:** Baughman, 1–2.

98 **"a prisoner released on bail":** James V. Hayes, "Contracts to Indemnify Bail in Criminal Cases," *Fordham Law Review* 6, no. 3 (November 1937): 395.

99 **tutelage of Jee Gam:** Jee Gam, "The Geary Act: From the Standpoint of a Christian Chinese," in *Chinese American Voices: From the Gold Rush to the Present*, ed. Judy Yung, Gordon H. Chang, and H. Mark Lai (Berkeley: University of California Press, 2006), 86.

99 **were turning violent:** "Eight Mongols Fiercely Resist Order Deporting Them to China," *San Francisco Call*, March 6, 1902; "Chinese Hide Many Weapons," *San Francisco Call*, March 8, 1902; "Penned Chinese Grow Desperate," *San Francisco Call*, April 11, 1902; "Orientals Plan to Escape from Detention," *San Francisco Examiner*, April 11, 1902; and "Chinese Detention Sheds Will Be Emptied," *San Francisco Examiner*, May 6, 1902.

99 **They intended to arrive:** For more on the arch, see "Memorial Arch," Oberlin College & Conservatory, accessed May 28, 2021, https://www.oberlin.edu/memorial-arch.

99 **day of their departure:** Fu Chi Hao, "My Reception in America," *Outlook*, August 10, 1907. It would also provide them cooler temperatures.

99 **The route was:** For maps of the railroad, see "Canadian Pacific Map: Railway Lines in Canada," University of British Columbia, accessed June 1, 2021, https://open.library.ubc.ca/collections/chung/chungtext/items/1.0228967#p4z-1r0f; and "Canadian Pacific Railway and Connecting Lines," Library of Congress, accessed June 1, 2021, https://www.loc.gov/item/2006627697/.

100 **encountered another fundamental:** Maya Schenwar and Victoria Law, *Prison by Any Other Name: The Harmful Consequences of Popular Reforms* (New York: New Press, 2020), 6.

100 **Newspapers throughout California:** "Ho Yow to Be Sued on the Forfeited Bonds," *San Francisco Call*, October 3, 1902.

101 **Chinese consul would lose:** "Ho Yow to Be Sued on the Forfeited Bonds"; "Suit to Be Brought against Consul Ho Yow," *San Francisco Call*, September 28, 1902.

101 **"The law required us":** Fu, "My Reception in America."

102 **"The problem of the twentieth":** W. E. B. Du Bois, *The Souls of Black Folk: Essays and Sketches* (Chicago: A. C. McClurg & Company, 1903), 13.

102 **"a new human unity":** Du Bois, *Souls of Black Folk*, 88.

103 **two friends had experienced:** Fu, "My Reception in America"; Miner, "Chinese Students and the Exclusion Laws"; and Edward Wagenknecht, *American Profile, 1900–1909* (Amherst: University of Massachusetts Press, 1982), 216.

103 **His chronicle was powerful:** Fu, "My Reception in America"; "The Woe of Fu Chi Hao," *Daily Morning Journal and Courier*, October 18, 1907; "Hardships of Chinese Student," *Boston Evening Transcript*, October 15, 1907; "Ill Treatment of Mongolians," *Joliet Evening Herald*, November 19, 1907; and Fu, "My Reception in America," *Santa Cruz Weekly Sentinel*, August 21, 1907.

103 **protest this discrimination:** Sin-Kiong Wong, "The Making of a Chinese Boycott: The Origins of the 1905 Anti-American Movement," *American Journal of Chinese Studies* 6, no. 2 (October 1999): 137.

103 **The year after Chi Hao:** Erika Lee and Judy Yung, *Angel Island: Immigrant Gateway to America* (New York: Oxford University Press, 2010), 11–12.

103 **requested twenty acres of land:** Lee and Yung, *Angel Island*, 11–12.

104 **"Ellis Island of the West":** Lee, *At America's Gates*, 75.

104 **Approximately 70 percent:** Lee and Yung, *Angel Island*, 57.

104 **While the detention facilities:** Lee and Yung, 56–57.

104 **still constituted 70 percent:** Lee and Yung, 70.

104 **Those labeled "Occidentals":** Lee and Yung, 56.

104 **The government subcontracted meals:** Lee and Yung, 61.

105 **One such poem read:** Poem 43, quoted from: Angel Island Immigration Station Foundation, "Poetry Examples," accessed August 25, 2023, https://www.aiisf.org/poems-and-inscriptions. For more poetry carved in the wooden walls of the barracks on Angel Island, see Him Mark Lai, Genny Lim, and Judy Yung, eds., *Island: Poetry and History of Chinese Immigrants on Angel Island, 1910–1940*, 2nd ed. (Seattle: University of Washington Press, 2014).

105 **In October 1919:** Lee and Yung, *Angel Island*, 101.

105 **fire in the immigration station:** Lee and Yung, 299–301.

CHAPTER 8

108 **Amid these now disquieting:** Edward A. Harris, "The Perplexing Case of Ellen Knauff," *St. Louis Post-Dispatch*, February 5, 1950.

109 **"test the right":** United States ex rel. Knauff v. Shaughnessy, 338 U.S. 537 (1950).

109 **the government's attorney provided:** Proclamation 2523, 55 Stat. 1696, 3 CFR, 1943 Cum. Supp., 270-272, at 175.57(b); Charles D. Weisselberg, "The Exclusion and Detention of Aliens: Lessons from the Lives of Ellen Knauff and Ignatz Mezei," *University of Pennsylvania Law Review* 143, no. 4 (April 1995): 956; Amending of the Act of May 22, 1918, 55 Stat. 252, 22 U.S.C. at 223; and Knauff v. Shaughnessy, 338 U.S. 537 (1950). The Act of June 21, 1941, passed amid fears of the Second World War, gave the president the right to impose additional restrictions on the entry of persons during national emergencies. Under the act, Franklin D. Roosevelt had issued Proclamation 2523, which authorized the attorney general to exclude any "alien" whose entry "would be prejudicial to the interests of the United States."

110 **"I don't know what to do":** I could not locate the letter anywhere in the archives to corroborate it.

110 **On a cold January day:** The case was decided on January 16, 1950. Weather data from "January 1950 Weather History in New York City," Weather Spark, accessed August 15, 2023, https://weatherspark.com/h/m/23912/1950/1/Historical-Weather-in-January-1950-in-New-York-City-New-York-United-States.

110 **"At the outset":** *Knauff,* 338 U.S. at 542.

110 **Three justices disagreed:** Frankfurter also wrote his own dissent.

110 **"says we must find":** *Knauff,* 338 U.S. at 551.

111 **Hiss swallowed once:** John Chabot Smith, "Hiss Guilty, Will Appeal," *Boston Sunday Globe,* January 22, 1950.

111 **Hiss had been an American exemplar:** Janny Scott, "Alger Hiss, Divisive Icon of the Cold War, Dies at 92," *New York Times,* November 16, 1996, https://www.nytimes.com/1996/11/16/nyregion/alger-hiss-divisive-icon-of-the-cold-war-dies-at-92.html.

111 **These "Pumpkin Papers":** Richard M. Fried, *Nightmare in Red: The McCarthy Era in Perspective* (New York: Oxford University Press, 1991), 19–20; and John Ehrman, "A Half-Century of Controversy: The Alger Hiss Case," *Studies in Intelligence* 44, no. 5 (2001), https://www.cia.gov/resources/csi/studies-in-intelligence/archives/vol-44-no-5/the-alger-hiss-case/.

111 **"thoroughly infested":** Jenny Scott, "Alger Hiss, Divisive Icon of the Cold War, Dies at 92," *New York Times,* November 16, 1996.

112 **McCarthy's accusations were outlandish:** Ted Morgan, *Reds: McCarthyism in Twentieth-Century America* (New York: Random House, 2004), 385.

112 **an "internal security emergency":** Internal Security Act, 64 Stat. 987 (1950).

112 **Within ninety days of the law's passage:** Harlan D. Unrau, *Ellis Island, Statue of Liberty National Monument, New York–New Jersey* (Washington, DC: U.S. Department of the Interior, National Park Service, 1984), 3:974–75.

112 **Harris, a muckraker:** "Edward A. Harris, Winner of Pulitzer for Reporting," *New York Times,* March 18, 1976, https://nyti.ms/2GEzkEy.

112 **"Such injustice cannot stand always":** Harris, "The Perplexing Case of Ellen Knauff."

113 **After Harris's piece came out:** Andrea Friedman, *Citizenship in Cold War America: The National Security State and the Possibilities of Dissent* (Amherst: University of Massachusetts Press, 2014), 49.

113 **Although Ellen never gained:** "Forgotten Woman," *Oakdale Journal,* April 4, 1963.

113 **"work on behalf of justice":** See, for instance, "Letters from the People," *St. Louis Post-Dispatch,* April 30, 1950.

113 **fought for the rights:** Lawrence H. Larsen, "William Langer: A Maverick in the Senate," *Wisconsin Magazine of History* 44, no. 3 (Spring 1961): 189; and Vincent J. Cannato, *American Passage: The History of Ellis Island* (New York: HarperCollins, 2009), 366.

113 **Seeing the popularity:** Edward A. Harris, "Bill Would Bar Deportation of Ellen Knauff," *St. Louis Post-Dispatch,* February 3, 1950; Edward A. Harris, "Bill in House to Cancel Knauff Exclusion Order," *St. Louis Post-Dispatch,* March 8, 1950; and Cannato, *American Passage,* 366.

113 **on May 2:** "House Votes to Let Mrs. Knauff into U.S.," *New York Times,* May 3, 1950.

114 **On May 16, 1950:** Edward A. Harris, "Ellen Knauff Deportation Stayed at Last Minute by Order of Justice Jackson," *St. Louis Post-Dispatch*, May 17, 1950.

114 **She set aside an elegant:** Royal Riley and James Davis, "GI Bride Gets Stay, Luggage Goes," *Daily News*, May 18, 1950.

114 **she could see the American:** Friedman, *Citizenship in Cold War America*, 48.

114 **mailed letter awaited him:** Story and timeline that follows from Harris, "Ellen Knauff Deportation Stayed at Last Minute."

115 **"Bundling this woman":** *A Scandalous Situation: The Knauff Case*, 81st Cong., 2nd sess., *Congressional Record* 96, pt. 15: A3751.

115 **"This is to inform you":** "Ellen Knauff Deportation Stayed at Last Minute by Order of Justice Jackson," *St. Louis Post-Dispatch*, May 17, 1950.

115 **"After 22 months of effort":** Riley and Davis, "GI Bride Gets Stay, Luggage Goes."

116 **Seeing Ellen's increasing anguish:** Alvin H. Goldstein, "Kurt Knauff Plans Flight to U.S. to Aid Wife," *St. Louis Post-Dispatch*, January 3, 1951.

116 **released "on parole":** The term "parole" can be confusing because in the criminal justice system, it refers to the conditional release of a person from prison prior to the end of the maximum sentence imposed, but immigration officials had long used "parole" to signify the concept of bail. Feingold's first name was Alfred, but he went by Al.

116 **"so happy at her unexpected":** Edward O'Neill and Art Smith, "GI Bride Ellen Knauff Paroled After 17 Mos. on Ellis Island," *Daily News*, January 31, 1951.

116 **her case was reevaluated:** Alvin H. Goldstein, "Attorneys Offer to Take Custody of Mrs. Knauff," *St. Louis Post-Dispatch*, February 13, 1951.

117 **fired questions at her:** These questions and answers paraphrase the original ones from "Record of Hearing before a Board of Special Inquiry," CIA-RDP59-00882R00100370034-1-FFS, Central Intelligence Agency, accessed June 18, 2023, https://www.cia.gov/readingroom/docs/CIA-RDP59-00882R000100370034-1.pdf.

117 **heavy Czech accent:** Edward A. Harris, "Knauff Exclusion Order Is Upheld after Hearing, She Plans Appeal," *St. Louis Post-Dispatch*, March 27, 1951.

118 **"January 3, 1947":** "Record of Hearing before a Board of Special Inquiry," CIA; also cited in Board of Immigration Appeals, "In re. Ellen Raphael Knauff or Boxhorn or Boxhornova in Exclusion Proceedings" (BIA, File A-6937471), August 29, 1951, reprinted in Ellen Raphael Knauff, *The Ellen Knauff Story* (New York: W. W. Norton, 1952), appendix.

118 **"not bound by the rules":** Cited in Board of Immigration Appeals, "In re. Ellen Raphael Knauff."

119 **"Testimony has been offered":** Alvin H. Goldstein, "Ellen Knauff Appeals Against Board's Decision," *St. Louis Post-Dispatch*, April 12, 1951.

119 **"'The Knauff case'":** Herbert A. Trask, "Basis of Knauff Case Is 'Hearsay,' Attorney Says," *St. Louis Post-Dispatch*, June 29, 1951.

120 ***Christian Science Monitor*:** "Entry Approval Reported in Case of Mrs. Knauff," *Christian Science Monitor*, November 2, 1951.

120 **"All of the testimony":** Board of Immigration Appeals, "In re. Ellen Raphael Knauff."

CHAPTER 9

123 **Public libraries throughout:** "Here's a List of New Books at the Library," *Auburn Journal*, April 2, 1953; "New Books Displayed at Corvallis Library," *Corvallis Gazette-Times*, May 27, 1952; "Book Loans Hit High Figure," *Daily Inter Lake*, August 24, 1952; "New Books at Adams Free Library," *North Adams Transcript*, October 23, 1952; and "Library Notes," *Placer Herald*, April 16, 1953.

124 **"most shocking perversions":** "How to Lose Our Friends," *Knoxville Journal*, March 30, 1952.

124 **"how far we have strayed":** John Oakes, "It Happened Here," *New York Times*, March 30, 1952.

124 **"A single red rose":** "Ellis Island Prisoner," *Salt Lake Tribune*, June 22, 1953.

124 **One of the most reported:** Ignatz Mezei had lived in the United States without papers for more than twenty years before heading back to Europe to visit his ailing mother. He returned to America in 1950, this time with a visa in hand.

124 **ruled in Ignatz's case:** Shaughnessy v. U.S. ex rel. Mezei, 345 U.S. 206 (1953).

124 **Desperate for freedom:** Charles D. Weisselberg, "The Exclusion and Detention of Aliens: Lessons from the Lives of Ellen Knauff and Ignatz Mezei," *University of Pennsylvania Law Review* 143, no. 4 (April 1995): 965.

124 **"The news media today":** General Joseph Swing, oral history interview by Ed Edwin, June 21, 1967, Eisenhower Administration Oral History Project, Columbia University.

125 **Canadian students picketed:** "Consulate Picketed Over Detention of Students," *Gazette and Daily*, January 7, 1954.

125 **"most dreaded 27 acres":** "Frustration Island," *Sydney Morning Herald*, August 14, 1954.

125 **The international repercussions:** Madeline Y. Hsu, *The Good Immigrants: How the Yellow Peril Became the Model Minority* (Princeton: Princeton University Press 2015), 36.

125 **"America has weighty reasons":** Luella Miner, "Chinese Students and the Exclusion Laws," *Independent*, April 24, 1902.

126 **year of peak immigration:** Ronald H. Bayor, *Encountering Ellis Island: How European Immigrants Entered America* (Baltimore: Johns Hopkins University Press, 2014), 39–40.

126 **only 6,752 were deported**: Bayor, *Encountering Ellis Island*, 39–40.

126 **90 percent of all Chinese:** Erika Lee and Judy Yung, *Angel Island: Immigrant Gateway to America* (New York: Oxford University Press, 2010), 84, 93.

126 **height of European migration:** Vincent J. Cannato, *American Passage: The History of Ellis Island* (New York: HarperCollins, 2009), 168. In April 1906, for

instance, an estimated forty-five thousand immigrants arrived at the island in a single week.

126 **1,004,756 immigrants:** Bayor, *Encountering Ellis Island*, 39.

126 **started issuing visas abroad:** For an understanding of visas during that period, see James Wright Morgan, "The Visa System as an Instrument of Immigration Control" (PhD diss., American University, May 1950).

127 **expensive, and ineffective:** In the immigration context, "parole" refers to what is treated as bail in the criminal justice system.

127 **"Unless this right to bail":** Stack v. Boyle, 342 U.S. 1, 4 (1951). It must be noted, however, that a year later, in *Carlson v. Landon*, a case that unsurprisingly dealt with alleged Communists who were resident aliens, the Supreme Court rejected the contention that the Constitution granted bail, noting that there was no right to bail in all cases and that the Eighth Amendment simply provided that bail not be excessive. Carlson et al. v. Landon, 342 U.S. 524 (1952). For citizens, however, the ideal remained that bail was to be set for pretrial release.

127 **Another 27 percent:** Caleb Foote, "Compelling Appearance in Court: Administration of Bail in Philadelphia," *University of Pennsylvania Law Review* 102, no. 8 (1954): 1048, https://scholarship.law.upenn.edu/penn_law_review/vol102/iss8/4.

128 **there remained the ideal:** As he considered pretrial release for entrants, Brownell abstained from using the term "bail" and used "parole," as this was the term used for immigration matters.

128 **first mass naturalization ceremonies:** "Miss Liberty Listens—US Has Mass Naturalization First Time in Its History" and "Changes Alien Policies," both in *The Sedalia Democrat*, November 11, 1954.

128 **"one more step forward":** "Address by Honorable Herbert Brownell, Jr., Attorney General of the United States," Naturalization Ceremonies, Ebbets Field & Polo Grounds, November 11, 1954, transcript, https://www.justice.gov/sites/default/files/ag/legacy/2011/09/12/11-11-1954.pdf.

128 **Its closure was in:** Cannato, *American Passage*, 375.

128 **a Norwegian seaman:** "Famed Island Now 'Closed,'" *Statesville Daily Record*, November 15, 1954; "The End of an Era," *Plain Speaker*, November 13, 1954; and "Ellis Island Ends Alien Processing," *New York Times*, November 13, 1954. Arne's surname is sometimes spelled as "Petterson," but it appears to have been "Pettersen"; see Megan Smolenyak, "Solving the Mystery of Arne Pettersen, the Last to Leave Ellis Island," accessed August 25, 2023, https://smolenyak.medium.com/we-finally-know-what-happened-to-arne-pettersen-the-last-to-leave-ellis-island-3529a692389d.

129 ***Barber*: "Physical detention of aliens":** Leng May Ma v. Barber, 357 U.S. 185 (1958).

129 **First Congregational Church of Oakland:** Jee Gam, "The Geary Act: From the Standpoint of a Christian Chinese," in *Chinese American Voices: From the Gold Rush to the Present*, ed. Judy Yung, Gordon H. Chang, and H. Mark Lai (Berkeley: University of California Press, 2006), 86.

130 **far from perfect or emancipatory:** For the same argument about individuals released from the criminal justice system, see Maya Schenwar and Victoria Law, *Prison by Any Other Name: The Harmful Consequences of Popular Reforms* (New York: New Press, 2020), 6.

130 **"prior written notice":** "Parole Conditions Re Ellen Knauff," February 20, 1951; and FOIA Request, Genealogy Records Request 50292674, Alien File/A-File A6937471, GEN2022001122.

130 **"giving both heart and conscience":** Herbert Brownell Jr., "Humanizing the Administration of the Immigration Law," conference remarks, Town Hall Club, New York, January 26, 1955, transcript, https://www.justice.gov/sites/default/files/ag/legacy/2011/09/12/01-26-1955.pdf. The number did increase throughout the 1956 fiscal year to 145 individuals held per day for all ports of entry, but it still remained much lower than the number before 1954. See Department of Justice, *Annual Report of the Immigration and Naturalization Service for the Fiscal Year Ended June 30, 1956* (Washington, DC: Government Printing Office, 1956), 13. A few other non-Mexican migrants seemed to have been held in facilities other than ports of entry during this year; while the total number of such detainees was not recorded, it is clear that the number of incarcerated non-Mexican individuals fell dramatically after 1954 and was small.

131 **94 percent of:** Department of Justice, *Annual Report of the Immigration and Naturalization Service for the Fiscal Year Ended June 30, 1955* (Washington, DC: Government Printing Office, 1955), 17.

131 **immigration officials offered:** For more on the history of voluntary departures during this period, see Adam Goodman, *The Deportation Machine: America's Long History of Expelling Immigrants* (Princeton: Princeton University Press, 2020), chap. 2.

132 **in his 1955 speech:** Brownell did address Operation Wetback in his speech, but he did so to show how Mexican migration had declined. He did not link it back to detention figures. For more on how the nation was not following "humane" detention practices in the period between 1954 and 1980, see Judith Irangika Dingatantrige Perera, "From Exclusion to State Violence: The Transformation of Noncitizen Detention in the United States and Its Implications in Arizona, 1891–Present" (PhD diss., University of Arizona, 2018); and Jessica Ordaz, *The Shadow of El Centro: A History of Migrant Incarceration and Solidarity* (Chapel Hill: University of North Carolina Press, 2021).

132 **constant stream of newspaper:** See, for instance, Gladwin Hill, "Two Every Minute across the Border," *New York Times*, January 31, 1954.

132 **Operation Wetback was led:** Swing, oral history interview.

132 **a military-style attack:** Mae M. Ngai, *Impossible Subjects: Illegal Aliens and the Making of Modern America* (Princeton: Princeton University Press, 2004), 155–56. Later, the operation expanded to Chicago as well.

133 **expanding the number of braceros:** Kitty Calavita, *Inside the State: The Bracero*

Program, Immigration, and the I.N.S. (New Orleans: Quid Pro Books, 2010), Appendix B, 238. Bracero contracts rose from 201,000 in 1953 to 309,000 a year later.

133 **had fallen to approximately:** Department of Justice, *Annual Report of the Immigration and Naturalization Service, 1959* (Washington, DC: Government Printing Office, 1959). Other migrants were also detained during this period and later. For instance, many Haitians remained behind bars because they could not pay bond. See Carl Lindskoog, *Detain and Punish: Haitian Refugees and the Rise of the World's Largest Immigration Detention System* (Gainesville: University Press of Florida, 2018), 18–25.

133 **acting as strikebreakers:** Ana Raquel Minian, *Undocumented Lives: The Untold Story of Mexican Migration* (Cambridge, MA: Harvard University Press, 2018), chap. 2.

133 **During its twenty-two years:** Mireya Loza, *Defiant Braceros: How Migrant Workers Fought for Racial, Sexual, and Political Freedom* (Chapel Hill: University of North Carolina Press, 2016), 2. Although the Bracero Program officially ended in 1964, contracts were actually issued until 1967. As such, the program unofficially lasted more than twenty-two years.

133 **braceros found themselves:** See Ana Raquel Minian, *Undocumented Lives*, chap. 1.

134 **With little work available:** See Minian, *Undocumented Lives*, 81–82.

134 **In the early 1960s:** Clemente Lomelí, interview by the author, January 2, 2009, Las Ánimas, Zacatecas, Mexico.

134 **caught about 30,000:** Manuel García y Griego and Mónica Verea, *México y Estados Unidos frente a la migración de indocumentados* (México: Universidad Nacional Autónoma de México, Coordinación de Humanidades, 1988), 119–21, chart 2.

134 **That number rose to:** García y Griego and Verea, *México y Estados Unidos frente a la migración de indocumentados*, 119–21, chart 2.

134 **31,000 migrants were detained:** Department of Justice, *Annual Report of the Immigration and Naturalization Service, 1964* (Washington, DC: Government Printing Office, 1964); and Department of Justice, *Annual Report of the Immigration and Naturalization Service, 1965* (Washington, DC: Government Printing Office, 1965). For more on the rise of detention during this period, see Perera, "From Exclusion to State Violence"; and Ordaz, *Shadow of El Centro*. The Bracero Program did continue until 1967 but in an almost insignificant manner.

134 **"largely the result of":** Department of Justice, *Annual Report of the Immigration and Naturalization Service, 1965*, 14.

134 **number of detentions mushroomed:** Department of Justice, *Annual Report of the Immigration and Naturalization Service, 1973* (Washington, DC: Government Printing Office, 1973), 15; and Department of Justice, *Annual Report of the Immigration and Naturalization Service, 1978* (Washington, DC: Government Printing Office, 1978), 23.

134 **journalist Jesús Saldaña:** Ordaz, *Shadow of El Centro*, 62.

135 **Ysidro activists denounced:** "Border Patrol Center Said to Need Money," *Chula Vista Star-News*, October 19, 1972.

135 **After Brownell's announcement:** "Address by Honorable Herbert Brownell, Jr., Attorney General of the United States"; and Department of Justice, *Annual Report of the Immigration and Naturalization Service, 1965*, 35.

135 **it reversed course:** Department of Justice, *Annual Report of the Immigration and Naturalization Service, 1973*, 23; and Department of Justice, *Annual Report of the Immigration and Naturalization Service, 1979*, 5.

135 **The guards forced him:** Manuel Jiménez, interview by the author, August 6, 2013, South San Francisco, California, digital recording.

135 **implemented Operation Wetback:** Numbers taken from all annual reports of the Immigration and Naturalization Service.

135 **But immigration officials still argued:** See INS Commissioner Chapman, as quoted in Lindskoog, *Detain and Punish*, 22.

CHAPTER 10

139 **forty-foot neon cowboy:** Steve Sebelius, "Horse-and-Rider Usher in Museum Dedicated to Neon," *Las Vegas Sun*, November 14, 1996, https://lasvegassun.com/news/1996/nov/14/horse-and-rider-usher-in-museum-dedicated-to-neon/.

141 **won a tidy pile:** Julia Martínez, oral history interview by the author, February 22– 24, 2019, Kissimmee, Florida, digital recording.

141 **their first child together:** "ULISES MANSUR Inmate X30606: Florida Prisoner," accessed February 1, 2020, https://www.rapsheetz.com/florida/doc-prisoner/MANSUR_ULISES/X30606. See also author's interview with Gerardo.

141 **"We were happy":** Martínez, oral history interview.

141 **An *Orlando Sentinel* article:** Maya Bell, "Marielitos in Trouble Arrive in Legal Limbo," *Orlando Sentinel*, April 22, 1990, https://www.orlandosentinel.com/1990/04/22/marielitos-in-trouble-arrive-in-legal-limbo/.

142 **with intent to sell:** Las Vegas Metropolitan Police Department, report on "Julia Martinez Leon," Julia Martínez, personal files.

142 **Gerry came into:** The sources provide conflicting dates of birth, but May 4, 1983, seems to be the correct one.

142 **court dropped the charge:** Las Vegas Metropolitan Police Department, report on "Julia Martinez Leon."

143 **January 4, 1984:** Las Vegas Metropolitan Police Department, report on "Julia Martinez Leon."

143 **A handful of other:** I could not confirm these charges through official records and relied solely on Gerardo's memory. However, government documents do show that Mariel Cubans were regularly arrested for infractions as slight as these.

144 **opened its gates in 1902:** Department of Justice, Federal Bureau of Prisons, "A

Report to the Attorney General on the Disturbances at the Federal Detention Center, Oakdale, Louisiana and the U.S. Penitentiary, Atlanta, Georgia," A1–A9, Folder 7, Box 8, Series II, Cuban Detainees' Litigation Papers, Atlanta History Center.

144 **they informed Congress:** Federal Bureau of Prisons, "A Report to the Attorney General on the Disturbances."

144 **each cell was meant:** Federal Bureau of Prisons, "A Report to the Attorney General on the Disturbances." Although Cellhouse B was closed by the time the report was written, it was open for most of Gerardo's time there. See also author's interview with Gerardo and *Atlanta Federal Penitentiary: Report of the Subcommittee on Courts, Civil Liberties, and the Administration of Justice of the Committee on the Judiciary*, 99th Cong. (1986).

144 **Across the corridor:** For a map of the facility, see Federal Bureau of Prisons, "A Report to the Attorney General on the Disturbances." See also author's interview with Gerardo and Committee on the Judiciary, *Atlanta Federal Penitentiary*, 1.

144 **There was also the dreaded:** Federal Bureau of Prisons, "A Report to the Attorney General on the Disturbances"; author's interview with Gerardo; Committee on the Judiciary, *Atlanta Federal Penitentiary*, 1.

144 **dormitories in better condition:** Federal Bureau of Prisons, "A Report to the Attorney General on the Disturbances."

144 **the decaying walls:** *Atlanta Federal Penitentiary*, 1. For more on the experiences, see Mark S. Hamm, *The Abandoned Ones: The Imprisonment and Uprising of the Mariel Boat People* (Boston: Northeastern University Press, 1995), 119–57; and Kristina Shull, *Detention Empire: Reagan's War on Immigrants and the Seeds of Resistance* (Chapel Hill: University of North Carolina Press, 2022), 29–63, 186–231.

145 **Alberto Herrera was one:** Hamm, *Abandoned Ones*, 60–65, 98, 110, 112, 133.

145 **Pedro was mugged:** Hamm, 66.

146 **"The seven of us":** El Pintor (pseudonym), oral history interview by the author, April 23, 2018, Miami, Florida, digital recording.

146 **Once he completed his:** El Pintor, oral history interview.

147 **Locked inside a maximum-security:** For an understanding of how the BOP classified its prisons and those it held, see *Federal Bureau of Prisons: Oversight Hearing before the Subcommittee on Courts, Civil Liberties, and the Administration of Justice of the Committee on the Judiciary*, 98th Cong. 480 (1984) (letter from Mark Mauer, American Friends Service Committee).

147 **five thousand Mariel Cubans:** *Atlanta Federal Penitentiary*, iii.

147 **they had no idea when:** *Mariel Cuban Detainees: Events Preceding and Following the November 1987 Riots: Hearing before the Subcommittee on Courts, Civil Liberties, and the Administration of Justice of the Committee on the Judiciary*, 100th Cong. 16 (1988) (letter from Alan Nelson, commissioner, INS).

147 **seemingly randomly chosen men:** *Mariel Cuban Detainees*, 293.

148 **Cubans were held in facilities:** Michael Welch, "The Role of the Immigration and

Naturalization Service in the Prison-Industrial Complex," *Social Justice* 27, no. 3 (2000): 73–88; and *Immigration and Naturalization Service Budget Authorization—Fiscal Year 1986: Hearings before the Subcommittee on Immigration, Refugees, and International Law of the Committee on the Judiciary*, 99th Cong. 110 (1985).

148 **"an additional 200,000 Cubans":** Department of Justice, Office of the Attorney General, "Report of the President's Task Force on Immigration and Refugee Policy," Folder: Immigration and Refugee Matters (3), Box 22, Edwin Meese Files, OA6518, Ronald Reagan Presidential Library.

148 **possible "enforcement options":** Office of the Attorney General, "Report of the President's Task Force on Immigration and Refugee Policy."

148 **"liberals, blacks, and church":** Office of the Attorney General, "Report of the President's Task Force on Immigration and Refugee Policy."

149 **"detention upon arrival":** Office of the Attorney General, "Report of the President's Task Force on Immigration and Refugee Policy."

149 **detention had been conceived:** For more on the Reagan administration's expansion of immigrant detention and the resistance to it, see Shull, *Detention Empire.*

149 **Maxine had previously made:** Peter McGrath et al., "Refugees or Prisoners?," *Newsweek*, February 1, 1982, 24–26, 28–29.

150 **Krome attempted suicide:** Robert Pear, "Suicide Attempts Reported Rising Among Haitians in U.S. Detention," *New York Times*, June 22, 1982.

150 **"ingestion of crushed glass":** Carl Lindskoog, *Detain and Punish: Haitian Refugees and the Rise of the World's Largest Immigration Detention System* (Gainesville: University Press of Florida, 2018), 75.

150 **"go back to Haiti":** Lindskoog, *Detain and Punish*, 75.

150 **The denial of parole:** David M. Margolick, "Suit by 6 Haitian Aliens Testing Detention Policy," *New York Times*, December 4, 1981.

150 **But the judge who delivered:** Gregory Jaynes, "Parole of Haitians Ordered," *New York Times*, June 30, 1982; Arthur C. Helton, "Imprisonment of Refugees in the United States," in *Mother of Exiles: Refugees Imprisoned in America*, ed. Lawyers Committee for Human Rights and Helsinki Watch (New York: Lawyers Committee for Human Rights, 1986), 68.

150 **parole would only be available:** Helton, "Imprisonment of Refugees in the United States," 68.

151 **"throwback to a policy":** Mary Thornton, "Haitian Release Appealed," *Washington Post*, July 10, 1982, accessed August 25, 2023, https://www.washingtonpost.com/archive/politics/1982/07/10/haitian-release-appealed/c6fefeb2-e250-42e3-a9b7-093b6bf83800/.

151 **idea of denying bail:** See, for instance, S.288: *A Bill to Amend section 3148(1) of Title 18, United States Code, in order to Authorize the Denial of Bail to Certain Individuals who are Charged with Crimes of Violence and who have Previously been Convicted of Similar Crimes, United States Senate*, 91st Cong. 1(1969).

151 **"To deny reasonable bail":** *Preventive Detention: Hearings before the Subcommittee on Constitutional Rights of the Committee on the Judiciary, United States Senate,*

91st Cong. 1 (1970) (statement of Senator Sam J. Ervin Jr., chairman of the Subcommittee on Constitutional Rights).

151 **"reform of the bail laws":** *Comprehensive Crime Control Act of 1983: Hearings before the Subcommittee on Criminal Law of the Committee on the Judiciary, United States Senate*, 98th Cong. 2 (1983) (opening statement of Hon. Strom Thurmond, chairman of the Committee on the Judiciary).

151 **"We face a serious problem":** *Comprehensive Crime Control Act of 1983: Hearings before the Subcommittee on Criminal Law of the Committee on the Judiciary, United States Senate*, 98th Cong. 3 (1983) (opening Statement of Hon. Edward M. Kennedy, a Massachusetts senator).

152 **the average bond:** *Comprehensive Crime Control Act of 1983: Hearings before the Subcommittee on Criminal Law of the Committee on the Judiciary, United States Senate*, 98th Cong. 2 (1983) (formal statement of the Department of Justice).

152 **their "freedom of movement":** "Address by Honorable Herbert Brownell, Jr., Attorney General of the United States," Naturalization Ceremonies, Ebbets Field & Polo Grounds, November 11, 1954, transcript, https://www.justice.gov/sites/default/files/ag/legacy/2011/09/12/11-11-1954.pdf.

152 **"endanger the safety of any":** *Comprehensive Crime Control Act of 1983: Hearings before the Subcommittee on Criminal Law of the Committee on the Judiciary, United States Senate*, 98th Cong. 1017 (1983) (letter from the Hon. Arthur L. Burnett, president of the National Council of United States Magistrates).

152 **the Democratic-majority House:** Elizabeth Hinton, *From the War on Poverty to the War on Crime: The Making of Mass Incarceration in America* (Cambridge, MA: Harvard University Press, 2016), 310.

153 **"put great additional pressure":** Edward C. Schmults to James A. Baker III, February 26, 1982, Folder: Immigration Policy: Cubans and Haitians, Box 10, James W. Cicconi Files, Ronald Reagan Presidential Library.

153 **"due to several factors":** "Termination of Ft. Chaffee Operations," n.d., Folder: Immigration Policy: Cubans and Haitians, Box 10, James W. Cicconi Files, Ronald Reagan Presidential Library.

153 **Senator Alfonse D'Amato:** *Federal Assistance to State and Local Law Enforcement—Prisons: Hearing before the Subcommittee on Juvenile Justice of the Committee on the Judiciary, United States Senate*, 98th Cong. 7 (1983) (prepared statement of the Hon. Alfonse M. Amato, a New York senator).

153 **French Smith's proposal:** *Federal Assistance to State and Local Law Enforcement—Prisons*, 6.

153 **a West Point graduate:** John Hurst, "Fried-Chicken Moguls Add Turnkey Division," *Record*, December 28, 1983, 83; Shull, *Detention Empire*, 202–11.

153 **After a fifteen-minute discussion:** Shull, 202–11.

154 **half a million dollars:** Shull, 209.

154 **$23.50 a day:** Hurst, "Fried-Chicken Moguls Add Turnkey Division," 83.

154 **When the facility opened:** Wayne King, "Contracts for Detention Raise Legal Questions," *New York Times*, March 6, 1984.

154 **CCA's immigration detention facility:** Mark Dow, *American Gulag: Inside U.S. Immigration Prisons* (Berkeley: University of California Press, 2004), 97. That same year, the Wackenhut Corporation, which would later become the GEO Group, opened another private immigration detention center as a prison in Aurora, Colorado.

154 **But CCA's facility represented:** For more on these differences, see Kristina K. Shull, "'Nobody Wants These People': Reagan's Immigration Crisis and America's First Private Prisons" (PhD diss., University of California, Irvine, 2014), 182, chap. 5. See also Shull, *Detention Empire*, 324.

154 **now rebranded as CoreCivic:** Shull, 443.

155 **Gerardo helped make:** *Atlanta Federal Penitentiary*, 3. Gerardo specified that the gloves were for the military, but the report did not. Still, this is almost certain. See Ian Urbina, "Prison Labor Fuels American War Machine," in *Prison Profiteers: Who Makes Money from Mass Incarceration*, eds. Tara Herivel and Paul Wright (New York: New Press, 2009), 114.

155 **He worked hard enough:** *Atlanta Federal Penitentiary*, 23.

155 **Gerardo's earnings paled:** Wage statistic is from "The Minimum Wage," *In-Context*, December 2005, http://www.incontext.indiana.edu/2005/december/pdfs/minwage.pdf.

155 **Congress had mandated:** Urbina, "Prison Labor Fuels American War Machine," 110. The official name was the Federal Prison Industries (FPI).

155 **Gerardo made $1.10:** *Atlanta Federal Penitentiary*, 3.

156 **People sent to Cellhouse C:** *Atlanta Federal Penitentiary*, 1.

156 **lithium and Haldol:** *Atlanta Federal Penitentiary*, 1.

156 **"no medication that was given":** Dow, *American Gulag*, 290.

156 **strains of wild-monkey malaria:** Loretta A. Cormier, *The Ten-Thousand Year Fever: Rethinking Human and Wild-Primate Malarias* (New York: Routledge, 2016), 123–36.

156 **Along with 274:** *Atlanta Federal Penitentiary*, 2.

157 **in front of Juan Alers:** The ministry would go on to remove Alers in 2002 because of accusations of sexual misconduct with minors during that same period, though Gerardo never knew this. "Diocese of Lake Charles Releases List of Credibly Accused Clergy," *KLFY* (blog), April 11, 2019, https://www.klfy.com/louisiana/diocese-of-lake-charles-releases-list-of-credibly-accused-clergy/; and "Database of Priests Accused of Sexual Abuse," Bishop Accountability, accessed August 25, 2023, https://www.bishop-accountability.org/?mo=Alers&post_type=accused&s=&order=ASC&orderby=post_name.

158 **a prison in Kentucky:** *Mariel Cuban Detainees*, 293.

158 **nicknamed her Mommy:** Martínez, oral history interview; and Margaret L. Knox, "A Mother's Nightmarish Predicament," *Atlanta Journal and Constitution*, July 13, 1986.

158 **communicated their love:** Martínez, oral history interview (alongside Gerardo's).

158 **Though almost four hundred:** Martínez, oral history interview; Knox, "A Mother's Nightmarish Predicament."
158 **On the weekends:** Martínez, oral history interview.
158 **She went to Mass:** Martínez, oral history interview.
158 **As she told a reporter:** Martínez, oral history interview.
158 **Julia sent regular postcards:** Martínez, oral history interview; "Notes from the Congressional Record," Sally Sandidge's personal collection, Decatur, Georgia; and Knox, "A Mother's Nightmarish Predicament."
159 **already loved the children:** Knox, "A Mother's Nightmarish Predicament."
159 **"I am their mother":** Martínez, oral history interview.
159 **"never let my children":** Knox, "A Mother's Nightmarish Predicament."
159 **Julia took on more:** Knox, "A Mother's Nightmarish Predicament"; and Martínez, oral history interview.
159 **"employee of the month":** "Notes on Gerardo Mansur Pineiro and Julia Martinez, husband and wife," from Sally Sandidge's personal collection, Decatur, Georgia.

CHAPTER 11

162 **Because adult migrants:** "Family Separation—a Timeline," Southern Poverty Law Center, March 23, 2022, https://www.splcenter.org/news/2022/03/23/family-separation-timeline.
162 **in July 2017:** "Timeline: Family Separation and Reunification Efforts," Kids in Need of Defense (KIND), accessed May 1, 2023, https://supportkind.org/wp-content/uploads/2022/02/Timeline-Family-Separation-Reunification.pdf.
162 **Kirstjen Nielsen tweeted:** Kirstjen Nielsen (@SecNielsen), Twitter, June 17, 2018, 5:52 p.m., https://twitter.com/SecNielsen/status/1008467510906228736.
162 **a class-action lawsuit:** The case was *Ms. L. v. ICE.*
163 **DHS officials told Reuters:** Julia Edwards Ainsley, "Trump Administration Considering Separating Women, Children at Mexico Border," Reuters, March 3, 2017, https://www.reuters.com/article/us-usa-immigration-children-idUSKBN16A2ES.
163 **"terribly dangerous network":** Daniella Diaz, "Kelly: DHS Is Considering Separating Undocumented Children from Their Parents at the Border," CNN, March 7, 2017, https://www.cnn.com/2017/03/06/politics/john-kelly-separating-children-from-parents-immigration-border/index.html.
163 **No plans were drafted:** Jacob Soboroff, *Separated: Inside an American Tragedy* (New York: HarperCollins, 2020), 139–90, 253–84.
163 **"I have a master's degree":** Jonathan Blitzer, "The Government Has No Plan for Reuniting the Immigrant Families It Is Tearing Apart," *New Yorker*, June 18, 2018, https://www.newyorker.com/news/news-desk/the-government-has-no-plan-for-reuniting-the-immigrant-families-it-is-tearing-apart.
164 **taken from their homes:** Margaret D. Jacobs, *A Generation Removed: The Fostering and Adoption of Indigenous Children in the Postwar World* (Lincoln: Uni-

versity of Nebraska Press, 2014), 93. For more on the idea that detention is built upon previous histories, see Kelly Lytle Hernández, *City of Inmates: Conquest, Rebellion, and the Rise of Human Caging in Los Angeles, 1771–1965* (Chapel Hill: University of North Carolina Press, 2017), 9.

164 **"tough on crime":** Elizabeth Hinton, *From the War on Poverty to the War on Crime: The Making of Mass Incarceration in America* (Cambridge, MA: Harvard University Press, 2016).

164 **imprisonment increased by 430:** Bruce Western, *Punishment and Inequality in America* (New York: Russell Sage Foundation, 2006), 39–40.

164 **one in ten Black children:** Western, 163.

164 **incarcerated juvenile population:** Western, 39–40.

166 **given to migrants:** The uniform code was similar to that of other detention centers. See, for instance, Leanna Garfield, "What Life Is Like Inside California's Largest Immigration Detention Center," *Business Insider*, May 9, 2017, https://www.businessinsider.com/alifornias-largest-immigration-detention-center-photos-2017-5.

166 **If migrants managed:** Zainab A. Cheema, "A Constitutional Case for Extending the Due Process Clause to Asylum Seekers: Revisiting the Entry Fiction After *Boumediene*," *Fordham Law Review* 87, no. 1 (2018): 291–93. Even if they passed their interview, their release was not guaranteed. The government could choose to continue detaining them—as it was in fact doing with thousands of such individuals.

167 **over a century old:** Eunice Lee, "The End of Entry Fiction," *North Carolina Law Review* 99, no. 3 (2021): 571.

167 **had placed the two:** Immigration and Nationality Act § 235(b)(1).

167 **This meant that undocumented:** Lee, "The End of Entry Fiction," 600–3; and Cheema, "A Constitutional Case for Extending the Due Process Clause to Asylum Seekers," 291–311.

167 **In January 1999:** See *Code of Federal Regulations* (Annual Edition) and *Code of Federal Regulations*, Aliens and Nationality, 8 C.F.R. § 3.19(h)(1)(i), (A), and (B) (1999), https://www.govinfo.gov/content/pkg/CFR-1999-title8-vol1/pdf/CFR-1999-title8-vol1.pdf.

168 **Cleivi held her youngest:** Cleivi Jerez, oral history interview by the author, August 21–28, 2021, Los Angeles, California, digital recording.

168 **turned into a furnace:** Jerez, oral history interview.

168 **Despite the ill-treatment:** Allyson Hobbs and Ana Raquel Minian, "A Firsthand Look at the Horrors of Immigration Detention," *Washington Post*, June 25, 2018, https://www.washingtonpost.com/news/made-by-history/wp/2018/06/25/a-firsthand-look-at-the-horrors-of-immigration-detention/.

169 **Although it was called:** Molly Hennessy-Fiske, "Immigrant Families in Detention: A Look Inside One Holding Center," *Los Angeles Times*, June 25, 2015, https://www.latimes.com/nation/la-na-dilley-detention-20150625-story.html.

169 **"your own bed":** Jerez, oral history interview.

170 **these homey touches diluted:** Hennessy-Fiske, "Immigrant Families in Detention."

170 **lawyer named Evelyn:** Jerez, oral history interview.

170 **"What does this mean?":** Jerez, oral history interview.

170 **"Mom! I thought":** Andrea Arredondo as remembered by Cleivi. Jerez, oral history interview.

171 **In her declaration for asylum:** "Asylum Declaration of Andrea Fernanda Arredondo Jerez, in the Matter of: CLEIVI MARILU JEREZ LARA et al.," File No.: A #216-590-956, personal records of Linda Dakin-Grimm.

171 **"It is impossible to overstate":** *The Department of Homeland Security's Family Separation Policy: Perspectives from the Border: Hearing before the Subcommittee on Border Security, Facilitation, and Operations of the Committee on Homeland Security*, 116th Cong. (2019) (statement of Michelle Brané, director for Migrant Rights and Justice, Women's Refugee Commission), https://www.govinfo.gov/content/pkg/CHRG-116hhrg36397/html/CHRG-116hhrg36397.htm.

171 **Ursula Processing Center:** Hobbs and Minian, "A Firsthand Look."

172 **Michelle described it:** *The Department of Homeland Security's Family Separation Policy.*

173 **shelter in San Antonio:** "Detainee Request Form, Rodriguez Esvin, 5/23/2018" in Fernando Arredondo's personal files; and Linda Dakin-Grimm, oral history interview by the author, August 18, 2021, by phone, follow-up on December 13, 2021, digital recording.

173 **Babies, toddlers, and children who were:** Caitlin Dickerson and Manny Fernandez, "What's Behind the 'Tender Age' Shelters Opening for Young Migrants," *New York Times*, June 20, 2018, https://www.nytimes.com/2018/06/20/us/tender-age-shelters-family-separation-immigration.html.

173 **According to an August:** Adam Isacson, Maureen Meyer, and Adeline Hite, "A National Shame: The Trump Administration's Separation and Detention of Migrant Families," Washington Office on Latin America, August 28, 2018, https://www.wola.org/analysis/national-shame-trump-administrations-separation-detention-migrant-families/.

173 **shelter in Tucson, Arizona:** Dan Barry et al., "Cleaning Toilets, Following Rules: A Migrant Child's Days in Detention," *New York Times*, July 14, 2018, https://www.nytimes.com/2018/07/14/us/migrant-children-shelters.html.

173 **a "tent city":** Julia Ainsley and Annie Rose Ramos, "Inside Tornillo: The Expanded Tent City for Migrant Children," *NBC News*, October 12, 2018, https://www.nbcnews.com/politics/immigration/inside-tornillo-expanded-tent-city-migrant-children-n919431.

174 **sleeping on mattresses:** Camila Domonoske and Richard Gonzales, "What We Know: Family Separation and 'Zero Tolerance' at the Border," NPR, June 19, 2018, https://www.npr.org/2018/06/19/621065383/what-we-know-family-separation-and-zero-tolerance-at-the-border.

174 **Between October 2014:** Matthew Haag, "Thousands of Immigrant Children

Said They Were Sexually Abused in U.S. Detention Centers, Report Says," *New York Times*, February 27, 2019, https://www.nytimes.com/2019/02/27/us/immigrant-children-sexual-abuse.html; and Caitlin Owens, Stef W. Kight, and Harry Stevens, "Thousands of Migrant Youth Allegedly Suffered Sexual Abuse in U.S. Custody," *Axios*, February 26, 2019, https://www.axios.com/immigration-unaccompanied-minors-sexual-assault-3222e230-29e1-430f-a361-d959c88c5d8c.html.

174 **"inappropriate pornographic magazines":** Edgar Walters, Ryan Murphy, and Darla Cameron, "Thousands of Children Still Live in Texas Shelters after End of 'Zero Tolerance,'" Houston Public Media, August 15, 2018, https://www.houstonpublicmedia.org/articles/news/2018/08/15/300200/thousands-of-children-still-live-in-texas-shelters-after-end-of-zero-tolerance/; and Office of Refugee Resettlement, Unaccompanied Alien Children Program, "Sexual Abuse Allegations Reported to DOJ," 2015–2018, https://www.documentcloud.org/documents/5751021-NadUAC1213-Sexual-Assaults-by-Date-of-Incident.html.

174 **In a strongly worded statement:** UN High Commissioner for Human Rights, "Press Briefing Note on Egypt, United States and Ethiopia," United Nations, June 5, 2018, https://www.ohchr.org/EN/NewsEvents/Pages/DisplayNews.aspx?NewsID=23174.

175 **The staff dealt:** Barry et al., "Cleaning Toilets, Following Rules."

175 **"Mommy, I love you":** Barry et al., "Cleaning Toilets, Following Rules."

175 **An investigation by:** Hajar Habbach, Kathryn Hampton, and Ranit Mishori, "'You Will Never See Your Child Again': The Persistent Psychological Effects of Family Separation," Physicians for Human Rights, February 25, 2020, https://phr.org/our-work/resources/you-will-never-see-your-child-again-the-persistent-psychological-effects-of-family-separation/.

175 **Psychologists also found:** Brief of Doctors Beth Van Schaack (J.D., Ph.D.), Daryn Reicherter (M.D.), and Ryan Matlow (Ph.D.) as Amici Curiae in Support of Plaintiffs' Opposition to Defendant's Motion to Dismiss the Complaint, D.J.C.V. and G.C. v. United States, No. 1:20-cv-5747-PAE (S.D.N.Y. 2020).

175 **to nothing less than torture:** Brief of Doctors Beth Van Schaack (J.D., Ph.D.), Daryn Reicherter (M.D.), and Ryan Matlow (Ph.D.) as Amici Curiae in Support of Plaintiffs' Opposition to Defendant's Motion to Dismiss the Complaint.

176 **The parents of over:** Associated Press, "9 Parents Separated from Families Return to Children in US," Courthouse News Service, January 24, 2020, https://www.courthousenews.com/9-parents-separated-from-families-return-to-children-in-us/.

176 **On October 15, 2017:** Declaration of David Xol-Cholom, No. 18-cv-00428-DMS-MDD, United States District Court Southern California, Ms. L. v. U.S. Immigration and Customs Enforcement, No. 1:19-cv-00017, Document 1—Exhibit 1, filed in TXSD on February 12, 2019.

176 **"Fearing the permanent loss":** Camilo Montoya-Galvez, "11 Migrant Parents Who Were Separated from Their Children Can Return to U.S, Judge Rules," *CBS*

News, September 5, 2019, https://www.cbsnews.com/news/family-separation-policy-some-migrant-parents-who-were-separated-from-their-children-can-return-to-u-s-judge-rules/.

177 **"Sir, do you have anything":** Erica Proffer, Anastasiya Bolton, and Jose Sanchez, "'This Is Not a Heartwarming Story. It's a Tragedy,'" KVUE, October 26, 2020, https://www.kvue.com/article/news/deep-dive-texas/family-separation- trauma-byron-and-david-reunion/269-da8fdaab-9908-416e-b014-f255f13a29d8. See also "Meet Byron, a Little Boy Who Was Separated from His Father at the Border," KVUE, streamed on October 26, 2020, YouTube video, https:// www.youtube.com/watch?v=AbMrWoUEeuw.

177 **after David pleaded guilty:** Proffer, Bolton, and Sanchez, "'This Is Not a Heartwarming Story."; and "Meet Byron," KVUE.

177 **"If you are going to":** Proffer, Bolton, and Sanchez, "'This Is Not a Heartwarming Story.'" Note that this translation is based on the video referenced in the article, but I am using my own translation from the Spanish.

177 **The judge replied:** Proffer, Bolton, and Sanchez, "'This Is Not a Heartwarming Story.'"

177 **Byron was designated:** Mark Reagan, "Despite Potential Sponsor, ORR Continues to Hold Child Separated from Father," *AP News*, February 17, 2019.

178 **he was so angry:** Nomaan Merchant, "One Boy's Tale of Family Separation Heads to Court," *AP News*, July 12, 2019, https://apnews.com/article/us-news-ap-top-news-courts-international-news-immigration-93126a9faa674c2b98697903386bd90c.

178 **"extraordinary medical negligence":** Declaration of Amy Cohen M.D., B.X. v. Jonathan Hayes and Servando Barrera, No. 1:19-cv-00017 (S.D. Tex., Brownsville Div.), Document 26-1, p. 2 of 11, Exhibit 1, filed on April 16, 2019.

178 **"We have enough room":** Holly Sewell, oral history interview by the author, August 20, 2021, by phone, digital recording.

178 **a federal court had approved:** Stipulated Settlement Agreement, Flores v. Reno, 507 U.S. 292 (1993).

179 **he couldn't sleep:** Merchant, "One Boy's Tale of Family Separation Heads to Court."

179 **"Were you threatened?":** Cleivi Marilu Jerez Lara, "Questions and Answers," Credible-Fear Interview, Form A216590956, Cleivi Jerez's personal files.

180 **consumed by anxiety:** Jerez, oral history interview.

CHAPTER 12

181 **Atlanta was sweltering:** "Atlanta, GA Weather History," Weather Underground, accessed March 4, 2020, https://www.wunderground.com/history/monthly/us/ga/atlanta/KATL/date/1984-10.

181 **read "Liberty Now":** Michael Moss, "Inmates Locked in Cells After Protest," *Atlanta Journal*, October 15, 1984; and Mark S. Hamm, *The Abandoned Ones:*

The Imprisonment and Uprising of the Mariel Boat People (Boston: Northeastern University Press, 1995), 85.

181 **a prison lockdown:** *Mariel Cuban Detainees: Events Preceding and Following the November 1987 Riots: Hearing before the Subcommittee on Courts, Civil Liberties, and the Administration of Justice of the Committee on the Judiciary*, 100th Cong. 12 (1988) (A Report to the Attorney General Disturbances—Atlanta).

182 **shattered the windows:** John Lancaster and James Alexander, "Cuban Inmates' Protest Escalates," *Atlanta Constitution*, October 18, 1984.

182 **Once the fires:** Hamm, *Abandoned Ones*, 86.

182 **Not two weeks passed:** "500 Cubans Riot at Prison," *Los Angeles Times*, November 2, 1984.

183 **cases of "self-mutilation":** Scott Thurston, "Life in the Cells," *Palm Beach Post*, July 6, 1986; and *Mariel Cuban Detainees: Events Preceding and Following the November 1987 Riots: Hearing before the Subcommittee on Courts, Civil Liberties, and the Administration of Justice of the Committee on the Judiciary*, 100th Cong. 12 (1988) (prepared statement, with attached remarks, by the Hon. John Lewis, congressman from Georgia).

183 **Herrera tried to strangle:** Hamm, *Abandoned Ones*, 63.

184 **about the unfair imprisonment:** Sally Sandidge, oral history interview by the author, May 6, 2018, Decatur, Georgia, digital recording.

184 **These events drew:** Sandidge, oral history interview.

184 **Three years after arriving:** Don Gentile, "Can Their Love Find Way Out?" *Daily News*, November 26, 1987.

185 **most active members:** Sandidge, oral history interview.

185 **"we'd lost most of it":** Gary Leshaw, oral history interview by the author, May 7, 2018, Atlanta, Georgia, digital recording.

185 **Gary decided to focus:** Leshaw, oral history interview.

185 **This was the moment that:** Brian O'Shea, "Congressional Panel Head Inspects Conditions at Pen," *Atlanta Constitution*, February 4, 1986.

186 **sixty group members:** Billy Mallard, "Candlelight Vigil at Penitentiary Protests Detention of 1,850 Cubans," *Atlanta Constitution*, February 10, 1986; and Carla Dudeck, "We Must Speak Out against Cubans' Incarceration," *Atlanta Constitution*, January 4, 1986.

186 **They cared so little:** William C. Rempel, "Health of Cuban Refugees Deteriorating," *Los Angeles Times*, May 1, 1980.

186 **It asserted that Cubans:** *Atlanta Federal Penitentiary: Report of the Subcommittee on Courts, Civil Liberties, and the Administration of Justice of the Committee on the Judiciary*, 99th Cong. iii (1986) (letter of transmittal from Robert W. Kastenmeier, chairman of the Subcommittee on Courts, Civil Liberties, and the Administration of Justice).

187 **he sat down on his bed:** Letter from Gerardo Mansur to Ms. Carl [*sic*] Dudeck, April 28, 1986, Sally Sandidge's personal files, Decatur, Georgia.

187 **"Today our distraught hearts":** Letter from Gerardo Mansur to Ms. Carl [*sic*] Dudeck.

187 **Carla received Gerardo's letter:** Letter from Gerardo Mansur to Ms. Carl [*sic*] Dudeck; and letters from detained Cubans, Boxes 13 and 14, Cuban Detainees' Litigation Papers, Atlanta History Center.

187 **One man wrote to Sally:** Letter to Sally from man with incomprehensible signature, May 4, 1987, Sally Sandidge's personal files, Decatur, Georgia.

187 **a happy Mother's Day:** Letter to Sally from Juan Carrasco Sanchez, postmarked May 19, 1987, and postcard from Carlos Cabrera to Sally Sandidge, n.d. Both letters from Sally Sandidge's personal files, Decatur, Georgia.

187 **Tito drew her flowers:** Letter from Tito to Sally, February 4, 1987, Sally Sandidge's personal files, Decatur, Georgia.

187 **Among the hundreds of letters:** Sandidge, oral history interview; and letter stored in Sally Sandidge's personal files, Decatur, Georgia.

188 **Julia and Gerardo's predicament:** Julia Martínez, oral history interview by the author, February 22–24, 2019, Kissimmee, Florida, digital recording; and Margaret L. Knox, "A Mother's Nightmarish Predicament," *Atlanta Journal and Constitution*, July 13, 1986.

188 **"We dared to dream we could":** Peggy Mulligan, "Alien Center Is Dedicated," *Alexandria Daily Town Talk*, March 22, 1986.

188 **A sense of confidence:** Frances Frank Marcus, "Louisianians Wait for Alien Center," *New York Times*, October 7, 1984, https://www.nytimes.com/1984/10/07/us/louisianians-wait-for-alien-center.html.

188 **director of the Federal Bureau of Prisons:** Mulligan, "Alien Center Is Dedicated."

189 **cut a red ribbon:** Mulligan, "Alien Center Is Dedicated."

189 **"The primary reason for":** Department of Justice, *Immigration and Naturalization Service Annual Report* (Washington, DC: Government Printing Office, 1986), 10.

189 **a fifty-two-year-old man:** Quotes from Mulligan, "Alien Center Is Dedicated"; photograph and birthdate from Katharine Q. Seelye, "Norman Carlson, Forceful Head of U.S. Prisons, Dies at 86," *New York Times*, August 20, 2020, https://www.nytimes.com/2020/08/20/us/norman-carlson-forceful-head-of-us-prisons-dies-at-86.html.

189 **Mowad had quit:** Kathy Des Jardins, "Life in Oakdale Has Changed Little," *Alexandria Daily Town Talk*, October 19, 1986; and "Dr. Mowad Is Candidate," *Alexandria Daily Town Talk*, February 10, 1972.

189 **But if anything:** Marcus, "Louisianians Wait for Alien Center." For Oakdale's total population, see Department of Commerce, *1980 Census of Population: Characteristics of the Population*, vol. 1 (Washington, DC: Government Printing Office, 1983), table 56, 11.

189 **the community had lost:** Marcus, "Louisianians Wait for Alien Center."

189 **California Department of Corrections:** Ruth Wilson Gilmore, *Golden Gulag: Prisons, Surplus, Crisis, and Opposition in Globalizing California* (Berkeley: University of California Press, 2007), 148.

189 **Mowad resolved that:** See Jenna M. Loyd and Alison Mountz, *Boats, Borders, and Bases: Race, the Cold War, and the Rise of Migration Detention in the United States* (Berkeley: University of California Press, 2018), chap. 3, for a broader discussion of how the prison came to be built in Oakland and its implications.

190 **Residents of Oakdale:** Kristina K. Shull, "'Nobody Wants These People': Reagan's Immigration Crisis and America's First Private Prisons" (PhD diss., University of California, Irvine, 2014), 182.

190 **Oakdale's Sacred Heart:** Des Jardins, "Life in Oakdale Has Changed Little."

190 **"recession-proof industry":** Marcus, "Louisianians Wait for Alien Center" and *Bureau of Prisons and the U.S. Parole Commission: Oversight Hearing before the Subcommittee on Courts, Civil Liberties, and the Administration of Justice of the Committee on the Judiciary*, 99th Cong. 55, 53 (1985).

190 **"With all the jobs":** Loyd and Mountz, *Boats, Borders, and Bases*, 109; and Marcus, "Louisianians Wait for Alien Center."

190 **a group of attorneys:** Wayne King, "Contracts for Detention Raise Legal Questions," *New York Times*, March 6, 1984, https://www.nytimes.com/1984/03/06/us/contracts-for-detention-raise-legal-questions.html.

190 **transfer to Oakdale:** Loyd and Mountz, *Boats, Borders, and Bases*, 112; and Frances Frank Marcus, "Prison for Aliens Opens in Louisiana," *New York Times*, April 9, 1986, https://www.nytimes.com/1986/04/09/us/prison-for-aliens-opens-in-louisiana.html.

190 **Mayor Mowad felt gloomy:** Des Jardins, "Life in Oakdale Has Changed Little."

191 **led prisons to hire:** Tracy Huling, "Building a Prison Economy in Rural America," Prison Policy Initiative, accessed August 25, 2023, https://www.prisonpolicy.org/scans/building.html#_ednref11.

191 **The government of Corcoran:** Tracy Huling, "Building a Prison Economy in Rural America."

191 **Shortly after 7:00 p.m.:** Hamm, *Abandoned Ones*, 3. For time, see Bill Carter, "NBC 'Nightly News' to Move to 6:30 from 7," *New York Times*, June 13, 1991. For what was happening, see "Cuba Will Honor Deal on Refugees," *Chicago Tribune*, November 21, 1987.

192 **"Somos los abandonados!":** Hamm, *Abandoned Ones*, 5; and *Mariel Cuban Detainees*, 317. See also Kristina Shull, *Detention Empire: Reagan's War on Immigrants and the Seeds of Resistance* (Chapel Hill: University of North Carolina Press, 2022), 186–232; and Elliott Young, *Forever Prisoners: How the United States Made the World's Largest Immigration Detention System* (New York: Oxford University Press, 2021), 133–52.

192 **They watched as eleven:** Hamm, *Abandoned Ones*, 5–6; and *Mariel Cuban Detainees*, 320.

192 **It offered the men:** *Mariel Cuban Detainees*, 63.

193 **"this explodes":** Rafael Quintana (pseudonym), oral history interview by the author, April 21, 2018, Miami, Florida, digital recording.

193 **One of the migrants:** *Mariel Cuban Detainees*, 439–40.

193 **"Doc, we have had":** *Mariel Cuban Detainees*, 439–40.
193 **Alarms rang throughout:** Quintana, oral history interview.
193 **José Peña Pérez:** Hamm, *Abandoned Ones*, 10–11.
193 **Ammunition continued to fly:** Quintana, oral history interview.
193 **Like in Oakdale:** El Pintor (pseudonym), oral history interviews by the author, January 4, 2018, and April 23, 2018, Miami, Florida, digital recordings.
194 **"This is war":** Quintana, oral history interview.
194 **die in there that day:** Quintana, oral history interview.
194 **The flyovers continued:** Hamm, *Abandoned Ones*, 16–17.
195 **He implored the Cubans:** Mary T. Schmich, "Cubans Believe Bishop's Words," *Chicago Tribune*, December 3, 1987; George Volsky, "Bishop Who Speaks for Downtrodden," *New York Times*, November 30, 1987; *Mariel Cuban Detainees*, 338; and Hamm, *Abandoned Ones*, 24.
195 **"We want the Bishop":** *Mariel Cuban Detainees*, 337.
195 **"We have reviewed the document":** Paul Weingarten, "All Hostages Released at 1 Prison," *Chicago Tribune*, November 30, 1987.
195 **Once the hostages:** Schmich, "Cubans Believe Bishop's Words."
195 **They were then taken:** *Mariel Cuban Detainees*, 339.
196 **Meese sent FBI agent:** Hamm, *Abandoned Ones*, 23, 27.
196 **Valladares had joined President Reagan:** Armando Valladares, *Against All Hope: A Memoir of Life in Castro's Gulag*, rev. ed. (New York: Encounter Books, 2001); and Tony Platt, "Cuba and the Politics of Human Rights," *Social Justice* 15, no. 2 (32) (Summer 1988): 41. Valladares was a Cuban political prisoner who had served a twenty-two-year sentence in Cuba. In his memoir, he described the terrible conditions in Cuba's prisons. Valladares was just the symbol President Reagan needed to criticize Communist Cuba. In a 1986 ceremony to mark Human Rights Day, the president even invited Valladares to the White House to decry the "horrors and sadism" of the Cuban prison system.
196 **angrily booed at them:** Hamm, *Abandoned Ones*, 24.
196 **Meese succumbed to:** Hamm, 28.
196 **They met with:** Leshaw, oral history interview.
196 **none would be deported:** Signed agreement, December 4, 1987, Gary Leshaw's personal archives, Atlanta, Georgia.

CHAPTER 13

197 **It all began:** *The Situation in Haiti and U.S. Policy: Hearing before the Subcommittees on Human Rights and International Organizations and Western Hemisphere Affairs of the Committee on Foreign Affairs*, 102nd Cong. 86 (1992) (testimony of Rep. Ronald V. Dellums).
198 **Upon taking office:** Elizabeth McAlister, "From Slave Revolt to a Blood Pact with Satan: The Evangelical Rewriting of Haitian History," *Studies in Religion / Sciences Religieuses* 41, no. 2 (2012): 197; and Carl Lindskoog, *Detain and Punish: Haitian*

Refugees and the Rise of the World's Largest Immigration Detention System (Gainesville: University Press of Florida, 2018), 100.

198 **"hundreds of people":** Amnesty International, "Haiti: Update on Amnesty International's Concerns," AI News Service 141/93, October 28, 1993, https://www.amnesty.org/en/wp-content/uploads/2021/06/nws111411993en.pdf.

198 **army did not limit:** *The Situation in Haiti and U.S. Policy*, 86.

198 **Some crossed the border:** Lindskoog, *Detain and Punish*, 102; Michael Ratner, "How We Closed the Guantanamo HIV Camp: The Intersection of Politics and Litigation," *Harvard Human Rights Journal* 11 (1998): 187–220, 189; and Barbara Crossette, "135 Feared Lost as Haitian Boat Sinks Off Cuba," *New York Times*, November 22, 1991.

198 **Twenty-eight-year-old Yolande Jean:** Yolande Jean, deposition, February 21, 1993, Camp Bulkeley, Guantánamo Bay, Rodger Citron personal archives.

198 **Before the coup:** Brandt Goldstein, *Storming the Court: How a Band of Law Students Sued the President—and Won* (New York: Scribner, 2005), 2–3.

199 **"to mobilize the people":** Jean, deposition.

199 **operation did not last long:** Jean, deposition.

199 **The nearing footsteps:** Goldstein, *Storming the Court*, 14.

199 **"Is this where Elsie lives?":** Goldstein, 14; and Jean, deposition.

199 **The men stopped hitting:** Goldstein, *Storming the Court*, 14.

199 **The truck stopped outside:** America's Watch, *The More Things Change . . . : Human Rights in Haiti, February 1989* (New York: Americas Watch Committee, 1989), 65–69.

200 **having a miscarriage:** Goldstein, *Storming the Court*, 15; and Jean, deposition.

200 **Police officers in the region:** Jean, deposition.

200 **She made arrangements:** Jean, deposition.

200 **Mariel boatlift had left such:** See, for instance, "Florida's Governor Unhappy about Influx of Haitians," *Weekend Chicago Defender*, November 23, 1991; David Dahl, "Mack Opposes Bush, Graham Backs Him," *St. Petersburg Times*, November 23, 1991; Zita Arocha, "Haitian Refugees Should Be Welcomed Ashore," *USA Today*, November 21, 1991; Dennis Gallagher, "The Haitians Surely Deserve Better," *Sun*, November 21, 1991; David Dahl and Rick Bragg, "Hundreds of Haitians to Be Sent Home," *St. Petersburg Times*, November 19, 1991; Melissa Healy, "U.S. Adrift in Bid to Put Haitians on Cuban Soil," *Los Angeles Times*, November 27, 1991; and "U.S. Military to Set Camp for Haitians," *Los Angeles Times*, November 26, 1991.

200 **When reporting on his candidacy:** David Shribman, "Clinton, Arkansas's Best-Known Overachiever, Widens His Horizons to Include the White House," *Wall Street Journal*, October 8, 1991; Cragg Hines," "Clinton Jumps in Race, Touts Economic Revival," *Houston Chronicle*, October 4, 1991; and Myron S. Waldman, "Arkansas Governor Enters Race," *Newsday*, October 4, 1991.

201 **Clinton's "Little Rock idyll":** Shribman, "Clinton, Arkansas's Best-Known Overachiever."

201 **incumbent president's cabinet:** See William P. Barr Oral History, April 5, 2001, George H. W. Bush Oral History Project, Presidential Oral History Program, Miller Center, University of Virginia, https://millercenter.org/the-presidency/presidential-oral-histories/william-p-barr-oral-history.

201 **administration decided to quell:** See, for instance, Mike Clary, "Haitians Held on Ship as U.S. Reviews Policy," *Los Angeles Times*, November 6, 1991.

201 **"You've got a potential":** Melissa Healy, "U.S. Military Will Shelter Haitians at Base in Cuba," *Los Angeles Times*, November 26, 1991, https://www.latimes.com/archives/la-xpm-1991-11-26-mn-209-story.html.

201 **When AIDS first emerged:** A. Naomi Paik, "Testifying to Rightlessness: Haitian Refugees Speaking from Guantánamo," *Social Text* 28, no. 3 (Fall 2010): 44–45; Paul Farmer, *AIDS and Accusation: Haiti and the Geography of Blame* (Berkeley: University of California Press, 2006), 237; Dorothy Nelkin, "AIDS and the News Media," *Milbank Quarterly* 69, no. 2 (1991): 299.

201 **To give the impression:** Exec. Order No. 12324, 46 Fed. Reg. 48109 (1981), https://www.archives.gov/federal-register/codification/executive-order/12324.html.

202 **According to the chief:** Clary, "Haitians Held on Ship as U.S. Reviews Policy."

202 **Days passed as:** Department of State, Daily Press Briefing, Tuesday, November 19, 1991, Collection: National Security Council, Series: Nancy Bearg Dyke Files, Subseries: Subject Files, OA/ID Number: CF01075, Haiti 1991 I (Post-coup) [1] [OA/ID CF01075-014], George Bush Presidential Library. After many days and much negotiation, Venezuela, Honduras, Belize, and Trinidad and Tobago agreed to take refugees, but only between 100 and 250 each. Not only was the number too low, but the countries did not even specify when they would admit the refugees.

202 **number of Haitians aboard:** Howard W. French, "U.S. Is Holding 200 Haitians on 2 Ships," *New York Times*, November 8, 1991.

202 **the number had climbed:** Mike Clary, "U.S. Pushes for Haitian Resettlement Plan," *Los Angeles Times*, November 16, 1991; "National Security Council Memorandum from WHSR_ROUTER@WHSR," November 19, 1991, File System: S, File Type: OF, Code: 73, Collection / Office of Origin: National Security Council, Series: Nancy Bearg Dyke Files, Subseries: Subject Files, OA/ID Number: CF01075, Haiti 1991 I (Post-coup) [1] [OA/ID CF01075-014], George Bush Presidential Library.

202 **Coast Guard set up tents:** "Haitian Refugees Held, for Now, in Floating Jails," *Sun*, November 11, 1991; and "Haitian Refugees Wait for Word on Status," *All Things Considered*, NPR, November 8, 1991.

202 **some of the Coast Guard:** "Haitian Refugees Wait for Word on Status"; "More Haitians Flee to the United States," *Chicago Defender*, November 14, 1991.

203 **As the media noted:** "Floating U.S. Jails Hold Haitian Refugees," *Orlando Sentinel*, November 11, 1991; and "Haitian Refugees Held, for Now, in Floating Jails."

203 **On November 13:** "National Security Council Memorandum, Subject FYI,"

November 13, 1991, File System: S, File Type: OF, Code: 73, Collection / Office of Origin: National Security Council, Series: Nancy Bearg Dyke Files, Subseries: Subject Files, OA/ID Number: CF01075, Haiti 1991 I (Post-coup) [2] [OA/ID CF01075-015], George Bush Presidential Library.

203 **administration presented this decision:** Office of the Assistant Secretary/Spokesman, "Haitian Boat People," *US Department of State Dispatch* 2, no. 46 (Washington, DC: Government Printing Office, November 25, 1991); Mike Clary, "U.S. Sending Boat People Back to Haiti," *Los Angeles Times*, November 18, 1991; and "Haitian Refugee Return Prompts Outcry," *All Things Considered*, NPR, November 19, 1991. See also William Barr to Honorable Jack Brooks, letter, February 20, 1992, File System: S, File Type: OF, Code: 78, Series: Marianne McGettigan Files, OA/ID Number: 08160 through 08161, Haitian Refugee Bills [OA/ID 08161-044], George Bush Presidential Library.

203 **deport Haitians back:** "National Security Council Memorandum from WHSR_ROUTER@WHSR."

204 **agreed with the center's lawyers:** Haitian Refugee Center, Inc. v. Baker, 789 F. Supp. 1552 (S. D. Fla. 1991). See also "Temporary Restraining Order," No. 91-2653-Civ-Atkins (S.D. Fla., filed Dec. 3, 1991), File System: S, File Type: OF, Code: 73, Collection / Office of Origin: National Security Council, Series: Nancy Bearg Dyke Files, Subseries: Subject Files, OA/ID Number: CF01075, Haiti 1991 I (Post-coup) [1] [OA/ID CF01075-014], George Bush Presidential Library.

204 **During the Mariel boatlift Bill Clinton:** Bill Clinton, *My Life* (New York: Vintage Books, 2005), 275.

205 **transferring the "excludable":** Frank Hodsoll, "Immigration: (A) Cuban Excludables (b) Detention Center," secret memorandum for the vice president et al., July 29, 1981, WHORM Subject File IM (Immigration-Naturalization), 198700-207074, Box 20, Folder IM 206000-206229, Ronald Reagan Presidential Library.

205 **"to hold the undesirables":** "Using Guantanamo to Hold the Undesirables Who Arrived in the Mariel Boatlift," Chaffee Working Files (5), Box 8, Frank Hodsoll Files, WH Staff Member and Office Files, Ronald Reagan Presidential Library. See also "Use of Guantanamo for Refugee Internment," confidential memorandum for the secretary of defense from the assistant secretary of defense, Detention Center and Chaffee Working Files (3), Box 8, Frank Hodsoll Files, WH Staff Member and Office Files, Ronald Reagan Presidential Library.

205 **If the US breached:** "Using Guantanamo to Hold the Undesirables," Chaffee Working Files.

205 **operational costs of opening:** "Using Guantanamo to Hold the Undesirables"; Frank Hodsoll, "Memorandum: Ft Chaffee Population," July 14, 1981, "Immigration and Refugee Matters" Box 22, Folder 4, Edward Meese III Files, OA6518, Ronald Reagan Presidential Library; and "Use of Guantanamo for Refugee Internment." See also Kristina Shull, *Detention Empire: Reagan's War on Immi-*

grants and the Seeds of Resistance (Chapel Hill: University of North Carolina Press, 2022), 58.

206 **access to Guantánamo:** Ratner, "How We Closed the Guantanamo HIV Camp," 192.

206 **entry fiction as precedent:** Haitian Refugee Center, Inc. v. Baker, 953 F. 2d 1498 (11th Cir. 1992) and Haitian Refugee Center, Inc. v. Baker, 789 F. Supp. 1552 (S.D. Fla. 1991). The district court cited Jean v. Nelson, 727 F.2d 957, 967 (11th Cir. 1984), and Landon v. Plasencia, 459 U.S. 21, 32, 103 S. Ct. 321, 329, 74 L. Ed. 2d 21 (1982), both of which depended on the Knauff ruling.

206 **Ellen Knauff's case:** Haitian Centers Council, Inc. v. McNary, 969 F. 2d 1326 (2d Cir. 1992), citing United States ex rel. Knauff v. Shaughnessy, 338 U.S. 537 (1950).

206 **"entrants" had the right:** 8 U.S.C. § 1362. "In any exclusion or deportation proceedings before a special inquiry officer and in any appeal proceedings before the Attorney General from any such exclusion or deportation proceedings, the person concerned shall have the privilege of being represented (at no expense to the Government) by such counsel, authorized to practice in such proceedings, as he shall choose."

207 **clothes clung to her:** Goldstein, *Storming the Court*, 66.

207 **refugees slept inside olive-green:** Goldstein, 101–2; Affidavit of Marcus Antoine, n.d., Rodger Citron personal archives.

207 **By the time Yolande:** Federation for American Immigration Reform, "Haiti: A Status Report on Repatriation," June 26, 1992, 14, File System: S, File Type: OF, Code: 73, Collection / Office of Origin: White House Office of Policy Development, Series: Betsy Anderson Files, OA/ID Number: 08755 through 08765, Haitians [1] [OA/ID 08756-010], George Bush Presidential Library. See also Exec. Order No. 12807, "Interdiction of Illegal Aliens," May 24, 1992, File System: S, File Type: OF, Code: 73, Collection / Office of Origin: National Security Council, Series: Virginia Lampley Files, Subseries: Subject Files, OA/ID Number: CF00750, Haiti [OA/ID CF01109-003], George Bush Presidential Library.

207 **To gain some semblance:** Haitian Centers Council, Inc. v. Sale, 823 F. Supp. 1028, 1037 (E.D.N.Y. 1993).

207 **There were long lines:** Goldstein, *Storming the Court*, 101; and Affidavit of Marcus Antoine.

207 **Yolande was escorted:** Goldstein, *Storming the Court*, 102–3.

208 **President Bush issued:** Exec. Order No. 12807, 57 Fed. Reg. 23133 (1992).

208 **administration defended its decision:** White House Office of the Press Secretary, "For Immediate Release," n.d., Stack: G, File System: S, File Type: OF, Code: 73, Collection / Office of Origin: National Security Council, Series: Nancy Bearg Dyke Files, Subseries: Subject Files, OA/ID Number: CF01480, Refugees: Haiti 1992 II [2] [OA/ID CF01480-018], George Bush Presidential Library.

208 **refugee population at Guantánamo:** "Status of Haitian Boat People as of June 3, 1992," File System: S, File Type: OF, Code: 73, Collection / Office of Origin:

National Security Council, Series: Nancy Bearg Dyke Files, Subseries: Subject Files, OA/ID Number: CF01480, Refugees: Haiti 1992 II [1] [OA/ID CF01480-017], George Bush Presidential Library.

208 **have mistakenly deported:** Affidavit of Marcus Antoine.

208 **chanted a song:** Affidavit of Marcus Antoine.

209 **some of Marie's relatives:** Affidavit of Marcus Antoine. The US government went to great lengths to discredit the story, claiming that Marie was not killed after she was deported back to Haiti. It is hard to know whether she was killed or not, but what is clear is that she was deported even though she had passed her credible-fear interview.

209 **she had "some germs":** Quoted in Jean, deposition.

209 **bus took Yolande:** *Haitian Centers Council v. Sale*, 823 F. Supp. at 1037.

209 **called himself Dr. Malone:** Jean, deposition.

210 **Yolande was being detained:** Ratner, "How We Closed the Guantanamo HIV Camp," 195.

210 **HIV-positive refugees:** Ratner, 196.

210 **even refused to guarantee:** In the spring of 1992, the Department of Justice released a plan for dealing with Haitians who remained at the detention facility. It maintained that it would only allow refugees who had AIDS to be transported to the United States "on a case-by-case basis." The department's plan entailed moving quickly to deport "any screened-in HIV-positive migrant who manifests symptoms of AIDS" and who had been denied parole. See "Plan for the Department of Justice to Assume a Greater Share of the Migrant Processing Effort in Guantanamo," May 7, 1992, File System: S, File Type: OF, Code: 73, Collection / Office of Origin: National Security Council, Series: Charles A. Gillespie Files, Subseries: Subject Files, OA/ID Number: CF01569, Haiti—General—May 1992 [3] [OA/ID CF01569-008], George Bush Presidential Library.

210 **Joel Saintil, a detained:** Joel Saintil is a pseudonym.

211 **denied the request three times:** Anna Quindlen, "Public & Private; A Death Watch," *New York Times*, May 30, 1993, https://www.nytimes.com/1993/05/30/opinion/public-private-a-death-watch.html.

211 **Yolande, who went from being:** Quindlen, "Public & Private; A Death Watch."

211 **state and federal prison systems:** Jordan B. Glaser and Robert B. Greifinger, "Correctional Health Care: A Public Health Opportunity," *Annals of Internal Medicine* 118, no. 2 (January 1993): 139.

211 **estimated 17 to 20 percent:** Members of the ACE Program of the Bedford Hills Correctional Facility, *Breaking the Walls of Silence: AIDS and Women in a New York State Maximum-Security Prison* (New York: Overlook Books, 1998), 23.

211 **Although the doctors:** Jean, deposition.

212 **medical staff pushed:** A. Naomi Paik, *Rightlessness: Testimony and Redress in U.S. Prison Camps since World War II* (Chapel Hill: University of North Carolina Press, 2016), 110.

212 **These lies and omissions:** "Haitians Scuffle at Guantanamo," *Washington Post*, July 19, 1992.

212 **just under three hundred Haitians:** Goldstein, *Storming the Court*, 140.

212 **refused to be subdued:** Jean, deposition.

213 **"They came with three tanks":** Jean, deposition.

213 **"give fleeing Haitians refuge":** Ratner, "How We Closed the Guantanamo HIV Camp," 200; and Paul Farmer, *Pathologies of Power: Health, Human Rights, and the New War on the Poor* (Berkeley: University of California Press, 2003), 63.

213 **and the other refugees assembled:** Goldstein, *Storming the Court*, 175–76.

213 **The camp erupted:** Goldstein, 176.

214 **gay and lesbian:** Ratner, "How We Closed the Guantanamo HIV Camp," 200.

214 **When similar numbers:** "For Haitians, Cruelty and Hope," *New York Times*, January 17, 1993.

214 **"Clinton has acknowledged":** Richard Estrada, "Haitian Reality Leaves Clinton with No Choice," *Sun Sentinel*, January 10, 1993.

214 **week into his presidency:** Mike Dorning, "The American Way? For Haitian Refugees with HIV, Freedom Is Still Miles Away," *Chicago Tribune*, January 25, 1993; Elaine Sciolino, "Clinton Says U.S. Will Continue Ban on Haitian Exodus," *New York Times*, January 15, 1993.

214 **despaired over Clinton's about-face:** Ratner, "How We Closed the Guantanamo HIV Camp," 202. As Michael Ratner, one of the lawyers working for the refugees, later recalled: "The Haitians had been kept in a barbed-wire camp for over a year, and it appeared more likely than ever that they would remain there indefinitely solely because they were HIV-positive." See also Lindskoog, *Detain and Punish*, 119.

214 **Their captors seemed intent:** For more on this idea of limbo and being halfway between life and death, see A. Naomi Paik, *Rightlessness*, 142–45, 203–11.

214 **"We have to go":** Goldstein, *Storming the Court*, 20.

215 **"We would prefer to die":** Claude LaGuerre, deposition, February 20, 1993, Rodger Citron personal archives.

215 **there was Robert Henry:** Goldstein, *Storming the Court*, 181.

215 **little left to lose:** Col. Stephen P. Kinder, telephone deposition, February 26, 1993, Rodger Citron personal archives.

215 ***There is no life*:** Jean, deposition.

215 **The press and famous activists:** Ratner, "How We Closed the Guantanamo HIV Camp," 208.

215 **Some Black clergy:** Lindskoog, *Detain and Punish*, 120.

215 **Amid this onslaught:** Lindskoog, 120.

215 **"made us, the lawyers":** Ratner, "How We Closed the Guantanamo HIV Camp," 208–9.

215 **legality of the detention facility:** Ratner, 202.

216 **lawyers made their case strongly:** Ratner, 202.

216 **"an HIV prison camp":** *Haitian Centers Council*, 823 F. Supp. at 1039.

216 **Yolande resettled in:** Yolande was allowed to leave Guantánamo shortly before Judge Sterling Johnson's decision.

216 **she drove to LaGuardia:** Goldstein, *Storming the Court*, 296–98.

216 **"U.S. Naval Base at Guantánamo Bay":** *Haitian Centers Council v. Sale*, 823 F. Supp. at 1041.

216 **This part of the ruling:** Brandt Goldstein, Rodger Citron, and Molly Beutz Land, *A Documentary Companion to Storming the Court* (Austin: Wolters Kluwer Law & Business, 2009), 219.

217 **One government official maintained:** Goldstein, *Storming the Court*, 298.

217 **The administration's appeal:** Goldstein, *A Documentary Companion to Storming the Court*, 298–300.

217 **administration officials ever intended:** Paik, *Rightlessness*, 149.

217 **Clinton's White House:** Lindskoog, *Detain and Punish*, 123; and "Cuban Balseros at GTMO," Guantánamo Public Memory Project, accessed August 25, 2023, https://gitmomemory.org/timeline/cuban-balseros/.

217 **last set of Cuban balseros:** "Guantánamo's Last Raft Refugees Leave for U.S.," *Los Angeles Times*, February 1, 1996.

217 **In 1997 and 1999:** Nancy San Martin, "Rescued Cubans Taken to Base," *Sun Sentinel*, March 13, 1997; Deborah Ramirez, "Cubans Questioned on Sea Escape," *Sun Sentinel*, September 28, 1997; "Guantanamo Gets Ready for Kosovars," *Orlando Sentinel*, April 7, 1999; and William Branigin and William Claiborne, "U.S. Prepares for 20,000 Refugees at Guantanamo," *Washington Post*, April 7, 1999.

218 **killing nearly three thousand people:** United States Congressional Serial Set, Serial No. 14801, H.R. Rep. Nos. 805–11, 107th Cong., 2nd sess. (2002), 74.

218 **"Terrorist attacks can shake":** George W. Bush, "Statement by the President in His Address to the Nation," September 11, 2001, White House press release, George W. Bush White House Archives, National Archives, transcript and RealMedia webcast, https://georgewbush-whitehouse.archives.gov/news/releases/2001/09/20010911-16.html.

218 **the Bush administration needed:** For more on this, see Mark P. Denbeaux and Jonathan Hafetz, eds., *The Guantánamo Lawyers: Inside a Prison Outside the Law* (New York: New York University Press, 2009), 2; and Joseph Margulies, *Guantánamo and the Abuse of Presidential Power* (New York: Simon & Schuster, 2006), 45.

218 **Donald Rumsfeld announced:** Margulies, *Guantánamo and the Abuse of Presidential Power*, 45.

219 **administration asked John Yoo:** Patrick F. Philbin and John C. Yoo, "Possible Habeas Jurisdiction over Aliens Held in Guantanamo Bay, Cuba," memo for William J. Haynes II, December 28, 2001, National Security Archive, George Washington University, https://nsarchive2.gwu.edu/torturingdemocracy/documents/20011228.pdf.

219 **"The great weight":** Philbin and Yoo, "Possible Habeas Jurisdiction over Aliens Held in Guantanamo Bay, Cuba."

219 **"We believe that these precedents":** Philbin and Yoo, "Possible Habeas Jurisdiction over Aliens Held in Guantanamo Bay, Cuba."

219 **Yoo issued another memorandum:** John Yoo and Robert J. Delahunty, "Application of Treaties and Laws to al Qaeda and Taliban Detainees," memo to William J. Haynes II, January 9, 2002, National Security Archive, George Washington University, https://nsarchive2.gwu.edu/torturingdemocracy/documents/20020109.pdf. Note that this memo was cowritten by Yoo and Delahunty.

219 **Rumsfeld publicly labeled:** Katharine Q. Seelye, "A Nation Challenged: The Prisoners," *New York Times*, January 12, 2002, https://www.nytimes.com/2002/01/12/world/nation-challenged-prisoners-first-unlawful-combatants-seized-afghanistan-arrive.html.

219 **Bush administration caged:** "20 Years of US Torture—and Counting," Human Rights Watch, January 9, 2022, https://www.hrw.org/news/2022/01/09/20-years-us-torture-and-counting.

220 **using "enhanced interrogation techniques":** *Report of the Senate Select Committee on Intelligence, Committee Study of the Central Intelligence Agency's Detention and Interrogation Program*, 113th Cong. 2 (2014), https://www.intelligence.senate.gov/sites/default/files/publications/CRPT-113srpt288.pdf.

220 **These "techniques" included:** Murtaza Hussain, "Tortured, Mentally Ill Guantánamo Prisoner Asks Court to Be Repatriated to Saudi Arabia," *Intercept*, April 19, 2018, https://theintercept.com/2018/04/19/torture-mohammed-al-qahtani-guantanamo; and Denbeaux and Hafetz, *Guantánamo Lawyers*, 240–41, 250–51. Mohammed al-Qahtani struggled with mental illness even before the US government tortured him.

220 **One of the most powerful:** Mohamedou Ould Slahi, *The Mauritanian*, ed. Larry Siems (Edinburgh, UK: Canongate Books, 2021).

220 **His account can be:** *Inquiry into the Treatment of Detainees in U.S. Custody, Report of the Committee on Armed Services, United States Senate*, 110th Cong. 2 (2008), at 135–41, https://www.govinfo.gov/content/pkg/CPRT-110SPRT48761/pdf/CPRT-110SPRT48761.pdf.

220 **Mohamedou was subjected:** Slahi, *Mauritanian*, 227.

221 **Donald Rumsfeld himself:** *Inquiry into the Treatment of Detainees*, at 135–41 (2008). Rumsfeld also agreed to other torture techniques against Slahi that had already been implemented against him without authorization.

221 **"replicate and exploit":** *Inquiry into the Treatment of Detainees*, at 137 (2008).

221 **It used these so-called:** Letta Tayler and Elisa Epstein, *Legacy of the "Dark Side": The Costs of Unlawful US Detentions and Interrogations Post-9/11* (Providence: Watson Institute for International and Public Affairs, 2022), https://watson.brown.edu/costsofwar/papers/2022/DetentionandTorture.

221 **very few knew:** David Johnston and Mark Mazzetti, "A Window into C.I.A.'s Embrace of Secret Jails," *New York Times*, August 12, 2009, https://www.nytimes.com/2009/08/13/world/13foggo.html.

222 **"Obama! Obama! Obama!":** Connie Bruck, "Why Obama Has Failed to Close

Guantánamo," *New Yorker*, July 25, 2016, https://www.newyorker.com/magazine/2016/08/01/why-obama-has-failed-to-close-guantanamo.

222 **"In the dark halls":** Barack Obama, "The War We Need to Win," remarks at the Woodrow Wilson International Center for Scholars, Washington, DC, August 1, 2007, transcript, https://www.presidency.ucsb.edu/node/277525.

222 **After it invaded Afghanistan:** Bruck, "Why Obama Has Failed to Close Guantánamo."

222 **but 242 remained:** "Guantanamo by the Numbers," Human Rights First, October 10, 2018, https://humanrightsfirst.org/library/guantanamo-by-the-numbers/.

223 **Obama administration's first serious:** Bruck, "Why Obama Has Failed to Close Guantánamo."

223 **Bush administration had previously:** A US district court in Washington, DC, had even ordered that the Uyghurs be brought into the United States, but the Departments of Justice, Defense, and Homeland Security had appealed the decision, and they had remained at Guantánamo.

223 **Obama focused on:** Bruck, "Why Obama Has Failed to Close Guantánamo." The White House made a similar compromise over a spending bill that prohibited funds from being used to transfer those at Guantánamo to the United States. Obama could have vetoed it but did not do so, because it also contained provisions to repeal the anti-gay "don't ask, don't tell" policy in the military.

224 **Obama finally put the nail:** "Guantanamo by the Numbers."

224 **In 2002, a Gallup survey:** Tom LoBianco, "CNN/ORC Poll: Americans Oppose Plan to Close Guantanamo Bay Prison," CNN Politics, March 4, 2016, https://www.cnn.com/2016/03/04/politics/guantanamo-bay-poll-north-korea; and Lydia Saad, "Few Americans Object to Treatment of Guantanamo Bay Captives," Gallup, February 7, 2002, https://news.gallup.com/poll/5302/few-americans-object-treatment-guantanamo-bay-captives.aspx.

224 **"some bad dudes":** David Welna, "Trump Has Vowed to Fill Guantanamo with 'Some Bad Dudes'—but Who?" *All Things Considered*, NPR, November 14, 2016, https://www.npr.org/sections/parallels/2016/11/14/502007304/trump-has-vowed-to-fill-guantanamo-with-some-bad-dudes-but-who.

CHAPTER 14

227 **two and a half weeks:** Linda Dakin-Grimm, *Dignity and Justice: Welcoming the Stranger at Our Border* (Maryknoll, NY: Orbis Books, 2020), 96.

228 **On June 19, 2018:** José Olivares, "ICE Review of Immigrant's Suicide Finds Falsified Documents, Neglect, and Improper Confinement," *Intercept*, October 23, 2021, https://theintercept.com/2021/10/23/ice-review-neglect-stewart-suicide-corecivic/.

228 **During his intake screening:** Olivares, "ICE Review of Immigrant's Suicide Finds Falsified Documents."

228 **This should have alerted:** José Olivares and Travis Mannon, "How Solitary Confinement Kills: Torture and Stunning Neglect End in Suicide at Privately Run ICE Prison," *Intercept*, August 29, 2019, https://theintercept.com/2019/08/29/ice-solitary-mental-health-corecivic/. In 2013, ICE itself had issued a policy document warning that solitary confinement could cause the "deterioration of the detainee's medical or mental health."

228 **"God was trying to kill":** Olivares and Mannon, "How Solitary Confinement Kills."

228 **Upon his return to Stewart:** Olivares and Mannon, "How Solitary Confinement Kills."

229 **night of July 10:** Olivares and Mannon, "How Solitary Confinement Kills."

229 **not the first time:** Olivares and Mannon, "How Solitary Confinement Kills."

231 **8 percent of *all* people:** E. Ann Carson, "Prisoners in 2018," U.S. Department of Justice, Bureau of Justice Statistics, 2020, 27–28, https://www.bjs.gov/content/pub/pdf/p18.pdf.

231 **In 2020, 81 percent:** "Detention Management," ICE, accessed August 25, 2023, https://www.ice.gov/detain/detention-management. In total, ICE detained 182,869 in fiscal year 2020. For the percentage of detention in private facilities, see Eunice Hyunhye Cho, Tara Tidwell Cullen, and Clara Long, *Justice-Free Zones: U.S. Immigration Detention Under the Trump Administration* (New York: ACLU, 2020), https://www.aclu.org/report/justice-free-zones-us-immigration-detention-under-trump-administration.

231 **The corporations that ran:** Cho, Tidwell Cullen, and Long, *Justice-Free Zones*, 17.

231 **The profit motive:** John Pfaff, "Private Prisons Aren't Uniquely Heinous. All Prisons Are Abusive," *Washington Post*, February 3, 2021, https://www.washingtonpost.com/outlook/2021/02/03/private-prisons-executive-order/; and Jacob Kang-Brown and Jack Norton, "More than a Jail: Immigrant Detention and the Smell of Money," Vera Institute of Justice, July 5, 2018.

231 **In 2016, a ten-minute:** Shannon Najmabadi, "Detained Migrant Parents Have to Pay to Call Their Family Members. Some Can't Afford To," *Texas Tribune*, July 3, 2018, https://www.texastribune.org/2018/07/03/separated-migrant-families-charged-phone-calls-ice/.

232 **"When did you say":** The government claims not to have a transcript of the interview; as such, I have relied solely on Fernando's memory to describe this interaction.

233 **asylum seekers are not guaranteed:** "Asylum Representation Rates Have Fallen amid Rising Denial Rates," TRAC Immigration, accessed August 25, 2023, https://trac.syr.edu/immigration/reports/491/.

234 **Cleivi also had a different:** Linda Dakin-Grimm, oral history interview, August 18, 2021, by phone, follow-up on December 13, 3021, digital recording. According to Fernando's lawyer, Fernando might have had a translator and simply not remembered during the oral history interview.

234 **In between these two dates:** 27 I&N Dec. 316 (A.G. 2018).

234 **"You know, [asylum officers]":** Dakin-Grimm, oral history interview and follow-up.

234 **something even more troubling:** Dakin-Grimm, oral history interview and follow-up.

235 **The form was in English:** "Record of Negative Credible Fear Finding and Request for Review by Immigration Judge," form signed by Fernando and checked "No, I do not request Immigration Judge review of the decision that I do not have a credible fear of persecution or torture," Fernando's personal files.

235 **He did not understand:** Dakin-Grimm, *Dignity and Justice*, 119.

235 **five days after ICE:** Lee Gelernt, "The Battle to Stop Family Separation," *New York Review*, December 19, 2018, https://www.nybooks.com/daily/2018/12/19/the-battle-to-stop-family-separation/.

236 **His first case:** Gelernt, "The Battle to Stop Family Separation."

236 **Lee filed a suit:** Gelernt, "The Battle to Stop Family Separation"; and Amended Complaint for Declaratory and Injunctive Relief with Class Action Allegations, Ms. L. v. ICE, No. 18-cv-00428-DMS-MDD (S.D. Ca.), Document 32, p. 9 of 15, filed on March 9, 2018, https://www.aclu.org/sites/default/files/field_document/2018.03.09_32_amended_complaint.pdf. See also Rex Huppke, "Congolese Mother and Child Finally Reunited in Chicago," *Chicago Tribune*, March 16, 2018.

236 **"you are the only one":** Gelernt, "The Battle to Stop Family Separation."

236 **"a humanitarian crisis":** Status Conference Transcript, Ms. L. v. ICE, No. 18-cv-0428-DMS-MDD (S.D. Ca.), June 12, 2018, https://www.aclu.org/cases/ms-l-v-ice?document=ms-l-v-ice-plaintiffs-reply-support-motion-classwide-preliminary-injunction.

236 **Judge Sabraw stated:** Order Granting Plaintiffs' Motion for Classwide Preliminary Injunction, Ms. L. v. ICE, No. 18-cv-00428-DMS-MDD (S.D. Ca.), Document 83, p. 12 of 24, filed on June 26, 2018, https://www.politico.com/f/?id=00000164-3f39-d1bc-afef-7fbbdf010001.

237 **formidable task, as officials:** Jacob Soboroff, *Separated: Inside an American Tragedy* (New York: HarperCollins, 2020), 139–90, 253–84.

237 **"reality is that for every parent":** Richard Gonzales, "Federal Judge Calls Government Plan to Reunify Migrant Families 'Disappointing,'" NPR, August 3, 2018, https://www.npr.org/2018/08/03/635502588/federal-judge-calls-government-plan-to-reunify-migrant-families-disappointing.

237 **The argument that:** Dakin-Grimm, *Dignity and Justice*, 122.

CHAPTER 15

240 **By early February 1988:** Elliott Young, *Forever Prisoners: How the United States Made the World's Largest Immigration Detention System* (New York: Oxford University Press, 2021), 153.

240 **spaces in halfway houses:** Young, *Forever Prisoners*, 153; El Pintor (pseudonym), oral history interview by the author, April, 25, 2018, Miami, Florida, digital recording; and Rafael Blanco (pseudonym), oral history interview by the author, April 21, 2018, Miami, Florida, digital recording.

240 **"That was hell":** Blanco, oral history interview.

240 **Another man imprisoned:** Young, *Forever Prisoners*, 153.

240 **thirty-eight hundred:** "System Still Sorting Out Cubans after Prison Riot," *Santa Cruz Sentinel*, November 21, 1988.

242 **"I felt so strange":** Julia Martínez, oral history interview by the author, February 22–24, 2019, Kissimmee, Florida, digital recording.

244 **Existing research shows:** For an analysis of the literature on this, see Beth M. Huebner and Regan Gustafson, "The Effect of Maternal Incarceration on Adult Offspring Involvement in the Criminal Justice System," *Journal of Criminal Justice* 35, no. 3 (2007): 283–96.

245 **Irania had chosen:** Irania Sori González, oral history interview by the author, February 23, 2019, Kissimmee, Florida, digital recording.

245 **He even shaved his head:** González, oral history interview.

245 **"a bad moment":** González, oral history interview.

245 **so attached to Gerardo:** González, oral history interview.

246 **they were police officers:** Dialogue as told to Irania by Jennifer. González, oral history interview.

247 **take back 2,746 Mariel Cubans:** Mark Dow, "Why Mariel Cuban Criminals Deserve Amnesty (and Anti-Castro Republicans Should Support It)," *Hill*, June 25, 2017, https://thehill.com/blogs/congress-blog/foreign-policy/339396-why-mariel-cuban-criminals-deserve-amnesty-and-anti-castro/.

247 **had deported 2,022:** Dow, "Why Mariel Cuban Criminals Deserve Amnesty."

247 **six days after Gerardo's arrest:** Department of State, "Migration and Refugees: Joint Statement Between the United States of America and Cuba," Havana, January 12, 2017, 2, https://www.state.gov/wp-content/uploads/2019/02/17-112-Cuba-Migration-and-Refugees.pdf. For more, see Young, *Forever Prisoners*, 157.

247 **With this agreement:** Frances Robles, "'Marielitos' Face Long-Delayed Reckoning: Expulsion to Cuba," *New York Times*, January, 14, 2017, https://www.nytimes.com/2017/01/14/us/cuba-us-migrants.html; and Dow, "Why Mariel Cuban Criminals Deserve Amnesty."

247 **Many were homeless:** For cases of people who had changed their identities and whose lives had changed dramatically or were going poorly, I consulted El Pintor, oral history interview; Blanco, oral history interview; Gorila (pseudonym), oral history interview by the author, December 28, 2018, Miami, Florida, digital recording; and Pedro Torres (pseudonym), oral history interview by the author, January 7, 2018, digital recording.

248 **Irania never questioned:** González, oral history interview.

CHAPTER 16

252 **"I felt like":** Cleivi Jerez, oral history interview by the author, August 21–28, 2021, Los Angeles, California, digital recording.

252 **lawyer was Linda Dakin-Grimm:** Linda Dakin-Grimm, oral history interview, August 18, 2021, by phone, follow-up on December 13, 3021, digital recording.

252 **Cleivi and the girls needed:** Linda Dakin-Grimm, *Dignity and Justice: Welcoming the Stranger at Our Border* (Maryknoll, NY: Orbis Books, 2020), 120–21.

253 **ACLU had reached an agreement:** Dakin-Grimm, oral history interview and follow-up; and Joel Rose, "Agreement Would Allow Separated Families to Seek Asylum in U.S.," NPR, September 13, 2018, https://www.npr.org/2018/09/13/647430277/agreement-would-allow-separated-families-to-seek-asylum-in-u-s.

253 **On July 12, 2019:** Dakin-Grimm, *Dignity and Justice*, 105.

254 **Holly Sewell, who was fostering:** Holly Sewell, oral history interview by the author, August 20, 2021, by phone, digital recording.

254 **She was not alone:** Dakin-Grimm, oral history interview and follow-up.

254 **"Welcome, Daddy":** Jerez, oral history interview; Brittny Mejia, "Families Reunite after Nearly Two Years Apart," *Los Angeles Times*, January 23, 2020, https://www.latimes.com/california/story/2020-01-23/families-reunite-after-nearly-two-years-apart-beginning-of-a-whole-other-journey.

254 **"Oh my God," Holly said:** Mejia, "Families Reunite after Nearly Two Years Apart."

254 **Fernando ran toward them:** Farida Jhabvala Romero, "9 Separated Migrant Parents Return to Reunite with Kids," KQED, January 23, 2020, https://www.kqed.org/news/11797579/9-separated-migrant-parents-return-to-reunite-with-kids.

255 **Now all he wanted:** Romero, "9 Separated Migrant Parents Return to Reunite with Kids."

255 **Alison cried inconsolably:** Mejia, "Families Reunite after Nearly Two Years Apart."

EPILOGUE

258 **In November 2018:** Ginger Thompson, "Families Are Still Being Separated at the Border, Months after 'Zero Tolerance' Was Reversed," *ProPublica*, November 27, 2018, https://www.propublica.org/article/border-patrol-families-still-being-separated-at-border-after-zero-tolerance-immigration-policy-reversed.

259 **threatened to impose a tariff:** The Mexican president also agreed to deploy Mexico's National Guard against Central American migrants who were crossing Mexico.

259 **While Central Americans waited:** "The Devastating Toll of 'Remain in Mexico' One Year Later," Doctors without Borders, January 29, 2020, https://www.doctorswithoutborders.org/latest/devastating-toll-remain-mexico-one-year-later; and Human Rights First, *Fatally Flawed: "Remain in Mexico" Policy*

Should Never Be Revived (Los Angeles: Human Rights First, 2022), https://humanrightsfirst.org/wp-content/uploads/2022/10/FatallyFlawed.pdf.

259 **"Sometimes you do things":** John Burnett, "'I Want to Be Sure My Son Is Safe': Asylum-Seekers Send Children Across Border Alone," NPR, November 27, 2019, https://www.npr.org/2019/11/27/783360378/i-want-to-be-sure-my-son-is-safe-asylum-seekers-send-children-across-border-alone. In the article, "Martinez" does not have an accent, but it is likely that he spelled it "Martínez."

259 **Health and Human Services identified:** Priscilla Alvarez, "At Least 350 Children of Migrant Families Forced to Remain in Mexico Have Crossed Over Alone to US," CNN, January 24, 2020, https://www.cnn.com/2020/01/24/politics/migrant-children-remain-in-mexico/index.html.

259 **little-known public health law:** 42 U.S.C. § 265, https://www.govinfo.gov/content/pkg/USCODE-2020-title42/html/USCODE-2020-title42-chap6A-subchapII-partG-sec265.htm.

260 **Biden suspended:** "Biden Administration Says 'Remain in Mexico' Policy Is Over," Associated Press, August 8, 2022, https://apnews.com/article/mexico-immigration-government-and-politics-5c7bb29c829d7f0711b23f9beb18755d.

260 **Holly Sewell, who fostered Byron:** Holly Sewell, oral history interview by the author, August 20, 2021, by phone, digital recording.

260 **Fear that ending:** Miriam Jordan, "Title 42 Is Gone, but Not the Conditions Driving Migrants to the U.S.," May 14, 2023, https://www.nytimes.com/2023/05/14/us/migrants-condition-title-42-ends.html.

260 **The app opened up:** "New Asylum Transit Ban Is Dangerous and Shortsighted," American Immigration Council, May 10, 2023, https://www.americanimmigrationcouncil.org/news/new-asylum-transit-ban-dangerous-and-shortsighted.

260 **Its effects thus mirrored:** Maria Abi-Habib et al., "Migrants Struggle to Get Appointments on Border Protection App," *New York Times*, May 11, 2023, https://www.nytimes.com/2023/05/11/us/migrants-border-app-cbp-one.html; and Sanya Mansoor, "'It's Like a Lottery.' Migrants Struggle to Make Asylum Appointments through U.S. Government App," *Time*, May 16, 2023, https://time.com/6280220/migrants-border-cbp-app-asylum/.

261 **fifteen thousand migrants detained:** Eunice Cho, "Unchecked Growth: Private Prison Corporations and Immigration Detention, Three Years into the Biden Administration," ACLU, August 7, 2023, https://www.aclu.org/news/immigrants-rights/unchecked-growth-private-prison-corporations-and-immigration-detention-three-years-into-the-biden-administration.

261 **average of thirty thousand people:** Cho, "Unchecked Growth."

261 **81 percent of migrants:** Cho, "Unchecked Growth."

261 **At the start:** "The Biden Plan for Securing Our Values as a Nation of Immigrants," Biden Campaign Website, accessed August 28, 2023, https://web.archive.org/web/20201122062835/https://joebiden.com/immigration/#; Cho, "Unchecked Growth."

261 **Neglect and mistreatment:** Cho, "Unchecked Growth."

261 **The list goes on:** See, for instance, the 911 call made from the Aurora ICE Processing Center: Tom Dreisbach, "A 'Shocking' 911 Call and Other Key Takeaways from NPR's ICE Detention Investigation," NPR, August 24, 2023, https://www.npr.org/2023/08/24/1195264716/a-shocking-911-call-and-other-key-takeaways-from-nprs-ice-detention-investigation.

262 **"Habeas Corpus secures":** Letter from Thomas Jefferson to Archibald H. Rowan, September 26, 1798, Series 1: General Correspondence 1651–1827, Thomas Jefferson Papers at the Library of Congress, https://www.loc.gov/item/mtjbib009131/.

263 **slightly over a century later:** In the 2020 case *Department of Homeland Security v. Thuraissigiam*, the court went even further, holding that these entrants had no right to file habeas petitions to challenge the government's failure to follow its own procedures. This case imposed a new and absolute limit on constitutional protections for entrants in a way that vitiates any procedural protections that Congress does provide for them.

263 **Even Americans were at risk:** Eric Lichtblau, "U.S., Bowing to Court, to Free 'Enemy Combatant,'" *New York Times*, September 23, 2004, https://www.nytimes.com/2004/09/23/politics/us-bowing-to-court-to-free-enemy-combatant.html.

263 **Americans make up only:** "Mass Incarceration," ACLU, accessed July 2, 2023, https://www.aclu.org/issues/smart-justice/mass-incarceration.

263 **one out of every three:** "Mass Incarceration," ACLU.

264 **the 2018 fiscal year:** Laurence Benenson, "The Math of Immigration Detention, 2018 Update: Costs Continue to Multiply," National Immigration Forum, May 9, 2018, https://immigrationforum.org/article/math-immigration-detention-2018-update-costs-continue-mulitply/.

264 **That very year:** "EPA's Budget and Spending," EPA, accessed August 15, 2023, https://www.epa.gov/planandbudget/budget.

265 **That percentage rose:** Nina Siulc and Noelle Smart, "Evidence Shows That Most Immigrants Appear for Immigration Court Hearings," Vera Institute of Justice, October 2020, https://www.vera.org/downloads/publications/immigrant-court-appearance-fact-sheet.pdf; and Ingrid Eagly, Steven Shafer, and Jana Whalley, *Detaining Families: A Study of Asylum Adjudication in Family Detention* (Washington, DC: American Immigration Council, 2018), https://www.americanimmigrationcouncil.org/sites/default/files/research/detaining_families_a_study_of_asylum_adjudication_in_family_detention_final.pdf.

266 **Even Trump's draconian family:** Suzanne Gamboa, "Border Apprehensions Were Up 88 Percent in Fiscal Year 2019, Agency Says," *NBC News*, October 29, 2019, https://www.nbcnews.com/news/latino/border-apprehensions-were-88-percent-fiscal-year-2019-agency-says-n1073486.

266 **"humane qualities of an enlightened":** Leng May Ma v. Barber, 357 U.S. 185 (1958).

267 **post-confinement regulations are:** Maya Schenwar and Victoria Law, *Prison by Any Other Name: The Harmful Consequences of Popular Reforms* (New York: New Press, 2020), 6.

267 **These programs are meant:** "Alternatives to Immigration Detention: An Overview," American Immigration Council, July 11, 2023, https://www.americanimmigrationcouncil.org/research/alternatives-immigration-detention-overview. From 2017 to 2022, the budget for such programs increased from $126 million to $443 million.

267 **People subjected to these:** For more on the problems of alternatives to detention, see American Immigration Council, "Alternatives to Immigration Detention"; "Government Alternatives to Detention," Detention Watch Network, accessed October 21, 2023, https://www.detentionwatchnetwork.org/issues/alternatives; Tosca Giustini et al., "Immigration Cyber Prisons: Ending the Use of Electronic Ankle Shackles," Benjamin N. Cardozo School of Law Kathryn O. Greenberg Immigration Justice Clinic, July 2021, https://larc.cardozo.yu.edu/faculty-online-pubs/3; "The Case Against 'Alternatives to Detention,'" Detention Watch Network, December 1, 2022, https://www.detentionwatchnetwork.org/sites/default/files/DWN_The%20Case%20Against%20ATDs_12.1.22.pdf.

268 **continued to hold Mexicans:** Carl Lindskoog, *Detain and Punish: Haitian Refugees and the Rise of the World's Largest Immigration Detention System* (Gainesville: University Press of Florida, 2018), 18–25. In certain years during this period, other migrants were also not released. Such was the case of Haitians who could not pay bond.

INDEX